Women in the Law Courts of Classical Athens

Intersectionality in Classical Antiquity
Series Editors: Mark Masterson, Victoria University of Wellington, Fiona McHardy, University of Roehampton and Nancy Sorkin Rabinowitz, Hamilton College

This series focuses on the intersection of gender and sexuality, in the Greco-Roman world, with a range of other factors including race, ethnicity, class, ability, masculinity, femininity, transgender and post-colonial gender studies. The books in the series will be theoretically informed and will sit at the forefront of the study of a variety of outsiders – those marginalised in relation to the 'classical ideal' – and how they were differently constructed in the ancient world. The series is also interested in the ways in which work in the field of classical reception contributes to that study.

Editorial Advisory Board
Patty Baker, Alastair Blanshard, Susan Deacy, Jacqueline Fabre-Serris, Cristiana Franco, Genevieve Liveley, Amy Richlin, Carisa R. Showden

Books available in the series
Exploring Gender Diversity in the Ancient World, ed. Allison Surtees and Jennifer Dyer
Women in the Law Courts of Classical Athens, Konstantinos Kapparis

Forthcoming books in the series
Marginalised Populations in the Ancient Greek World: The Bioarchaeology of the Other, Carrie L. Sulosky Weaver

Visit the series web page at: edinburghuniversitypress.com/series-intersectionality-in-classical-antiquity

Women in the Law Courts of Classical Athens

Konstantinos Kapparis

EDINBURGH
University Press

Edinburgh University Press is one of the leading university presses in the UK. We publish academic books and journals in our selected subject areas across the humanities and social sciences, combining cutting-edge scholarship with high editorial and production values to produce academic works of lasting importance. For more information visit our website: edinburghuniversitypress.com

© Konstantinos Kapparis, 2021, 2022

Edinburgh University Press Ltd
The Tun – Holyrood Road,
12(2f) Jackson's Entry,
Edinburgh EH8 8PJ

First published in hardback by Edinburgh University Press 2021

Typeset in 11/13 Adobe Garamond by
IDSUK (DataConnection) Ltd

A CIP record for this book is available from the British Library

ISBN 978 1 4744 4672 3 (hardback)
ISBN 978 1 4744 4673 0 (paperback)
ISBN 978 1 4744 4674 7 (webready PDF)
ISBN 978 1 4744 4675 4 (epub)

The right of Konstantinos Kapparis to be identified as the author of this work has been asserted in accordance with the Copyright, Designs and Patents Act 1988, and the Copyright and Related Rights Regulations 2003 (SI No. 2498).

Contents

Abbreviations	viii
Introduction	1
Women and the legal system of the Athenian democracy: Why is it important?	1
The intersection of the law with the lives of women	8
Sources	12
The modern literature	14

Part I Cases Involving Women Litigants

1. Lysias, *To Antigenes, on the Abortion* — 23
2. Lysias, *On the Daughter of Antiphon* — 26
3. Hypereides, *Against Aristagora, Aprostasiou (Two Speeches)* — 29
4. Deinarchos, *That the Daughters of Aristophon Are Not Heiresses*; or, *Diamartyria that the Daughter of Aristophon Is Not an Heiress* — 36
5. Pericles, *In Defence of Aspasia, for Impiety* — 39
6. [Demosthenes] 40, *To Boiotos on his Mother's Dowry* — 43
7. Hypereides, *Against Demetria, Apostasiou* — 46
8. Lysias 32, *Against Diogeiton: A Mother's Compelling Speech* — 47
9. Deinarchos, *Synegoria to Hegelochos, for the Epikleros*, or *Against Hegelochos, Synegoria on Behalf of the Epikleros* — 51
10. Deinarchos, *Against Hedyle, Apostasiou* — 52
11. Lysias, *To Lais* — 53
12. [Deinarchos], *Dispute Between the Priestess of Demeter and the Hierophant* — 56

13. Lycurgus, *On the Priestess*	60
14. Deinarchos, *For an Epikleros: For the Daughter of Iophon*	66
15. Euboulides, *Against the Sister of Lakedaimonios, for Impiety*	67
16. Hypereides, *In Defence of Mika*	67
17. Apollodoros, *Against Neaira*	68
18. Lysias, *For Nikomache*	68
19. Menekles, *Against Ninos the Priestess, for Impiety*	69
20. Lysias, *On the Daughter of Onomakles*	73
21. Isaios 3, *On the Estate of Pyrrhos*	73
22. Lysias, *Against Philonides for Rape*	75
23. Hypereides, *In Defence of Phryne*	76
24. Lysias, *On the Daughter of Phrynichos*	82
25. Isaios, *To Satyros, for the Epikleros*	83
26. Antiphon 1, *Against the Stepmother for Poisoning*	84
27. Demosthenes, *Against Theoris, for Impiety*	85
28. Hypereides, *To Timandra*	88

Part II Women and the Athenian Justice System

1. Women's Participation in the Athenian Justice System — 105
Women's access to the various layers of the justice system — 105
Representation versus exclusion — 112
Not all women are the same — 117
Conclusions — 120

2. Judicial Procedures Involving Women — 124
An overview of processes in the Athenian justice system — 124
Women and politics — 129
Citizenship and immigration violations — 131
Prosecutions for religious offences — 136
Economic disputes — 143
Violent crime — 147
Personal responsibility before the law — 149

3. Gender as a Factor in the Construction of the Argument — 155
Gender stereotypes as a factor in trials involving both men and women: An introduction — 155
The dutiful wife and mother — 157
The indecent women of Athens — 164
The poisoner and the witch — 169
Images of the body and sexuality — 172
A woman with a past — 175
Conclusions — 180

4.	**Women's Empowerment, Social Groups and the Justice System**	187
	Introduction	187
	Citizen women in the Athenian polis	188
	Metic women in the Athenian polis	197
	The working women of Athens: Legal implications	202
	Conclusions	207
5.	**Conclusions**	217

Appendix: The Main Laws Affecting the Lives of Athenian Women   227

1. The law on marriage — 227
2. The law on the *epidikasia* — 228
3. The law on the *epidikasia* of a poor *epikleros* — 229
4. The Periclean citizenship law — 230
5. The laws prohibiting mixed marriages between Athenians and non-Athenians — 231
6. The law on divorce — 232
7. The laws on adultery affecting women — 233
8. The laws on succession and inheritance directly affecting women — 234
9. The social network: the laws requiring the archon to protect women, children and orphans from abuse of their person or property — 237
10. All priests and priestesses are equally responsible under the law — 240

Select Bibliography   242
Index of Ancient Authors   271
General Index   274

Abbreviations

Abbreviations for Greek authors are mostly as in the Liddell–Scott–Jones Ancient Greek Lexicon (*LSJ*), and abbreviations for Roman authors as in Lewis & Short. Following the Thesaurus Linguae Graecae (*TLG*), all references to Athenaios are by book and chapter of Kaibel's edition. A similar principle has been applied to other authors: I tend to follow the numbering of the *TLG* in order to make it easier for the reader to check references, as electronic databases are increasingly becoming the dominant form. For the fragments of ancient authors I indicate the editor. I am not fond of Latinising the names of Greek authors, and I tend to keep them as close to their original form as possible, but for some commonly used names in English (for example, Plato or Epicurus) one must keep the Latinised spelling. Inevitably this creates an inconsistency, but since it is not likely to cause any confusion, I find it acceptable.

Introduction

WOMEN AND THE LEGAL SYSTEM OF THE ATHENIAN DEMOCRACY: WHY IS IT IMPORTANT?

The majority of studies on Athenian law do not have much to say about the interactions of Athenian women with the legal system of the democracy in the classical period.[1] The *dikasteria*, the two *boulai* and the *ekklesia* were the domain of men, and women simply did not belong. Narratives about the status of Athenian women often advance images of a society divided along lines of gender so impermeable that women transgressing into the world of men in any capacity or form should be viewed as aberrations, like those tragic heroines who violently crossed the boundaries of their gender and sought to take male roles, always with bad consequences, as for example Klytemestra did when she sought to rule in her husband's place.[2] Such narratives assume roles for the women of the Athenian democracy based on obedience, subservience, silence and fragility, where women did not engage with the institutions of the democracy, but relied on their fathers or husbands to take care of anything and everything that happened beyond their doorstep. These narratives were sometimes influenced by 1980s struggles over gender equality; they were based upon the assumption that men and women have been engaged in a perpetually and intensely antithetical relationship, and in some extreme cases divided women in society along the lines of crisply defined roles either as respectable citizen wives and mothers, or as shady outsiders.[3] However, real life rarely fits well into such neat normative patterns; real life is nuanced, complex and often random, chaotic and unpredictable, and this is where these narratives fell short. They failed to take into account shades and variable patterns between the absolute positions which they often advocated. Somewhere between the full engagement or the full exclusion of Athenian women from the justice system and public life altogether there may be shades, and more variable and flexible patterns. Therefore, the question should not be whether women were included in the Athenian justice system on the same level as men, but whether there were degrees and patterns of inclusion somewhere in between equal inclusion and total exclusion.

This is the primary premise of this study; I argue that women had significant interactions with the Athenian legal system, but the shape and patterns of these interactions were different from those of their male counterparts, and that these differences were generated by law, tradition and powerful social norms. It is my contention in this study that differences in the approaches to the legal system of the Athenian democracy between male and female litigants should not automatically be interpreted as exclusion or obstructive practices. Instead, they should be studied carefully within the social context of classical Athens, with the ultimate objective of understanding better how these different approaches affected the administration of justice in each case, if at all, and how women were able to safeguard their rights, property and person within these confines of the Athenian legal system.

The assumption that women were excluded from the Athenian legal system is primarily based upon the fact that, unlike free men, they could not speak in court either as witnesses or as litigants, not even in their own defence. I argue that this assumption is based upon a very simplistic view of the Athenian legal system. This view does not take into account the multiple tiers before a case could go to trial before the *dikasterion*, nor does it take into account important practices in the Athenian legal system, such as those of the *synegoria*, where a supporting advocate could always deliver part of or the entire speech of a litigant, or the shadow speechwriters, the *logographoi*, who operated quietly in the background, prepared the case, chose the tactic and best vector of approach, offered legal advice, prepared litigants for what was to come, and even wrote the speech to be delivered during the trial. All these factors, and many more facets of the legal system of the Athenian democracy, are critically important for the issue at hand. As I will be arguing in the following chapters, women were not totally excluded from access to the Athenian legal system, first of all because they had access to the first tier of it, the magistrates of the state, who initiated lawsuits, and always retained the right to summarily impose a quite substantial fine of up to 50 drachmas on any offender, without the possibility of an appeal.[4] A woman could always approach a magistrate, launch a complaint and ask for his help. Could it be the case that the modest punitive powers of magistrates were often sufficient to resolve minor disputes that we do not get to hear about because they never made it to the next stage? A woman could also appear and give evidence before an arbitrator. Public arbitration, where an arbitrator was appointed by the state, was the mandatory second tier in all private lawsuits.[5] Alternatively private arbitration, where the litigants agreed to resolve their dispute outside the courts by entrusting it to the judgement of friends or relatives, was another possibility for both public and private lawsuits. Women had direct access to this second tier too.[6] Matters became more rigid when it came to the final tier, the appeal before the heliastic courts and the trial before a large jury, where women's physical presence was mandated only when they had been prosecuted for a crime.

I will be arguing that it was not any specific law but rather custom, tradition and expectations of respectability which kept women away from the heliastic courts. However, regardless of the reasons, their inability to appear as witnesses or speak as litigants created an inescapable need for representation. A practice which was optional for male litigants was mandatory for female litigants. But our focus should not be on the differences, in this case; instead, it should be on the similarities, because they are particularly instructive. These similarities allow us to see how women could actually defend their person, rights and property, even though they could not speak in court. Whether he was supporting a man or a woman, a *synegoros* should have been speaking not for profit but out of friendship or familial duty, and within the available time limits he needed to make the best possible case for the litigant. Whether it was Demosthenes speaking on behalf of Timarchos, or Xenokles speaking on behalf of his wife Phile, the duty of a *synegoros* was to win the case for the person whom he was supporting. He could have written the speech himself, as Apollodoros did in his *synegoria* for Theomnestos,[7] or he could have memorised a speech composed by an expert logographer, as the *synegoros* speaking on behalf of Phormion did.[8] All the same, the primary duty of the *synegoros* was to employ the best possible tactics and to help the person whom he was supporting. In this respect, there was no inherent disadvantage to the need of women to employ a *synegoros* for a court appearance. If anything, it may have been a slight advantage because a man with exaggerated confidence in his own ability to speak in public might actually harm his case by not asking for help, while a woman, since she had no choice, would need to rely on a representative who might have been chosen, among other things, for his skill with the laws and experience with the courts and public speaking.[9] While the merits of the case, the skills and tactics of a *synegoros*, and a myriad of additional and often unpredictable factors could have decided the outcome of the case, the fact that women needed a *synegoros*, while men had a choice, did not necessarily put the former at a disadvantage when it came to their chances of winning the case.

The employment of expert speechwriters was certainly a widespread practice. If someone had a trial coming, either as a prosecutor or as a defendant, and did not have enough confidence in his ability to speak, or indeed in his knowledge and understanding of the law and the tactics and skills needed to win, he could seek help from a professional advocate, who, working in the shadows, could advise his client and write the speech, building a case in the most advantageous way for his client. The tactics which different speechwriters used varied significantly. Each had their preferences, their own weapons, and their own tropes for tackling the needs of the case at hand. The famous *ethopoieia* of Lysias, the unstoppable torrent of Demosthenic oratory, the slick tactics of Aeschines, the overwhelmingly effective point-by-point argumentation of Isaios, the urbanity and elegance of Hypereides, or the expert and adventurous storytelling of Apollodoros are lasting monuments to the high level of expertise put into the *agones* of litigants before Athenian juries. All these exceptional skills were for sale to the person who could afford to pay the fee of the logographer, and we know for sure that the great representatives of Attic oratory were wealthy men, and also that at least in the case of Lysias, as well as that of Demosthenes, most of this wealth had been acquired from hiring out their skills as speechwriters and litigators. A wealthy woman like Phryne could afford the high price for the services of Hypereides, and the famous hetaira Nais could afford the services of Lysias when she took Philonides to court for sexual assault. Once the speechwriter was hired on behalf of a male or female client the chances of winning would depend largely on *his* skill to convince a jury. Speech, storytelling, arguments, evidence, the overall handling and presentation of the case, and performance in court[10] would all be critical for the outcome. In this process a woman was not necessarily disadvantaged compared to a male litigant because it was up to her logographer's tactics and eloquence, and the performative skills of her *synegoros*, to carry the day. If they proved to be more adept at the task than the opposing litigant and his or her entourage, victory was hers.

If we were to agree that despite some obstacles, indirect access routes and differences in procedure, the women of Attica were able to obtain justice and pursue rightful claims, then why is the issue of their involvement with the legal system of any further significance? Two important issues come to mind. The first has to do with our perceptions of the gender relations and position of women in Athenian society, and their interactions with the institutions of the democracy. The second has to do with our overall understanding of Athenian law and how it served the entire community which it was supposed to serve, and not only the minority of adult male citizens. Both of these important issues are interwoven into the discussions contained in this volume, and I hope that they will be sufficiently explored. Here I will present a brief outline of these issues and how they affect the intersection of Athenian law with the lives of women living in Attica.

The first question is particularly significant in the light of modern narratives developed before and during the 1980s about the subdued and silenced women of Attica, locked away in the dark quarters of the *gynaeconitis* and leading an uninteresting existence at the mercy of the men who dominated their lives, like fathers, husbands and sons.[11] Although research in later years has partially corrected this dark and pessimistic image of the lives of Athenian women,[12] still such perceptions have not gone away altogether, and from time to time they return with a vengeance.[13] Accusations of misogyny, oppression and double standards are frequently thrown at the Greeks in some modern studies.[14] Yet, while modern perspectives can be informative and can make history relevant for us, there is a certain futility in the criticism of the past when it does not conform to our values and standards.

In the early years of the third millennium, during an MA thesis defence at the University of Florida, the late David Young, the great Pindaric scholar, wondered what 'space studies' were, since the subject did not exist in the early 1960s, when he was at graduate school. Space studies in classical scholarship took shape as part of the debate on the position of women in Athenian society from the 1980s.[15] A sharp divide between the indoors (ἔνδον) and outdoors (ἔξω), the front of the house, which belonged to the men (ἀνδρωνῖτις),[16] and the back of the house or the upper floor, which belonged to the women (γυναικωνῖτις), ultimately between the *oikos*, where women ruled, and the polis, which was the domain of the men, evolved into a ubiquitous narrative which defined every aspect of gender relations in classical Athens. As a result space studies became the investigative tool for the contrast between the outdoors, the world of men, and the indoors, the world of women. Any crossing of the dividing boundary, in drama, in fiction, in poetry or in real life, was to be interpreted as a transgression with, almost invariably, bad consequences, except in comedy, where such reversals formed the foundation of the humour and were an inextricable part of the plot.

This volume will build on studies which have mounted a serious challenge to these assumptions, and argue that any divide between the indoors and outdoors or the female and male spheres of influence was very much permeable and could be crossed when necessary without adverse consequences. It will be argued that crossing such boundaries was imperative for Athenian households to function in real life, and especially in challenging times of war and the calamities of defeat and tyrannical regimes, which were ubiquitous for a good part of the classical period. The narrative which limited the universe of Athenian women to the doorstep of their household was based upon certain assumptions, such as sufficient financial prosperity to allow the women not to worry about money, a living, healthy *kyrios* on whom the rest of the household could rely for their maintenance and for taking care of all the affairs outside the *oikos*, relative stability and prosperity in public life, and altogether a supportive infrastructure, which would allow women to focus on their roles as wives, mothers and managers of the household. It is certainly not an accident that Xenophon in the *Oeconomicus* chose to place his description of an idealised Athenian household in the *pentekontaetia*,[17] those fifty golden years of prosperity and stability under the Athenian Empire between the end of the Persian wars and the outbreak of the Peloponnesian war. However, for much of the classical period warfare was almost constant; men of all ages, and especially young husbands and fathers, were killed in large numbers; wives and children were left behind without a protector and breadwinner; and Athens went through some seriously trying times involving hostile invasions, siege, hunger, deadly epidemics, defeat, military occupation, tyrannical regimes, and periods of political and economic instability.

This cosy image of the Athenian household, with the *kyrios* dealing with outside affairs and his loyal and dutiful wife efficiently running her little indoors empire, sounds more like nostalgia for the Athenian household of the golden age when viewed from the perspective of an ageing and displaced Xenophon, as the Peloponnesian war, the Corinthian war and the realignment of the Greek city-states after the rise of Thebes had taken a heavy toll upon Athenian families. Intriguingly, the historian might have been playing a trick on his readers when he placed Ischomachos and his wife Chrysilla as the ideal Athenian couple, if he was – and he should have been – aware of the events which followed as described by Andocides:[18] Chrysilla took her daughter's husband Kallias as a lover and had a child with him out of wedlock; her daughter, deeply ashamed, tried to commit suicide, but when she recovered she divorced her husband; Kallias publicly refused to acknowledge his son by Chrysilla, but later changed his mind, married her and acknowledged his son. Quite plausibly Xenophon expected his readers to understand the difference between an idealised household and the tangled mess that a real family could actually be at any point in history. Whether he meant to do this or not is not important; however, the lesson which this teaches us is meaningful. We should not be making assumptions about the lives of real families in challenging historical circumstances based on abstractions which remove from the picture a number of important parameters, such as poverty, disease, dysfunctional relationships, almost incessant warfare, periods of political instability, and limited welfare options for a household led by a disabled or infirm *kyrios*. On the contrary, we should weigh heavily the impact of such factors when we try to synthesise a more accurate reflection of the lives of real Athenian families in the classical period, taking into account the full diversity of the population living in Attica, in terms of wealth, status, gender, religious practices, sexual preferences, possibilities and lifestyles.

Once we start correcting the image and allowing for such variables, then the widow and mother of five in the *Thesmophoriazousai* of Aristophanes who is struggling to make a living by selling wreaths to partygoers, as the Peloponnesian war has reached its twentieth year, stops being a caricature of comic fantasy, and becomes a very real character, the on-stage representation of many real Athenian women who were in the same position. The widow of the *Thesmophoriazousai* cannot stay indoors, she does not have the luxury of worrying about matters such as respectability, she cannot afford to maintain the paleness of her skin by staying away from the sun or take pleasure in the vanities of women, at which Aristophanes and other comedians so often poke fun;[19] her domain extends far beyond her doorstep to the hillsides and mountains of Attica where she collects the materials for her wreaths, and to the marketplace and the whole network of clients where she can sell her product. She does not have a husband to be the breadwinner, the protector of the household and its property, and the representative of the household in the legal system and the institutions of the polis. If someone were to wrong the persons of the *oikos* or misappropriate its property, there would be no *kyrios* to take care of these matters without her full involvement. In so many ways she is the effective *kyrios* of the household, and the indoors and outdoors, the *oikos* and the polis, or the private and the public, are converging on her. She may not be able to take care of some of these matters without help from male relatives, but she needs to be the driving force behind everything, even if that means pleading with or cajoling and ultimately using sometimes reluctant male relatives whose help she needs, as Steven Johnstone has suggested.[20] She needs to be the breadwinner, the defender and protector, the manager and caretaker, the guardian and the ruler of her family, the single parent who, as Demosthenes emphasises when he speaks about the widowhood of his own mother, needs to put her own life on hold so as to be able to take care of her children and household.[21]

High demands such as these upon Athenian women were not a rare exception. Thousands of men were killed in the constant warfare between the Greek city-states, leaving behind widows and children.[22] Perhaps not all widows were facing the same predicament. For example, the mother of Demosthenes, coming from an affluent household and having married a rich man, surely was never in a position as precarious as that of the Aristophanic widow, and many of the households which were left without a *kyrios* had substantial property and supporting families behind them. But we cannot make the same assumption for all households. How this changes our perception of the direct interactions of women with the justice system and institutions of the Athenian democracy becomes obvious when we consider the simple principle that the larger the exposure of women to the world of the outdoors, the marketplace, the business centres and practices of an open economy like that of classical Athens, the greater the danger and the need for direct encounters with the legal system of the city. As men needed to have recourse to the courts of justice in order to defend their property and business interests, or to fend off attacks by enemies upon their person, family or property, so did women who had to work and function outside their homes.

But there is more to it than that, since the *oikos* was no safe haven either. Relatives could be laying counterclaims to property which belonged to the *oikos*, and such quarrels could turn out to be vicious and prolonged affairs.[23] If an attack by relatives was directed towards property which either the woman had brought into the household or she was entitled to inherit from her natal family, to which she always retained inheritance rights, albeit secondary to the agnatic line, someone needed to step in and defend the woman and her property rights. If the *kyrios* was incapacitated, absent or dead, another relative would need to champion her case, and if the dispute ended up in court he would need to act as a representative, and/or hire the services of a professional advocate to maximise the chances of winning, especially when substantial property was at stake. Perhaps things became more complicated when the dispute was about relatively small sums of money, not worth much time and attention, and/or the woman's relationship with her relatives was strained. How could she go about defending her rights? For the metic innkeepers in the underworld of Aristophanes' *Frogs*, who had been defrauded of payment by Herakles, the only protectors of their interests were public figures like Kleon and Hyperbolos.[24] This complicates the picture further, and we do need to take into account factors like wealth and citizen status as we try to understand the particulars and the precise avenues open to women of citizen or metic status, if they needed to access the legal system, in order to seek redress for a crime or to lay a claim on property. In the following chapters I have tried to discuss these matters in their full complexity, and I hope that I have at least succeeded in portraying the women of Attica as a very diverse group in their interactions with the legal system and institutions of the polis. I also hope that this discussion will contribute to a richer and more accurate understanding of the lives of the lesser-known half of Attica's population.

THE INTERSECTION OF THE LAW WITH THE LIVES OF WOMEN

An important fact about classical Athenian law was that it had evolved over centuries and continued to evolve all the way to the end of the Athenian polis and beyond. Athenian law must not be understood as a static concept, nor should it be understood as the product of democratic processes in its entirety. It was firmly rooted in the two law codes, by Drakon and Solon, introduced under the aristocratic state in the archaic period and intended to serve as responses to the acute problems of a society significantly different from that classical Athens. And yet, the Athenian democracy had found effective and successful ways of incorporating those antiquated codes and the legal concepts and assumptions behind them into the laws of the democracy, which were inspired by very different principles like those of equality before the law (*isonomia*), equality of political rights (*isopoliteia*), free speech (*parrhesia*) and the rule of the people (*demokratia*). As I have suggested in a previous publication, the Athenian democracy through its laws recognised basic human rights, like the rights to life, property, family and personal fulfilment and happiness, for all free persons living in Attica, while the right to life and some very rudimentary legal protections against excessive cruelty were even extended to slaves. The democracy also aspired to offer open and equal access to the justice system for all free persons, even though such aspirations had their limitations in real life. Wealth and status created inequalities, as rich persons could afford to hire pricey and effective speechwriters and advocates, while the poorest among the citizens had to rely on their own skills or those of a well-intentioned, but possibly less effective, relative or friend who could act as a *synegoros*.[25]

The legal system of classical Athens was based on principles intended to secure a fair trial.[26] Each litigant received an equal allocation of time and an equal opportunity to present supporting witnesses, laws or other relevant evidence. In order to prevent bribery and corruption from affecting verdicts, the Athenian state operated a complex system of allocation of judges by lot to each court in the morning before the trial, and never earlier, and asked the judges to take an oath that they would judge according to the laws and the merits of the case.[27] The random selection and the large number of judges in each court offered some guarantees that they were a representative cross-section of society, and that individual prejudices or politics would not have a decisive influence on the outcome. The secret ballot at the end of each trial was meant to guarantee that each judge cast his vote according to his conscience, and not under the influence of extraneous factors, such as political pressures or group psychology. Were such measures enough to guarantee a free and fair trial for all litigants? This is a very difficult question to answer since we know the verdicts in a very small number of cases; all we can tell is that these measures reflect the firm desire of the Athenian democracy to ensure fairness and justice through its legal system.

No state in history, before or after, has subjected its magistrates and public officials to greater scrutiny than classical Athens. Not only did officials have to undergo a scrutiny before their entry to office (δοκιμασία),[28] and a gruelling auditing of their accounts and conduct at the end of their office (εὔθυνα),[29] with dire consequences which could go as far as disfranchisement for those who failed, but also all officials were continuously monitored throughout their tenure of office, and could be suspended if some serious failing was brought to the attention of the *demos*. The result of this incessant scrutiny should have inspired fair and thoughtful interactions of magistrates with the public, if not out of a sense of duty, at least out of a sense of apprehension for the approaching auditing in the not too distant future.

The question of how women fit into this system is a complicated one. Did Athenian law view them as individual citizens, or were they seen as mere appendages attached to a family? How much personal responsibility did they have before the law? Were the existing laws of Athens sufficient to ensure women's rights to life, safety, property and personal happiness? Which lawsuits applied to women, since they were excluded from a large chunk of public life? It is not easy to provide simple, straightforward answers to most of these questions. First, there is a temporal dimension which complicates things. The place of women in the Solonean *oikos* was very different from their place in the classical *oikos*, and yet, most of the legislation which directly affected the lives and fortunes of women in classical Athens had been introduced by Solon. While Solonean laws treated women as part of a family, attached to a certain *oikos*, their father's, husband's, brother's or that of some other male relative who was serving as their guardian, and viewed their rights and obligations through the spectrum of this network, classical Athenian law under the democracy operated on the basis of personal responsibility and viewed free persons as individuals, personally responsible before the law. These two concepts may seem contradictory and impossible to accommodate at the same time, and yet the Athenian democracy found ways to do it. As a result, the property and inheritance rights of women could not even be understood outside the context of family law, and the archaic concepts of the laws of Solon about property only made sense within the context of an *oikos*. Although Solon's property and inheritance laws guaranteed and safeguarded the property rights of individual women, they did so through a series of bizarre provisions which had families rather than individuals in mind, like that of an *epikleros* (heiress), and astonishingly removed from women any sense of choice or personal responsibility about their married life, personal happiness and fate in life.

On principle, Athenian magistrates as the first tier of the justice system, public and private arbitrators as the second tier, and the *dikasterion* as the final, top tier in the process were not expected or encouraged by the fundamental principles of the Athenian democracy to treat women unfairly on account of their gender. But how this translated into actual practice is more complicated, especially when the judges themselves did not perceive men and women as equal in many important aspects. Gender could affect the build-up of cases, the types of lawsuits in which women were involved, the types of arguments that would be brought before the juries, the *ethopoeia* and tactics in the construction of the case and many other factors. It is impossible to answer the question whether these differences produced biased verdicts, but the difference in gender certainly played an important role in the tactics used to win a case involving a female litigant as well as the types of lawsuits in which women could be involved.

All these issues are discussed in more detail in the following chapters and I hope that the final conclusions can throw some light upon those less studied aspects of Athenian law. For more than a century, ever since scholars began to study more thoroughly the laws of classical Athens, the focus has been on the male citizen, his interactions with the *dikasteria*, and how these interactions shaped the democracy and its institutions, the history of the city-state and the lives of everyone in it. And while this is a very important part of the story, it is not the whole story, because it leaves out half the population of Attica and the way its interactions with the justice system and the institutions of the democracy influenced political developments, social structures and the largely invisible aspects of economic activity involving women, since women's labour and its contribution to the economy have been barely acknowledged. For these important reasons it is necessary to focus upon the intersection of the lives of Athenian women with the law and institutions of the democracy, and to study how this allows us to form a more complete image of life in fifth- and fourth-century Athens, for all its inhabitants, and a more encompassing and complete view of the interactions between the Athenian legal system and the entirety of the population which it was expected to serve.

This volume, as part of the series on Intersectionality in Classical Antiquity, stands at the intersection between law and the lives of Athenian women, and explores the interactions of Athenian women with the law. During this investigation it will become necessary to explore how gender intersects with issues such as race[30] and ethnicity, especially as we study the interactions of metic women with the law of Athens. The metic women of Attica were themselves a very diverse group coming from every corner of the known world, from the Greek cities of the mainland, Asia minor and Southern Italy and Sicily, to the shores of North Africa and the Black Sea, and sometimes from faraway lands, like sub-Saharan Africa and the depths of the Persian Empire and beyond. They could be high-born Greek women from other cities, or liberated slaves, like the sly Antigona, the former prostitute and procuress who led astray the naïve speaker in the speech of Hypereides *Against Athenogenes*. They could be rich, like Archippe,[31] who married Pasion and then Phormion, two of the richest men in Athens, or dirt-poor and scraping a living in the marketplace; they could be attractive, like Phryne, highly educated intellectuals, like Aspasia, ordinary, respectable housewives in metic households, notorious prostitutes, like Sinope, low-class businesswomen like the two innkeepers in the *Frogs* of Aristophanes, and so on.

What united this very diverse and to a large extent marginalised population under one category was the contrast with Athenian citizen women who could marry Athenian men and give birth to citizens. The latter I will call 'Athenian women', or 'citizen women', when it is necessary to distinguish them from the rest of the free female population of Attica, whom I will comprehensively call 'the women of Attica'.[32] The interactions of all women living in Attica with the legal system of the Athenian democracy also intersect with matters of class, ability, wealth, status and overall social standing. It is a stated purpose of this study to explore these intersections.

Finally, it may seem like a contradiction in terms to consider the majority of the population of Attica as a marginal group, but I hope that it will become clear to the reader that this large group, the free female population of Attica, was marginalised in some very important ways and needed to depend on male friends and relatives in order to be able to safeguard basic rights which the democratic constitution guaranteed for all free persons, such as safety, property and personal dignity. While the emphasis in this volume has been placed not so much on the obstacles which women faced as upon the possibilities afforded to them so as to overcome these obstacles, the reader should always keep in mind that the women of Attica were subject to serious legal disabilities. I will not be arguing against this core position; our purpose here is to explore the possibilities open to women in their efforts to secure and safeguard their legal rights within the confines of these restrictions and disabilities.

SOURCES

The main source for our understanding of the interactions between the legal system of the Athenian democracy and the women of Attica is a number of speeches where a woman was either one of the litigants or the main person of interest behind the dispute. This leaves us with a very limited number of extant speeches – in fact only three where one of the litigants was a woman: Antiphon *Against the Stepmother*, Apollodoros *Against Neaira*, and the speech for a claim entered by Xenokles on behalf of his wife Phile to the estate of her father Pyrrhos (Is. 3). If we cast the net wider we can include the case *To Boiotos* (D. 40), which revolves around his mother Plangon and her relationship with his father Mantias, and also the case involving the wife of Diodotos and daughter of Diogeiton (Lys. 32), because even though on the surface it is a dispute between men – her son-in-law has sued her father on behalf of her young sons – she stands at the centre of this dispute and in all but name she is the true prosecutor of her father. The vast majority of cases involving women litigants has come to us in the form of fragmentary speeches. Sometimes these fragments allow an adequate understanding of the events leading to the trial, but more often they do not. They tantalise us with vague and yet exciting clues, they invite us to guess, to reconstruct, to imagine, to reach tentative conclusions, but they offer little certainty. We cannot ignore this evidence, even though there's always a danger that it might lead us down the wrong path. My understanding of these cases is based upon a reconstruction which could be incorrect, or partially incorrect, but the conclusions which I have been drawing from these cases and the contribution they make to the bigger picture stand on safer ground, because on many occasions they can be cross-referenced and corroborated by additional evidence and comparisons with similar cases on which we are better informed.

In Part I of this volume I have mostly included the relevant fragments with English translation and as much commentary as I felt that it was safe to make, short of resorting to wild speculation. The entries are roughly in alphabetical order of the person named in the entry title, according to the Roman alphabet. This seemed to be the only sensible arrangement, considering that in many cases we cannot even be sure about the author, and we certainly do not have enough information to date most of these speeches even approximately. I have also included summaries of the main issues at hand and a few pointed extracts from the extant speeches, enough to inform the reader about the merits and facts of the case, and how they help us understand better women's interactions with the Athenian justice system. Mindful of space, I have not included extant speeches in their entirety, considering that there are excellent online translations and resources readily available, as well as some high-quality modern commentaries for some of them. I have not cast the net so wide as to include cases where men's claims to properties could have originated from the enatic line, for example the messy and complicated dispute on the estate of Hagnias, where claims and counterclaims were entered for decades allegedly on behalf of female relatives who had been dead for some time, or might not even have been real persons.[33]

I have also left out evidence from other literary genres, like the 'trial' of Antigone by Kreon, after she has been caught disobeying his orders. I believe that such evidence, especially from drama, and maybe even from the Hellenistic novel, which often follows classical sources, may have much to tell us about a woman's brush with the law and the authorities, but this is a discussion for another day, as the approaches and methodologies for the study of such indirect sources would be vastly different from those employed for the study of more direct evidence from the Attic orators. By turning the spotlight on the actual court cases, for which we have evidence, even if not the entire speech, we can build a relatively clear, factual construct, which is not distorted by literary fantasy or philosophical discourse. Since the main historians of classical Athens, like Thucydides and Xenophon, offer no factual information for such cases, and even the *Athenaion Politeia*, that invaluable source for our understanding of Athenian constitution and law, does not help much in this case, our most reliable sources are the actual court documents of classical Athens, in the form they have reached us. Some of them may be revisions of the actual speeches read in court, but we cannot tell which ones are, if any, and in any case it does not matter for our purposes. Whether revised or not, they still provide very important information about the interactions of Athenian women with the legal system of the city, and this information is discussed in a more synthesised form in Part II. This may create some duplication, but it is necessary, if we are to put these cases in context, and join the pieces of evidence they provide into a more complete picture.

Finally, the Appendix contains a selection of the most important laws which affected the lives and fortunes of Athenian women, accompanied by a brief commentary on each law. I hope that this selection will be helpful to the reader for a better understanding of the legal background against which most of these cases were introduced into court. I have not provided an extensive discussion of these legal documents, as there are numerous high-quality studies to which the reader can turn. On the whole, the aspiration for this volume has been to contain discussions sufficiently comprehensive to adequately explore the main aspects of a subject which stands at the intersection between legal history and gender studies, each a topic with vast bibliography and unlimited extensions.

THE MODERN LITERATURE

The study of the lives of women in the ancient world was a very peripheral subject before the 1980s. Historians studied the political history of the Athenian democracy, students indulged in the tactics employed in the countless battles fought on Greek soil, memorised a plethora of names and dates and learned to admire the great men of the past. The gradual emergence of a more inclusive culture after the 1960s brought about some changes in the way we view history, and generated a number of pioneering studies exploring the history, status and lives of Greek women, like Sarah B. Pomeroy's *Goddesses, Whores, Wives, and Slaves* (1975), or Mary R. Lefkowitz's *Heroines and Hysterics* (1981), and a number of collections starting with Helene Foley (1981), and a decade later Elaine Fantham et. al. (1994). Already in the 1970s David Schaps, in a significant article published in 1975, and shortly after in his authoritative monograph *Economic Rights of Women in Ancient Greece* (1979), had mapped out complex patterns in inheritance law which suggested that women had substantial property rights and an influential presence in the finances of the *oikos*. These spirited efforts to shift the focus to the unknown half of Attica's population and shed some light on the lives and contribution of its female population culminated in two important books in the mid1990s: Sue Blundell's *Women in Ancient Greece* (1995), and Christine Schnurr-Redford's *Frauen im klassischen Athen* (1996). As the new millennium approached, an ever-increasing number of high-impact studies on the lives of women explored numerous topics, from literary and artistic representations to the real lives of women in Athens and other parts of the Greek world.

The literature of the 1990s somewhat softened the edges of the confrontational gender politics of the 1980s and generated more nuanced images of the lives of women. They started being seen not as mere victims of history, but as creators and contributors to the societies in which they lived. The important work of Cynthia Patterson (1976; 1998) and Claude Mossé (1993), and more recently of Susan Lape (2010) and Josine Blok (2017), especially on citizenship and what it meant for women, allowed for a better understanding of some important background issues and made clear that although citizenship was understood differently for women, in terms of rights and duties, there was no doubt that classical Athenian law saw a very clear difference between citizen and alien women. This more encompassing view of the lives of Athenian women was also reflected in the most significant study on the legal status of Athenian women, the classic and still largely relevant volume by Roger Just, *Women in Athenian Law and Life* (1989). Just opens the chapter discussing the legal capabilities of women as follows:

> A woman's life long supervision by a guardian, her *kyrios*, summarizes her status in Athenian law. She was not considered a legally competent, autonomous individual responsible for her own actions or capable of determining her own interests.[34]

This sentence says it all. Just was restating the orthodox view that since women needed to rely on a *kyrios* for their dealings with the law, they were considered to be legal minors, and therefore had no interactions with the law of the city in their own right. However, it must be said that thoughout his study Just explores the issues at hand in their full complexity, and this is why his work remains influential more than three decades after its publication. Near the end of the millennium Steven Johnstone (1998) reinforced the traditional position by pointing out the difficulties and complications in interpersonal relations within families as women were trying to secure representation for legal matters from male relatives.

Lin Foxhall was the first, as far as I know, to mount a direct challenge to the established orthodoxy on the absence of women from the Athenian legal system in an important article entitled 'The law and the lady: Women and legal proceedings in classical Athens' (1996), where she argued that the picture is more nuanced. Two years later the pioneering study by Michael Gagarin, 'Women in Athenian courts' (1998), presented and discussed a substantial amount of evidence about the interactions of the women of Attica with the courts, but still largely upheld the established view of women's exclusion from the justice system. A few years later Gagarin presented another important study, entitled 'Women's voices in Attic oratory' (2001), offering some valuable insights into the way the Attic orators present women. More recently Esther Eidinow, in an adventurous and insightful volume entitled *Envy, Poison, and Death: Women on Trial in Classical Athens* (2016), has presented a wide-ranging exploration of the possible motives, emotions and background behind the trials of several women in fourth-century Athens. Around the same time Rebecca Kennedy (2014) engaged in a thorough discussion of the lives of women in classical Athens which, although focused on metics, presented the women of Attica in all their diversity, and painted a rich and realistic image of their lives.

These important works, and many more consulted throughout this volume, have contributed to a more encompassing picture. I owe a heavy debt in particular to four major studies on Athenian law: MacDowell (1978), Schaps (1979), Todd (1993) and Just (1989). If I were to acknowledge every occasion I have relied upon the scholarship in one of these books as background reading, it would get tedious. Many more studies have served as background readings on the complex issues discussed in this volume. The actual cases involving women litigants, as presented in Part I, support the view of Lin Foxhall for a more nuanced understanding of the topic. The question is not whether women had a presence equal to that of men in the justice system, but whether within the confines of the system they were able to obtain justice without prejudice and safeguard their rights, property and safety within the *oikos* and the polis. This is why taking black-and-white positions on this issue has not been helpful for our understanding of the interaction between women's lives and the law. The questions we are facing are complex and they have no easy 'yes-or-no' answer. We need to take for granted the fact that the ancient world perceived women to be a different kind of citizen from men, with a different set of obligations towards the city, the community and the family, a different set of rights, even a different set of virtues and vices, and if we were to subscribe to the views of some philosophers like Xenophon and Aristotle, a different nature altogether manifesting itself with different strengths and weaknesses from those of men.[35] Beyond this point we need to try and understand how these perceived differences affected not only the legal standing of Athenian women, but also their avenues to the justice system of the Athenian democracy, the litigation tactics and their chances of success. With these considerations in mind, my ultimate objective in this volume is to shed light upon the complex relationship which the women of Attica had with the justice system of the democracy. Somewhere between complete exclusion from the legal system and access equal to that of men there was a compromise, a softer position where representation did not mean exclusion, support by a family member or an advocate was not exactly equal to legal minority, and *synegoria*, a common practice which benefited both men and women litigants, was not equal to tutelage. This approach has been the guiding principle of this volume, and its primary purpose has been to add this crucial piece of the puzzle, which will give us a fuller picture of the lives and fortunes of women under the first democracy in history, as well as a more complete understanding of the legal system of democratic Athens and how it served the entire community.

NOTES

1. See for example, Goldhill 1994: 347–69, where it is stated that the Athenians were 'remarkably unwilling' to allow women into the space of the law court; Carey 2007: 429: 'In Athenis mulieribus litem agere non licebat'; Todd 1993: 201: 'Citizenship at Athens was a man's business, in that the active exercise of citizen rights in the public sphere was confined to men'; Tetlow 2004: 59–160; among others. While these conclusions are correct and truthful, it will be argued in this volume that the full picture is more complex and nuanced.

    By 'classical period' I refer to fifth- and fourth-century Athens. This study focuses upon this time frame, although when necessary I go back to the archaic period (seventh to sixth centuries), especially the time of Solon, when the core laws, which largely governed the lives and fortunes of Athenian women, were introduced. It has been a conscious choice to stay focused upon these two all-important centuries for Athenian history, when the polis remained independent and democratically governed, except some brief periods of political upheaval at the end of the fifth century.

2. In fact, there are several different approaches to women transgressing into the world of men, moving from the *oikos* to the polis sphere, in Athenian drama. For some scholars these crossings are primarily violations of gender norms limited to the world of fiction (e.g. Taaffe 1993: 139; Stehle 2002: 369–406; Fletcher 1999:

108–12; Zeitlin 1981: 169–217; Shaw 1975: 255–66; Finnegan 1990: 100–6). Other scholars see a dialectic between the indoors and the outdoors, the *oikos* and the polis (e.g. Summons 2005: 10–14; Compton-Engle 2005: 163–76; Foley 1981: 1–21. However, Foley in a more recent study (2014: 259–74) emphasises the greater adherence of women than of men to gender stereotypes; see also Gerolemou 2011, where madness is presented as either an excuse or an explanation for women stepping out into the world of men; Papadopoulou 2008: 149–77, where such transgressions typically enforce but also challenge gender stereotypes; a similar argument is put forward by Des Bouvrie 1990.

3. The works of Eva Keuls (1985) and Carola Reinsberg (1989) are a good example of such antitheses.
4. See Rubinstein 2018b: 104–43. Rubinstein discusses fines recorded in inscriptions and their legal context.
5. An important study on arbitration is Roebuck 2001. On public arbitration see Miyazaki 1996: 73–83.
6. See e.g. D. 40.10–11, where Plangon appears before a public arbitrator and gives evidence about the paternity of her sons with Mantias, and 59.45–6, where Neaira appears before three private arbitrators, and speaks in defence of her status as a free person. Both women succeeded in their objectives.
7. D. 59; see also the discussion in Part I, p. 68.
8. The *synegoria* for Phormion (D. 36) was composed by Demosthenes in its entirety, with the thin excuse that Phormion did not feel confident of his Greek. Of course, a man capable of performing large financial transactions and detailed contract negotiations, to the point of becoming one of the richest people in the city and being able to secure for himself Athenian citizenship, from very humble beginnings since he had started life as a slave, surely had enough intellect and understanding of Greek to speak for himself. Instead, he chose not to risk it and paid handsomely for one of the best orators in town to write an effective speech for him. The success of Phormion in that trial surely vindicated his choice. An authoritative study of *synegoria* is Rubinstein 2000, esp. pp. 25–41, where all known cases of *synegoria* are listed and briefly presented.
9. Theomnestos, for example, explains to the court that he has chosen Apollodoros as his *synegoros*, because he is young and inexperienced, while Apollodoros is older and more experienced in legal matters (D. 59.14–5: δέομαι οὖν ὑμῶν, ὦ ἄνδρες δικασταί, ἅπερ ἡγοῦμαι προσήκειν δεηθῆναι νέον τε ὄντα καὶ ἀπείρως ἔχοντα τοῦ λέγειν, συνήγορόν με κελεῦσαι καλέσαι τῷ ἀγῶνι τούτῳ Ἀπολλόδωρον. καὶ γὰρ πρεσβύτερός ἐστιν ἢ ἐγώ, καὶ ἐμπειροτέρως ἔχει τῶν νόμων, καὶ μεμέληκεν αὐτῷ περὶ τούτων ἁπάντων ἀκριβῶς, καὶ ἠδίκηται ὑπὸ Στεφάνου τουτουί, ὥστε καὶ ἀνεπίφθονον αὐτῷ τιμωρεῖσθαι τὸν ὑπάρξαντα. 'Therefore I am asking you, men of the jury, what I think I should be asking as a young man and an inexperienced speaker – to allow me to invite Apollodorus as my advocate for this trial. He is older and has more experience in the laws, he has paid close attention to all these matters, and he suffered injustice at the hands of Stephanus; so he has every right to punish the man who started it').

10. A number of important studies in recent years have emphasised the performance of litigants in court and its importance for the outcome of the case. See in particular the excellent monograph of Andreas Serafim (2017) and the rich collection of articles in the recent volume edited by Sofia Papaioannou, Serafim and Beatrice de Vela (2017), with references to previous scholarship.
11. E.g. Wright 1923; Flacelière 1965: 55, 65–7; Gilmore 1987; Rahe 1984: 2; Walcot 1994: 27–50; Brulé 2001; Pritchard 2014: 173–93, who accepts that seclusion was only an ideal, but nonetheless asserts that the Athenians endorsed it; and most of the articles in the earlier collections on women in antiquity; for the entire discussion see the very useful review article by Katz (1995: 21–43).
12. Voices of dissent were raised even before the 1980s (e.g. Gomme 1925: 1–25; Sainte Croix 1970: 273–8, who, while accepting that women's property rights were inferior, objects to the concept of an oppressive segregation; Richter 1971; Gould 1980: 38–59, with emphasis on the infinite complexities of the issues at hand). Later studies for the most part have supported a more nuanced picture, where the boundaries between separate spheres of influence for men and women were neither impermeable nor oppressive, and there were many shades and complexity in the norms and patterns governing the lives of Athenian women and their relationship with their menfolk and the polis (e.g. Blundell 1998; Schnurr-Redford 1996; Hartmann 2002; Konstantinou 2018; Cohen 1989a: 3–15; Just 1989: 106–25; Wolpert 2002: 415–24; Kennedy 2014; Sourvinou-Inwood 1995: 111–20; Siropoulos 2000: 181–96; Rosen 1997: 149–76; Brock 1994: 336–46; Henderson 1991: 133–47; Davidson 2013: 107–24; among others).
13. See for example the pessimistic point of view of Pierre Brulé (2001) on the lives of Athenian women, the equally dark and pessimistic point of view of Elizabeth Tetlow (2004) on the legal position of Athenian women, and the deeply flawed and problematic book by Morris Silver (2018) on marriage, concubinage and the *oikos*.
14. E.g. Brulé 2001; DuBois 1992: 97–116.
15. See Gilhuly and Worman 2014; Westgate 2015: 47–95; Davidson 2013: 107–24; Morris 1998: 193–220; Wolpert 2000: 415–24; Isaacs 2010; Konstantinou 2018; Antonaccio 1999: 517–33; Rehm 1999: 363–75; Easterling 1987: 15–26; Corner 2011: 60–85.
16. How exaggerated this division of spheres has been may be obvious from the fact that the term ἀνδρωνῖτις for the men's part of the house is only used three times in classical literature, all three in an intentionally forced and artificial division of the house. It is used twice in the *Oeconomicus* of Xenophon (9.5.3, 9.6.6), where Ischomachos wants to emphasise that male and female slaves should not be allowed to mix without the permission of their master, and once in Lysias 1 (9), where the orator has an interest in drawing a very strict separation of the spheres of male and female dominance. The *gynaeconitis* is somewhat better attested (ten references), but even in these cases there is always an underlying objective to emphasise any divisions. On the basis of this evidence it is highly doubtful that a separation with lock and key between male and female quarters was universal practice, and when it came to poorer households such a division would have been totally impractical. Moreover, such a strict division would undermine the role of

the senior female figure as the manager and leader of her household, because how could she possibly fulfil such a role locked away? On balance I am in favour of the view of Carla Antonaccio (1999: 517–33) that the *gynaeconitis* was a flexible space, where women could retreat when the men of the house were hosting male friends. Sonia Isaacs (2010) broadly agrees in her thorough account of the subject.

17. X. *Oec.* 7; see also Pomeroy 1994, esp. the introduction; Nelsestuen 2017: 74–104, who examines the underlying political thought and emphasises the relationship between the *Oeconomicus* of Xenophon and Aristotle and the theory of empire; Föllinger and Stoll 2018: 143–58, who emphasise that the advice of Ischomachos, far from being 'emotional', is motivated by economic sense and purpose. On gender issues in the *Oeconomicus* see Larivée 2012: 276–98; Oost 1977: 225–36.
18. And. 1.124–7, with MacDowell's note ad loc., and also MacKenzie 1985: 95–6.
19. E.g. Ar. *Lys.* 1–253; Fr. 317–44; Eub. Fr. 97 (= Fr. 98 Hunter).
20. Johnstone 2003: 247–74.
21. D. 29.26–33.
22. For a dramatic but accurate presentation of widowhood in Athens as a result of war and other calamities see the authoritative account by Richard Cudjoe on the subject (2010: 1–5).
23. On the issue of family feuds as part of inheritance disputes see the important work which Brenda Griffith-Williams has done in a series of articles, especially 2012: 145–62; 2016: 111–16; 2019: 375–88, and her 2013 commentary on several speeches of Isaios; see also the excellent commentary by Rozalia Hatzilambrou on Isaios 3 (2018); Hunter 1993: 100–21; Patterson 1998; Cox 1998; and the earlier authoritative work of David Schaps, especially 1975: 53–7 and his 1979 monograph on the property rights of Athenian women.
24. Ar. *Ra.* 549–78.
25. Kapparis 2019a: 30–6, 46–9, 96–101. Conceptual studies on human rights in classical Athens include Burnyeat 1994: 19–27; Ténékidès 1988: 605–37; Garver 2014: 510–27; Zoumpoulakis 2015 (with emphasis on the concept of justice); and the recent review article on the Athenian democracy by Carol Atack (2017: 576–88).
26. Important studies on this are Harris 2013 and Adamidis 2017; Lanni 2016 takes a different approach emphasising the preventative aspects of the law in classical Athens.
27. Arist. *Ath.* 63–6 with Rhodes com. ad loc., and D. 24.149–51.
28. See Lysias' *dokimasia* speeches (16, 25, 26, 31) and Weißenberger 1987; Feyel 2009; Lepri Sorge 1987: 427–34; Adeleye 1983: 295–306; Todd 2010: 73–108, with response by Gagliardi.
29. On *euthyna* see Efstathiou 2007: 113–35; Carawan 1987: 167–208; Adshead 1984: 1–6.
30. I understand the term 'race' in its broadest sense as a social construct intended to define and separate one group from another. I think this broader definition better matches the realities of the ancient world, which did not define race on the basis of skin colour, but certainly had clear concepts of outsider groups, 'us' and 'the others': even though a Spartan might look like an Athenian to the point where from a

modern perspective we would consider them to be of the same race, a fourth-century Athenian would consider a Spartan to be of a different race as a Dorian, and sufficiently different to evoke racial tensions, familiar to us, under certain circumstances. An important study on race in classical Athens is Lape 2010.

31. While Archippe was certainly of metic status when she married Pasion, also still a metic, her status may have been redefined after his naturalisation. For this complicated and rather inconclusive debate see Carey 1991: 84–9; Whitehead 1986a: 109–14.
32. Unless otherwise indicated, I typically exclude female slaves from this larger group, because their legal status was very different from that of free women, and they were viewed as assets rather than persons, in almost all aspects of public and private life.
33. See Humphreys 1983: 219–25.
34. Just 1989: 18.
35. See Deslauriers 2003: 213–31; Hall 2016: 35–42; Karbowski 2012: 323–50; Yates 2015: 1–16; Inglis 2011.

PART I

Cases Involving Women Litigants

1. Lysias, Πρὸς Ἀντιγένη, Περὶ τῆς ἀμβλώσεως

To Antigenes, on the Abortion

Among the speeches of Lysias we encounter a few fragments of an extraordinary and truly intriguing case, which seemingly pushed the boundaries of Athenian legal procedure with arguments which were more akin to philosophy and medicine than Athenian homicide law and process. The speech made an impression upon several rhetoricians of later antiquity, who recommended it precisely because of its unorthodox argumentation as a good exercise for students of rhetoric.

> Fr. 20b Carey = Theon *Progymnasmata* ii 69, Spengel: ἤδη δέ τινα καὶ παρὰ ῥήτορσιν εἴρηται θετικὰ κεφάλαια, ... ὡς ὅ τε ... ἐπιγραφόμενος Λυσίου καὶ ὁ περὶ τῆς ἀμβλώσεως· ἐν μὲν γὰρ θατέρῳ ζητεῖται, εἰ ... εἰ τὸ ἔτι ἐγκυούμενον ἄνθρωπός ἐστι, καὶ εἰ ἀνεύθυνα τὰ τῶν ἀμβλώσεων ταῖς γυναιξί, Λυσίου μὲν οὔ φασιν εἶναι τούτους τοὺς λόγους, ὅμως δὲ οὐκ ἀχάριστον τοῖς νέοις γυμνασίας ἕνεκα καὶ τούτοις ἐντυγχάνειν.

A number of disputable arguments have already been put forward by the orators ... as in the speech of Lysias *On the Abortion*. ... In that speech the question is whether what is carried in the womb is a human being, and whether women can have abortions without fear of a penalty. Some people claim that these speeches were not written by Lysias, but it would be beneficial for young people to read these too for the sake of exercise.

> Fr. 20d Carey = Sopater Ἐκ διαφόρων τινα χρήσιμα (ed. H. Rabe *RHM* 64 [1909] 576): Ὅτι Λυσίᾳ μεμελέτηται ἰατρικὸν πρόβλημα παραδόξως ῥητορικῶς μεθοδευθὲν <ἐν τῷ> Περὶ τοῦ ἀμβλωθριδίου, ἐν ᾧ Ἀντιγένης κατηγορεῖ τῆς ἑαυτοῦ γυναικὸς φόνου ἀμβλωσάσης ἑκουσίως, φάσκων ὡς ἐξήμβλωκε καὶ κεκώλυκεν αὐτὸν πατέρα κληθῆναι παιδός.

Lysias is dealing with a medical question, which he paradoxically converts into a rhetorical subject in the speech *On the Abortion*, where Antigenes is accusing his wife of homicide because she had an induced abortion; he maintains that she had an abortion and prevented him from being called the father of a child.

Fr. 20c Carey = Sopater *Commentary on Hermogenes*, 5,3 Walz: εἰσὶ γὰρ καὶ ἰατρικὰ καὶ φιλόσοφα ζητήματα· καὶ ἰατρικοῦ μὲν ζητήματος παράδειγμα, ὃ καὶ μεμέληται τῷ Λυσίᾳ· εἰ ὁ ποιήσας ἐξαμβλῶσαι γυναῖκα φόνον ἐποίησεν· δεῖ γὰρ γνῶναι πρῶτον, εἰ ἔζη, πρὶν ἐτέχθη. ὅπερ φυσικῶν καὶ ἰατρικῶν ἐστι·

There are also medical and philosophical questions; an example of a medical question is the one discussed by Lysias, namely whether a man who made a woman have an abortion has committed murder; for it is necessary to know if it (sc. the foetus) was a living being before it was born. And this is a matter pertinent to medicine and natural philosophy.

Fr. 20a Carey = *Prolegomena on the Staseis*, 7,15 Walz (= *Prolegomenon Sylloge* 13,200 Rabe): ὡς καὶ ὁ Λυσίας ἐν τῷ περὶ ἀμβλώσεως, κρίνων φόνου τὸν αἴτιον, βιάζεται ζῷον τὸ βρέφος ἀποδεικνύναι καὶ πανταχοῦ φησιν, ὥσπερ οἱ ἰατροὶ καὶ αἱ μαῖαι ἀπεφήναντο.

For example Lysias in the speech *On the Abortion* where the person responsible is on trial for murder goes to great lengths to prove that the foetus (*brephos*[1]) is a living being, and says everywhere '*as the doctors and the midwives have stated*'.

Fr. 22 Carey = Harpokration s.v. *amphidromia*: Ἀμφιδρόμια: Λυσίας ἐν τῷ περὶ τῆς ἀμβλώσεως, εἰ γνήσιος ὁ λόγος.

Lysias in the speech *On the Abortion,* if the speech is authentic (cf. Apostolius Paroem. *Centuria* 2,56)

Fr. 23 Carey = Harp. s.v. *themisteuein*: Θεμιστεύειν: ἀντὶ τοῦ χρησμῳδεῖν Λυσίας ἐν τῷ περὶ τῆς ἀμβλώσεως, εἰ γνήσιος.

themisteuein (to give oracles) instead of *chresmodein*: Lysias in the speech *On the Abortion,* if authentic.

Hip. *Epid.* 2.2.19: Ἡ Ἀντιγένεος, ἡ τῶν περὶ Νικόμαχον, ἔτεκε παιδίον, σαρκῶδες μὲν, ἔχον δὲ τὰ μέγιστα διακεκριμένα, μέγεθος δὲ ὡς τετραδάκτυλον, ἀνόστεον, ὕστερον δὲ παχὺ καὶ στρογγύλον· αὕτη δὲ ἀσθματώδης ἐγένετο πρὸ τοῦ τόκου· ἔπειτα ἅμα τῷ τόκῳ πῦον ἀνήμεσεν ὀλίγον, οἷον ἐκ δοθιῆνος.

The wife of Antigenes, the one living near Nichomachos' place, produced a foetus which was fleshy, with the major organs already shaped, about four fingers long, but without bones, and then round and thick. Before labour she became asthmatic; then during labour some pus came out, as if from a boil.

Compare Galen's comment on this passage (*Comm. Hip. Epid.* 2, 17a 371 Kühn): θαυμαστὸς εἴη ὁ τόκος οὗτος, εἰ μὴ ὑποψίαν παρέχῃ αὐτὸν ἐξ ἀμβλώσεως γεγονέναι.

This birth would have been wondrous if it did not create suspicions that it was the product of an induced abortion.

This mysterious and intriguing case is only known to us from these few citations in grammarians and rhetoricians. What we know about it is not enough to allow us to form a clear picture, but it is sufficient to excite our curiosity. A more detailed discussion of this case and the fragments has been provided in a previous publication.[2] Here I will focus upon the battle before the Areopagos between Antigenes and his wife. It seems clear that an Athenian man named Antigenes prosecuted his wife for homicide because he suspected that she had taken drugs to induce an abortion. If there is any chance that the passage from the second book of the *Epidemics* of Hippocrates refers to this particular case then we understand why the husband became very suspicious.[3] Galen in his commentary on the passage confirms that the appearance of the abortus raised strong suspicions that drugs had been taken intended to induce a miscarriage.[4] Whatever the case, once Antigenes became suspicious of his wife he had no mechanism for prosecuting her simply because Athenian law did not prohibit abortion, or tried to restrict it in any way. Patients were free to seek abortions and doctors were free to perform them, without fear of interference from the law. It is a fair bet to assume at this point that Antigenes divorced his wife. He then proceeded with a prosecution for homicide. His argument was that his wife with her actions had deprived him of fatherhood, and that she had killed his child. Both Theon and Sopater emphasise the speculative and philosophical nature of the arguments used in this case, while the author of the *Prolegomena* emphasises that the orator was pushing the argument to breaking point (βιάζεται). Theon explicitly recommends the speech to students of rhetoric exactly for this reason, because he believes that the unusual nature of these arguments would be instructive.

It seems that the unnamed woman was defended by one of her relatives, who responded to Antigenes with a speech which was attributed to Lysias, even though some doubts were expressed by Harpocration and Theon. A possible strategy of the defence may be revealed in the messy and probably inaccurate citation in the *Prolegomena on the Staseis*, where it is stated that the case largely depended on the expert testimony of some doctors and midwives, intended to shed light upon the question whether the foetus at that stage of its development could be considered to be a human being, and therefore the actions of the wife of Antigenes tantamount to homicide. Doctors in the classical period typically believed in the gradual animation of the foetus at some point during the pregnancy, when the limbs became visible and therefore the foetus took on the appearance of a human being.[5] Consistent with this dominant view, the doctors and midwives invited to testify in this trial probably stated that in their opinion this particular foetus was not a human being, and therefore the wife of Antigenes had not committed homicide. Beyond this point it is not clear how the prosecution could have proved that drugs harmful to the pregnancy had been taken on purpose, and a skilful defendant could have generated a lot of sympathy for a woman who not only had miscarried but also had been so horribly mistreated by her own husband and cruelly cast aside. But above all, it is difficult to see how the Areopagos, this sober-minded and highly experienced court, famous for the fairness of its verdicts, could have been swayed into taking such a big leap and equating the miscarriage of a foetus in early pregnancy with the killing of a human being as defined in Drakon's homicide law. The confluence of these factors turned the balance against Antigenes, and his former wife was acquitted. Never again was an abortion going to be equated with homicide in Athenian law before its criminalisation with the rescript of Severus and Caracalla at the beginning of the third century AD.[6] The modern reader may feel disappointed because this intriguing speech did not survive; it could have been fascinating to watch whether the same arguments made two and a half millennia before our time resembled arguments still made by politicians and lawmakers in the present day.

2. LYSIAS, Περὶ τῆς Ἀντιφῶντος θυγατρός

On the Daughter of Antiphon

Several new fragments included in Carey's edition have enriched our understanding of this case in recent years, but still, the existing evidence is too scanty.[7] It appears to be a case of ἐπιδικασία, namely a process intended to decide who was the closest male relative of a deceased man named Antiphon, and eligible to marry his only daughter, who was an *epikleros*. If so, it is the only case of *epidikasia* of which we have at least some fragments, while the procedure is often mentioned by the orators in the background of property and inheritance disputes.[8]

> Fr. 25a Carey = Plu. *Vitae Decem Oratorum* 833 A: μετὰ δὲ τὴν κατάλυσιν τῶν τετρακοσίων εἰσαγγελθεὶς (sc. ὁ Ἀντιφῶν) σὺν Ἀρχεπτολέμῳ, ἑνὶ τῶν τετρακοσίων, ἑάλω, καὶ τοῖς περὶ τῶν προδοτῶν ἐπιτιμίοις ὑπαχθεὶς ἄταφος ἐρρίφη καὶ σὺν τοῖς ἐκγόνοις ἄτιμος ἐνεγράφη. οἱ δ' ὑπὸ τῶν τριάκοντα ἀνῃρῆσθαι αὐτὸν ἱστοροῦσιν, ὥσπερ Λυσίας ἐν τῷ

ὑπὲρ τῆς Ἀντιφῶντος θυγατρὸς λόγῳ· ἐγένετο γὰρ αὐτῷ θυγάτριον, οὗ Κάλλαισχρος ἐπεδικάσατο. ὅτι δ' ὑπὸ τῶν τριάκοντα ἀπέθανεν, ἱστορεῖ καὶ Θεόπομπος (*FGrH* 115 F 120) ἐν τῇ πεντεκαιδεκάτῃ τῶν Φιλιππικῶν. ἀλλ' οὗτός γ' ἂν εἴη ἕτερος, Λυσιδωνίδου πατρός, <οὗ> καὶ Κρατῖνος ἐν Πυτίνῃ (Fr. 212 KA) <ὡς> οὐ πονηροῦ μνημονεύει· πῶς <γὰρ> ἂν ὁ προτεθνεὼς καὶ ἀναιρεθεὶς ἐπὶ τῶν τετρακοσίων πάλιν ἐπὶ τῶν τριάκοντα εἴη;

But when those Four Hundred were overthrown, he with Archeptolemus, who was likewise one of the same number, was accused of the conspiracy, condemned, and sentenced to the punishment due to traitors, his body cast out unburied, and all his posterity infamous on record. But there are some who tell us, that he was put to death by the Thirty Tyrants; and among the rest, Lysias, in his oration for Antiphon's daughter, says the same; for he left a little daughter, whom Callaeschrus claimed for his wife by the law of propinquity. And Theopompus likewise, in his Fifteenth Book of Philippics, tells us the same thing. But this must have been another Antiphon, son of Lysidonides, whom Cratinus mentions in his Pytine as a rascal. But how could he be executed in the time of the Four Hundred, and afterward live to be put to death by the Thirty Tyrants?

Fr. 25b Carey = Vat. Gr. 7, Fr. 88 Ucciardello: Δαπανᾶν οὐ τὸ ἀναλίσκειν ἁπλῶς, ἀλλὰ τὸ λαμπρῶς ζῆν . . . 'ἀνήλισκεν αὐτός', ὥς φησι Λυσίας ἐν τῷ περὶ τῆς Ἀντιφῶντος θυγατρὸς 'καὶ δι' ὑπεροβὴν φιλοτιμίας <πλείω> τῶν ὑπὸ τῆς πόλεως προσταττομένων ἐδαπανᾶτο'

To spend lavishly is not simply to spend money, but to live in style . . . 'himself was spending', as Lysias says in the speech *On the Daughter of Antiphon* 'because of excessive generosity he was spending more than what was required by the city'.

Fr. 26 = P. Vindob. Gr. 29816, Fr. 2, col. 2, 2–8: π[εφ]ευγότο[ς Ἀν]τιφῶντος ἀναλαβὼν τὸν ἀρρα[βῶ]να πα[ρ]ὰ Πυρωνίδου ἐδικάζετο [αὐτ]ῷ βεβαιώσε[ως

When Antiphon went on the run, receiving the deposit from Pyronides this man sued him for verification.[9]

Fr. 27 = P. Vindob. Gr. 29816, F. 1, col. 1, 1–14: Ἐπίστρατος δὲ φάσκων αὐτοῦ εἶναι, ἵν[α δ]ιασώσειε τῇ θ[υγ]ατρὶ τῇ Ἀντιφῶντος, εἶχε τὸ χωρίον πλέον ἢ πέντε μῆνας ἕως ἡγ[ησ]άμενοι οἱ τρ[ιά]κοντα οὐδὲν αὐτοῖς προσήκειν τὸν δῆμον ἀνακαλε[σάμ]ε[ν]ο[ι ἐπην]άγκασαν . . .[10]

Epistratos maintained that the field belonged to him, in order to preserve it for the daughter of Antiphon. He held on to the field for more than five months until the Thirty came to the conclusion that they had no claim on it, and then they summoned the people and compelled . . .

Fr. 28 = P. Vindob. Gr. 29816, F. 4, 1–8: οἰκίας [ὡς] προσῆκον ἦν α[ὐ]τοῖς ἠμφεσβήτησαν, τὸ δὲ χωρί[ον] ἔτι ἔχειν ἐκεῖ[νον ἠξίωσ]αν, τῆς [δὲ ἐπικα]ρπίας [αὐ/τοὺς λα]μβάν[ειν.[11]

They laid claim to the house as their own, but they were willing to allow him to keep the field, so long as they retained the usufruct.

Fr. 29 = P. Vindob. Gr. 29816, F. 3, 1–9: ἐκ δ]ὲ τῶν [εἰρημέ]νων σκοπ[οῦντας] ἡγήσασθαι χρ[ὴ Πυ]ρωνίδου τὸν [κλῆρον] εἶναι, εἴ τω μ[ὴ κά]κιστος περὶ τ[οὺς ἑ]αυτοῦ προσήκ[ον]τας Ἀντιφῶν [εἶ]ναι δοκεῖ.

Considering what has been said you can reach the conclusion that the property belongs to Pyronides, unless someone believes that Antiphon was a terrible man towards his relatives.

The case seems to revolve around a woman whom we only know as the daughter of Antiphon. Several ancient sources have tried to identify Antiphon with the orator (Fr. 25a), but this is undoubtedly wrong. Antiphon the orator was convicted of treason and executed not long after the fall of the Four Hundred (c. 410 BC).[12] However, the father of the woman around whom this case revolves was among the men who fled the city during the Thirty (404–3 BC), fearing for his life because it seems that members of the regime had set their eyes on his property (Fr. 26–8).[13] By that time Antiphon the orator had been dead for several years. Some ancient authors tried to reconcile the evidence, invoking the testimony of Lysias and Theopompos (Fr. 25a and b). Lysias indeed says that Eratosthenes was responsible for the death of his own associate Antiphon, but he explicitly places the events in the time of the restoration of the democracy around 410, and suggests that Eratosthenes turned against his friends out of disloyalty and self-serving interest.[14] It is likely that this passage gave rise to the confusion; a careless reader could easily think that Eratosthenes turned on Antiphon as a member of the Thirty in 404–3. The man concerned in this case seemingly died during or shortly after the time of the Thirty. By the looks of it, he never came back from his self-imposed exile.

Unlike the descendants of the orator Antiphon, who were permanently disfranchised while the property of the family was confiscated in its entirety,[15] the daughter of our Antiphon, seemingly an only child (Fr. 27), became an *epikleros* and found herself at the epicentre of a legal battle over who was going to marry her. Either she was supremely attractive, or the efforts of the Thirty to grab her father's property were thwarted by clever, determined and perhaps influential relatives. One of them, a man named Pyronides, seems to be a close relative of her father and one of the claimants of the *epikleros* and her estate. Fr. 29, which looks like the concluding section of the speech of a *synegoros* of Pyronides, defends his right to the estate (and the woman who came with it) on the basis of his close relationship to Antiphon, even though we do not know what that relationship was. This was an important issue, since legally the *epikleros* and her property were to go to the closest male relative of her father willing and able to marry her. Yet it seems that the person who won the *epidikasia* was a man named Kallaischros, if we understand the aorist ἐπεδικάσατο as an indication of the outcome of the *epidikasia*, and not merely of the claim. This in itself is intriguing, because a man named Kallaischros was a powerful oligarch involved in the regime of the Four Hundred, and according to Lysias, an antagonist of Eratosthenes.[16] If the influential oligarch is the same man as the one who was claiming the daughter of Antiphon as her closest relative, this might help us understand how the family succeeded in saving all or most of the property of Athiphon from the rapacious appetites of the Thirty. An influential oligarch with the right connections could be successful in his attempts to thwart the regime and safeguard the property of Antiphon, so as to be able to legally claim it along with the *epikleros* at a later date, without having to share it with the Thirty.

It appears that the relatives of Antiphon employed a number of tactics in order to thwart the rapacity of the Thirty. One of them, a man named Epistratos, pretended that a piece of land (χωρίον) belonged to him, and he held on to it for more than five months until the Thirty were convinced that they could not claim it as part of Antiphon's estate (Fr. 27). However, the success of Epistratos may have been short-lived, because Fr. 28 suggests that the Thirty were willing to allow him to keep the field, but work it for their benefit, since they would keep the usufruct. A compromise solution like this might be one of the means the family employed to safeguard the property of the *epikleros*, and connections with members of the regime could have made such advantageous arrangements possible in these perilous times. We should be in no doubt that the daughter of Antiphon had little or no say in all this bargaining about her life and fortune amidst powerful and rapacious men circling around her father's property.

3. HYPEREIDES, Κατὰ Ἀρισταγόρας ἀπροστασίου (λόγοι β')

Against Aristagora, Aprostasiou (Two Speeches)
The two speeches of Hypereides *Against Aristagora* were delivered in trials related to an alleged immigration violation, but we should be in no doubt that, as in similar cases against other alien women in the fourth century, the true motives

behind this prosecution had nothing to do with immigration offences. Several lexicographers and rhetoricians preserve quotes from the seemingly popular speeches.

Fr. 13.1 Jensen = Athen. 13.52: καὶ Ὑπερείδης μέμνηται ἐν τῷ κατὰ Ἀρισταγόρας β' λέγων οὕτως· 'ὥστε Λαΐς μὲν ἡ δοκοῦσα τῶν πώποτε διενηνοχέναι τὴν ὄψιν καὶ Ὤκιμον καὶ Μετάνειρα'

Hypereides has also mentioned her in the second speech *Against Aristagora* saying the following: 'Lais who appeared be the most beautiful woman ever, and Okimon and Metaneira'

Fr. 14: Harp. s.v. ὅτι χιλίας ἐξημιοῦντο αἱ κατὰ τὰς ὁδοὺς ἀκοσμοῦσαι γυναῖκες Ὑπερείδης ἐν τῷ κατ' Ἀρισταγόρας β'.

Women misbehaving in the streets were fined 1,000 drachmas. Hypereides in the second speech *Against Aristagora*.

Fr. 15: ἀπροστασίου εἶδος δίκης κατὰ τῶν προστάτην μὴ νεμόντων μετοίκων Ὑπερείδης ἐν τῷ κατ' Ἀρισταγόρας β'.

aprostasiou: a type of lawsuit against those who were not using a mentor. Hypereides in the second speech *Against Aristagora*.

Fr. 16: Harp. s.v. 16.5 διαμαρτυρία. Ὑπερείδης δ' ἐν τῷ κατ' Ἀρισταγόρας ἀπροστασίου β' φησὶν ὡς οἱ νόμοι κελεύουσι διαμαρτυρεῖν ἐπὶ ταῖς γραφαῖς ταῖς τοῦ ἀπροστασίου τὸν βουλόμενον ὁμοίως τῶν ξένων καὶ τῶν ἐπιχωρίων.

Diamartyria. Hypereides in the second speech *Against Aristagora* says that the laws ordain that anyone who wishes, Athenian or foreigner, can serve as a witness disputing the admissibility of an *aprostasiou* lawsuit.

Fr. 17: Harp. s.v. νοθεῖα. τίνων δ' οὐκ ἐξῆν τοῖς νόθοις μετέχειν, δεδήλωκεν Ὑπερείδης ἐν τῷ κατ' Ἀρισταγόρας β'.

Who could not be classed among illegitimate persons is indicated by Hypereides in the second speech *Against Aristagora*.

Fr. 18: Harp. s.v. πωληταὶ καὶ πωλητήριον. οἱ μὲν πωληταὶ ἀρχή τίς ἐστιν Ἀθήνησι – Ὑπερείδης ἐν τῷ κατ' Ἀρισταγόρας β'.

The 'sellers' is an office in Athens. Hypereides in the second speech *Against Aristagora*.

Fr. 19: Harp. s.v. φαλάγγια. Ὑπερείδης ἐν τῷ κατ' Ἀρισταγόρας β', ὅτι τῶν δακετῶν τι ζῷόν ἐστι τὸ φαλάγγιον.

Hypereides in the second speech *Against Aristagora* says that the spider is one of those animals that bite.

Fr. 20: Harp. s.v. δωροξενία ἐπεὶ καὶ ὁ τῆς δωροξενίας νόμος ἁρμόττων ἐστὶ τῷ νῦν ἀγῶνι παραχθῆναι· εἰ γὰρ καὶ τοὺς ἀποφυγόντας ξενίας εἴρηκεν ἐξεῖναι τῷ βουλομένῳ πάλιν γράψασθαι, ἐὰν μὴ δοκῶσι δικαίως τὸ πρῶτον ἀποπεφευγέναι, πῶς οὐ φανερόν ἐστι κατ' Ἀρισταγόρας τὸ δίκαιον;

The law on *doroxenia* applies to this case, because if it says that those who were acquitted in a *xenia* case can be indicted again by anyone who wishes, if they appear to have been unjustly acquitted, how is justice not against Aristagora?

Fr. 21: Sud. ν 166: Ὑπερείδης· ὥστε κελευστέον τοὺς μαρτυροῦντας τὰ τοιαῦτα καὶ τοὺς παρεχομένους . . . . . <μὴ> μάτην ἀπατᾶν ὑμᾶς, <ἐὰν> μὴ τυγχάνωσι δικαιότερα λέγοντες· καὶ νόμον ὑμῖν ἀναγκάζετε παρέχεσθαι, τὸν κελεύοντα μὴ νέμειν προστάτην.

Hypereides: Thus those who give such testimony must be asked . . . not to deceive you without reason, if they do not speak justly, and you compel them to present the law which says that one is not to have a sponsor.

Fr. 22: Theon. prog. I p. 162 W. ὁμοίως τὸν καλούμενον τόπον παρὰ τοῖς παλαιοῖς ἔστιν εὑρεῖν· καθάπερ τὸ Δημοσθενικὸν ἐν τῷ ὑπὲρ τοῦ στεφάνου· . . . καὶ Ὑπερείδου κατὰ τῶν ἑταιρῶν ἐν τῷ κατὰ Ἀρισταγόρας.

This topos (namely that Athens was full of people who were enemies of the gods) can be found in the ancient orators, like the Demosthenic passage in the speech *On the Crown*, and in Hypereides, against the hetairai, in the speech *Against Aristagora*.

Fr. 23: Harp. s.v. ἀφαίρεσις ἰδίως λέγεται ἡ εἰς ἐλευθερίαν· Ὑπερείδης ἐν τῷ κατ' Ἀρισταγόρας

Removal to freedom; Hypereides in *Against Aristagora*.

Fr. 24: Athen. 13.50. (Quote from the speech *Against Aristagora*) καὶ πάλιν τὰς Ἀφύας καλουμένας τὸν αὐτὸν τρόπον ἐκαλέσατε.

Again, the so-called Aphyai ('Sardines') you nicknamed in this manner (because they were pale-skinned and very thin with large dark eyes).

Fr. 25: Anecd. Bek. 102. κακολογεῖν Ὑπερείδης κατὰ Ἀρισταγόρας.

'to speak ill'. Hypereides *Against Aristagora*.

Fr. 26: Harp. s.v. μετοίκιον· Ὑπερείδης ἐν τῷ κατ' Ἀρισταγόρας.

Metoikion: Hypereides *Against Aristagora*.

The fragments of the speech allow some insights into the basics of the case, but they do not answer some of the most fundamental questions, like the reason why we have two speeches for a public case, or whether the tradition which states that Aristagora was the mistress of Hypereides is genuine. Outside these fragments there is some independent evidence confiming that she was a notorious hetaira. The most significant is the testimony of Idomeneus, cited by several authors, that Aristagora was one of the pricey mistresses of Hypereides, whom he had set free for a large sum of money and established in his house in Piraeus as his concubine.[17] Apparently she was not the only one; Idomeneus mentions two other mistresses, the 'very luxurious' (πολυτελεστάτην) Myrrhine, who seems to have been the favourite concubine since she was the one established in his main residence in the city, and Phila, who was established in his house in Eleusis.

The passage of Idomeneus allows us a glimpse into the potential problems of such greedy arrangements. First we are told that Hypereides had a big fight with his son Glaukippos, who one might think was understandably upset to watch his father lavishly spend the family's wealth on the fickle affections of not one but three extravagant mistresses. Hypereides expelled his son from the house to make room for Myrrhine. Then, it seems that his infatuation with Phila passed at some point, but perhaps not his affection for the woman, and this is why, when he no longer desired her as his mistress, he made her the housekeeper of his residence in Eleusis. The third woman in this strange quartet, Aristagora, might not have been as pliable and easy-going as Phila, and when she felt neglected she was not willing to settle for less. A reference to an illegitimate son (Fr. 17) might add complications to the already explosive mix.[18] We do not know what the precise circumstances were which led to a bad break-up, but it seems very likely that the two former lovers fell out, and love was replaced by hatred. Eventually Aristagora was prosecuted by her former lover for immigration violations, and a protracted, increasingly bitter legal battle ensued.

A public lawsuit for 'lacking a sponsor' (*graphe aprostasiou*) was the process employed for the prosecution of aliens living in Attica but not registered as metics. The law allowed visitors to the city to stay for some time (perhaps a month) until they concluded their business, but anyone who wanted to stay longer would need to register as a metic. In order to do so, the alien man or woman needed to be sponsored by an Athenian citizen (προστάτης), whose role, it seems, was limited to supporting the alien during initial registration. No further role for the *prostates* is attested, even though theoretically, at least, he was perhaps supposed to function as a mentor and supporter of the metic in his or her new city of residence, especially in his or her dealings with the law.[19] Metics paid a flat-rate tax set at twelve drachmas a year for a man and his family and six drachmas for independent women (*metoikion*), and in exchange they were officially recognised as free persons permanently residing in Attica, under the protection of the Athenian polis and its justice system.[20]

I have argued elsewhere that alien women who were part of an Athenian *oikos* as concubines, or non-citizen relatives of Athenian men, such as illegitimate daughters or half-sisters, did not need to register independently as metics and pay the *metoikion*, because the tax was normally paid by the head of the household, and only non-Athenian households paid this tax.[21] This grey area in Athenian immigration law may be the root of all troubles for alien women prosecuted for not having a sponsor in fourth-century Athens. Women like Aristagora who were concubines of Athenian men never needed to register as metics, but after a break-up, they became independent and had to register. If they failed to do so, they were subject to a *graphe aprostasiou*, and a disgruntled former lover had the perfect pretext to pursue them through the courts, with serious consequences if he succeeded.[22] If this interpretation of Athenian immigration law is correct, it means that alien hetairai attached to Athenian or metic men did not themselves need to register as metics, and only needed to do so when they decided to live and work independently. So, while Aristagora was the concubine of Hypereides living in his house in Piraeus she did not need to register as a metic, but after the break-up she needed to do so, but perhaps she was too slow, and this provided the platform for her former lover to launch his vicious attack against her.

A *graphe aprostasiou* was a public prosecution which could be introduced by any Athenian citizen (Ἀθηναίων ὁ βουλόμενος). In public trials introduced through a *graphe* each litigant delivered only one long speech, and then the jury voted. However, two speeches *Against Aristagora* are attested, as if the case were a private lawsuit. I have argued that the solution to the puzzle probably lies in Fr. 20, which mentions *doroxenia*, a process employed for cases of *graphe xenias* where the defendant had been acquitted, but the prosecutor alleged that this had happened through bribery. Exceptionally in this case Athenian law allowed double jeopardy, and the prosecutor could reopen the case. Possibly Hypereides used the *doroxenia* process against Aristagora, after her acquittal in the first *aprostasiou* trial. The fact that the initial prosecution was not a *graphe xenias* might not be significant if we supposed that *doroxenia* had been extended to all immigration offences by the time of Hypereides. On the other hand this fact could be significant, and Hypereides may be struggling to expand the definition of *doroxenia* here, in order to make it apply to the case of Aristagora, as Fr. 20 seems to imply. Either way, the prospect that the second speech was delivered in a *doroxenias* trial offers a good explanation for the existence of the second speech, the line of argumentation in it, and the reason why the grammarians of later antiquity did not separate the two speeches, but considered them to be part of one and the same case, related to the alleged immigration law violation.

Among the citations from the speech found in the lexicographers and grammarians of later antiquity we find, not surprisingly, references to immigration law. Fr. 15 and 21 imply that the orator at some point cited the law on the *graphe aprostasiou*. Fr. 21 suggests that he quoted the law verbatim, because Suda feels the need to explain the unusual phrase νέμειν προστάτην (to have a sponsor), found in Hypereides as part of the actual legal language. Fr. 26 refers to the *metoikion*, the flat-rate tax which all metics needed to pay (see above). The reference to the πωληταί becomes clear from comparison with a passage of the first speech *Against Aristogeiton*.[23] Demosthenes there explains that metics who had been sentenced to slavery for serious violations of immigration law were handed over to the *poletai*, the public auctioneers, to be sold as slaves. Fr. 17, an entry on *notheia*, the property which illegitimate children were allowed to inherit, may suggest that Hypereides and Aristagora had an illegitimate son, but this interpretation is not inevitable. The ἀφαίρεσις εἰς ἐλευθερίαν (Fr. 23) is well described in extant speeches,[24] and it was the appropriate procedure for rescuing a free person from slavery. If someone treated another person as a runaway slave, but a citizen was prepared to provide sureties on his or her behalf, he could rescue this person from the clutches of the alleged master until a trial decided the status of the alleged slave. Although the law did not specify it, such a process in reality was only applicable to liberated slaves or low-class metics who could be mistaken for slaves; otherwise to hale away a citizen or an obviously free metic as a slave was a serious crime in Athenian law (ἀνδραποδισμός), liable to *apagoge*, and the penalty for the ἀνδραποδιστής was death.[25] Finally, Harpocration informs us that the second speech *Against Aristagora* was an important source for the process of the *diamartyria*, and made clear that the process was not limited to citizens; any free person could serve as a witness challenging the legality of a certain lawsuit.[26]

The remaining fragments, although much more difficult to interpret, present some alluring possibilities about themes and motifs which made these speeches memorable for centuries. Fr. 13 suggests that Hypereides employed a topos found for the first time in the speech of Lysias *To Lais*, and subsequently in other speeches delivered at trials of hetairai.[27] As I argue there, the main function of this topos was to establish an emotional bond between the speaker and his audience through the sharing of common memories and experiences, to give the impression that he is well informed, and perhaps to compare the behaviour and conduct of famous hetairai with those of the litigant. This is probably the context of a reference to two sisters, both hetairai, nicknamed 'Aphyai' (Sardines) because of their appearance (Fr. 24). Athenaios tells us that they were pale and thin with dark eyes, and this is why they were thus nicknamed. Hypereides mentions them along with other hetairai, but unlike the famous past beauties, the two sisters seem to be contemporaries of Aristagora, and perhaps, from the tone of this reference, unfavourably compared to the past beauties mentioned in Fr. 13. A reference to speaking ill of someone (Fr. 25) might have something to do with such unsavoury comparisons.

A reference to a topos where Athens is presented as a place full of enemies of the gods (Fr. 22) is fascinating, because such comments on men who are enemies of the gods, including the related noun θεοισεχθρία,[28] are frequent in the public forensic speeches of Demosthenes, but absent from private speeches, with the notable exception of an insult by Apollodoros against his arch-enemy Phormion.[29] It appears that it was a favourite expression of Demosthenes, found only once in a non-Demosthenic public forensic text (D. 58.67), and this is why it is interesting to hear from Theon that Hypereides used it too in this speech.

A law attributed to Solon (but probably from the classical period, at least in its present form), penalising women misbehaving in the streets with a fine of 1,000 drachmas, undoubtedly was introduced to curb lewd acts in back alleys, and had prostitutes in mind. No woman except the most highly paid hetairai had the financial capacity to pay such a fine, and this is why the most likely interpretation of this law is that it was a measure intended to curb improper acts involving prostitutes in outdoor spaces. This interpretation also fits with other topics in these speeches related to prostitution and the past of Aristagora.

The most intriguing of these references is one to spiders, cited by Harpocration with the seemingly superfluous comment that they bite. Perhaps this is a helpful clue for our understanding of this reference, in conjunction with the accusations against Theoris of Lemnos that she was an expert in poisons. Conceivably Hypereides, among others, threw into the mix this accusation against Aristagora in order to incite fear and prejudice. It appears that exaggerated views of the apocryphal powers of women with mysterious poisons and philtres, which could entrap men, harm them or even kill them easily and subtly, could scare and upset male juries.[30]

The surviving fragments suggest that Hypereides used every weapon in his arsenal in this bitter vendetta against his former mistress. He passionately pursued

Aristagora through the courts not once but twice, not accepting defeat after her acquittal in the first trial, but coming back stronger and seemingly with dirtier tactics. He argued that Aristagora had broken the immigration laws of the city, that she had all the negative traits associated with prostitutes, and that she was a trap and dangerous for men associated with her, because of her expertise with philtres and poisons, among other things. The themes which these meagre fragments suggest are familiar to us from other speeches where similar vectors of attack have been used against women, especially alien hetairai. It is unfortunate that the grammarians, rhetoricians and lexicographers who transmit these fragments did not take greater care to neatly separate them by speech. This might have allowed us a better idea of how the tactics of the orator evolved and changed from the first speech to the second. If the reference to spiders and their poison, positively attributed to the second speech by Harpocration, offers any indication, it may suggest that the second speech was less inhibited and that the orator used dirty tricks which had worked in the case of Theoris, and possibly of other women accused of apocryphal powers within the frame of prosecutions of impiety. If this is correct, Hypereides decided that veering off the beaten track and appealing to the irrational fears of the jury might succeed where more rational arguments had failed in the first trial.[31]

4. DEINARCHOS, Ὡς οὐκ εἰσὶν ἐπίδικοι αἱ Ἀριστοφῶντος θυγατέρες sive Διαμαρτυρία περὶ τοῦ μὴ ἐπίδικον εἶναι τὴν Ἀριστοφῶντος θυγατέρα (FR. 60 CONOMIS)

That the Daughters of Aristophon Are Not Heiresses; or, Diamartyria that the Daughter of Aristophon Is Not an Heiress

Α' Β'

60.1. Dionys. Halic. *de Din.* 12, p. 318, 2 R. Διαμαρτυρία, ὡς οὔκ εἰσιν ἐπίδικοι <αἱ> Ἀριστοφῶντος θυγατέρες· <τοῦ νόμου δεδωκότος, ὦ ἄνδρες>.

Witness statement (*Diamartyria*), that the daughters of Aristophon are not heiresses. 'The law allows, men'.

60.2. Harpocr. s.v. <διαμαρτυρία> καὶ <διαμαρτυρεῖν>· τρόπος τις ἦν παραγραφῆς ἡ διαμαρτυρία· ... Δείναρχος μέντοι τὸ διαμαρτυρῆσαι τέθεικεν οὐκ ἐπὶ τοῦ μαρτυρήσαντος αὐτοῦ, ἀλλ' ἐπὶ τοῦ παρασχόντος τινὰ διαμαρτυρήσαντα ἐν τῇ διαμαρτυρίᾳ περὶ τοῦ μὴ ἐπίδικον εἶναι τὴν Ἀριστοφῶντος θυγατέρα ...

'Witness statement', and 'to offer a witness statement'; the 'witness statement' was a form of blocking lawsuit. . . . However, Deinarchos is using 'to offer a witness statement' not for the witness himself, but for the person who presented someone as a witness, in the witness statement that the daughter of Aristophon is not an heiress.

60.3. Harpocr. s.v. <ἐπίδικος> καὶ ἐπίκληρος καὶ ἐπίπροικος καὶ ἐπικληρῖτις. ἐπίκληρος μέν ἐστιν ἡ ἐπὶ παντὶ τῷ κλήρῳ ὀρφανὴ καταλελειμμένη, μὴ ὄντος αὐτῇ ἀδελ- φοῦ (ἡ δὲ αὐτὴ καὶ ἐπικληρῖτις)· ἐπίπροικος δὲ ἡ ἐπὶ μέρει τινὶ τοῦ κλήρου ὥστε προῖκα ἔχειν, ἀδελφῶν αὐτῇ ὄντων· ἐπίδικος δὲ ἡ ἀμφισβητουμένη ἐπίκληρος ὅτῳ χρὴ αὐτὴν γαμηθῆναι. ταῦτα δὲ δηλοῦσιν Ἰσαῖος ἐν τῷ πρὸς Σάτυρον ὑπὲρ ἐπικλήρου καὶ Δείναρχος ἐν τῷ ἐπιγραφομένῳ Διαμαρτυρία περὶ τοῦ μὴ ἐπίδικον εἶναι τὴν Ἀριστοφῶντος θυγατέρα· ἐν δὲ τούτῳ τῷ λόγῳ δείκνυται καὶ ὅτι τὰς ἀπορουμένας κόρας ἐξεδίδοσαν οἱ ἄγχιστα γένους πέντε μνᾶς ἐπιδιδόντες. ὁ δὲ Ἰσαῖος ἐν τῷ πρὸς Λυσίβιον τὴν ἐπίκληρον ἐπικληρῖτιν κέκληκεν.

Harpocration under 'epidikos' and 'epikleros' and 'epiproikos' and 'epikleritis'. 'epikleros' is the orphan woman who has been left as an heiress to the entire fortune, in the absence of a brother (the same woman is also called 'epikleritis'). 'epiproikos' is the woman who has been left as an heiress to part of the fortune, in the presence of brothers. 'epidikos' is the disputed 'epikleros', and the question is to whom she is to be given in marriage. This is what Isaios says in the speech *To Satyros, for the Epikleros*. And Deinarchos in the speech *Witness Statement that the Daughter of Aristophon Is Not an Epikleros*. In the same speech it is demonstrated that poor maidens were given in marriage by their nearest relatives with a dowry of five minae. Isaios in the speech *To Lysibios* gave the name 'epikleritis' for an 'epikleros'.

According to Dionysios Halicarnasseus the case concerned more than one woman, but the title as given by Harpocration indicates that only one woman was involved. It is not possible to tell who remembered incorrectly on the basis of our sources, but I find it slightly easier to assume that one woman only was involved when we consider more closely the details of the case. The dispute seems to have been about the status of the daughter of a man named Aristophon after his death. Clearly some relative was claiming her as an *epikleros*, an heiress to the estate of her father, which would go with her when she married the closest male relative of her father. The law did not allow the suitor to simply marry the woman; this was explicitly prohibited by the law, in order to prevent unscrupulous relatives from illegally getting their hands on the properties of female orphans through shady arrangements.[32] The suitor needed go through the archon and ask him to legally authorise the marriage through a process of adjudication (ἐπιδικασία).[33] Only when the archon had adjudicated and allotted the woman to him was the marriage legal, and during this process another man could enter a counterclaim arguing that he was the closest male relative. In a society which did not keep registers of births, mistrusted written documents, and primarily relied upon witnesses to verify family relations, establishing an accurate family tree might be more challenging than it seems.[34]

In this particular instance a counterclaim was made, but the counterclaimant, instead of arguing that he had a stronger case, presented a witness asserting that the woman was not really an heiress. This could mean one of two things. Either the woman had a brother, natural or adopted, or she was already married and had children with her husband. Which of the two applied to this case we cannot tell for sure, but since a brother, especially a natural one, could not be conjured out of nowhere, it seems more likely that the witness testified to the presence of children in the marriage. Let's say, if the *epidikasia* was taking place many years after the death of Aristophon, and perhaps even of his daughter, then in the legal battle among more distant relatives and descendants over the property the status of the daughter of Aristophon could be an important factor. In this instance our evidence is too scarce to form a better idea of the specifics of the case. We can probably conclude that the status of one woman rather than many was in question if we assume that she was married with children, and therefore not an *epikleros*, but the matter becomes much more complicated if we assume that the status of more than one daughter of Aristophon was in question.

The process of *diamartyria* was the standard procedure for blocking an unlawful lawsuit until the introduction of the *paragraphe* in the early fourth century, and continued to be in use in parallel with the new procedure throughout the fourth century.[35] A litigant who believed for some reason that his opponent had introduced an improper lawsuit could introduce a witness willing to testify to this effect. This would stop the lawsuit from going ahead. At this junction his opponent had the option of prosecuting the witness for false testimony (*pseudomartyrion*), and if he prevailed the way was open again to pursue the initial lawsuit. Alternatively, he could abandon the case altogether. In this instance the counterclaimant presented a witness asserting that the daughter(s) of Aristophon was or were not an *epikleros* or *epikleroi*, and if the initial claimant of the woman and her property wanted to proceed with his claim, he first needed to successfully prosecute the witness for false testimony. There are several attested cases where this legal manoeuvre was used in an effort to block the claim of an *epikleros*.[36]

5. PERICLES, Ὑπὲρ Ἀσπασίας, Ἀσεβείας

In Defence of Aspasia, for Impiety

Two later sources mention a prosecution of Aspasia of Miletos, the concubine of Pericles, for impiety, and attest that Perikles spoke in her defence.

Plu. *Per.* 32 (= Aeschin. Socr. Fr. 25 Dittmar): Περὶ δὲ τοῦτον τὸν χρόνον Ἀσπασία δίκην ἔφευγεν ἀσεβείας, Ἑρμίππου τοῦ κωμῳδιοποιοῦ διώκοντος καὶ προσκατηγοροῦντος, ὡς Περικλεῖ γυναῖκας ἐλευθέρας εἰς τὸ αὐτὸ φοιτώσας ὑποδέχοιτο, καὶ ψήφισμα Διοπείθης ἔγραψεν εἰσαγγέλλεσθαι τοὺς τὰ θεῖα μὴ νομίζοντας ἢ λόγους περὶ τῶν μεταρσίων διδάσκοντας, ἀπερειδόμενος εἰς Περικλέα δι' Ἀναξαγόρου τὴν ὑπόνοιαν. δεχομένου δὲ τοῦ δήμου καὶ προσιεμένου τὰς διαβολάς, οὕτως ἤδη ψήφισμα κυροῦται Δρακοντίδου γράψαντος, ὅπως οἱ λόγοι τῶν χρημάτων ὑπὸ Περικλέους εἰς τοὺς πρυτάνεις ἀποτεθεῖεν, οἱ δὲ δικασταὶ τὴν ψῆφον ἀπὸ τοῦ βωμοῦ φέροντες ἐν τῇ πόλει κρίνοιεν. Ἅγνων δὲ τοῦτο μὲν ἀφεῖλε τοῦ ψηφίσματος, κρίνεσθαι δὲ τὴν δίκην ἔγραψεν ἐν δικασταῖς χιλίοις καὶ πεντακοσίοις, εἴτε κλοπῆς καὶ δώρων εἴτ' ἀδικίου βούλοιτό τις ὀνομάζειν τὴν δίωξιν. Ἀσπασίαν μὲν οὖν ἐξῃτήσατο, πολλὰ πάνυ παρὰ τὴν δίκην, ὡς Αἰσχίνης φησίν, ἀφεὶς ὑπὲρ αὐτῆς δάκρυα καὶ δεηθεὶς τῶν δικαστῶν, Ἀναξαγόραν δὲ φοβηθεὶς <τὸ δικαστήριον> ἐξέκλεψε καὶ προύπεμψεν ἐκ τῆς πόλεως. ὡς δὲ διὰ Φειδίου προσέπταισε τῷ δήμῳ, [φοβηθεὶς τὸ δικαστήριον] μέλλοντα τὸν πόλεμον καὶ ὑποτυφόμενον ἐξέκαυσεν, ἐλπίζων διασκεδάσειν τὰ ἐγκλήματα καὶ ταπεινώσειν τὸν φθόνον, ἐν πράγμασι μεγάλοις καὶ κινδύνοις τῆς πόλεως ἐκείνῳ μόνῳ διὰ τὸ ἀξίωμα καὶ τὴν δύναμιν ἀναθείσης ἑαυτήν. αἱ μὲν οὖν αἰτίαι, δι' ἃς οὐκ εἴασεν ἐνδοῦναι Λακεδαιμονίοις τὸν δῆμον, αὗται λέγονται· τὸ δ' ἀληθὲς ἄδηλον.

About this time also Aspasia was put on trial for impiety, Hermippus the comic poet being her prosecutor, who alleged further against her that she received free-born women into a place of assignation for Pericles. And Diopeithes brought in a bill providing for the public impeachment of such as did not believe in the gods, or who taught doctrines regarding the heavens, directing suspicion against Pericles by means of Anaxagoras. The people accepted with delight these slanders, and so, while they were in this mood, a bill was passed, on the motion of Dracontides, that Pericles should deposit his accounts of public moneys with the prytanes, and that the jurors should decide upon his case with ballots which had lain upon the altar of the goddess on the acropolis. But Hagnon amended this clause of the bill with the motion that the case be tried before fifteen hundred jurors in the ordinary way, whether one wanted to call it a prosecution for embezzlement and bribery, or malversation. Well, then, Aspasia he begged off, by shedding copious tears at the trial, as Aeschines says, and by entreating the jurors; and he feared for Anaxagoras so much that he sent him away from the city. And since in the case of Pheidias he had come into collision with the people, he feared a jury in his own case, and so kindled into flame the threatening and smouldering war, hoping thereby to dissipate the charges made against him and allay the people's jealousy, inasmuch as when great undertakings were on foot, and great perils threatened, the city entrusted herself to him and to him alone, by reason of his worth and power. Such, then, are the reasons which are alleged for his not suffering the people to yield to the Lacedaemonians; but the truth about it is not clear.[37]

Athen. *Deipnosophists. Epitome* 2,2. 117: Περικλῆς ... ἦν δὲ πρὸς ἀφροδίσια πάνυ καταφερής· ὃς καὶ τῇ τοῦ υἱοῦ γυναικὶ συνῆν, ὃς καὶ φευγούσης ποτὲ Ἀσπασίας γραφὴν ἀσεβείας λέγων ὑπὲρ αὐτῆς πλείω ἐδάκρυσεν ἢ ὅτε ὑπὲρ τοῦ βίου καὶ τῆς οὐσίας ἐκινδύνευεν.

Pericles ... was very prone to erotic matters. He slept with the wife of his son and when one time Aspasia was prosecuted for impiety, as he was speaking in her defence he shed more tears for her than he did when his own life and fortune were in danger.

The historicity of these events may at first appear to be suspect. Madeleine Henry raises the possibility of an onstage fantasy trial in a play by Hermippos, which cannot be completely discounted, since the two Second Sophistic sources which mention this trial have a propensity for fancy tales when it comes to this almost mythical and mesmerising figure of Aspasia of Miletos.[38] However, it is noteworthy that Plutarch cites Aeschines Socraticus, the student of Aspasia who wrote an encomiastic work in honour of his teacher entitled 'Aspasia'. This speaks in favour of the reliability of this evidence because the reference is specific, and Aeschines would be a trustworthy source, if indeed Plutarch has drawn information from his work. On balance, I would be inclined to accept the historicity of this trial, even though I am convinced that the decree of Diopeithes never existed,[39] and if anything, I think that the text of Plutarch strongly points in this direction. He says that Aspasia was prosecuted for impiety with a *graphe asebeias* (and Athenaios agrees). This was the standard, traditional procedure for religious offences of any kind. However, Plutarch in the same breath speaks about the decree of Diopeithes, leaving us wondering why, if that decree was real, Aspasia was not prosecuted for *eisangelia*, since the impiety case against her was largely based on the activities of her intellectual circle, and the decree of Diopeithes was tailor-made to match such activities. In a previous publication I have argued that the decree of Diopeithes is probably a Second Sophistic invention on the basis of the *Clouds* of Aristophanes, on the grounds that it would have been impossible for research into scientific subjects, which exploded in Periclean Athens, to have taken place under the threat of such legal provisions.[40] Although we can be fairly certain that the decree of Diopeithes never existed, this does not mean that the rest of the information in the passage need be inaccurate. After all, Plutarch's and Athenaios' information is reminiscent of other prosecutions against women, and fits the pattern well in several important ways.[41]

First, we should not be surprised to find that if political opponents wanted to attack a man so powerful that he was beyond their reach, they could try to hurt him by attacking the people in his immediate circle. Such a case would bear strong similarities with the prosecution of Neaira. Apollodoros does not even try to hide the fact that his primary target is not an elderly woman he has never met before, but Stephanos, her powerful and well-connected partner, and his own bitter political enemy. This lawsuit was really targeting Stephanos, and the ultimate objective was to have him removed from public life. Neaira, who stood to lose her freedom, was merely collateral damage. The case of Aspasia bears strong similarities, but also some differences. Plutarch categorically asserts that Pericles was the true target behind the prosecutions of Aspasia, Anaxagoras and Pheidias, because of his office and power (διὰ τὸ ἀξίωμα καὶ τὴν δύναμιν). Then, both Plutarch and Athenaios leave no room for doubt that Aspasia was a bargaining chip between Pericles and the *demos*. By prosecuting her his enemies put him in a weak spot where he had to beg the people in court with tearful pleas to give her back to him.[42] Plutarch says that this information comes from Aeschines Socraticus, and if this is correct, this evidence should be reliable. We can easily understand that Pericles acted as her advocate, and that the great politician and orator, fully aware of both the reasons behind the prosecution and the danger in which Aspasia was, appeared before the judges with a humble demeanour and tears in his eyes to beg for her life. We do know for sure that Pericles knew how to carry the people with him, and in this instance too he won the day, but apparently he was rattled and this is why he did not take the same risk with Anaxagoras, and chose instead to help him escape Athens.

Aspasia was an iconoclast who, like Phryne, another legendary figure who lived a century later and also came close to losing her life through a *graphe asebeias*, was crossing new frontiers for the women of her time.[43] She was a scholar, an intellectual and a teacher who clearly enjoyed the profound admiration of her students, such as Aeschines Socraticus, and the respect of some of the most brilliant minds of Periclean Athens, most notably Socrates. Plutarch informs us that she was keen to adopt the rhetorical skills of Gorgias, and she initiated Pericles into them. Plato also speaks of her as one of the leading intellectuals in the city.[44] It is easy to imagine that such accomplishments would have elicited apprehension, envy, maybe even contempt and certainly anger in the most conservative sectors of Athenian society and, moreover, if this woman was the partner of the most powerful, the most loved and most hated man in the city, we can understand why she was an easy target. Comedians vilified her on stage, sometimes with really nasty comments like the 'dog-faced concubine' of Cratinus,[45] and even Aristophanes, who seemingly belonged to the same intellectual circle and had probably met Aspasia and conversed with her in real life, calls her a brothel-keeper in his *Acharnians*.[46] It is not a coincidence that, according to Plutarch, her prosecutor in the impiety case was Hermippos, another comedian. This is not impossible, but perhaps we need to be sceptical, because this is the kind of detail too convenient to be true. A comic poet not content with on-stage attacks, but willing to take to court the concubine of the most powerful man in the city, risking at the same time a huge fine and his entire career,[47] seems very far-fetched. Perhaps a prosecution motivated and encouraged by an on-stage onslaught in a play by Hermippos, or even a stage trial as Henry has suggested, just as the prosecution of Socrates was facilitated and fuelled by Aristophanes' *Clouds*, seems like a more logical explanation for Plutarch's comment.

Plutarch seems to imply that the impiety charge was based on conversations about the natural world and the principles of all things in Aspasia's intellectual gatherings. We can get an idea of how such charges could be shaped and argued from Aristophanes' *Clouds*, where Socrates in his school is teaching young men that the traditional gods do not exist, that the new gods are a meteorological phenomenon, the Clouds (an unmistakbable allusion to scientific inquiry and natural philosophy), and that the moral world order which the Olympian gods represented is also extinct, and has been replaced by the moral relativism of rhetorical skill. In the prosecution of Socrates for impiety one of the primary charges was that he did not believe in the gods, and that, like the character of Socrates in the play, the actual Socrates was trying to replace the traditional gods with new deities.[48]

The other charge, which Plutarch presents as the primary charge of impiety, namely that Aspasia was having a corrupting influence upon the respectable women of the city, echoes the charges against Socrates, and also against Phryne, that they were having a corrupting influence upon the young men of the city. Aspasia was allegedly procuring respectable women, and brought them together with Pericles. To think that Aspasia would be arranging for her partner to have illicit sexual encounters with free women does stretch the limits of credibility, because it would assume a very open-minded relationship, which, although not impossible for someone as accomplished and secure in herself, is still not easy to accept as factual.

The trial of Aspasia for impiety preceded the trial of Socrates by four or five decades, and the trial of Socrates in turn preceded the trial of Phryne by four or five decades. But there is much more that these three cases have in common than a somewhat symmetrical date arrangement. The actual charges in all three cases sound remarkably similar. All three defendants were accused of undermining the traditional state religion and trying to introduce strange new deities, but more importantly of representing a threat to the established moral order, Aspasia by corrupting the respectable women of the city, and Socrates and Phryne by corrupting its young men. But in all three cases we can clearly see that there is much more than meets the eye in these charges. The accused had close connections with strong public figures, like Pericles, Alcibiades or Hypereides, and surely this made them a target; perhaps less so in the case of Phryne, but then again we don't know anything about the political connections of her prosecutor Euthias, and whether these played any role in her prosecution, as such connections did in the cases of Aspasia and Neaira. All three were iconoclastic figures who challenged traditional boundaries, each in his or her own way. All three were consequential figures who questioned fundamental assumptions of their contemporaries, refused to play by the rules, and broke the glass ceiling, eliciting fear, envy, indignation and rejection in the process. Their unconventional ways turned them into symbols of ridicule and fear.

From our perspective, we may think that the reaction of their contemporaries was disproportionate, unjustified and paranoid. But if we were to see things from the point of view of their contemporaries, each one of these three pioneers was opening doors which many adamantly believed should remain shut. No one wanted, after all, intelligent women acting as if they were equal with men and organising colloquia; no one wanted pesky philosophers questioning every aspect of society's norms and long-standing assumptions; nor did anyone want rich, independent women breaking the bonds of traditional family life, living their lives without having to account to any man, while spending their fortune for their own self-aggrandisement and vanity projects. Surely such persons were not only a menace to society, but, like the Aristophanic Peisetairos, were threatening to block out the gods themselves.

6. [DEMOSTHENES] 40, Πρὸς Βοιωτὸν περὶ μητρὸς προικῷας

To Boiotos on his Mother's Dowry

This is the second speech in a set surviving in the Corpus Demosthenicum, delivered by a man named Mantitheos against his half-brother whom he calls Boiotos, but whose official name was also Mantitheos.[49] In order to avoid confusion I will also call the half-brother Boiotos. The first speech of the set was composed by Demosthenes, and concerns the dispute between the two men about the name 'Mantitheos'. Boiotos won the case, one would imagine because it was not against the law for two half-brothers to have the same name. The speech is a competent sample of Demosthenic oratory, and surely it was not the reason why Mantitheos lost; one can imagine why a jury would find that his half-brother had every right to be called Mantitheos, too, if this is what he wanted. But the case was not an innocent and petty sibling quarrel about favourite names. It was very much a bitter argument among members of a highly dysfunctional family about property and legitimacy. The actual facts of the case are complicated and there is much uncertainty about many important details, but to cut a long story short, the most likely sequence of events seems to be that an affluent Athenian called Mantias married a very attractive woman named Plangon, also from an affluent family.[50] Following a time-honoured Greek custom, which survives to the present day, Mantias named his first son Mantitheos, probably after his father, and then he named his second son Pamphilos, after his wife's father. At some point it seems that the older Pamphilos lost all of his property when he was sentenced to pay a very heavy fine of five talents to the state. As he was unable to pay off that fine, in addition to losing his property, he was also disenfranchised (ἀτιμία). After his death his sons inherited his disenfranchisement along with his debts. The entire family was impoverished, with no realistic hope of financial recovery.

It is difficult to tell whether this was a contributing factor to the acrimonious break-up of the marriage between Mantias and Plangon, but by the looks of it, their relationship was tempestuous to start with, and very probably he suspected her of infidelity. This is the only reasonable explanation behind his refusal to publicly acknowledge his sons by registering them to the phratry and later the deme. Common sense suggests that even if Mantias hated the mother of his sons, he would not have abandoned them to a life of destitution and dishonour unless he believed that they were not his, because their mother had been unfaithful. The subsequent actions of Mantias support this understanding of the events. Not long afterwards it seems that Mantias was remarried, he had a son and named him Mantitheos, after his father, since he no longer acknowledged the son of Plangon with this name as his own. When his second wife died it seems that there was a rapprochement between Mantias and Plangon, and the passionate relationship between the two was rekindled, but it remained an extramarital affair to which, if we believe Mantitheos, his father refused to give legitimacy.[51]

When the two boys reached adulthood they sued their father in an effort to arm-twist him to acknowledge them. At that point Mantias asked for formal assurances for the one issue that had been troubling him all along, namely whether the boys were truly his sons. He challenged their mother to take an oath confirming the paternity before the arbitrator.[52] When Plangon publicly swore that the boys were his sons, Mantias did what was necessary and registered the boys with his phratry and deme. Mantitheos presents a version of events in which Mantias was duped by a cunning plan orchestrated by Plangon, and acknowledged the two boys against his wishes, but we need not give much credence to this, because, oath or not, Mantias was under no obligation to acknowledge the two boys and thus divide into three parts his property, until then destined to go to Mantitheos, his one recognised son. He only did so because through the oath he and the entire community were reassured in a public and formal setting that the other two boys were also his own sons. One wonders whether an unmistakable physical similarity between the young men and their father, which it is to be expected his youngest son would not acknowledge, played a role in Mantias' decision.

Understandably, Mantitheos did not receive his half-brothers into his father's *oikos* with open arms. He had just lost two thirds of his very sizeable inheritance at a single stroke, and there was going to be no love lost in the family in subsequent years. We are aware of at least three lawsuits, two on financial matters, the third a serious prosecution for deliberate wounding with trumped-up charges and self-inflicted wounds, in which if Boiotos had won he would have succeeded in sending his half-brother away to permanent exile from Attica; fortunately for Mantitheos, that lawsuit failed. The second speech of the set preserved in the Demosthenic corpus was almost certainly composed by a different logographer, and we can understand why. Mantitheos had paid dearly for the services of Demosthenes and he had lost the lawsuit on the name. Understandably he would not employ him again. The new logographer took a very different approach. Instead of the sophisticated and dignified arguments employed by Demosthenes, in the second speech we find more cunning and ruthless tactics, including a vitriolic attack on Plangon. While in the case on the name Plangon was a marginal figure and she is mentioned by name only once, because it was absolutely necessary for the identity argument which the orator was trying to make at that point, in the second speech she is brought centre-stage and essentially becomes the opposing litigant.

The unknown composer of the second speech places her in the spotlight in order to illustrate her flaws and suggest to the jury that she was a mere paramour, a hetaira, and not the wife of Mantias at any point. Mantitheos' strategy in some ways resembles the tactics which the mother and brother of Endios used against Phile in Is. 3 *On the Estate of Pyrrhos*, when they tried to delegitimise her and her claim by arguing that her mother was a hetaira, and therefore not a wife. Mantitheos' plan was to argue that Plangon had only been a mistress of his father, the object of an irrational passion, and this is why she never brought any dowry to the house. If the jury believed Mantitheos in his assertion that Plangon had been nothing more than a mistress, then he did not need to say much more in order to make a credible case against any claim to a dowry. This is why the second speech against Boiotos focuses upon the tempestuous relationship between Mantias and Plangon.

As I have argued elsewhere, Mantitheos goes to great lengths to build the identity of an Athenian hetaira, pushed into prostitution by hopelessness and destitution.[53] In order to outline how desperate she was Mantitheos presents her as the main breadwinner in her entire natal *oikos*, a very attractive woman who exploited her charms in order to feed her children and her brothers. Manthitheos attributes to Plangon several characteristics and behaviours which his audience would identify as typical of a hetaira, such as a very attractive appearance combined with shaky morals and easy virtue, a taste for an extravagant lifestyle beyond her means, an explosive temperament combined with charm and the ability to have men do her bidding, and an argumentative nature. Moreover, he does not hesitate to mention her by name eight times in the second speech, which as far as I know is unprecedented in the entire corpus of the Attic orators, once we set aside women who were recognisably hetairai.[54]

Mantitheos has created the character of a woman who could never be ignored or pushed into respectable anonymity, a flashy personality appropriate for a hetaira but not for an Athenian wife. His strategy is clear, but what surprises us is that he actually never uses a word meaning 'prostitute' (like *hetaira* or *porne*) to describe the mother of his opponent. The reason for this was probably that this would break a strong taboo. No matter how many insults Athenian litigants were trading with each other in court they never seem to stoop so low as to call each other's womenfolk whores, and one imagines that a jury might also react very badly to such insults, with detrimental consequences for the litigant who broke with convention. The only women who are ever called *hetaira, porne* or some other synonym in court are women widely recognised as prostitutes at some point in their lives, like Neaira, Sinope or Timandra. As I have argued elsewhere, I do not find it unlikely that Plangon, pressed by desperate circumstances, took in lovers.[55] However, if this happened, as Mantitheos unmistakably implies, it happened discreetly. We should be in no doubt that if Plangon had run some kind of recognisable establishment, like that of Theodote or Sinope, Mantitheos would not have hesitated to describe it with every sleazy detail. The fact that he is circumspect about it, even though it is clearly a major part of his strategy to suggest to the judges that Plangon was a hetaira, should be taken as an indication that if she had taken lovers it would have been done quietly and with some consideration for social standards and her own reputation as an Athenian woman.

7. HYPEREIDES, Κατὰ Δημητρίας ἀποστασίου (FR. P. 93 JENSEN)

Against Demetria, Apostasiou

There is only one reference preserved from this case concerning the actual charge against Demetria, the *dike apostasiou*.

> Harp. s.v. ἀποστασίου δίκη. πολλάκις δ' ἐστὶ παρὰ τοῖς ῥήτορσιν, παρὰ τῷ Λυσίᾳ ἐν τῷ πρὸς Ἀριστόδημον καὶ Ὑπερείδης ἐν τῷ κατὰ Δημητρίας ἀποστασίου.

> Defection lawsuit: it is attested many times in the orators, in Lysias in the speech *To Aristodemos*, and Hypereides in the speech *Against Demetria* for defection.

We have no further information about the defendant. The fact that she is mentioned by her first name in the title may suggest that she was a hetaira, like Neaira, Aristagora and several other women who faced charges for immigration violations in the fourth century, and probably a former slave since the *dike apostasiou* applied only to liberated slaves. The charge against her, the *dike apostasiou*, is not a clearly understood process. Despite Harpocration's assertion that it was attested often in the orators, which is backed by the preservation of several titles for such cases,[56] we know very little about it, and it seems that the ancient lexicographers were not much better informed either. We cannot be sure whether this was a public (*graphe*) or private (*dike*) lawsuit, because our sources seem to be using the terms interchangeably.[57]

Some lexicographers attest that it was a dispute or claim between a liberated slave and his or her former master.[58] I have argued in a previous publication that what they probably mean is that if a former slave had been set free under a *paramone* condition and breached the terms of the manumission contract, his or her former master could pursue him or her through an *apostasiou* lawsuit, seeking to restore control over the former slave.[59] If Demetria had been a hetaira she could have been set free under terms similar to those included in the manumission contract of Neaira, namely that she could no longer practise prostitution under certain conditions. Neaira was not allowed to stay and practise prostitution in Corinth, because clearly her former masters wanted a clean break from her and their youthful indiscretions. Perhaps in other *paramone* cases involving hetairai the opposite was required. A former master/procurer might be willing to continue profiting from a former slave prostitute, and the threat of an *apostasiou* trial offered him or her an excellent tool in their attempts to never let go. This is why I am inclined to believe that *apostasiou* was a *dike*, not a *graphe*. It would make much better sense if a procedure which concerned the contractual obligations between two parties was a *dike*, and there would be no good reason for the law to impose such a high-risk process as a *graphe* upon a former master, when he was simply trying to enforce the privileges granted by an existing contract. Whatever the terms were in the case of Demetria, her former master claimed that she had breached them, and through this lawsuit he was trying to re-establish his control over her. If convicted, Demetria would have become a slave again.

8. LYSIAS 32, *Κατὰ Διογείτονος*

Against Diogeiton: A Mother's Compelling Speech

Lysias's speech *Against Diogeiton* deals with the affairs of another dysfunctional Athenian family. A man named Diogeiton gave his only daughter in marriage to his brother Diodotos, but only after the latter became a successful merchant and had made a great fortune. We are explicitly given this piece of information in the opening sections of the speech, no doubt because it contributes to an understanding of Diogeiton as a heartless, money-oriented man with no regard for anyone else, even his only daughter. When Diodotos was killed in a campaign, Diogeiton was appointed guardian of the three underage children of Diodotos, as was expected. Shortly after the older of the two boys came of age, Diogeiton, who in the meantime had remarried and had more children with his second wife, handed over to his grandson only a tiny fraction of the property which his father had left him. Given the size of the property which Diodotos owned, a massive quarrel erupted in the family, and when challenged Diogeiton made a preposterous claim, that he had spent seven talents on the upbringing of the three children and the maintenance of Diodotos' widow. Besides the fact that such a claim would be ridiculous to start with, his widowed daughter had remarried at some point, and he did not even have to pay for her maintenance after that. His daughter was outraged and decided to take action in order to defend the best interests of her children. First, it seems that she turned to her new husband, Hegemon, but reading between the lines it seems that he did not want to get involved in this bitter family feud between Diogeiton and his daughter and grandchildren. The determined mother then turned to her son-in-law and asked him to summon a wider family meeting. Diogeiton was reluctantly persuaded to attend.

We are told that in the meeting his daughter stood up and, after making a few commonplace apologies for speaking among men even though it was not her custom as a respectable Athenian woman, she gave an eloquent and emotionally charged speech which moved to tears all those attending and spurred them to action. While witnesses summoned immediately afterwards should have been able to confirm that the meeting took place, that the daughter of Diogeiton spoke and that she chastised her father, her speech as we have it is composed by Lysias, and it is a rhetorical device. Nonetheless, it is interesting in itself, because it is the longest sample of a speech attributed to a woman in the extant corpus of Attic oratory, and is the closest we can get to a glimpse of how an Attic logographer might have composed a speech for a female client, if he ever had the chance in real life. It also reinforces what we know from other sources, that the Athenians did not believe women to be inherently incapable of public eloquence,[60] but custom and respectability were the main reasons why Athenian women did not directly speak before male judges in court:

> In the end, their mother implored and entreated me to assemble her father and friends together, saying that even though she had not before been accustomed to speak in the presence of men, the severity of their misfortunes would compel her to give us a full account of their hardships. I went first and expressed my indignation to Hegemon, the husband of this man's daughter; I then discussed the matter with the other relations; and I called upon this man to allow his handling of the money to

be investigated. Diogeiton at first refused, but finally he was compelled by his friends. When we held our meeting, the mother asked him what heart he could have, that he thought fit to take such measures with the children, 'when you are their father's brother,' she said, 'and my father, and their uncle and grandfather. Even if you felt no shame before any man, you ought to have feared the gods. For you received from him, when he went on the expedition, five talents in deposit. I offer to swear to the truth of this on the lives of my children, both these and those since born to me, in any place that you yourself may name. Yet I am not so abject, or so fond of money, as to take leave of life after perjuring myself on the lives of my own children, and to appropriate unjustly my father's estate.' And she convicted him further of having recovered seven talents and four thousand drachmae of bottomry loans, and she produced the record of these; for she showed that in the course of his removal from Collytus to the house of Phaedrus the children had happened upon the register, which had been mislaid, and had brought it to her. She also proved that he had recovered a hundred minae which had been lent at interest on land mortgages, besides two thousand drachmae and some furniture of great value; and that corn came in to them every year from the Chersonese. 'After that,' she said, 'you had the audacity to state, when you had so much money in your possession, that their father bequeathed them two thousand drachmae and thirty staters, – just the amount that was bequeathed to me, and that I gave you after his decease! And you thought fit to turn these, the children of your daughter, out of their own house, in worn-out clothes, without shoes or attendant or bedding or cloaks; without the furniture which their father bequeathed to them, and without the money which he had deposited with you. And now you are bringing up the children you have had by my step-mother in all the comforts of affluence; and you are quite right in that: but you are wronging mine, whom you ejected from the house in dishonor, and whom you are intent on turning from persons of ample means into beggars. And over proceedings of this sort you feel neither fear of the gods nor shame before me who am cognizant of the facts, nor are you mindful of your brother, but you put money before us all.' Thereupon, gentlemen of the jury, after hearing all the severe things spoken by the mother, the whole company of us there were so affected by this man's conduct and by her statements.[61]

Several studies have discussed this remarkable piece of Attic oratory, all agreeing that it is an artificial construct with limited value for our understanding of women's discourse and influence in the household. Nonetheless, it undoubtedly suggests that women had a voice and significant influence within the *oikos* and its affairs. Even if the speech was not a real reflection of what the daughter of Diogeiton actually said, still it needed to be a convincing reconstruction of what an Athenian jury could believe that she said.[62] The short speech which Lysias puts in the mouth of Diogeiton's daughter contains in abbreviated form the main elements which we would expect to find in an epitropic speech, when compared with similar works in the Corpus Demosthenicum (D. 27–31). In the opening section there is an emotional plea outlining the close relationships between Diogeiton and those he had wronged. Then a narrative follows where his daughter provides a full list of all the assets of the family which were in her father's possession and belonged to Diodotos' children. The information which she is able to provide comes not only from her own memory of the family assets but also from the family books and detailed knowledge of all leases, income from interest and other resources. Like the capable widow of Polyeuktos (D. 41), or the devoted mother of Demosthenes (D. 27–31), the daughter of Diogeiton apparently had full knowledge of the family's finances. And, like Polyeuktos' widow, she was not only literate, but also skilled in keeping an eye on the assets of the household.

A short argumentation follows in which the entire dispute is placed in context. Diogeiton's daughter makes clear her father had remarried and had more children of his own, and also that she had more children with her new husband. From a legal point of view this is a significant point, because neither Diogeiton nor she should be spending any of the property which belonged to her children from Diodotos to provide for the new children in her father's family or her own. And yet she claims that Diogeiton was doing exactly this. Contrary to the law, he was spending the orphans' fortune on his own children. His daughter could have taken a more high-handed approach and reminded him that he had no legal right to do that. But instead, she argues in more moderate tones. Given the size of Diodotos' property (around fifteen talents, according to her calculations), she maintains that there is enough money for everyone. Diogeiton could and should provide well for her young half-brothers or half-sisters, but not while the children of Diodotos, who at the end of the day were the rightful owners of all this property, were forced to live in destitution. Her argument with her father doesn't seem to be about small sums or details, but about his refusal to return to the orphans the bulk of the property which their father had left for them. If there is any truth in what is said here, Diogeiton was prepared to return to the orphans only the spending money which Diodotos had left to his wife when he went away, and which she handed over to her father after the death of her husband, when he was appointed guardian. This was approximately twenty-seven minae,[63] a mere pittance, less that a thirtieth of what their father had left them. According to his daughter, Diogeiton was only prepared to admit that he was in possession of the money that his daughter had handed him over, but not an obol more than that. His daughter alleges that he intended to appropriate the bulk of his deceased brother's fortune.

The daughter of Diogeiton closes her speech with the customary plea to the gods, and in a climactic outburst she accuses her father of putting money above family. We are told that the effect of her speech was overwhelming. There was no response, no counter-argument, but only a pregnant silence. Those present were moved to tears, and walked away quietly, but this was not the end of the argument. Her powerful speech was only the opening salvo of aggressive litigation against Diogeiton initiated by his daughter on behalf of her children by Diodotos. In the ensuing legal proceedings she was represented by her son-in-law, probably because her elder son had only recently passed his scrutiny for the deme, and as an ephebe he was not permitted to bring any lawsuits for the next two years. Perhaps this tells the whole story of how outraged Diogeiton's daughter was at the conduct of her father. She wanted him to be held immediately accountable and was not willing to wait for her son to finish his military training and then prosecute his guardian, as for example Demosthenes did.[64] Although the case against Diogeiton would be fought between men in court, the brain behind the entire operation and the true accuser of Diogeiton before the wider family was his determined daughter, who was clearly prepared to do what it took in order to defend the interests of her children and protect them from exploitation, even if this brought her onto a direct collision course with her own father.

9. DEINARCHOS, Συνηγορία Ἡγελόχῳ Ὑπὲρ Ἐπικλήρου

Synegoria to Hegelochos, for the Epikleros
or
Κατὰ Ἡγελόχου Συνηγορία Ὑπὲρ Ἐπικλήρου
Against Hegelochos, Synegoria on Behalf of the Epikleros

Fr. 57.1 Conomis = D. H. *Din.* 12. Συνηγορία Ἡγελόχῳ ὑπὲρ ἐπικλήρου· <ὥσπερ καὶ ἡμῶν ἕκαστος>.

Synegoria to Hegelochos, in Defence of the *Epikleros*; <as each one of us>

Fr. 57a. 1. Conomis = Harp. s.v. ληξιαρχικὸν γραμματεῖον· Αἰσχίνης ἐν τῷ Κατὰ Τιμάρχου (1, 18), εἰς ὃ ἐνεγράφοντο οἱ τελεωθέντες τῶν παίδων, οἷς ἐξῆν ἤδη τὰ πατρῷα οἰκονομεῖν, παρ' ὃ καὶ τοὔνομα γεγονέναι, διὰ τὸ τῶν λήξεων ἄρχειν· <λήξεις> δ' εἰσὶν οἵ τε κλῆροι καὶ αἱ οὐσίαι, ὡς καὶ Δείναρχος ἐν τῇ Κατὰ Ἡγελόχου συνηγορίᾳ ὑπὲρ ἐπικλήρου.

'*Lexiarchikon Grammateion* (The deme's register)'; Aeschines in the speech *Against Timarchos*, in which the scrutinised youths were inscribed. Then they could manage their parental estate, and thus the name, from the act of taking possession of their properties. *Lexeis* are the estates and properties, as Deinarchos says in *Against Hegelochos, Synegoria in Defence of the Epikleros*.

The two sources which mention this speech disagree about the title. Dionysius Halicarnasseus suggests that the *synegoros* was on the same side as a man named Hegelochos, in a case which revolved around an *epikleros*. Harpocration, on on the other hand, suggests that Hegelochos was on the opposite side from a man who was acting as a *synegoros* for the *epikleros*. Thus, while the first title implies a straightforward claim of an *epikleros* in an *epidikasia* case, the second may suggest otherwise, namely that the *epikleros* herself was one of the litigants in this case and was represented in court by her *synegoros*, while Hegelochos was the opposing litigant. If Harpocration cites the title accurately, then we can assume that Hegelochos had somehow wronged the *epikleros*, and he was being challenged in court by the woman and her representative, who is delivering here either the entire case for the prosecution against Hegelochos, or maybe a part of it. The only information which we can draw from these fragments is that it involved a property dispute, which, at any rate, we could have guessed from the title alone, since typically claims of or around an *epikleros* had much to do with property. What is unusual about this case is the possibility that the wronged *epikleros* employed a *synegoros*, perhaps even hired Deinarchos himself, to defend her interests in court. This interpretation of the fragment (57 a.1) is not inevitable as several other scenarios could be at play, but it is certainly intriguing.

10. DEINARCHOS, Κατὰ Ἡδύλης ἀποστασίου

Against Hedyle, Apostasiou

Little is known about another case of *apostasiou* brought up against an otherwise unknown woman named Hedyle, possibly a hetaira.

Fr. 55. 1. Conomis = DH. *Din.* 12, p. 317, 19 R. Κατὰ Ἡδύ[λ]ης ἀποστασίου· <καταλιπόντος [ἐμοὶ τοῦ] πατρός>.

Against Hedyle *apostasiou*. My father left me

Fr. 55. 2. Conomis = Harp. s.v. διαμαρτυρία καὶ <διαμαρτυρεῖν>· ... Δείναρχος μέντοι τὸ διαμαρτυρῆσαι τέθε[ι]κεν οὐκ ἐπὶ τοῦ μαρτυρήσαντος αὐτοῦ, ἀλλ᾽ ἐπὶ τοῦ παρασχόντος τινὰ διαμαρτυρήσαντα ἐν τῇ διαμαρτυρίᾳ περὶ τοῦ μὴ ἐπίδικον εἶναι τὴν Ἀριστοφῶντος θυγατέρα. οὗτος δὲ ὁ ῥήτωρ ἐν τῷ Κατὰ Ἡδύλης καὶ τὸν τρόπον διαγράφει τῆς διαμαρτυρίας.

Harp. s.v. *diamartyria*: Deinarchos used *diamartyresai* not for the person who gave testimony, but for the person who produced a witness to testify that the daugher of Aristophon was not an *epikleros*.[65] The same orator describes the process of the *diamartyria* in the speech *Against Hedyle*.

The name Hedyle was quite common in Attica, as a number of references in inscriptions suggests, and there is no way of knowing whether one of the women mentioned in the inscriptions is our Hedyle.[66] The scant fragments of the speech offer no insight into the particulars of the case. The first fragment, from the essay by Dionysios Halicarnasseus on Deinarchos, may be a citation of the opening line. The other fragment, cited by Harpocration, attests that the speech was an important source for the understanding of the process of *diamartyria*, because in it Deinarchos explained in detail how the procedure of *diamartyria* worked.[67] Conceivably Hedyle was another hetaira, like several of the women against whom lawsuits were filed around that time on the pretext of immigration offences, but there is no evidence to confirm this.

11. LYSIAS, Πρὸς Λαΐδα

To Lais
or
Κατὰ Λαΐδος
Against Lais

A single fragment has survived from the speech of the unknown defendant responding to a prosecution brought by Lais.

> Fr. 208 Carey = Λυσίας δ' ἐν τῷ πρὸς Λαΐδα, εἴ γε γνήσιος ὁ λόγος, τούτων μνημονεύει· 'Φιλύρα γέ τοι ἐπαύσατο πορνευομένη ἔτι νέα οὖσα καὶ Σκιώνη καὶ Ἱππάφεσις καὶ Θεόκλεια καὶ Ψαμάθη καὶ Λαγίσκα καὶ Ἄντεια καὶ Ἀριστόκλεια.[68]

> Lysias in the speech *To Lais*, if it is authentic, mentions these women: 'Philyra gave up prostitution while still young, and so did Skione, Hippaphesis, Theokleia, Psamathe, Lagiska and Anteia and Aristokleia.

The authenticity of the speech was questioned by Athenaios, but we do not have sufficient evidence to tell whether he was right. At any rate, even if the speech was not actually written by Lysias, the case probably went to court in the time of Lysias (first quarter of the fourth century), since several other sources firmly fix these women to the turn of the century. The plaintiff in this lawsuit could be Lais of Hykkara (aka Lais of Corinth),[69] the most famous hetaira in the ancient world, or more likely one of her copycats, for example her junior contemporary Lais the Athenian, the daughter of Damasandra.[70] The famous Lais lived in Corinth and there is no firm evidence suggesting that she ever even travelled to Athens (or anywhere else, as a matter of fact, probably because she never needed to do so; her fame brought to her doorstep rich clients down to her more mature years). This is why it is more likely that this lawsuit was introduced to court by the Athenian Lais.

Carey finds it difficult to accept that Lais was the plaintiff because, in his words, 'In Athenis mulieribus litem agere non licebat' ('Women could not bring prosecutions in Athens'). However, he acknowledges the possibility that she could have brought the lawsuit through a representative, and in his edition he prefers the title 'Πρὸς Λαΐδα' (*To Lais*), implying that she was the plaintiff, instead of Κατὰ 'Λαΐδος' (*Against Lais*), which would imply that she was the defendant. It is more likely that Lais was the plaintiff.[71] Beyond this point the circumstances of the case remain a mystery.

The women mentioned here were notorious hetairai and some of them are known from other sources. Philyra (literally 'lime-tree') was probably the inspiration for a play by Ephippos (first half of the fourth century) entitled *Philyra*. Skione is also mentioned by the scholiast of Aristophanes among several Corinthian hetairai.[72] Hippaphesis is otherwise unknown. Theokleia was nicknamed Korone, according to Athenaios, but this information may be mistaken.[73] Psamathe is otherwise unknown. Lagiska was a well-known hetaira mentioned in several plays and seemingly the concubine of Isocrates.[74] Undoubtedly a man as rich as Isocrates had the means to liberate an attractive hetaira, and keep her as his concubine. Anteia and Aristokleia are also mentioned in Apollodoros's list, which included the women owned and procured by Nikarete of Elis at her brothel in Corinth.[75] Anteia, in particular, was a famous beauty, and several plays by Eunikos (or Phillylios), Antiphanes and Alexis were named after her, while she also makes an appearance in Anaxandrides' *Gerontomania*,[76] which is important for our understanding of the purpose of this reference to past beauties in the speech *To Lais*.[77]

> {Α.} τὴν ἐκ Κορίνθου Λαΐδ' οἶσθα; {Β.} πῶς γὰρ οὔ;
> τὴν ἡμετέρειον. {Α.} ἦν ἐκείνη τις φίλη
> Ἄντεια. {Β.} καὶ τοῦθ' ἡμέτερον ἦν παίγνιον.
> {Α.} νὴ τὸν Δί' ἤνθει τότε Λαγίσκιον, τότ' ἦν
> καὶ Θεολύτη μάλ' εὐπρόσωπος καὶ καλή,
> ὑπέφαιν' ἐσομένη δ' Ὤκιμον λαμπρὸν πάνυ.

> {A.} Did you know Lais from Corinth? {B.} How couldn't I?
> Our own sweetie. {A.} She had a friend
> Anteia. {B.} And she was also our plaything.

{A.} By Zeus, the lovely Lagiska was blooming at that time,
And so was Theolyte, with a very pretty face, and very beautiful,
And Okimon was promising to become a shining beauty.

Benjamin Millis correctly understands that there is a nostalgic tone to this passage, but his suggestion that the speakers may be hetairai makes no sense. Why would a hetaira call Anteia her plaything?[78] We should be in no doubt that the speakers are old men reminiscing about conquests involving hetairai in their youth. I have argued in a previous publication that this theme is intended to establish a bond between the members of the audience who knew those famous beauties, or had heard about them, and create a warm, fuzzy feeling by reminding them of the vivacious days of their youth.[79] Very probably a similar intent is to be detected in the employment of this theme by the orators. When Apollodoros is employing a similar theme in the speech *Against Neaira* he seems to have in mind a twofold objective.[80] First he intends to do just that: bond with the audience, just as veterans bond around war stories. He invites the older members of the jury, who might easily be the majority, to reminisce about the days of their youth and their raucous pursuits of hetairai. Then, he intends to show to the jury how well informed he is. They should recognise these women, as several of them were so notorious that they had inspired comic plays named after them.[81] Through this device the judges themselves become participants in the narrative, and more likely to believe that what the orator is saying is truthful. They know some of the protagonists, who had been notorious hetairai and, by the sound of it, concubines set free by their lovers for a high price. Beyond this point it becomes easier to believe Apollodoros, and his tall tales about these women, and especially Neaira.

It is reasonable to extrapolate that the same theme in the speech *To Lais* had a similar function: it sought to establish a bond between the orator and his audience and also to suggest to the judges that the orator was well informed and knew the details and facts of the case. Having identified with the orator through the references to these old beauties it might be easier for the judges to believe his story in its entirety. Such references to notorious hetairai appear to be a topos in those speeches where a hetaira, active or retired, was one of the litigants. There is one more example of the motif in the fragments of the speech of Hypereides *Against Aristagora*, but there it seems that those past beauties are contrasted with low-end hetairai contemporary with Aristagora, like the two sisters called Aphyai.[82] Athenaios, quoting the lost study of Apollodoros *On the Athenian Hetairai*, goes on to say that they were named Ἀφύαι (Sardines) because they were thin, with pale skin and large eyes. More importantly, Athenaios confirms that the reference to the women was hostile. Hyperides, by insulting these women, was attempting to bond with his audience in condemnation, add credibility to his narrative and evoke negative emotions against Aristagora, with whom somehow the two women were connected.

Prosecutors through this motif invited juries to identify with their version of events, and believe their story based on their own knowledge of the people mentioned. However, there was a deeper emotional level to this topos, a cultivated connection between the orator and his audience through shared memories and life experiences. It is an intriguing possibility to think that when Apollodoros half a century later listed the women who supposedly had belonged to Nikarete, rather than citing his own research of the facts and providing a dry catalogue, he was actually taking advantage of an established litigation tool, a motif with a proven value in Athenian courtrooms for more than fifty years, every time hetairai were on trial.

12. [DEINARCHOS], ΔΙΑΔΙΚΑΣΙΑ ΤΗΣ ΊΕΡΕΙΑΣ ΤΗΣ ΔΗΜΗΤΡΟΣ ΠΡΌΣ ΤΌΝ ΊΕΡΟΦΑΝΤΗΝ

Dispute Between the Priestess of Demeter and the Hierophant

A few citations of a speech attributed to Deinarchos and delivered in a formal dispute (*diadikasia*) between the priestess of Demeter and the Hierophant have been preserved by Harpocration and Pollux. Harpocration expresses doubt about Deinarchos' authorship. The contents of these fragments, for the most part, have to do with the myth of Demeter and Persephone, and cultic objects, and in this respect they offer little help for a better understanding of the case, and what the dispute was about. However, I argue that an unexpected source, the speech of Apollodoros *Against Neaira*, may be offering important information pertaining to this case. The main sources are the following:

> Fr. 35. 1. Conomis = DH *Din.* 11, p. 314, 12 R. Διαδικασία τῆς ἱερείας τῆς Δήμητρος πρὸς τὸν ἱεροφάντην· <πολλῶν καὶ παραδόξων, ὦ ἄνδρες δικασταί>. οὗτος ὁ λόγος ἤδη πεφευγότος αὐτοῦ εἴρηται, ὡς ἐξ αὐτοῦ γίγνεται φανερόν. μέμνηται γὰρ ἐν αὐτῷ τῆς κατασχούσης ὀλιγαρχίας.

> Dispute between the priestess of Demeter and the hierophant: 'This speech has been delivered while he (sc. Archias) was already in exile, as it becomes apparent in the speech itself, because he mentions in it the establishment of the oligarchy.

> Fr. 35. 2. Conomis = Harp. s.v. <Δυσαύλης>· Δείναρχος ἐν τῇ {περὶ} τῆς ἱερείας διαδικασίᾳ, εἰ γνήσιος. Ἀσκληπιάδης δ' ἐν δ' Τραγῳδουμένων (*FGrH* 12 F 4) τὸν Δυσαύλην αὐτόχθονα εἶναί φησι, συνοικήσαντα δὲ Βαυβοῖ σχεῖν παῖδας Πρωτονόην τε καὶ Νῖσαν. Παλαίφατος δ' ἐν α' Τρωικῶν (*FGrH* 44 F 1) σὺν τῇ γυναικί φησιν αὐτὸν ὑποδέξασθαι τὴν Δήμητρα.

'Dasaules': Deinarchos in the *Dispute About the Priestess*, if authentic. Asklepiades in the fourth book *On Tragedy* (*FGrH* 12 F 4) says that Dasaules was a native born of the ground (*autochthon*), and that he married Baubo, and had two daughters Protonoe and Nissa. Palaiphatos in the first book of the *Trojan War* (*FGrH* 44 F 1) says that Dasaules together with his wife received Demeter.

Fr. 35. 3. Conomis = Pollux 7, 69 <ὀρθάπτου> δὲ μέμνηται Δείναρχος ἐν τῇ τῆς ἱερείας δοκιμασίᾳ· ἔστι δ' ἐξ ἐρίου πίλημα φοινικοῦν, ᾧ φαιδρύνουσι τὰ ἔδη τῶν θεῶν.

'*orthaptes*'. It is mentioned by Deinarchos in the *Dispute About the Priestess*. It is a dark red cushion made of wool, which is used to decorate the temples of the gods.

D. 59.116–17: Ἄξιον δὲ κἀκεῖνο ἐνθυμηθῆναι, ὦ ἄνδρες Ἀθηναῖοι, ὅτι Ἀρχίαν τὸν ἱεροφάντην γενόμενον, ἐξελεγχθέντα ἐν τῷ δικαστηρίῳ ἀσεβεῖν θύοντα παρὰ τὰ πάτρια τὰς θυσίας, ἐκολάσατε ὑμεῖς, καὶ ἄλλα τε κατηγορήθη αὐτοῦ καὶ ὅτι Σινώπῃ τῇ ἑταίρᾳ Ἁλῴοις ἐπὶ τῆς ἐσχάρας τῆς ἐν τῇ αὐλῇ Ἐλευσῖνι προσαγούσῃ ἱερεῖον θύσειεν, οὐ νομίμου ὄντος ἐν ταύτῃ τῇ ἡμέρᾳ ἱερεῖα θύειν, οὐδ' ἐκείνου οὔσης τῆς θυσίας ἀλλὰ τῆς ἱερείας. οὔκουν δεινὸν τὸν μὲν καὶ ἐκ γένους ὄντα τοῦ Εὐμολπιδῶν καὶ προγόνων καλῶν κἀγαθῶν καὶ πολίτην τῆς πόλεως, ὅτι ἐδόκει τι παραβῆναι τῶν νομίμων, δοῦναι δίκην (καὶ οὔθ' ἡ τῶν συγγενῶν οὔθ' ἡ τῶν φίλων ἐξαίτησις ὠφέλησεν αὐτόν, οὔθ' αἱ λῃτουργίαι ἃς ἐλῃτούργησε τῇ πόλει αὐτὸς καὶ οἱ πρόγονοι αὐτοῦ, οὔτε τὸ ἱεροφάντην εἶναι, ἀλλ' ἐκολάσατε δόξαντα ἀδικεῖν)· Νέαιραν δὲ ταυτηνὶ εἴς τε τὸν αὐτὸν θεὸν τοῦτον ἠσεβηκυῖαν καὶ τοὺς νόμους, καὶ αὐτὴν καὶ τὴν θυγατέρα αὐτῆς, οὐ τιμωρήσεσθε;

It is worth remembering this, too, men of Athens: that you punished Archias the hierophant after he was found guilty of impiety because he had performed sacrifices contrary to the ancestral custom. Among other things, he was accused of sacrificing for the courtesan Sinope a victim she had provided, on the altar in the courtyard of the sanctuary at Eleusis during the Haloa, although it was not permissible to sacrifice victims on that day, and the sacrifice was not one of his functions but the priestess's. Is this not terrible? A man from the *genos* of the Eumolpidae and a citizen with worthy ancestry was punished for a minor transgression of the traditional ritual. Neither the pleas of his relatives and friends nor the liturgies he and his ancestors had performed for the city nor the fact that he was a hierophant did him any good, but you punished him, nonetheless, because he appeared to have done something wrong. Will you not punish Neaera here, who has committed crimes against the same god and the laws – she and her daughter too.[83]

Plu. *Pel.* 10.6: ἧκε γάρ τις ἐξ Ἀθηνῶν παρ' Ἀρχίου τοῦ ἱεροφάντου πρὸς Ἀρχίαν τὸν ὁμώνυμον, ξένον ὄντα καὶ φίλον, ἐπιστολὴν κομίζων οὐ κενὴν ἔχουσαν οὐδὲ πεπλασμένην ὑπόνοιαν, ἀλλὰ σαφῶς ἕκαστα περὶ τῶν πρασσομένων φάσκουσαν, ὡς ὕστερον ἐπεγνώσθη. τότε δὲ μεθύοντι τῷ Ἀρχίᾳ προσαχθεὶς ὁ γραμματοφόρος καὶ τὴν ἐπιστολὴν ἐπιδούς 'ὁ ταύτην' ἔφη 'πέμψας ἐκέλευσεν εὐθὺς ἀναγνῶναι· περὶ σπουδαίων γάρ τινων γεγράφθαι.' καὶ ὁ Ἀρχίας μειδιάσας 'οὐκοῦν εἰς αὔριον' ἔφη 'τὰ σπουδαῖα,' καὶ τὴν ἐπιστολὴν δεξάμενος ὑπὸ τὸ προσκεφάλαιον ὑπέθηκεν.

Someone came from Athens sent from Archias the hierophant to Archias his namesake, who was his friend and former guest, bringing a letter which did not contain some kind of empty or made-up suspicion, but explained with clarity what was about to happen, as it transpired later. The bearer of the letter was brought in before Archias, and after he handed him the letter said 'the person who is sending it is asking you to open it immediately, because it contains important information'. Then, Archias smiling said 'let us leave the important things for tomorrow', and taking the letter he put it under his pillow.

The narrative of Apollodoros in *Against Neaira* is critically important for our understanding of this case. In all probability, a dispute which seemingly started from religious differences and ended up in the punishment of Archias took more than one court case. At least two can be ascertained from the combined testimony of several sources. The first appears to be a dispute about jurisdiction between the hierophant and the priestess of Demeter at Eleusis. This one could not have resulted in the punishment of the hierophant, because it was a *diadikasia*, an open dispute between two parties entering competing claims, without prosecutor or defendant. The logical sequence of events, as outlined by Apollodoros, would be that the hierophant lost, and this outcome paved the way for a prosecution of the hierophant, very likely with a *graphe asebeias*. This resulted in his punishment. How a dispute over religious duties between two servants of the sanctuary resulted in a criminal prosecution and the punishment of one of them becomes clear when we take into account the testimony of Plutarch, who suggests that these cases were about much more than religious correctness. As is often the case with the *graphe asebeias*, a thin veneer of religious argument was seemingly masking darker political motives.[84]

However, Dionysios Halicarnasseus intriguingly suggests that the *diadikasia* did not precede the criminal trial which had resulted in the exile of Archias, but actually followed it. This version would flatly contradict the assertion of Apollodoros that Archias was punished because of religious transgressions related to his dispute over jurisdiction with the priestess of Demeter, and implies that Archias was exiled as a result of political actions. According to Dionysios, once Archias was in exile, his enemies took advantage of his fall and pursued their own interests through the *diadikasia*. We can be certain that the *diadikasia*, whether it preceded or followed the criminal trial, was not really about religious correctness but about economics and the profits from the rich offerings to the sanctuary of the Two Goddesses.

According to Plutarch, Archias the hierophant had a long-standing friendship with another man also named Archias, one of the leaders of the oligarchic regime of Thebes in the early 370s, which was supported by a Spartan garrison. Before the Theban coup of 378, the hierophant sent a warning letter to his namesake, but the latter postponed to the next day the reading of the epistle, which outlined the intentions and plans of Pelopidas in great detail, and as a result the pro-Spartan government was caught by surprise and overthrown.[85] Official Athenian policy at the time was strongly supportive of the Theban exiles, and Pelopidas and his men had orchestrated the entire conspiracy while living in Athens. Athens reinforced with troops the efforts of Pelopidas and his political allies to expel the Spartan garrison, which was occupying the Kadmeia, and at this junction the enemy, as far as Athenian foreign policy was concerned, was domineering Sparta.[86] Clearly the oligarchic sympathies of Archias and his activities in support of the pro-Spartan government in Thebes were offensive enough to his compatriots to result in his exile.

While the sequence of events suggested by Dionysios Halicarnasseus emphasises the political dimension and asserts that the *diadikasia* followed the exile of Archias, and sought to take advantage of his weakened position, the one suggested by Apollodoros presents a more logical pattern, where the religious dispute offered a platform for the political enemies of Archias to orchestrate their eventually successful attack. It must be noted at this point that these two sources are not of comparable authority. A fourth-century orator speaking to a jury about relatively recent events ought to be a more trustworthy source than a historian who lived three centuries later. Apollodoros is explicitly telling the jury that Archias was punished because he overstepped his authority and appropriated duties which belonged to the priestess of Demeter. Clearly the *diadikasia* case attested among the fragments of Deinarchos was introduced to court in order to clarify the boundaries between the duties of the priestess and those of the hierophant, and consequently the correct share of the profits. Although we may infer that the hierophant lost that case, his punishment with exile must have come as a result of subsequent litigation. Apollodoros has telescoped two trials into one, because it suited his purpose to present the relatively minor religious transgressions of Archias as the primary reason for which the hierophant suffered such a severe punishment. Plutarch and Dionysios correct the picture by adding the true motive behind the exile of Archias, namely his oligarchic sympathies and treasonous attempts to support the hostile, pro-Spartan regime of Thebes.

One difficult issue which cannot be easily resolved is the date of these trials. The most reasonable time frame for the *diadikasia* and subsequent litigation (the *graphe asebeias*?) against Archias would be between the time of the Theban coup in 378 and the battle of Leuctra in 371, which signals a dramatic shift in Athenian foreign policy against Thebes and in favour of the old enemy, Sparta. However, Deinarchos had not even been born then, and even if we tried to place these events later in the fourth century, on account of the fact that Athenian foreign policy was often messy and unpredictable, especially towards neighbouring Thebes, still we could not go past 342, when the speech *Against Neaira* was delivered. Even at this latest possible date Deinarchos was barely an adult. So either the squabbling hierophant and priestess in the speech of Deinarchos are different people from our Archias and the priestess with whom he quarrelled, and a new dispute over jurisdiction came to court in the later part of the fourth century, when Deinarchos was active as a speechwriter, or the *diadikasia* speech has wrongly been attributed to Deinarchos. Given how many coincidences we would need to set aside if we accepted the latter option, I am convinced that by far the easiest solution to our dilemma is to consider the *diadikasia* speech a *pseudepigraphon*, a speech composed in the 370s and later wrongly attributed to Deinarchos. The remaining fragments from the *diadikasia* trial (Fr. 35. 2–3) offer no helpful clues, as they discuss matters of religion and the myths of Eleusis,[87] which we would expect to find in the argumentation of a case like this.

13. LYCURGUS, *Περὶ τῆς ἱερείας*

On the Priestess

There are numerous fragments, especially in lexicographers, from a speech of Lycurgus involving a priestess of Athena, which attracted the lexicographers' attention because they contain unusual cultic or religious terms:

> Fr. 6.1. Conomis = Harpocr. s.v. <παράκλησις>· ἀντὶ τοῦ προτροπή· ... τίθεται μέντοι σπανίως καὶ ἀντὶ τῆς δεήσεως· Λυκοῦργος ἐν τῷ *Περὶ τῆς ἱερείας* προειπὼν <εἰ μὲν ὑπὲρ ἰδίου τινὸς ἦν ὁ ἀγών, ἐδεόμην ἂν ὑμῶν μετ' εὐνοίας ἀκοῦσαί μου>· μετ' ὀλίγον φησίν· <νυνὶ δὲ αὐτοὺς ὑμᾶς οἶμαι τοῦτο ποιήσειν καὶ χωρὶς τῆς ἐμῆς παρακλήσεως>.

<*paraklesis* (request)> instead of *protrope*. Sometimes it is also used instead of *deesis*. Lycurgus In the speech *On the Priestess* said in the opening section 'if this trial were about a private matter I would be begging you to listen to me with favour'. After a while he says 'However, on this occasion I think you will do it even without my request.'

Fr. 6.2. Conomis = Harpocr. s.v. <ἐπιτελεοῦν> καὶ <ἐπιτελέωμα>· ἀμφότερα πολλάκις ἐστὶ τὰ ὀνόματα ἐν τῷ Περὶ τῆς ἱερείας Λυκούργου· ἔοικε δὲ ἐπιτελέωμα λέγεσθαι τὸ ἐπὶ πᾶσι θυόμενον ὑπὲρ τοῦ ἐπιτελεῖς γενέσθαι τὰς πρότερον θυσίας. αὐτὸς γοῦν ὁ ῥήτωρ ἐν τῷ λόγῳ φησίν· <ἔτι τοίνυν> ἔφη <πάντων ὕστατα ταῦτα θύεσθαι καὶ ἐπιτελεώματα εἶναι τῶν ἄλλων θυμάτων>.

<*epiteleoun* 'sacrificial victim'> and <*epiteleoma*>. Both terms are used frequently in the speech of Lycurgus *On the Priestess*. It appears that *epiteleoma* is the term for the final sacrificial victim so that all previous sacrifices are successful. The same orator says in the speech '"even now" he said "the last victims are offered as a prayer for the success of all previous victims"'.

Fr. 6.3. Conomis = Harpocr. s.v. <Μίκων>· Λυκοῦργος ἐν τῷ Περὶ τῆς ἱερείας. <καὶ Μίκωνα τὸν γράψαντα † ἕως τοὺς λ' μῆνας ἐζημίωσαν>.[88]

<Mikon> Lycurgus in the speech on the priestess. 'And they punished Mikon who introduced it † up to thirty months.'

Fr. 6.4. Conomis = Suda s.v. <συσσημαίνεσθαι>· ὃ καλοῦσι κατασφραγίζεσθαι, τοῦτο οἱ ῥήτορες συσσημαίνεσθαι λέγουσι. Λυκοῦργος ἐν τῷ Περὶ <τῆς>[89] ἱερείας· <ὥστε προστεταγμένον ὑπὸ ψηφίσματος καὶ τὴν ἱέρειαν συσσημαίνεσθαι τὰ γραμματεῖα> . . .

<*syssemainesthai* 'to mark'> What this called 'to seal' the orators call *syssemainesthai*. Lycurgus in the speech *On the Priestess* says 'as was ordained by a decree, the priestess sealed the documents'.

Fr. 6.5. Conomis = Priscian. 18, 267 (p. 346, 3 Hertz) Attici 'περὶ τόσους' καὶ 'περὶ τόσοις'. – – Lycurgus ἐν τῷ Περὶ τῆς ἱερείας· <ὡς περ<ὶ> εἴκοσιν ἀνθρώποις> . . .

The Attic authors *peri tosous* and *peri tosois*. Lycurgus in the speech *On the Priestess* says 'about twenty people'.

Fr. 6.6. Conomis = Harpocr. s.v. <Ἀλόπη>· Λυκοῦργος ἐν τῷ *Περὶ τῆς ἱερείας*· Κερκύονος θυγάτηρ, ἐξ ἧς καὶ Ποσειδῶνος Ἱπποθῶν ὁ τῆς Ἱπποθωντίδος φυλῆς ἐπώνυμος, ὡς . . .

Alope: Lycurgus in the speech *On the Priestess* says that she was the daughter of Kerkyon, and from her a Poseidon Hippothon was born, the eponymous hero of the Hippothontis tribe.

Fr. 6.7. Conomis = Harpocr. s.v. <διήλλαξεν>· ἀντὶ τοῦ μετήλλαξεν, ἐτελεύτησεν. Λυκοῦργος ἐν τῷ *Περὶ τῆς ἱερείας*.

diellaxen instead of *metellaxen*, passed away. Lycurgus in the speech *On the Priestess*.

Fr. 6.8. Conomis = Harpocr. s.v. <ἐπίβοιον>· Λυκοῦργος ἐν τῷ *Περὶ τῆς ἱερείας*. Φιλόχορος δ' ἐν β' (*FGrH* 328 F 10) φησὶν οὕτως· 'ἐὰν δέ τις τῇ Ἀθηνᾷ θύῃ βοῦν, ἀναγκαῖόν ἐστι καὶ τῇ Πανδρόσῳ θύειν οἶν, καὶ ἐκαλεῖτο τὸ θῦμα ἐπίβοιον' . . .

epiboion: Lycurgus in the speech *On the Priestess*. Philochoros in the second book says this 'If someone sacrifices an ox to Athena, it is also necessary to sacrifice a sheep to Pandrosos, and this victim was called *epiboion* (in addition to the ox).'

Fr. 6.9. Conomis = Harpocr. s.v. <ἐπιμήνια>· Λυκοῦργος ἐν τῷ Περὶ τῆς ἱερείας. ἔοικεν εἶναι ἐπιμήνια ἤτοι τὰ καθ' ἕκαστον μῆνα θυόμενα ὑπὲρ τῆς πόλεως, ἢ τὰ ὑπὲρ ὅλου τοῦ μηνὸς ἅπαξ ποτὲ γιγνόμενα θύματα.

epimenia (monthly sacrifices): Lycurgus in the speech *On the Priestess*. It appears that the *epimenia* were the victims offered each month on behalf of the city, or victims sacrificed once for the entire month.

Fr. 6.10. Conomis = Harpocr. s.v. <ἐσχάρα>· Λυκοῦργος ἐν τῷ *Περὶ <τῆς> ἱερείας*. Ἀμμώνιος ἐν τοῖς Περὶ βωμῶν (*FGrH* 361 F 1) ἐσχάραν φησὶ καλεῖσθαι τὴν μὴ ἔχουσαν ὕψος {ὡς} ἑστίαν, ἀλλ' ἐπὶ γῆς ἱδρυμένην κοίλην, παρ' ὃ καὶ τοὺς ἰατροὺς τὰ ἐν τοῖς σώμασι κοῖλα ἕλκη ἐσχάρας καλεῖν.

eschara: Lycurgus in the speech *On the Priestess*. Ammonios in the study *On Altars* says that a hearth which has no height, like the *hestia*, but is built in the ground, is called *eschara*. The doctors also call *escharas* the hollow ulcers on the body.

Fr. 6.11. Conomis = Harpocr. s.v. <Ἐτεοβουτάδαι>· Λυκοῦργος ἐν τῷ Περὶ τῆς ἱερείας. γένος <παρ'> Ἀθηναίοις, οἷον οἱ ἀληθῶς ἀπὸ Βούτου· ἐτεὸν γὰρ τὸ ἀληθές. ἐκ δὲ τούτων καθίστατο ἡ ἱέρεια τῆς Πολιάδος Ἀθηνᾶς, καθά φησι Δράκων Περὶ 6.11.5 γενῶν (FGrH 344 F 1).

Eteoboutadai: Lycurgus in the speech *On the Priestess*. A *genos* among the Athenians, which means 'those who are true descendants of Boutos', because *eteon* means 'true'. The priestess of Athena was appointed from this *genos*, as Drakon says in the study *On the Gene*.

Fr. 6.12. Conomis = Harpocr. s.v. <κύρβεις>· Λυκοῦργος ἐν τῷ Περὶ τῆς ἱερείας. κύρβεις φησὶν Ἀπολλόδωρος ἐν τοῖς Περὶ θεῶν (FGrH 244 F 107a) ἔχειν ἐγγεγραμμένους τοὺς νόμους.

kyrbeis: Lycurgus in the speech *On the Priestess*. Apollodoros, in the study *On the Gods*, says that the *kyrbeis* contain the laws inscribed.

Fr. 6.13. Conomis = Harpocr. s.v. <Νίκη Ἀθηνᾶ>· Λυκοῦργος ἐν τῷ Περὶ τῆς ἱερείας. ὅτι δὲ Νίκης Ἀθηνᾶς ξόανον ἄπτερον, ἔχον ἐν μὲν τῇ δεξιᾷ ῥόαν, ἐν δὲ τῇ εὐωνύμῳ κράνος, ἐτιμᾶτο παρ' Ἀθηναίοις, δεδήλωκεν Ἡλιόδωρος ὁ περιηγητὴς ἐν α' Περὶ ἀκροπόλεως (FGrH 373 F 2).

Nike Athena: Lycurgus in the speech *On the Priestess*. Heliodoros the periegete in the first book of the study *On the Acropolis* says that a wooden statue of Nike Athena without wings, holding a pomegranate in the right hand and a helmet in the left, was honoured by the Athenians.

Fr. 6.14. Conomis = Harpocr. s.v. <πάρεδρος>· Λυκοῦργος ἐν τῷ Περὶ τῆς ἱερείας. πολύ ἐστι τοὔνομα παρά τε τοῖς ῥήτορσι καὶ ἐν τῇ ἀρχαίᾳ κωμῳδίᾳ. Ἀριστοτέλης δ' ἐν τῇ Ἀθηναίων Πολιτείᾳ (56, 1) φησὶ κτέ.

paredros (assessor): Lycurgus in the speech *On the Priestess*. The word appears often in the orators and Old Comedy. Aristotle in the *Athenian Constitution* says . . .[90]

Fr. 6.15. Conomis = Harpocr. s.v. <πέλανος>· Λυκοῦργος ἐν τῷ Περὶ τῆς ἱερείας ... Ἀπολλώνιος δ' ὁ Ἀχαρνεὺς ἐν τῷ Περὶ τῶν <Ἀθήνησιν> ἑορτῶν (FGrH 365 F 1) οὕτω γράφει· 'ὁμοίως δὲ καὶ ὁ προσαγορευόμενος πέλανος· λέγεται δὲ πέμματά τινα τοῖς θεοῖς γινόμενα ἐκ τοῦ ἀφαιρεθέντος σίτου ἐκ τῆς ἅλω'

pelanos. Lycurgus in the speech *On the Priestess*... Apollonios the Acharnian in the study *On the Festivals of Athens* writes this: 'likewise the so-called *pelanos*; this is the name for cakes made from the wheat removed from the threshing-floor'.

Fr. 6.16. Conomis = Harpocr. s.v. <Πλυντήρια>· Λυκοῦργος ἐν τῷ Περὶ τῆς ἱερείας. ἑορτὴ παρ' Ἀθηναίοις.

Plynteria. Lycurgus in the speech *On the Priestess.* A festival in Athens.

Fr. 6.17. Conomis = Harpocr. s.v. <Πολύγνωτος>· Λυκοῦργος ἐν τῷ Περὶ τῆς ἱερείας. Περὶ Πολυγνώτου τοῦ ζωγράφου, Θασίου μὲν τὸ γένος, υἱοῦ δὲ καὶ μαθητοῦ Ἀγλαοφῶντος, τυχόντος δὲ τῆς Ἀθηναίων πολιτείας ἤτοι ἐπεὶ τὴν Ποικίλην στοὰν {ἂν}ἔγραψε προῖκα, ἢ ὡς ἕτεροι, τὰς ἐν τῷ † θησαυρῷ καὶ τῷ Ἀνακείῳ γραφάς, ἱστορήκασιν ἄλλοι τε καὶ Ἀρτέμων ἐν τῷ Περὶ ζωγράφων καὶ Ἰόβας ἐν τοῖς Περὶ γραφικῆς.[91]

Polygnotos. Lycurgus in the speech *On the Priestess.* On Polygnotos, the painter. He was from the island of Thasos, son and student of Aglaophon. He was rewarded with citizenship by the Athenians either because he painted the Poikile Stoa free of charge, or, as others say, including Artemon in the study *On the Painters,* and Iobas in the study *On Painting,* because he painted the images on the treasure and the Anakeion.

Fr. 6.18. Conomis = Harpocr. s.v. <προτέλεια>· Λυκοῦργος ἐν τῷ Περὶ τῆς ἱερείας. τὰ πρὸ τοῦ τελεσθῆναί τι τῶν εἰς τὸ θεῖον ἀναφερομένων γινόμενα ἢ διδόμενα καλεῖται προτέλεια.

proteleia. Lycurgus in the speech *On the Priestess.* What is performed or offered before some religious ritual is called *proteleia*.

Fr. 6.19. Conomis = Harpocr. s.v. <σκίρον>· Λυκοῦργος ἐν τῷ Περὶ τῆς ἱερείας. φασὶ δὲ οἱ γράψαντες περί τε ἑορτῶν καὶ μηνῶν Ἀθήνησιν, ὧν ἐστι καὶ Λυσιμαχίδης (*FGrH* 366 F 3), ὡς τὸ σκίρον σκιάδειόν ἐστι μέγα, ὑφ' ᾧ φερομένῳ ἐξ ἀκροπόλεως εἴς τινα τόπον καλούμενον Σκίρον πορεύονται ἥ τε τῆς Ἀθηνᾶς ἱέρεια καὶ ὁ τοῦ Ποσειδῶνος ἱερεὺς καὶ ὁ τοῦ Ἡλίου· κομίζουσι δὲ τοῦτο Ἐτεοβουτάδαι, κτέ.

skiron. Lycurgus in the speech *On the Priestess.* Those who have written on the festivals and months in Athens, among whom is Lysimachides, say that the *skiron* is a large parasol, under which the priestess of Athena, the priest of Poseidon and the one of the Sun are transported while it is carried; the Eteoboutadai are carrying it . . .

Fr. 6.20. Conomis = Harpocr. s.v. <τραπεζοφόρος>· Λυκοῦργος ἐν τῷ Περὶ τῆς ἱερείας. ὅτι ἱερωσύνης ὄνομά ἐστιν ἡ τραπεζοφόρος, <καὶ> ὅτι αὕτη τε καὶ ἡ κοσμὼ συνδιέπουσι πάντα τῇ τῆς Ἀθηνᾶς ἱερείᾳ, αὐτός τε ὁ ῥήτωρ ἐν τῷ αὐτῷ λόγῳ δεδήλωκε καὶ Ἴστρος ἐν ιγ' τῶν Ἀττικῶν Συναγωγῶν (*FGrH* 334 F 9).

trapezophoros: Lycurgus in the speech *On the Priestess*. The *trapezophoros* (table bearer) is the name of a priestess, and that herself and the one called *kosmo* (the decorator) arrange everything for the priestess of Athena. The orator himself says this in the same speech, and Istros in the thirteenth book of the *Attic Collections*.

Fr. 6.21. Conomis = Harpocr. s.v. <τριτομηνίς>· Λυκοῦργος ἐν τῷ Περὶ τῆς ἱερείας. τὴν τρίτην τοῦ μηνὸς τριτομηνίδα ἐκάλουν, δοκεῖ δὲ γεγενῆσθαι τότε ἡ Ἀθηνᾶ. Ἴστρος δὲ (*FGrH* 334 F 2) καὶ Τριτογένειαν αὐτήν φησι διὰ τοῦτο λέγεσθαι.

tritomenis (third of the month): Lycurgus in the speech *On the Priestess*. They called the third day of the month *tritomenis*, and Athena seems to have been born on that day. Istros also says that she is called Tritogeneia (third birth) on account of this.

Fr. 6.22. Conomis = Harpocr. s.v. <Ὑγίεια Ἀθηνᾶ>· Λυκοῦργος ἐν τῷ Περὶ τῆς ἱερείας. ἔστι δὲ ἐπώνυμον τῆς Ἀθηνᾶς· καὶ γὰρ Ὑγίεια καλεῖται καὶ Νίκη καὶ Ἱππία καὶ Ἐργάνη.

Hygeia Athena (Athena Health): Lycurgus in the speech *On the Priestess*. It is an eponym of Athena. For she is also called Hygeia, and Nike (Victory) and Hippia (Horse Goddess) and Ergane (the Worker).

The fragments of the speech offer very little information about the facts of the case. We do not know who was prosecuting whom and for what reason; we only know for sure that the case revolved around the priestess of Athena (Fr. 6.8, 11, 13, 15, 16, 18–22), a citizen woman always appointed from the ancient *genos* of the Eteoboutadai to fill this prestigious public office, who tactfully is not mentioned here by her personal name.[92] The surviving fragments suggest that the speech was loaded with cultic and mythological references, and unusual vocabulary related to religion, which attracted the attention of later grammarians and lexicographers (Fr. 6.2, 4, 6 etc.).

Whatever the case may have been about, one thing is certain: Lykourgos put traditional religion and mythology to work for his case, creating an awesome effect in the courtroom. The opening lines (Fr. 6.1) suggest that the speaker was trying to emphasise in his prologue the public interest in this case, when appealing to the jury to listen to him favourably. This is a customary topos, especially in public forensic speeches. Aeschines for example, in the opening sections of his *Against Timarchos*, just as he tries to convince the jury that this is a case of great public interest, admits to private motives for bringing a public lawsuit, but also says 'personal animosities often correct public affairs'.[93] A cynical reader might detect in this an excuse for using public religion to air private differences and interests. However, since we know so little about the case, it is not possible to tell how religion, gender and the law intersect in this instance.

14. DEINARCHOS, Ἐπικληρικὸς Ὑπὲρ τῆς Ἰοφῶντος θυγατρός

For an Epikleros: For the Daughter of Iophon

Dionysios Halicarnasseus transmits the opening lines of the two speeches from a case over an *epikleros*, known to us only as 'the daughter of Iophon'. The first speech began as follows:

> Din. Fr. 58 Conomis = D.H. *Din.* 12: ἄνδρες δικασταί, οὐ πένης ὤν
>
> Men of the jury, although I[94] was not poor

Since this was a private lawsuit, each side delivered two speeches. Dionysios also had the second speech, which started as follows:

> Din. Fr. 59 Conomis = D.H. *Din.* 12: ἄμαχον γὰρ ἦν, ὦ ἄνδρες
>
> Men, it was irresistible

This is too little information to allow any understanding of the case, beyond the fact that it was a dispute involving an *epikleros*. It seems that the speaker began by telling the jury that he was well off before he became eligible to marry the *epikleros*. By starting the speech in this manner he wanted to underline that it was not greed but other, morally superior, reasons for which he wanted to marry the *epikleros*, as Andocides does in the speech *On the Mysteries*.[95] But, of course, alternative interpretations are wide open.

15. EUBOULIDES, Κατὰ τῆς Λακεδαιμονίου ἀδελφῆς, ἀσεβείας

Against the Sister of Lakedaimonios, for Impiety

This case is mentioned in the speech *Against Euboulides* (D. 57). We know the outcome but little else:

> D. 57.8: Εὐβουλίδης γὰρ οὑτοσί, ὦ ἄνδρες Ἀθηναῖοι, ὡς ὑμῶν ἴσασι πολλοί, γραψάμενος ἀσεβείας τὴν ἀδελφὴν τὴν Λακεδαιμονίου τὸ πέμπτον μέρος τῶν ψήφων οὐ μετέλαβεν. ὅτι δὴ ἐν ἐκείνῳ τῷ ἀγῶνι τὰ δίκαια, τούτῳ δὲ τἀναντί' ἐμαρτύρησα, διὰ ταύτην τὴν ἔχθραν ἐπιτίθεταί μοι.

> This man here, Euboulides, men of Athens, as many of you know, prosecuted the sister of Lakedaimonios for impiety, but he did not even receive one fifth of the votes. Now he is attacking me for this enmity, because I testified in that trial what was fair, against him.

The name of the woman's brother implies an aristocratic Athenian family. In the fifth and early fourth century, Athenians from aristocratic families with pro-Spartan oligarchic sympathies gave their sons names like this one.[96] This passage implies that there was more in this case than meets the eye, and it is quite possible that the sister of Lakedaimonios, like Neaira, was attacked as part of a plan to injure her brother politically. This would also explain why Demosthenes identifies her with the name of her brother rather than in the standard way, with the name of her father or husband. Like the rest of the suits and countersuits between Euboulides and Euxitheos, it seems that politics were behind it all. In this instance, the prosecutor failed miserably because, by the look of it, the woman's family with their political friends rallied behind her. Euboulides must have been a well-off man, since he was clearly able to pay the fine of 1,000 drachmas after his bad loss, and continued to be involved in the politics of the deme of Halimous, and perhaps the city.

16. HYPEREIDES, Ὑπὲρ Μίκας

In Defence of Mika

This seems to be one more instance where Hypereides accepted the defence of a hetaira. We do not know the charge or much else about the case:

> Hyp. Fr. 125 Jensen = Poll.7.191: Ὑπερείδης δὲ ἐν τῷ ὑπὲρ Μίκας ἔφη· ἐμισθώσατο τυλυφάντας.

Hypereides in the speech *In Defence of Mika* said that she (?) hired weavers of luxurious cushions.

That Mika was probably a hetaira is suggested by the fact that her first name is used in a defence speech, while a more respectful title would probably have been used for a family woman. Moreover, a vase found in the Vari cave, near the ancient deme of Anagyrous, has the inscription Μίκα καλὴ ἀνέθηκεν ('Dedicated by the beautiful Mika'), which again, if we are talking about the same woman, suggests a hetaira.[97] In general, women's names from walls or other public spaces with the inscription *kale* suggest a hetaira.[98] The one meagre reference to luxury from the speech corroborates this understanding, as extravagance was typically associated with hetairai.

17. APOLLODOROS, *Κατὰ Νεαίρας*

Against Neaira
The prosecution of Neaira, a former hetaira, who had settled down as the respectable concubine of Stephanos, an Athenian politician, was the culmination of political animosities and realignments in the last days of the independent Athenian polis, a few short years before Philip's overwhelming victory at Chaironeia, which effectively ended the Greek city-state. The case went to court around 342, and it was a prosecution for illegal marriage between a citizen and an alien. The prosecution was trying to prove that Stephanos and Neaira were living together as a family, had male children together who had been introduced to the deme as citizens, and a daughter who had been given in marriage twice to Athenian men as a citizen woman. The prosecution argued that this proved an illegal marriage, or at least fraudulent pretence of a legal marriage. The defence countered that none of these children (all adults by the time of this trial, with children and families of their own) were Neaira's; they were the offspring of Stephanos with an unnamed citizen woman, his first wife, and Neaira was only a concubine. The prosecution had no proof for any of the claims, and Apollodoros bet on a complex and adventurous narrative to carry the case by appealing to the worst fears and instincts of his audience. We do not know the outcome. The case is probably the most important source for the lives of fourth-century women and their dealings with the law, and has been extensively discussed here and elsewhere. The reader could turn to these discussions for a more thorough overview of the case.[99]

18. LYSIAS, *Ὑπὲρ Νικομάχης*

For Nikomache
A small fragment is the only surviving extract from this speech:

Fr. 257 Carey = Marcellinus *Scholia in Hermogenem*. 4. 324 Walz: ὁ Λυσίας ἐν τῷ ὑπὲρ Νικομάχης διώκων Ἐκφαντίδην καὶ Διοφάνην οὐκ ἦλθεν ἐπὶ τὸ κεφάλαιον τοῦτο, διὰ τὸ μίαν εἶναι ἀμφοτέρων τὴν ποιότητα.

Lysias in the speech *For Nikomache* prosecuting Ekphantides and Diophanes did not reach this conclusion, because they both had the same quality.

This seems to be another case involving a hetaira, since she is mentioned by her first name. Yet this almost incomprehensible citation acquires special significance if we take διώκων as a forensic verb in its primary sense to mean literally 'prosecuting'. It would indicate that Lysias was not defending Nikomache, in a case brought against her, but was introducing a prosecution to court against two men, Ekphantides and Diophanes, on her behalf, as her supposedly unpaid *synegoros*, and thus ὑπὲρ Νικομάχης in this instance would literally mean 'on behalf of Nikomache'.

19. MENEKLES, *Κατὰ Νίνου τῆς ἱερείας, ἀσεβείας*

Against Ninos the Priestess, for Impiety
The successful prosecution of a priestess called Ninos by a man named Menekles is well attested in two speeches from the Demosthenic corpus (D. 39 and 40), which are sources hostile towards Menekles, because the speaker Mantitheos considered Menekles to be one of the prime conspirators with his alleged half-brothers, Boiotos and Pamphilos, and their mother Plangon. Their objective was to compel his father Mantias to acknowledge the two sons of Plangon as his own.[100] As a result of this conspiracy Mantitheos believes that he has been unfairly deprived of two thirds of his inheritance, which went to his half-brothers:

D. 39.2: νῦν δὲ λαχὼν δίκην τῷ πατρὶ τῷ ἐμῷ καὶ μεθ' ἑαυτοῦ κατασκευάσας ἐργαστήριον συκοφαντῶν, Μνησικλέα τε, ὃν ἴσως γιγνώσκετε πάντες, καὶ Μενεκλέα τὸν τὴν Νῖνον ἑλόντ' ἐκεῖνον, καὶ τοιούτους τινάς, ἐδικάζεθ' υἱὸς εἶναι φάσκων ἐκ τῆς Παμφίλου θυγατρὸς καὶ δεινὰ πάσχειν καὶ τῆς πατρίδος ἀποστερεῖσθαι.

He brought suit against my father, and having got up a gang of blackmailers to support him – Mnesicles, whom you all probably know, and that Menecles who secured the conviction of Ninus, and others of the same sort – he went into court, alleging that he was my father's son by the daughter of Pamphilus, and that he was being outrageously treated, and robbed of his civic rights.[101]

D. 39.13: ὁρᾶτε μὲν γὰρ ἅπαντες αὐτὸν χρώμενον, ἕως μὲν ἔζη, Μενεκλεῖ καὶ τοῖς περὶ ἐκεῖνον ἀνθρώποις, νῦν δ' ἑτέροις ἐκείνου βελτίοσιν οὐδέν, καὶ τὰ τοιαῦτ' ἐζηλωκότα καὶ δεινὸν δοκεῖν εἶναι βουλόμενον·

You all know, for instance, that he was intimate with Menecles during his lifetime, and with his crowd, and that he now associates with others no better than Menecles, and that he has cherished the same ambitions, and desires to be thought scary;[102] and, by Zeus, I dare say he is.

D. 40.9: ἐπειδὴ δὲ οὗτος αὐξηθεὶς καὶ μεθ' αὑτοῦ παρασκευασάμενος ἐργαστήριον συκοφαντῶν, ὧν ἡγεμὼν ἦν Μνησικλῆς καὶ Μενεκλῆς ἐκεῖνος ὁ τὴν Νῖνον ἑλών, μεθ' ὧν οὗτος ἐδικάζετό μου τῷ πατρὶ φάσκων υἱὸς εἶναι ἐκείνου

But after Boeotus had grown up and had associated with himself a gang of blackmailers, whose leaders were Mnesicles and that Menecles who secured the conviction of Ninus, in connection with these men he brought suit against my father, claiming that he was his son.

D. 40.10. τελευτῶσα ἡ Πλαγγών, ὦ ἄνδρες δικασταί (πάντα γὰρ εἰρήσεται τἀληθῆ πρὸς ὑμᾶς), μετὰ τοῦ Μενεκλέους ἐνεδρεύσασα τὸν πατέρα μου καὶ ἐξαπατήσασα ὅρκῳ

Finally Plangon, men of the jury (for the whole truth shall be told you), having in conjunction with Menecles laid a snare for my father, and deceived him by an oath that among all mankind is held to be the greatest and most awful.

D. 40.32: οὗτος δὲ ἐμοὶ μετὰ Μενεκλέους τοῦ πάντων τούτων ἀρχιτέκτονος ἐπιβουλεύσας

Boeotus, plotting against me with Menecles, who is the prime mover in all these schemes

Din. Fr. 33.1 Conomis (= D.H. *Din.* 11): ὁ μὲν γὰρ κρινόμενός ἐστι Μενεκλῆς, ὁ τὴν ἱέρειαν Νῖνον ἑ[λ]ών, ὁ δὲ κατηγορῶν υἱὸς τῆς Νίνου.

The defendant is Menekles, the person who secured the conviction of the priestess Ninos, and the prosecutor is the son of Ninos.

Sch. Dem. 19.495a <ἐφ' οἷς ἑτέρα τέθνηκεν ἱέρεια>] ἐφ' οἷς φαρμάκοις καὶ ἄλλη ἱέρεια τέθνηκεν. λέγει δὲ τὴν Νῖνον λεγομένην. κατηγόρησε δὲ ταύτης Μενεκλῆς ὡς φίλτρα ποιούσης τοῖς νέοις.

<for which another priestess was put to death> For these poisons another priestess was also put to death. He means the so-called Ninos. Menekles charged her that she was making love-philtres for young people.

Sch. Dem. 19.495b. ἐφ' . . . ἱέρεια] ἐξ ἀρχῆς γέλωτα εἶναι καὶ ὕβριν κατὰ τῶν ὄντως μυστηρίων [ὅτι] τὰ τελούμενα ταῦτα <νομίζοντες> τὴν ἱέρειαν ἀπέκτειναν· μετὰ τοῦτο τοῦ θεοῦ χρήσαντος ἐᾶσαι γενέσθαι τὴν Αἰσχίνου μητέρα μυεῖν ἐπέτρεψαν.

From the outset they considered that these rites were a mockery and an insult against the true Mysteries, and this is why they put to death the priestess; after that because the god gave an oracle that these rites ought to continue to be held, they allowed the mother of Aeschines to initiate people.

Menekles is a common name and this is why it is difficult to figure out how many of its numerous occurrences in the orators and Attic inscriptions are referring to the prosecutor of the priestess Ninos. The ones which certainly have to do with this man are those in the two speeches *Against Boiotos*, the fragment of a speech wrongly attributed to Deinarchos,[103] where the son of the convicted priestess is going after her prosecutor, and two notes by the scholiast of Demosthenes on the speech *On the False Embassy*. Esther Eidinow accepts one more piece of evidence, a passage of Josephus where the name 'Ninon (in the accusative)', has been added by an emendation of Weil.[104] This emendation is far from certain, because other than a superficial similarity between the reading of the manuscripts νῦν and the name of the priestess Νῖνον, there is no other evidence suggesting that Ninos was accused of introducing new gods. The possibility is alluring and at the same time pernicious, because it reminds us of similar accusations brought up in the trial of Phryne, as well as the trial of Socrates. Much caution is needed because it could be a case of similar charges brought up in this case too, but equally it could be all made up on the basis of what the well-read Josephus knew from these famous cases.

Two more possibilities are put forward by the scholiast of Demosthenes. One of the notes says that Ninos was prosecuted because, like Theoris of Lemnos, she was somewhat of a sorceress making love-philtres for young people. The way this note is written suggests that this is what the scholiast inferred from the words 'another priestess was put to death' (καὶ ἄλλη ἱέρεια τέθνηκεν) and his own knowledge of the speeches against Boiotos. He may have inferred correctly, but then again there is no evidence to support the possibility that he did. He could just as easily have made it all up. Even weaker is the connection of the second note to Ninos, where an unnamed priestess was allegedly put to death because she was perceived to be mocking the Eleusinean Mysteries. All these three could be accusations levelled against Ninos, but we must be aware of the fact that the evidence is late and tenuous, and we really do not know for sure whether or why Ninos was put to death, because the sources from the classical period are ambiguous about the precise outcome of her trial, and do not elaborate on the reasons for her conviction. The participle ἑλών used three times in classical sources can simply indicate that Menekles won the case against Ninos, but not necessarily that he secured the death penalty. Since we do not really know why he was prosecuting her we cannot infer with certainty that she was sentenced to death. But this is precisely what the scholiast of Demosthenes and the corrected text of Josephus infer, and this is why they should be treated with suspicion, because they could have been misled by the ambiguity of ἑλών to assume the worst possible outcome.

Ninos must have been an Athenian citizen, unless the term 'priestess' (ἱέρεια) is improperly used by Pseudo-Deinarchos and the scholiast of Demosthenes. In the state religion of Athens, while worship was open to all, only citizen women could occupy priestly offices, and sometimes these were restricted even further to specific families. Priestesses, like male priests, were viewed as officials of the Athenian state and in the fourth century they were subject to a *dokimasia* and an *euthyna* like all other magistrates. Understandably, free non-citizen women were excluded from such offices. While the term is sufficiently broad to be used for any leading figure in a cult, the fact that the son of Ninos prosecuted Menekles, the man responsible for the conviction of his mother, probably suggests that this was a citizen family, and that, like Lakedaimonios' sister, Ninos was a citizen woman. The fact that sympathetic classical sources use her first name, instead of a more respectful way of identification, may indicate that she was actually put to death, but this is not a decisive argument.

Menekles, the man who secured her conviction, was clearly a small-time political sleazebag, if one can judge by the way Mantitheos describes him repeatedly. Mantitheos considered him the brain behind the operation which trapped and compelled Mantias into acknowledging the sons of Plangon as his own, and suggests that Menekles inspired some fear and apprehension (δεινός), exactly because of actions like the successful prosecution of Ninos. The impression which we obtain is that of a low-life gang leader capable of doing real damage, and this is why he elicited fear and loathing.

20. LYSIAS, Περὶ τῆς Ὀνομακλέους θυγατρός

On the Daughter of Onomakles

We only have the title of this speech, transmitted in two entries of Harpocration.[105] Although nothing is known about the case, the father of the woman in question is known from other sources. Onomakles was a general who was arrested along with Antiphon and Archeptolemos on charges of treason, but unlike the other two he was acquitted, and then he was appointed as one of the Thirty.[106] Clearly Onomakles was a staunch and unrepentant oligarch, and we can imagine that he had legal problems after the restoration of the democracy, since, as one of the Thirty, he was not covered by the terms of the general amnesty. Some of this litigation seemingly revolved around his daughter; my guess is that she was an *epikleros* and quite possibly had inherited property stolen under the Thirty.[107]

21. ISAIOS 3, Περὶ τοῦ Πύρρου κλήρου

On the Estate of Pyrrhos

This is probably the most popular of Isaios' speeches, and was delivered as part of an inheritance dispute surrounding the sizeable estate of an Athenian man named Pyrrhos.[108] Pyrrhos adopted his nephew Endios, the son of his sister, because he had no sons of his own, but he had a daughter. When Pyrrhos died, Endios succeeded him and gave Phile, the daughter of the family, in marriage to an Athenian man named Xenokles, with a dowry of ten minae (although this may not be true, because the speaker has strong reasons for underestimating the actual amount of the dowry, which could have been much more substantial).[109] For twenty years Endios remained in possession of Pyrrhos' estate, but when he died childless a vicious inheritance dispute erupted between his natal family, who were claiming the estate on behalf of their mother, the sister of Pyrrhos, and Phile, who after the death of her adopted brother was claiming the property as the only surviving child of Pyrrhos. Thus, the two women were locked in prolonged litigation, each represented by a close family member. Pyrrhos's sister was represented by her other son, Endios' brother, who would be the ultimate beneficiary if she won, and Pyrrhos' daughter was represented by her husband Xenokles. Clearly the family had children, because the possibility that Phile was an *epikleros* is never raised.

Phile's claim was undoubtedly much stronger. For all intents and purposes, she should have inherited the property of her father in the absence of a male heir. The only way for Pyrrhos' sister to inherit would be if Phile was out of the picture, and this is precisely what the speaker and his mother tried to achieve from the outset. They claimed that Phile was not entitled to inherit from her father because she was illegitimate, the daughter of a hetaira. As evidence for that they cited some unusual behaviour, like singing, merriment and spirited parties in Pyrrhos' house, with his wife present along with the guests, which would be inappropriate in a respectable Athenian household. The fact that Pyrrhos' wife was Athenian, and her brother was around to testify that he had betrothed her to Pyrrhos with *engye* in the presence of no fewer than four witnesses, and also that Pyrrhos' daughter had been given in marriage to an Athenian man with *engye* as a properly born Athenian woman, did not deter Endios' brother, and it is a testament to the exceptional skills of Isaios as a litigator that he could build a case for him and his mother literally out of thin air. Moreover, marriages between Athenians and non-Athenians were declared illegal at some point around 380, and unless we assume that the speech was delivered before the introduction of this law, Phile could not have been the wife of an Athenian man unless she was a legitimately born Athenian herself.

After the death of Endios, Xenokles on behalf of his wife tried to move into Pyrrhos' property, understandably assuming that now Phile was the sole heiress, only to be thwarted by the determined brother of Endios. What followed was a number of blocking lawsuits the purpose of which was to eliminate crucial witnesses for Phile, like her maternal uncle, who could verify that he had betrothed her mother to her father with proper *engye*, and her husband, who was representing her in this fight and was living proof that she was a properly born Athenian woman given in marriage to an Athenian man several years before the trial, and with whom she had legitimately born Athenian children. The details of this protracted litigation are outside our purposes for this discussion. Suffice to say that the strategy was clever, and the single narrow path that could actually lead Endios' brother to success. One would think that the entire strategy was desperate, and that the attempts of Pyrrhos' sister and her son to seize the property from Pyrrhos' daughter were tragically hopeless. However, one should not underestimate skilful litigators like Isaios, and what they could do in court. It seems that Endios' borther had already won the first blocking lawsuit (*diamartyria*), and was now on course with the second trial for false witness (*pseudomartyrion*), against Xenokles. The confusion which the crafty rhetoric of Isaios has caused among modern scholars suggests that this case was far from a foregone conclusion before an Athenian jury, and could still have gone his way. If he had succeeded in the second lawsuit too, the road would have been open for him to lay a successful claim to the estate of Endios/Pyrrhos. But even if he ultimately failed, and Phile was reinstated in her parental estate, Endios' brother still had the opportunity to enjoy the income of the large estate for years while litigation was going on. The case decidedly underlines how precarious the position of women could be when ruthless and determined relatives had set eyes upon their inheritance.

Even if what Endios' brother says about the conduct of Phile's mother is true (and I strongly doubt it), still the entire case is presented as a zero-sum game between the roles of the wife and the hetaira. If an Athenian wife deviated even mildly from established behavioural stereotypes and standards she could not be considered a proper wife, but had to be a hetaira. According to this logic, if a household happened to have somewhat relaxed attitudes towards proper etiquette in a party, it did not belong to a proper citizen family. The argument about Phile's mother is also based upon a false dichotomy between the roles of the wife and the hetaira, according to which a hetaira could not be a wife. The topic is explored to its fullest by Apollodoros in the speech *Against Neaira*, with one important difference: Neaira was a foreigner, while the wife of Pyrrhos was beyond reasonable doubt Athenian.[110] There was no law in Athens prohibiting a citizen man from marrying a hetaira, if she was an Athenian woman, and we encounter cases like this in the plays of New Comedy. The stock character of the pseudo-hetaira is a woman of good character, whom the audience likes, forced into prostitution by inescapable necessity. Later through some recognition plot she is discovered to be a citizen and can marry her beloved in a happy ending. Even if Pyrrhos' wife had been a hetaira in her younger days (and this is a big 'if'), and even if the morals of their household were somewhat too liberal for the tastes of their neighbours, she could still be a legally married citizen wife and a mother. It is clear that Pyrrhos was willing to enter into a proper marriage contract (*engye*) with her brother, in the presence of no fewer than four witnesses, which rendered her marriage fully legal, and any offspring from it unquestionably legitimate. The dichotomies upon which the case against Phile and her mother has been built are false, based on widespread but not universal gender assumptions and stereotypes. However, it must be noted that in a manner rather typical of legal disputes involving women, such assumptions seem to be playing a disproportionate role in the build-up of the case. Ultimately Phile might have been deprived of her inheritance solely because her parents were a somewhat unconventional and rowdy couple for their times.

22. LYSIAS, *Κατὰ Φιλωνίδου Βιαίων*

Against Philonides for Rape

Fr. 299 Carey = Athen. 13.62: τὴν δὲ Ναΐδα ταύτην Λυσίας ἐν τῷ κατὰ Φιλωνίδου βιαίων, εἰ γνήσιος ὁ λόγος, ἐρωμένην φησὶ γενέσθαι Φιλωνίδου γράφων ὧδε· 'ἔστιν οὖν γυνὴ ἑταίρα Ναῒς ὄνομα, ἧς Ἀρχίας κύριός ἐστιν, ὁ δ' Ὑμέναιος ἐπιτήδειος, ὁ Φιλωνίδης δ' ἐρᾶν φησιν.'

Lysias in the speech *Against Philonides for Rape*, if it is authentic, says that this Nais had been a mistress of Philonides in these words: 'There is a woman, a hetaira, called Nais, whose *kyrios* is Archias, while Hymenaios is her friend, and Philonides claims that he is in love with her.'

Ar. *Plu.* 179: ΧΡ. Ἐρᾷ δὲ Ναῒς[111] οὐ διὰ σὲ Φιλωνίδου;

(Chremes speaking to Wealth). Isn't Nais in love with Philonides because of you?

The details of this rather fascinating case have been discussed in a previous study, and the reader should turn to it for more information.[112] Here I will only be providing a brief summary of the case as I understand it. The hetaira Nais reached her floruit at the turn of the century, and she must have been quite famous in her time because she's mentioned by a number of authors, including Aristophanes, and Alcidamas, who had even written an encomium for her.[113] Several authors (e.g. Athenaios and Harpocration) are uncertain about the authorship of the speech, but the issue is not important because either way these events need to be placed in the early years of the fourth century. The speech attributed to Lysias is a prosecution speech against the well-known Athenian Philonides of Melite, who was the butt of numerous jokes in contemporary comedy, ridiculed for his very large size, uncouth manners and extravagant lifestyle.[114] Philonides is accused of rape or sexual assault of the hetaira Nais. The procedure (*dike biaion*) was sufficiently broad to include crimes of violence, seizing someone else's property by force, sexual assault or rape (which the Athenians perceived primarily as crimes of violence). We do not know exactly what Philonides was accused of; what seems clear is that Nais and her representative (probably a man named Archias, acting as her *kyrios*, quite possibly under the direction of her alien procurer Hymenaios)[115] were accusing him of trying to take something by force. Given that Philonides was one of the richest men in Athens at the time it is most unlikely that this was an object or a property item. What he probably tried to take by force was Nais herself. If this is correct, this would be the only real case of rape or attempted rape that we know about from the legal documents of classical Athens, and it is even more interesting if we take into account the fact that she was a prostitute, because it would mean that Athenian law did not make exceptions for acts of sexual assault against a free woman, prostitute or not. This would also be the only case that we know about where a woman took her assailant to court seeking his punishment for non-consensual sexual advances. If she won she could have extracted hefty compensation. This understanding of the events may be supported by the fictional account in the second mime of Herodas, *The Pimp*, where a procurer takes a sailor to court because he physically assaulted and tried to take by force one of the girls in his brothel. In both instances an aggressive client is assaulting and trying to rape a prostitute against her procurer's consent. Given these intriguing aspects of the case against Philonides, it is most unfortunate that so little of it has reached us.

23. HYPEREIDES, Ὑπὲρ Φρύνης

In Defence of Phryne
The case against Phryne has intrigued scholars, artists, grammarians and rhetoricians, politicians and even laypersons for two and a half millennia, and the

reasons behind this widespread and lasting appeal are complex.[116] I have discussed my views on this case in several previous publications, and the reader could further consult these works.[117] Here I will present the main fragments and a brief outline of the case as I understand it.

Fr. 171 Jensen. ὡμιληκὼς δὲ καὶ Φρύνῃ τῇ ἑταίρᾳ ἀσεβεῖν κρινομένῃ συνεξητάσθη· αὐτὸς γὰρ τοῦτο ἐν ἀρχῇ τοῦ λόγου δηλοῖ. (Plu. 849 E). – ἐν τῷ ὑπὲρ Φρύνης λόγῳ Ὑπερείδης ὁμολογῶν ἐρᾶν τῆς γυναικός. (Ath. 13.171) – διελέχθην αὐτῇ καὶ διειλεγμένος εἰμὶ (de concubitu) ὡς Ὑπερείδης (Poll. 5. 93). – Ὑπερείδης δὲ διειλεγμένος ἐπὶ ἀφροδισίων. (Poll. 2.124). διαλέγεσθαι καὶ τὸ πλησιάζειν ταῖς γυναιξίν, ὡς Ὑπερείδης (Moeris 195).

Because he (sc. Hypereides) had been a lover of Phryne the hetaira, he supported her in the trial when she was accused of impiety; he says so himself in the beginning of his speech. – In the speech *In Defence of Phryne* Hypereides confessed that he was in love with the woman. – 'I have been associated with her in the past, and I am still associated with her now.' – Hypereides used the word *dieilegmenos* (to be in a discussion) for sexual intercourse. *dialegesthai* is to get intimate with women, as Hypereides says.

Fr. 172 Jensen (= Syrian. *ad Herm.* 4 p. 120 Walz = 2. 31 Rabe). Ὑπερείδης δὲ πάλιν ἐν τῷ ὑπὲρ Φρύνης, ἐξισάζοντος, ὅτι αὐτός τε καὶ Εὐθίας ὡμιληκότες ἦσαν τῇ Φρύνῃ ... εὑρών τινα διαφορὰν ἔφυγε τὸ ἐξισάζον φήσας· οὐ γὰρ ὅμοιόν ἐστι τὸν μὲν ὅπως σωθήσεται ἐκ παντὸς τρόπου ζητεῖν, τὸν δὲ ὅπως ἀπολέσει.

Hypereides in the speech *Against Phryne*, when he appeared to be on the same footing as Euthias, because both had associated with Phryne ... he found one difference and avoided the false equation by saying 'it is not the same when one man will go to any lengths to save her, while the other to kill her'.

Fr. 176 Jensen (= Harp. s.v.). Εὐθίας· Ὑπερείδης ὑπὲρ Φρ. τῶν ἐπὶ συκοφαντίᾳ διαβεβλημένων ἦν ὁ Εὐθίας. Harp.

Euthias: Hypereides in the speech *In Defence of Phryne*. Euthias was among those accused of sycophantic activities.

Fr. 177 Jensen (= Harp. s.v.). Ἰσοδαίτης· Ὑπερείδης ἐν τῷ ὑπὲρ Φρ. ξενικός τις δαίμων, ᾧ τὰ δημώδη γύναια καὶ μὴ πάνυ σπουδαῖα ἐτέλει.

Isodaites: Hypereides in the speech *In Defence of Phryne*. It was a foreign deity, worshipped by public, insignificant women.

Fr. 178 Jensen (= Athen. 13.59). ὁ δὲ Ὑπερείδης συναγορεύων τῇ Φρύνῃ, ὡς οὐδὲν ἤνυε λέγων ἐπίδοξοί τε ἦσαν οἱ δικασταὶ καταψηφιούμενοι, παραγαγὼν αὐτὴν εἰς τοὐμφανὲς καὶ περιρρήξας τοὺς χιτωνίσκους γυμνά τε τὰ στέρνα ποιήσας τοὺς ἐπιλογικοὺς οἴκτους ἐκ τῆς ὄψεως αὐτῆς ἐπερρητόρευσεν δεισιδαιμονῆσαί τε ἐποίησεν τοὺς δικαστὰς <καὶ> τὴν ὑποφῆτιν καὶ ζάκορον Ἀφροδίτης ἐλέῳ χαρισαμένους μὴ ἀποκτεῖναι.

Hypereides when he was speaking as an advocate for Phryne, because he was getting nowhere with his speech, and the judges were leaning towards conviction, brought her before them and tearing her garments and showing her breasts he made the closing pleas from her appearance, put the fear of god in the judges and made them take pity on the servant and attendant of Aphrodite and refrain from killing her.

Fr. 179 Jensen (= Alciphr. I.32): αἴτησόν τι παρ' αὐτοῦ (Euthia), καὶ ὄψει σεαυτὴν ἢ τὰ νεώρια ἐμπεπρηκυῖαν ἢ τοὺς νόμους καταλύουσαν

Ask him (Euthias) for something and you will find yourself accused of burning the dockyards or abolishing the laws.

Anon. Seg. *Ars Rhet.* 215 Hammer: From the speech of Euthias (possibly composed by Anaximenes): ἀσεβείας κρινομένη ἡ Φρύνη· καὶ γὰρ ἐκώμασεν ἐν Λυκείῳ καὶ καινὸν εἰσήγαγε θεὸν καὶ θιάσους ἀνδρῶν καὶ γυναικῶν συνήγαγεν· 'ἐπέδειξα τοίνυν ὑμῖν ἀσεβῆ Φρύνην, κωμάσασαν ἀναιδῶς, καινοῦ θεοῦ εἰσηγήτριαν, θιάσους ἀνδρῶν ἐκθέσμους καὶ γυναικῶν συναγαγοῦσαν'. ψιλὰ γὰρ νῦν τὰ πράγματα διηγεῖται.

Phryne is on trial for impiety, because she was carousing in the Lycaeum and introduced a new god, and put together groups (θίασοι) of men and women. 'I have demonstrated to you that Phryne is impious, and that she was shamelessly carousing, and introduced a new deity, and gathered together illicit groups of men and women.' At this point he is only providing the mere facts of the case.

The prosecution and acquittal of the hetaira Phryne, which took place around the middle of the fourth century, is one of the most celebrated episodes in the history of Athenian legal practice, and has been the subject of numerous paintings, sculptures and engravings since the Renaissance. And yet, despite the fascination the actual facts about this case, which we must extrapolate from a few fragments and some references in authors of later antiquity, are obscure and entwined with the legend of Phryne to such an extent that some scholars have questioned most of the evidence,[118] and some have concluded that the trial of Phryne and the events surrounding it are largely or entirely fictional.[119] On balance I am in agreement with the conclusion of James Davidson that 'It is a travesty to treat the Greek courtesan as a literary figment and equally mistaken to see her as pure unadulterated fact. She operates at the intersection and belongs to both art and reality, an artfulness in everyday reality, an everyday reality in art.'[120] While a great deal of scepticism is indeed necessary, the two speeches for the prosecution and the defence were well known to grammarians and rhetoricians in later antiquity, and were seemingly preserved intact well into the Byzantine period. Scholars in later antiquity have preserved for us a few direct quotations. A citation from the closing of the prosecution speech of Euthias in the rhetorical manual of *Anonymus Seguerianus* sums up the case for the prosecution, and its importance cannot possibly be overestimated, because without it we would have the impossible task of trying to understand why Phryne was prosecuted through the misleading legends of later antiquity.[121] This critically important citation gives us the bullet points of the case for the prosecution.

The case was a γραφὴ ἀσεβείας,[122] and the charges, probably intentionally, mirror the successful prosecution of Socrates half a century before, and that of Aspasia a century earlier. Like Socrates, Phryne was presented as a bad influence upon the young men of the city, and hence the accusations about indecent partying at the Lycaeum. While there was nothing extraordinary about celebrations in temples and sanctuaries, the prosecutor of Phryne probably argued that the *komos* in which Phryne was involved was indecent. The next accusation was that she had introduced a new deity, a god named Isodaites, related to the sympotic space and thus a favourite of prostitutes.[123] Like Socrates, who in the play of Aristophanes was presented as trying to replace the traditional Olympian gods with the Clouds, Phryne was probably accused of subverting traditional religion in order to satisfy personal ambition (of which she was by no means short). In the same spirit we must read the third accusation, according to which Phryne organised illicit religious groups of men and women (*thiasoi*). While such organisations had existed in Attica for centuries, it appears that under the increasingly more visible syncretism of the late classical period anxieties arose about the role and place of many such associations, especially the more exotic ones, in the traditional Athenian religion, which were translated into prosecutions or threats of prosecution. Moreover, the prosecution of Aspasia for impiety on similar grounds suggests that suspicions could always be raised about subversive activities in such groups. Considering the nature of these charges one might be justified in thinking that the enemies of Phryne were scraping the bottom of the barrel trying to find some evidence that could link her to charges of impiety and all their grave consequences.

The rather unimaginative style of the real charges against Phryne was not consonant with the legend of the woman and the fame of her trial in the rhetorical schools of the Second Sophistic and beyond. Surely something larger, more dramatic, more in tune with the legend of the famous hetaira needed to be behind her prosecution. This seems to be the reason why later antiquity almost certainly invented a story according to which Phryne was prosecuted because during the festival of Poseidon at Eleusis she stripped naked and jumped into the sea, inviting the admiration of the onlookers, some of whom thought that Aphrodite herself was coming out of the water.[124] Quite possibly later antiquity also invented an incident during her trial according to which Hypereides, sensing danger and afraid of losing the case, bared her breasts (her entire body in Quintilian's version) and through this stunt secured her acquittal.[125] Earlier research, especially after the influential article by Craig Cooper, considered this story to be yet another fiction about the legendary hetaira, but recent scholarship is prepared to put more faith in this story, on the grounds that surprising stunts were sometimes part of the trial strategy of the Attic orators, and were intended to compensate for failures of the actual defence strategy, or more often to complement it.[126] What counts against an easy acceptance of the truthfulness of the story is the fact that it is not mentioned anywhere in classical sources. Of course, this could be accidental; yet again, such an impressive and successful stunt should have received considerable attention in the literature of the classical period, and subsequently in every handbook of rhetoric. On balance, we need to be content with some uncertainty in this instance.

What the true motives behind Phryne's prosecution were may be harder to pinpoint in this case, because of the incomplete and confusing state of our evidence. As with the prosecutions of Aspasia and Socrates before her, the true motives appear to be both personal and broader, and they certainly have little to do with genuine piety. Both Euthias, the prosecutor, and Hypereides, the defending advocate, admitted that they had a personal relationship with Phryne as former lovers. Hypereides, however, successfully demolished the false equation between the two men by pointing out that while he was trying to save Phryne his opponent was trying to destroy her. Euthias' vicious and determined attack makes better sense if it is seen as part of a personal vendetta against a former mistress. However, the reasons behind the attack were also broader. Esther Eidinow has correctly emphasised that envy probably played a major part.[127] Phryne, in an attempt to promote herself and create a legend around her person which would satisfy her vanity and appeal to lovers, took some extraordinary actions which pushed the boundaries for a woman of her time, even a wealthy and independent hetaira. Her famous statue, a splendid work by Praxiteles, stood by the side of kings and heroes in Delphi, along with a statue of Aphrodite and one of Eros forming what is known as the Thespian triad.[128] Her physical form could be recognised in a statue of Aphrodite by Praxiteles, and in a story told by Kallistratos in his work *On Hetairai* (= Athen. 13.60) she provocatively offered to restore the walls of Thebes on condition that an inscription would be added saying 'Alexander destroyed, but Phryne the hetaira restored.' If there is any truth in this story, we can see how insensitive this triumphalism towards a fallen neighbour would have seemed to many Athenians, who felt a great deal of sympathy for the woes of the Thebans in the aftermath of Chaironeia.[129] We can see purpose behind such provocative actions, but also the mechanism which would eventually lead to the prosecution of the uppity alien woman who did not know her place.

Hypereides' speech in defence was one of the most admired works of Attic oratory, and one of few Attic law court speeches to be translated into Latin, undoubtedly on account of its literary virtues. Messala's Latin translation is praised by Quintilian for preserving that rare quality of *urbanitas* which, in his judgement, eluded Roman orators. Quintilian preserves the opening words of the Latin translation 'bene fecit Euthia'.[130] We recognise in these words an opening to the speech similar to that of Lys. 24 *For the Disabled Man*:

Ὀλίγου δέω χάριν ἔχειν, ὦ βουλή, τῷ κατηγόρῳ, ὅτι μοι παρεσκεύασε τὸν ἀγῶνα τοῦτον, εἰ πρότερον οὐκ ἔχων πρόφασιν ἐφ' ἧς τοῦ βίου λόγον δοίην, νυνὶ διὰ τοῦτον εἴληφα.

I almost owe the prosecutor my thanks, members of the Council, for getting me involved in this trial. In the past I did not have an excuse to give an account of my life, but now I have, because of him.

Another opening with the same motif is adopted in the speech *For Mantitheos* (Lys. 16. 1–2):

Εἰ μὴ συνῄδειν, ὦ βουλή, τοῖς κατηγόροις βουλομένοις ἐκ παντὸς τρόπου κακῶς ἐμὲ ποιεῖν, πολλὴν ἂν αὐτοῖς χάριν εἶχον ταύτης τῆς κατηγορίας· ἡγοῦμαι γὰρ τοῖς ἀδίκως διαβεβλημένοις τούτους εἶναι μεγίστων ἀγαθῶν αἰτίους, οἵτινες ἂν αὐτοὺς ἀναγκάζωσιν εἰς ἔλεγχον τῶν αὐτοῖς βεβιωμένων καταστῆναι. ἐγὼ γὰρ οὕτω σφόδρα ἐμαυτῷ πιστεύω, ὥστ' ἐλπίζω καὶ εἴ τις πρός με τυγχάνει ἀηδῶς [ἢ κακῶς] διακείμενος, ἐπειδὰν ἐμοῦ λέγοντος ἀκούσῃ περὶ τῶν πεπραγμένων, μεταμελήσειν αὐτῷ καὶ πολὺ βελτίω με εἰς τὸν λοιπὸν χρόνον ἡγήσεσθαι.

If I did not know, members of the Council, that my accusers were planning to harm me in every possible manner, I would have been very thankful to them for their accusation. I believe that such men provide the greatest service to those unfairly slandered, by compelling them to undergo a review of their life. I am so very confident in myself that I even expect anyone who dislikes me to change his opinion and think much more highly of me in the future once he has heard me describe my conduct.[131]

While the poor old man delivering Lys. 24 spoke of the opportunity for a public appraisal of his life with a hint of self-deprecating humour, a true celebrity like Phryne would be justified in seizing the opportunity and placing her life at the centre of public attention. And like Mantitheos, she could appear so confident about her innocence that she might even gain new friends through this process. Undoubtedly the publicity from this trial would enhance her legend, already in the making during her lifetime, first and foremost by Phryne herself, according to Eleonora Cavalini and Helen Morales.[132] Thus, like Mantitheos, she should have greatly welcomed the opportunity to have one of the most eloquent men in the city, and a former lover, praising her to the high heavens, if only she was not facing such a mortal danger.

We do not know much more about the content of the speech,[133] but we do know the outcome. Unlike several unlucky women who had been convicted of impiety and put to death around that time, such as Ninos and Theoris, Phryne was acquitted. Was it the brilliant speech of Hypereides, or maybe the extraordinary stunt of her bare breasts in the courtroom? Or could it be the fact that the case for the prosecution was inherently weak and failed to turn the jury against a popular and iconic figure? Perhaps it was all these factors put together. The verdict seems to have been overwhelmingly in her favour, if the information in some sources that Euthias never spoke again is to be interpreted as evidence that, after a bad loss with less than one fifth of the vote, he was unable to pay the 1,000 drachmas fine and was disenfranchised.[134] For Phryne this must have been a fearful experience, but if she could have looked into the future, to the publicity which this trial generated and how it solidified her legend through the centuries, she might have been truly grateful to her prosecutor for bringing this lawsuit, just as her advocate said in the opening lines of his speech.

24. LYSIAS, *Περὶ τῆς Φρυνίχου θυγατρὸς*

On the Daughter of Phrynichos

Not much is known about a case involving a woman known as the daughter of Phrynichos. Harpocration, our main source for this speech, was interested only in some religious vocabulary from the cult of Artemis at Brauron.

Fr. 309 Carey = Harp s.v. Ἀρκτεῦσαι: Λυσίας ἐν τῷ ὑπὲρ Φρυνίχου θυγατρὸς, εἰ γνήσιος, τὸ καθιερωθῆναι πρὸ γάμων τὰς παρθένους τῇ Ἀρτέμιδι τῇ Μουνυχίᾳ ἢ τῇ Βραυρωνίᾳ.

arkteusai: Lysias in the speech *On the Daughter of Phrynichos*, if it is authentic, calls *arkteusai* the dedication of young woman to Artemis of Brauron or Mounichia before their marriage.

Harp. s.v. δεκατεύειν. . . . Δίδυμος ὁ γραμματικὸς περὶ τούτου βιβλίον γράψας φησὶν ὅτι τὸ δεκατεῦσαι Λυσίας ἐν τῷ περὶ τῆς Φρυνίχου θυγατρὸς ἀρκτεῦσαι εἴρηκεν. δεκατεῦσαι μέντοι, φησίν, κυρίως ἐλέγετο τὸ καθιερῶσαι, ἐπειδήπερ ἔθος ἦν Ἑλληνικὸν τὰς δεκάτας τῶν περιγινομένων τοῖς θεοῖς καθιεροῦν. ἴσως δὲ τὸ ἀρκτεῦσαι δεκατεῦσαι εἴρηκεν ὁ ῥήτωρ, ἐπειδὴ αἱ δεκέτιδες ἤρκτευον.

Didymus the grammarian, who wrote a book about this, says that Lysias called the *dekateusai* '*arkteusai*' in the speech *On the Daughter of Phrynichos*. '*Dekateusai*', he says, meant 'to dedicate', because it was a Greek custom to dedicate the tenth of one's income to the gods. It is possible that the orator called *arkteusai* '*dekateusai*' because ten-year-old girls were dedicated to Artemis.

Carey is uncertain about the identity of Phrynichos, with good reason; it is a common name, and very little is known about this case. This is why it is probably best not to try and guess who was the father of the woman at the centre of this lawsuit. The few citations of the speech are only concerned with the unusual usage of the term *arkteusai* to indicate the dedication of young girls to the goddess Artemis. The bear (*arktos*) was connected to the cult of Artemis, and young girls dressed as bears participated in a ritual at the sanctuary of Artemis in Brauron.[135] Since this is the only piece of information we have about the speech, it is impossible to construct a plausible hypothesis of how this was connected to the facts of the case. The possibility that this was another case related to a *graphe asebeias* is just as open as the prospect that it was an inheritance dispute.

25. ISAIOS, *Πρὸς Σάτυρον ὑπὲρ ἐπικλήρου*

To Satyros, for the Epikleros

Harp. s.v. ἐπίδικος (= Or. 39 Thalheim). . . . ἐπίδικος δὲ ἡ ἀμφισβητουμένη ἐπίκληρος ὅτῳ χρὴ αὐτὴν γαμηθῆναι. ταῦτα δὲ δηλοῦσιν Ἰσαῖος ἐν τῷ πρὸς Σάτυρον ὑπὲρ ἐπικλήρου.[136]

epidikos is the disputed heiress, who needs to be given in marriage to a certain man. This is what Isaios denotes in the speech *To Satyros, for the Epikleros*.

The only information we have about this speech comes from an entry of Harpocration on *epidikos*, which he defines as the disputed heiress. The case appears to be related to an inheritance dispute involving an *epikleros*.

26. ANTIPHON 1, Φαρμακείας κατὰ τῆς μητριᾶς

Against the Stepmother for Poisoning

This is the only extant homicide case brought against a woman, and one of the earliest speeches in the corpus of Attic oratory. The prosecutor is the stepson of a woman whom he accuses of the premeditated killing of his father. The alleged murder took place several years before the trial, when the speaker was still a boy. He argues that his stepmother manipulated a slave concubine owned by a friend of his father into giving the two men what was supposedly a love potion in their drink. It was actually poison and killed both men. The stepmother was not physically present in the house where the poisoning happened during a sacrificial dinner, nor was she involved in any way in the preparation of the potion; no motive is given for the murder; and there is absolutely not a shred of proof connecting the stepmother in any way to these unfortunate events. For all we know, the entire incident may have been an accident. The speaker was convinced that it was not, and this is why as soon as he reached adulthood he prosecuted the stepmother for the death of his father. The woman's natural son, the half-brother of the prosecutor, is speaking in her defence. The slave concubine who accidentally poisoned the two men, and knew what had transpired, had been executed several years before the trial with summary procedures.

The speaker tries to compensate for the inherent weakness of his case by making a very deliberate connection with the tragic stage, and calling his stepmother a 'Klytemestra'. Kostas Apostolakis in an insightful article argues that this connection is deliberate and intended to subconsciously influence the jury into accepting the speaker's version of events. Michael Edwards rightly emphasises the skilful narrative of the speech, which does much to compensate for the weakness of the case. Victoria Wohl on the other hand makes a connection with Sophocles' *Women of Trachis*, and the unintentional poisoning of Herakles by Dieaneira. These fascinating links with drama notwithstanding, the case is inherently weak, and it is doubtful that an experienced court like the Areopagos could have been swayed by such trickery. We do not know the outcome.[137]

27. DEMOSTHENES, Κατὰ Θεωρίδος, ἀσεβείας

Against Theoris, for Impiety
The case is attested in the first speech *Against Aristogeiton*, and Plutarch states that Demosthenes was actually her prosecutor, which is implicitly supported by the account of Demosthenes.

1. D. 25. 79–80: τὰ μὲν ἄλλα σιωπῶ, ἀλλ' ἐφ' οἷς ὑμεῖς τὴν μιαρὰν Θεωρίδα, τὴν Λημνίαν, τὴν φαρμακίδα, καὶ αὐτὴν καὶ τὸ γένος ἅπαν ἀπεκτείνατε, ταῦτα λαβὼν τὰ φάρμακα καὶ τὰς ἐπῳδὰς παρὰ τῆς θεραπαίνης αὐτῆς, ἣ κατ' ἐκείνης τότ' ἐμήνυσεν, ἐξ ἧσπερ ὁ βάσκανος οὗτος πεπαιδοποίηται, μαγγανεύει καὶ φενακίζει καὶ τοὺς ἐπιλήπτους φησὶν ἰᾶσθαι, αὐτὸς ὢν ἐπίληπτος πάσῃ πονηρίᾳ. οὗτος οὖν αὐτὸν ἐξαιρήσεται, ὁ φαρμακός, ὁ λοιμός, ὃν οἰωνίσαιτ' ἄν τις μᾶλλον ἰδὼν ἢ προσειπεῖν βούλοιτο, ὃς αὐτὸς αὑτῷ θανάτου τετίμηκεν ὅτε τοιαύτην δίκην ἔλαχεν.

It was this brother – I pass over the other facts – who got possession of the drugs and charms from the servant of Theoris of Lemnos, the filthy sorceress whom you put to death on that account with all her family. She gave information against her mistress, and this rascal has had children by her, and with her help he plays juggling tricks and professes to cure fits, being himself subject to fits of wickedness of every kind. So this is the man who will beg him off! This poisoner, this public pest, whom any man would ban at sight as an evil omen rather than choose to accost him, and who has pronounced himself worthy of death by bringing such an action.[138]

2. Plu. *Vita Demosthenis* 14.6.2: κατηγόρησε δὲ καὶ τῆς ἱερείας Θεωρίδος ὡς ἄλλα τε ῥᾳδιουργούσης πολλὰ καὶ τοὺς δούλους ἐξαπατᾶν διδασκούσης, καὶ θανάτου τιμησάμενος ἀπέκτεινε.

He (sc. Demosthenes) prosecuted the priestess Theoris, for plotting on many other matters, and teaching slaves to deceive, and after demanding the death penalty he had her killed.

3. Harp. s.v. Θεωρίς: Δημοσθένης ἐν τῷ κατ' Ἀριστογείτονος, εἰ γνήσιος. μάντις ἦν ἡ Θεωρίς, καὶ ἀσεβείας κριθεῖσα ἀπέθανεν, ὡς καὶ Φιλόχορος ἐν ϛ' γράφει.

Demosthenes in the speech *Against Aristogeiton*, if it is authentic. Theoris was an oracle and after a prosecution for impiety she was sentenced to death. Philochoros also says so in the sixth book.

The passionate reference to 'the filthy Theoris' and the second person plural referring to the judges[139] in the first speech *Against Aristogeiton* support Plutarch's informtaion that Demosthenes was the actual prosecutor of Theoris. The combined evidence of our sources (1–3 above) leaves no room for doubt that the prosecution of Theoris for impiety was successful, and that when it came to the assessment of the penalty Demosthenes succeeded in securing the death penalty. His comment that it was not only Theoris that was put to death but also all her progeny (τὸ γένος ἅπαν) is difficult to interpret, because Athenian courts did not impose sentences upon entire families. The most likely interpretation of the passage is that the children of Theoris were prosecuted too for the same offence, and they were also convicted and put to death along with her. An alternative possibility could be that Demosthenes is speaking metaphorically, meaning that when Theoris was put to death her entire evil bloodline ended, but this is less likely. The fact that her prosecution was the result of a denunciation by her maid may suggest that procedures were followed similar to the mass denunciations and convictions of 415, for allegedly major religious violations in both instances, and this is how the entire family of Theoris ended up in the dock.[140]

Why Theoris was prosecuted is somewhat of a mystery. Derek Collins, in a thorough investigation of the accounts of the trial, concludes that what has reached us is essentially incompatible with Athenian legal procedure and probably contains much rhetorical embellishment. He believes that Theoris in the end was convicted for poisoning, not magic.[141] Esther Eidinow, on the other hand, attributes Theoris' conviction to a complex web of factors, which Edinow sets out to investigate in her enchanting 2016 monograph.[142] Both would agree that the smoking gun is missing. Our sources offer a few tantalising clues but no clarity on the matter. A denunciation by her maid seems to have triggered the case against Theoris, and this may offer some clues not only for the procedure but also for the motives and the way the case was presented to the authorities. In 415 Alcibiades and several of his friends were denounced by a servant for mimicking the Eleusinian Mysteries before the eyes of uninitiated persons. The assembly was so outraged by these revelations that Alcibiades was recalled to face trial in Athens while he was on the high seas on his way as leader of the large Sicilian expedition. It appears that some people successfully stoked up fears about the fate of the campaign if a man who had offended the Two Goddesses remained at the helm of the entire project. We can see the possibility that the revelations of Theoris' maid generated similar fears and indignation, and prompted one of the leading politicians in the city to prosecute her for impiety, and aggressively seek the death penalty for the priestess and her descendants.

We cannot be sure about the content of the denunciations by the maid. Our sources allude to three different accusations. The first, which was seemingly supported by abundant material evidence, was that Theoris was in possession of potions, philtres and other magical objects that came with a full set of spells. But potions and philtres with real or alleged miraculous qualities were circulating in abundance in fourth-century Athens, as a hefty amount of medical and pharmacological literature confirms. In this pluralism of often toxic potions and treatments making big promises to customers and patients, why were those in Theoris' possession perceived to be so dangerous? The answer seems to be hidden in the actual wording of Demosthenes, who uses two verbs that would not really apply to any medicinal potion or philtre. The first of these, μαγγανεύει, means 'to charm and deceive someone'. A passage of Achilles Tatius refers to the kisses of a woman as the means to deceive,[143] and probably this is the direction in which we should be looking. Theoris' philtres and potions were dangerous because they could make a man lose his senses and fall in love against his wishes, with detrimental effects. They had the power to remove from a man his most precious commodity, his ability to reason, and made him a slave to the wishes and desires of a woman. The second verb used by Demosthenes, φενακίζει, also has to do with deception. I think we can see the argument: that Theoris' dangerous philtres had the potential to deceive, to take control of someone's mind and make him do things which he would not do in his right mind. And was it not against the law for a man to make a will under the influence of a woman?[144] Such influences were viewed as detrimental because, among other things, they deprived the family of its assets and spelled trouble for the entire *oikos*.

The second set of accusations which emerges from Plutarch's brief reference to the case is related to deception, but it is much broader. Here we are not dealing with love-philtres and deceptive women, but, it seems, with an entire network of plots (ἄλλα τε ῥᾳδιουργούσης). Plutarch singles out one which seemed especially heinous: Theoris was instructing slaves in tricks and techniques to deceive their masters. Could it be the case that Theoris was presented in court as a female Spartacus, scheming and plotting against families and the safety of the state itself, by teaching servants not to obey their masters? The third set of accusations emerges from the note by Harpocration, repeated in later lexicographers, that Theoris was an oracle. While something like this in itself would not be offensive to Greek religion, pretending to be an oracle and perhaps mimicking sacred rituals from more established oracles, which had been sanctified in public perception for aeons, would have been sufficient reasons to give grave offence to the gods, and demand the execution of the impious woman who had polluted sacred rituals, and the members of her family participating in such impious acts.

It is difficult to be sure about the true reasons behind the accusations against Theoris, and nothing other than mass hysteria comparable to that of 415 seems to suggest itself. From the fourth century onwards, more and more alien cults with strange customs and outlandish promises to the believers were invading the cosmopolitan centres of the Greek world like Athens, and this invasion would rapidly accelerate under the Hellenistic kingdoms and the Roman Empire. Why in this religious, cultural and ideological pluralism Theoris and her family were singled out and punished so vengefully is not certain, but perhaps we cannot understand from a rational perspective a reaction which was instinctively emotional and motivated by fears, anxieties and paranoia.

28. HYPEREIDES, Πρὸς Τιμάνδραν

To Timandra

The case involving the hetaira Timandra, the mistress of Alcibiades in his latter days, was yet another sensational trial of a former hetaira, which scandalised later rhetoricians with the explicit images of prostitutes and brothels that the orator evoked:

> Fr. 164 Jensen. (= Sud. s.v.) παιδάριον. οὐ μόνον ἐπὶ τῶν ἀρρένων κέχρηνται τῷ ὀνόματι οἱ ῥήτορες, ἀλλὰ καὶ ἐπὶ παρθένων. Ὑπερείδης ἐν τῷ πρὸς Τιμάνδραν· Καταλειφθέντων γὰρ τούτων, δυοῖν ἀδελφαῖν, ὀρφανῶν καὶ πρὸς πατρὸς καὶ πρὸς μητρὸς καὶ παιδαρίων.

> *paidarion* (youngster). The orators use it not only for boys but also for girls. Hypereides in the speech *To Timandra*. These two sisters were left orphaned by their father and mother and as youngsters.

> Fr. 165 Jensen. (= Demetr. *Eloq.* 302) καθάπερ ὁ τῆς Τιμάνδρας κατηγορῶν ὡς πεπορνευκυίας τὴν λεκανίδα καὶ τοὺς ὀλίσβους καὶ τὴν ψίαθον καὶ πολλήν τινα τοιαύτην δυσφημίαν ἑταιρῶν κατήρασε τοῦ δικαστηρίου.

> As the accuser of Timandra, since she had been a prostitute, uttered profanities involving bathtubs, dildos, straw mats and other such distasteful items appropriate for hetairai.

While very little is known about the actual facts of this case, the scanty fragments preserved by rhetoricians and lexicographers offer valuable hints about the tactics which Hypereides employed. The woman involved was the notorious hetaira Timandra.[145] She had reached her floruit at the end of the fifth century and was reportedly with Alcibiades in his last days. If she was in her twenties around that time, she would probably be in her sixties when this trial took place. We do not know what the lawsuit was about. If the title has been accurately preserved in the Suda we should assume that she had initiated the legal proceedings. Demetrius, on the other hand, may imply that she was the defendant in a vicious prosecution which dragged her through the mud. We can recognise two techniques broadly employed in lawsuits involving women. The fragment of the Suda, which contains a quotation from the speech of Hypereides, is clearly reminiscent of the technique of Apollodoros in *Against Neaira* (59.18 ff.). As Apollodoros begins his narrative from the time that Neaira was a small child, Hypereides also opened his narrative with the observation that Timandra and her sister were left orphaned from a young age. We can reasonably extrapolate that he went on to describe how Timandra was initiated into prostitution, as Apollodoros does, when he relates her initiation into prostitution at a very young age during a visit to Athens with her procuress (D. 59.22).

The brief reference to the judgement of Demetrios on the unsavory terminology extensively used in the speech is truly intriguing because it suggests that, despite the convention of keeping court speeches within the bounds of polite discourse, prosecutors of women who were widely recognised as prostitutes took more liberties and employed scandalous language in order to shock and entertain juries, and secure votes through the vilification of the 'other woman', the one who was totally unlike their wives, mothers, daughters or sisters. By stoking up fears and social anxieties about the dangerous influence of the 'other woman' on Athenian men, which seem to be prevalent around the middle of the fourth century if the argumentation of the speech *Against Neaira* is any indication (107–24), the orators attempt to drive a wedge between the 'us' and 'them', and taking the judges on their side. Several sources attest that such tactics were employed in the prosecutions of hetairai, and among those this small fragment from Demetrius is important because it enlists the actual words and items which he found too distasteful to be mentioned in court. The passage clearly suggests that these items were associated with low-class prostitution (πεπορνευκυίας). The dildo is an item associated with prostitutes, lesbian sex and lonely women.[146] The straw mats must be associated with brothels and cheap sex. In the notorious scene from Juvenal where Messalina visits a brothel and offers herself to clients all night long, the mat (*teges*) is a necessary accessory in the cubicle where she works.[147] The term *lekane* and its derivatives, like *lekanis*, were in broad use to indicate any kind of bowl or tub, from expensive golden and silver dining bowls to functional large tubs of metal, clay or stone. In this instance it probably indicated the tubs or bowls used in brothels. I think we get the picture. Through references to such objects Hypereides was trying to recreate in the courtroom images of low-end prostitution, the objects, the odours and the sensations of a brothel, just as Juvenal does so successfully in the aforementioned scene that the reader can almost smell the stench of the soiled mats. With such connotations of filth and cheap sexuality, this was a world almost antithetical to the images of the respectable Athenian household stereotypically portrayed in the Attic orators, or even to polished establishments of upper-end prostitution, like the house of Theodote in Xenophon's *Memorabilia*.[148]

The passage of Demetrios sheds light on the vector of attack which Hypereides adopted against Timandra. As in the cases of Neaira, Aristagora or Phryne, Timandra's past as a prostitute played a major role in the build-up of the case, even though, like Neaira, at the time of her trial she was an old woman in her sixties or seventies, with her days as a glamorous hetaira a distant memory.

NOTES

1. The term typically refers to a child after it is born.
2. Kapparis 2002: 185–93; see also Carey's discussion in his subsequent edition of the fragments (2007: 319–24).
3. Most cases in the *Epidemics* typically come from other cities, but there is no way of telling for sure whether the travelling physician(s) had visited Athens and included this case because they thought that it was relevant. This particular entry does not mention location, and the highly fragmentary and rather archival nature of this work leaves all options open.
4. The size of the abortus suggests that the pregnancy when interrupted was of around twelve weeks' duration, but the foetus is not properly formed. By that stage the limbs should be clearly visible, and this was significant, because Hippocratic doctors believed that the foetus acquires human identity from the moment when it is formed to resemble a human being with the limbs clearly visible. By the looks of it, the prosecution (and Galen seven centuries later) attribute the abnormalities to the effects of drugs taken to inhibit and ultimately to terminate the pregnancy. However, without further proof of foul play, such an interpretation was far from inevitable, and we do not know whether Antigenes had such proof in his hands.
5. See the discussion in Kapparis 2002: 33–52; Hanson 2008: 95–108; Dasen 2007; Brisson et al. 2008.
6. Kapparis 2002: 167–94.
7. See also the relevant article by Carey (2004: 123–50).
8. E.g. D. 43.16, 44.13, 46.22; Is. 3.41 al. On the *epikleros* and the process of the *epidikasia* see Karnezis 1972; Katz 1992: 692–708; Leão 2001a: 113–32; 2005: 5–31; Cudjoe 2005: 55–88 (a useful article, but I do not agree with the conclusion that the *epidikasia* did not amount to lawful marriage); Paoli 1943: 19–29 (on the *epikleros* in Roman plays inspired by Greek originals).
9. According to Harpocration (s.v.) a δίκη βεβαιώσεως was introduced by someone against a man who sold him something, because a third party was laying claim to the same piece of property. Through this lawsuit the introducer was asking the seller to formally verify that the property item was his to sell, and therefore not subject to any third-party claims. The same procedure could be followed if the property transfer had not been completed but the introducer had paid the seller a deposit in order to secure it, as seems to be the case here.
10. I am following the text of Carey, except for a minor difference in punctuation. Carey places a comma after τὸν δῆμον, but it seems that τὸν δῆμον is the object of ἀνακαλεσάμενοι, and this is how I have translated it here.

11. I have supplemented τῆς [δὲ ἐπικα]ρπίας [αὐ/τοὺς λα]μβάν[ειν by comparison with passages like Isoc. 17.125 τούτους δὲ τὰς ἐπικαρπίας λαμβάνοντας. I have also added ὡς before προσῆκον.
12. Th. 8.68; Plu. 833 E–F.
13. For these tactics of the Thirty see the detailed presentation in Lys. 12 (esp. 5ff.) and 13.47. For the events surrounding those years see Wolpert 2002.
14. Lys. 12.67: βουλόμενος δὲ τῷ ὑμετέρῳ πλήθει δοκεῖν πιστὸς εἶναι Ἀντιφῶντα καὶ Ἀρχεπτόλεμον φιλτάτους ὄντας αὐτῷ κατηγορῶν ἀπέκτεινεν, εἰς τοσοῦτον δὲ κακίας ἦλθεν, ὥστε ἅμα μὲν διὰ τὴν πρὸς ἐκείνους πίστιν ὑμᾶς κατεδουλώσατο, διὰ δὲ τὴν πρὸς ὑμᾶς τοὺς φίλους ἀπώλεσε. 'Since he wanted to appear loyal to the multitude of you, he accused Antiphon and Archeptolemus, although they were his closest supporters, and he had them executed. He went so far in his depravity that he enslaved you to gain their trust and killed his friends to gain yours' (trans. Andrew Wolpert).
15. Plu. 834 A.
16. Lys. 12.66.
17. Idomeneus *FGrH* 338 F 4; cf. Athen. 13.58; Plu. 849 D; Theon *Prog.* 68 Spengel, al.
18. I conclude that *notheia* must refer to an illegitimate son, rather than an illegitimate daughter, because a daughter would get a dowry, albeit smaller than that of a legitimate daughter, while the *notheia* was the maximum legally permissible share of the family property which a father could leave to an illegitimate son (property up to the value of 1,000 drachmas). See Harp. s.v. νοθεῖα.
19. There is some evidence suggesting that metic women used a *prostates* in their dealings with the law, but what exactly this means is less clear (D. 25.58; Ar. *Ra.* 569–70). They needed a male representative to speak for them, who could reasonably be called '*prostates*', but we cannot tell for sure that this was the originally appointed *prostates*. While it is possible that the original *prostates*, a citizen with whom the alien might have a personal and trusting relationship, could represent him or her for many years, the law surely could not be requiring that this relationship lasted for ever. Reason suggests that the term was flexible and we need to understand it in its broader sense as 'protector', applying to any male citizen representative or *synegoros* of a metic woman, for a specific case or maybe for all her dealings with the state over a lengthy time period, depending on the circumstances and the individuals involved.
20. On the metic women of Attica see Kennedy 2014; Bakewell 2008: 97–109; Carey 1991: 84–9; Whitehead 1986a: 109–14. On metics in general Whitehead's classic monograph (1977) remains important; see also Bakewell 1999: 5–22; Sosin 2016: 2–13 (convincingly reaffirming Whitehead's position that all free non-citizens were considered to be metics in Athens); Watson 2010: 259–78 (on the origins of the institution).
21. See Kapparis 2019a: 90–1.
22. The penalty after a conviction for *graphe aprostasiou* was slavery.
23. D. 25.57–8; cf. Harp. s.v. μετοίκιον; Arist. *Ath.* 47.2; Rhodes com. ad loc. The process followed by Aristokrates against Zobia in 25.57–8 was irregular, at least in the form described to us by Demosthenes, and this is why Zobia was released.

A free person could not be sold into slavery prior to a court ruling imposing this penalty upon him or her, for certain offences, mostly related to citizenship and immigration violations. Procedures against aliens which could lead to enslavement were the *graphe xenias*, the *graphe aprostasiou*, the *dike apostasiou*, the 'pretence of lawful marriage to a citizen' (in the fourth century), or an *ephesis* to the court after rejection from the deme (see my previous discussion in Kapparis 2019a: ch. 2; 2005: 71–113; MacDowell 1978: 76–8; Todd 1993: 111, 139).

24. D. 59.40; Aesch. 1.62; Lys. 23.11, al. See also the discussion in Kapparis 1999: 248–50.
25. The ἀφαίρεσις εἰς ἐλευθερίαν was often employed as a legal manouevre to deflect pressure and confuse the issues (as in Isoc. 5.14), or to force a reluctant opponent to accept arbitration (as in D. 59.40), rather than simply decide on someone's status.
26. The *diamartyria* was the traditional process through which someone could challenge the legality of a lawsuit on technical grounds, before the introduction of the more evolved procedure of the *paragraphe* in the early fourth century Until then, if someone believed that a lawsuit was inadmissible for some reason, he needed to present a witness willing to testify to this effect. If this happened, the initial lawsuit was frozen until the *diamartyria* was decided, and if the challenger won, the initial lawsuit was automatically dropped. If he lost, the initial trial would resume as normal. See Lys. 23. 13–14; Isoc. 18.2–3; see also Schönbauer 1964: 203–31; Gernet 1955: 83–102; MacDowell 1978: 212–19, 216–19; Wolff 1966; Isager and Hansen 1975.
27. See Lys. Fr. 208 Carey, D. 59.19 and also the discussion in the speech *To Lais*.
28. The noun appears twice in classical literature, once in Demosthenes (22.59) and once in Aristophanes (*V.* 418), in both instances related to the public life of the city.
29. D. 45.79. See also D. 18.46, 61, 199, 245; 19.61, 95, 197, 223, 250, 268, 315; 21.150, 197; 22.59; 23.119, 201; 24.6, 195; 25.66.
30. See also Eidinow 2010: 9–35; 2016; Frankfurter 2014: 319–39; Spaeth 2014: 41–70; Stratton 2014: 1–37; and the useful collection of essays edited by Stratton and Kalleres (2014); see also the discussion in the entry on the prosecution of Theoris.
31. Such a shift in tactics would remind us the two speeches in the cases against Boiotos. The first speech *To Boiotos, on the Name*, is an authentic Demosthenic text, rational, eloquent and urbane, but it failed in court; probably the case was inherently weak. The court had no good reason to ban the use of the name Mantitheos, if this is what the speaker's half-brother wished to be called. The second speech *To Boiotos* is far less urbane. It is angrier, dirtier and more aggressive, and does not hesitate to pile up heavy insults against the opponent, his brothers and especially his mother. See the discussion on D. 40 below, pp. 43–6.
32. D. 46.22 ἀνεπίδικον δὲ κλῆρον μὴ ἔχειν 'one is not allowed to have the estate without prior adjudication'.
33. On the *epikleros* see Kapparis 2019a: 167–70; Maffi 1990: 21–36; Karnezis 1979: 145–71; Katz 1992: 692–708.

34. See for example D. 43 in conjunction with Is. 11 for a super-complicated case of claims and counterclaims over the estate of Hagnias which went on for years.
35. See note 26 above.
36. E.g. Is. 3.3; 5.16; 6.4; 7.3.
37. Trans. B. Perrin.
38. Henry 1995: 24.
39. Plu. *Per.* 32: ψήφισμα Διοπείθης ἔγραψεν εἰσαγγέλλεσθαι τοὺς τὰ θεῖα μὴ νομίζοντας ἢ λόγους περὶ τῶν μεταρσίων διδάσκοντας. 'Diopeithes introduced a decree according to which those who did not believe in the gods or taught about celestial phenomena were to be prosecuted for *eisangelia*.'
40. For this larger and more complex discussion see Kapparis 2019a: 259; MacDowell 1978: 200–2; Whitmarsh 2015: 71–137; Filonik 2013: 11–96; 2016: 125–40; Wallace 1994: 127–55; 1996: 226–40; O'Sullivan 2011: 167–85.
41. On Aspasia the standard study is the excellent monograph by Madeleine Henry (1995).
42. Ἀσπασίαν μὲν οὖν ἐξῃτήσατο, πολλὰ πάνυ παρὰ τὴν δίκην, ὡς Αἰσχίνης φησίν, ἀφεὶς ὑπὲρ αὐτῆς δάκρυα καὶ δεηθεὶς τῶν δικαστῶν.
43. Henry (1995: 29–56) correctly emphasises this aspect of Aspasia's legend.
44. Pl. *Mx.* 835 e ff.
45. Crat. Fr. 241 παλλακὴν κυνώπιδα.
46. Ar. *Ach.* 526–37; see also Henry 1995: 19–28.
47. If he had lost with less than one fifth of the votes, which he might have done since he was going against the mighty Pericles, and had been unable to pay the fine, as an *atimos* he would not have been able to attend the theatre or compete in dramatic contests.
48. X. Mem. 1.1.1: ἡ μὲν γὰρ γραφὴ κατ' αὐτοῦ τοιάδε τις ἦν· ἀδικεῖ Σωκράτης οὓς μὲν ἡ πόλις νομίζει θεοὺς οὐ νομίζων, ἕτερα δὲ καινὰ δαιμόνια εἰσφέρων. Pl. *Ap.* 19 b 4–c 7: Σωκράτης ἀδικεῖ καὶ περιεργάζεται ζητῶν τά τε ὑπὸ γῆς καὶ οὐράνια καὶ τὸν ἥττω λόγον κρείττω ποιῶν καὶ ἄλλους ταὐτὰ ταῦτα διδάσκων.' τοιαύτη τίς ἐστιν· ταῦτα γὰρ ἑωρᾶτε καὶ αὐτοὶ ἐν τῇ Ἀριστοφάνους κωμῳδίᾳ, Σωκράτη τινὰ ἐκεῖ περιφερόμενον, φάσκοντά τε ἀεροβατεῖν καὶ ἄλλην πολλὴν φλυαρίαν φλυαροῦντα, ὧν ἐγὼ οὐδὲν οὔτε μέγα οὔτε μικρὸν πέρι ἐπαΐω. καὶ οὐχ ὡς ἀτιμάζων λέγω τὴν τοιαύτην ἐπιστήμην, εἴ τις περὶ τῶν τοιούτων σοφός ἐστιν ('"Socrates is an evil-doer, and a curious person, who searches into things under the earth and in heaven, and he makes the worse appear the better cause; and he teaches the aforesaid doctrines to others." That is the nature of the accusation, and that is what you have seen yourselves in the comedy of Aristophanes; who has introduced a man whom he calls Socrates, going about and saying that he can walk in the air, and talking a deal of nonsense concerning matters of which I do not pretend to know either much or little – not that I mean to say anything disparaging of anyone who is a student of natural philosophy' (trans. B. Jowett).
49. See *IG* ii² 1622, where all three sons of Mantias are mentioned as Πάμφιλος [Θορίκιος] / . . . / Μαντίθεος Θ[ορίκ –]/ Μαντίθεος [Θορίκ –]; and 4883, where a daughter and grandson of one of the two Mantitheoi are mentioned

(Ἱππάρχη Μαντιθέο Θορικίο θυγάτηρ ὑπὲρ τō ὑέος καὶ ἑαυτῆς ἀνέθηκεν). Further on the question of identity see Griffith-Williams 2020: 32–46.
50. Thus Miles 1951: 38–46.
51. For further discussion of the legal aspects of this case see Maffi 1985: 261–311, as a response to Jean Rudhardt (1962: 39–64).
52. On challenges to take an oath or torture of a slave see Durand and Otis-Cour 2002; Mirhady 1996: 119–31; 2000: 53–74; Gagarin 1996: 1–18; Thür 1996: 132–4. Akiko Yamauchi (2005: 59–67) discusses Mantias's challenge to Plangon, correctly outlining that it was exceptional when compared to similar challenges elsewhere in the Attic orators. This has been a long debate as scholars are struggling to understand how the Athenians could attach any value to such challenges as evidence when they knew, as we know, that they were nothing more than rhetorical devices. My view on the subject, which I outlined in the 1999 commentary on the speech *Against Neaira* (424–36), has been that these rhetorical devices are generally of very low demonstrative value, used only when no other form of proof could be produced, in order to offer some compensation for the lack of evidence. However, as Yamauchi correctly points out, Mantias' challenge is different. Maybe he truly wanted the paternity of his sons formally and publicly verified in an official setting, so as to avoid future challenges to their citizenship, or possibly he was double-crossed by Plangon, as Mantitheos suggests. In either case, he should have known that he had little room for manoeuvre if Plangon accepted the challenge and swore that the boys were his children. Would he have risked it and trusted his former wife, if he did not want to hear that the two boys were his sons? Probably not, if the previous relationship between the two is any indication. This is why I am inclined to take the first option and accept that he wanted formal and public verification of the paternity of the boys before he acknowledged them. This would make his challenge to take an oath different, because Mantias genuinely wanted the truth to come out, while ordinarily through such challenges litigants were not in pursuit of the truth; they were simply trying to score points against their opponent.
53. See Kapparis 2020: 63–80.
54. Occasionally a speaker might have very good reasons to mention an Athenian woman by name (e.g. Is. 3.30; And. 1.16; D. 57.68), but in these few instances the woman's name was mentioned only once, not repeatedly. By contrast, Neaira's name is mentioned eighty times in a single speech (D. 59). See Schaps 1997: 323–30, and also Stephanie Larson (2005: 225–44).
55. Kapparis 2019a: 442.
56. E.g. Lysias: *Πρὸς Ἀνδοκίδην ἀποστασίου, Ὑπὲρ Δεξίου ἀποστασίου, Πρὸς Πυθόδημον ἀποστασίου*; Deinarchos: *Κατὰ Ἡδύλης ἀποστασίου* (see also the discussion below, pp. 52–3), *ἀποστασίου πρὸς Ἀρχέστρατον, ἀποστασίου ἀπολογία Αἰσχύλῳ πρὸς Ξενοφῶντα*.
57. E.g. D. 35.48; Arist. *Ath.* 58.3; Sud. α 3546; Phot. s.v. ἡγεμονία δικαστηρίου; Harp. s.v. ἀποστασίου and s.v. διαμαρτυρία.
58. E.g. Ptolemy Gramm. *De Differentia Vocabulorum* 397.26 Heylbut; Ammon. 60 Nickau; Harp. s.v. ἀποστασίου.

59. Kapparis 2019a: 91. It was common for manumission contracts to contain a passage through which the former master sought to extend his control over the former slave. Let's say a master might want to reward a loyal slave with his freedom, but did not want to completely lose out on the financial side of things, by losing the labour which the slave provided. So he wrote a condition into the manumission contract (*paramone*) under which the former slave still had some duties to perform for his former master, sometimes for a short period of time, but often for a very long period of time, even a lifetime. Such an arrangement was seen as mutually beneficial. The slave gained his freedom, but the master did not lose out financially. Sometimes the arrangements were of a more personal nature, for example the obligation for a former slave to perform funeral rites after the death of his former master who had no relatives to do this. On *paramone* see: Calderini 1908; Silver 2015: 139–61; Samuel 1965: 221–311; Sosin 2015: 325–81; Westermann 1948: 9–50.
60. There are several instances where women were praised for their eloquence: e.g. Ar. *Ec.* 241–5; Plu. *Per.* 24 (about the eloquence of Aspasia), Cic. *N.D.* 1.93.3 (where Cicero expresses his indignation because the hetaira Leontion dared to deliver a retort to a speech by the great Theophrastus, but also admits that it was done with learning [*scito sermone*] and in elegant Attic Greek).
61. Lys. 32. 13–18. Trans. W. R. M. Lamb.
62. For the relevant discussion see Gagarin 2001: 161–76; Blok 2001: 95–116; Walters 1993: 194–214.
63. Lys. 32.7: 2,000 drachmas = 20 minae, 30 Cyzicus staters × 25 = 750 drachmas = 7.5 minae. The total is approximately 27 minae, roughly equal to the sum of an average dowry.
64. D. 30.6–7. But even in the case of Demosthenes there was a certain urgency to bring the guardians to court ὡς τάχιστα.
65. See the discussion above, pp. 129–31.
66. E.g. *IG* ii² 1514 col. II. 58; 1516, col. II, 34; 1523, col. II, 20; 1524, face B, col. II, 194; 1527, face B, 25 (and several other inscriptions around 350 BC); 4358: [Ἡ]δύ[λ]η Εὔφρο[νος –]; 5492: Ἡδύλη Καλλικλέους Ἁλαέως; 6218: Ἡδύλη Ἀττάβου Θορικίου al.
67. On the process of *diamartyria* see note 26 above.
68. The text is that of Carey (2007) Fr. 208. Carey combines the testimony of Athen. 13.51 and 13.62 to produce a better text. He obelises the unnecessary {καὶ} ἔτι νέα οὖσα encountered in 13.62, while he adds καὶ Ἀριστόκλεια from 13.62, omitted in 13.51. He also accepts Harpokration's suggestion that the correct name of the hetaira is probably Ἄντεια instead of Ἄνθεια transmitted in A of Athenaios. The manuscripts of D. 59.19, where the same woman is mentioned, are also divided and transmit the forms (Ἀντία [SFQ] or Ἄντεια [YRD]). Given the way the manuscripts are split in D. 59.19, it is most likely that the name of the woman was Ἄντεια, the mythical queen of Argos (*Il.* 6.160).
69. Kapparis 2018a: 416–18.
70. Damasandra was one of the women linked with Alcibiades in his latter years, and the one who buried him after his death (see Kapparis 2018a: 107–8, 299).

Alcibiades was killed in 404. Lais the Younger, the daughter of Damasandra, would have reached her floruit around 380, if she was born when her mother was in her twenties or thirties around 400. This would be consonant with a date for the speech around 380. By then, those legendary beauties who had reached their floruit around 400, and had given up prostitution while at the top of their game, could still be remembered fondly.

71. Athenaios confuses matters, transmitting the title as *Πρὸς Λαΐδα* in 13.51 and *Κατὰ Λαΐδος* in 13.62. Carey, along with the majority of scholars, has adopted *Πρὸς Λαΐδα*, probably because between the two it is the *lectio difficilior*. It would be easier for someone to use the title *Κατὰ Λαΐδος* in a speech attacking her, than the more involved *Πρὸς Λαΐδα*.
72. Sch. Ar. Plu. 149; this reference is not necessarily independent, as the scholiast could be using the speech by Lysias as his source, but then again, he could be quoting the play by Ephippos or another source.
73. Athen. 13.46. For the arguments see Kapparis 2018a: 451.
74. Kapparis 2007: 415–6, and 108–9.
75. D. 59.19; see also Kapparis 1999: 208–10.
76. Benjamin Millis (2015: 66–72) questions the traditional understanding of the title of the play as 'old men struck with madness', because in parallels like γυναικομανία (Chrysippos, Fr. 667 von Arnim), ὀρνιθομανία (Chrysippos, Fr. 667 von Arnim) or ἱππομανία (Luc. *Nigr*. 29) the first compound is the object of the madness, not its subject. He would prefer an understanding of the title along the lines of 'mad about old men'. For a speaker of Modern Greek an understanding of γεροντομανία as 'old age madness' would have many parallels, like γεροντοέρωτας (old age love), γεροντοπαλλήκαρο (an ageing bachelor), γεροντόπαχο (old age weight gain), γεροντόπαιδο (a child born to older parents). In all these instances the first compound γεροντο- simply defines the second, which is the case with γεροντομανία. The question is when this usage came into the language, and in my opinion the few instances which Millis mentions can also be interpreted in this context: the first compound simply defines the second (women-madness, bird-madness, horse-madness). On these grounds I think the traditional understanding as 'old age madness' is the correct one. In this particular context the old men conversing here are crazy about hetairai, maybe like Philoxenus and Nicobulus, the two old men visiting a brothel in the final scenes of Plautus' *Bacchides*.
77. Anaxandrides Fr. 9. Kapparis 2018: 388–9.
78. As far as we can tell, such a bold homoerotic reference would be unheard of in the stylised world of character-driven Middle Comedy.
79. Kapparis 2019b: 193–208.
80. D. 59.19: Ἑπτὰ γὰρ ταύτας παιδίσκας ἐκ μικρῶν παιδίων ἐκτήσατο Νικαρέτη, ..., Ἄντειαν καὶ Στρατόλαν καὶ Ἀριστόκλειαν καὶ Μετάνειραν καὶ Φίλαν καὶ Ἰσθμιάδα καὶ Νέαιραν ταυτηνί. 'Nikarete bought these seven slave-girls when they were little children . . . Anteia, Stratola, Aristokleia, Metaneira, Phila, Isthmias and Neaira here.' I have argued that the list is roughly chronological (Kapparis 1999: 208–10). Anteia, who seems to be the eldest, reached her floruit

at the turn of the century, Metaneira in the 380s and Neaira, who seems to be the youngest, in the 370s. Without being too rigid about it, the pattern seems to be that every five years or so, one of these women would be sold by her mistress at a very high price, while still in her prime, and another one would be ready to take her place, to be exploited by Nikarete for the next five years.

81. Plays with the title *Anteia* are attributed to Eunikos, Phillylios, Antiphanes and Alexis. *Neaira* was the title of plays by Timokles and Philemon, while Lais probably inspired the *Antilais* of Kephisodoros.
82. Hyp. Fr. 24 Jensen = Athen. 13.50; Apollodoros *FGrH* 244 F 210. See also Kapparis 2018: 390.
83. Trans. K. Kapparis, in Wolpert and Kapparis 2011.
84. See Filonik 2013: 11–96; 2016: 125–40.
85. See also X. *HG* 5.4.1–18.
86. The situation would be reversed in the 360s after the stunning successes of the Thebans against Sparta, when the Athenians became worried that all along they had been harbouring a potentially dangerous adversary on their doorstep. In a very dramatic narrative describing the impact of the battle of Leuctra, Xenophon (*HG* 6.4.19–20) relates how a very upset *boule* did not even offer the herald the customary meal and hospitality (*xenia*).
87. For the myths of Eleusis see Hom. *H. Cer.*[, and also Foley 1994; Arthur 1977: 7–47; Parker 1991: 1–17; Faulkner 2011; Gasparro 1986.
88. This form of punishment makes no sense, unless we are to understand that Mikon was punished even though thirty months had elapsed since the introduction of the decree. This would be basically illegal, because the law allowed the punishment of a person who had introduced an unconstitutional law or decree for up to a year. After that, while a decree or law judged to be unconstitutional could still be annulled, the introducer was no longer liable to punishment. However, the case of Mikon seems to be extraordinary.
89. The addition of the definite article is probably unnecessary. Although the title given in most sources is Περὶ τῆς ἱερείας, it is very likely that the author of the *Suda* simply omitted it, as Harpocration also does in 6.10.
90. On the *paredroi* see my 1998 study.
91. The text does not seem to me to be as damaged as Conomis thought. I think that the crux before θησαυρῷ is unnecessary, as it must refer to a dedication with a painting on it, and the addition of ἄν before ἔγραψε is also unnecessary as ἔγραψε on its own can mean 'to paint'. (e.g. ζῷα γράφεσθαι Hdt. 4.88; Pl. *R.* 420c).
92. On Greek priestesses the main study is Connelly 2007; see also Skov 1975: 136–47 (useful about the priestess of the Two Goddesses, but I am not convinced that the Haloa contained initiation rituals); about the role of women in religion in a broader sense see Cole 2004; Goff 2004; Dillon 2002.
93. Aesch. 1.2: αἱ γὰρ ἴδιαι ἔχθραι πολλὰ πάνυ τῶν κοινῶν ἐπανορθοῦσι. Likewise Apollodoros in *Against Neaira* employs *amplificatio* to elevate this trial to a matter of grave public concern, first in the opening section (1), and then in the argumentation of the speech and the epilogue (107–26).
94. I assume that the subject of the participle is 'I', but it could really be anyone.

95. And. 1.117–19.
96. See for example *SEG* 16.39, middle of the fifth century, where the admirer of an attractive youth has written in a graffiti Λακεδαιμόνιος καλός 'Lakedaimonios is handsome.'
97. See Shaw King 1903: 327–8.
98. See also my previous discussion in Kapparis 2019a: 351–4; 2019b: 193–208.
99. Since I have written extensively on the subject, the reader could be informed on my views from previous publications, esp. Kapparis 1999, and in a lighter version Wolpert and Kapparis 2011. Moreover, the case and its particulars are discussed in relevant sections in Part II of this study, esp. Chapter 2, pp. 129–43, on the political background, and pp. 129–32 on the actual build-up of the case. See also Hamel 2003; Patterson 1993: 199–216; Spatharas 2011: 99–120; Glazebrook 2005b: 161–87; Bakewell 2008: 97–109; Campa 2019: 257–79.
100. See the discussion on the speech above, pp. 129–43.
101. All translations from D. 39 and 40 here are by A. T. Murray.
102. Murray translates δεινόν as 'a clever fellow', and understands it as 'possibly "an eloquent speaker"'. I have changed the translation here to 'scary', because I think it means that Boiotos wanted to inspire fear in public life, like Menekles and other men like him.
103. Dionysios correctly points out that Deinarchos would have been too young to compose the speech.
104. Eidinow (2016: 17–23) accepts the version of the text of Josephus as amended by Weil: Νῖνον (νῦν codd.) γὰρ τὴν ἱέρειαν ἀπέκτειναν, ἐπεί τις αὐτῆς κατηγόρησεν, ὅτι ξένους ἐμύει θεούς· νόμῳ δ' ἦν τοῦτο παρ' αὐτοῖς κεκωλυμένον καὶ τιμωρία κατὰ τῶν ξένον εἰσαγόντων θεὸν ὥριστο θάνατος. 'They put to death the priestess Ninos, because someone accused her of introducing new gods; for this was prohibited among them, and the punishment against those who introduced a foreign god was death.'
105. Harp. s.v. πεντακοσιομέδιμνοι and Ὑβάδαι = Fr. 260 and 261 Carey.
106. Th. 8.25–30; Plu. 833F; X. *HG* 2.3.2.
107. For property losses under the Thirty, and their impact after the amnesty of 403, see the recent study of Lene Rubinstein (2018a: 123–44).
108. The most recent edition of the speech, with rich, informative commentary and bibliography, is Hatzilambrou 2018. For a reliable translation see Edwards 2007. For useful background discussions on women, families and inheritance disputes see also Griffith-Williams 2012: 145–62; 2013; 2016: 111–16; 2019: 375–88. I take a stronger position than both Hatzilambrou and Griffith-Williams, as well as most scholars before, on the issue of Phile's legitimacy. While the majority of scholars are prepared to put some faith in the claim that Phile may have been illegitimate, or at least adopt cautious scepticism, I have no doubt that a woman born to a married Athenian couple, and given in marriage to an Athenian husband with whom she evidently had citizen children, ought to be considered legitimate, and this is why I have unequivocally maintained that Phile was legitimate and the lawful heiress of her father's property, and that the case against Phile was nothing more than a property grab, made more convincing

by the superb skill of Isaios. But even the most accomplished property litigator in classical Athens could not ultimately obscure the fact that his clients had no lawful claim.

109. Ten minae was the maximum legal amount permitted as a dowry to an illegitimate daughter (Harp. s.v. *notheia*). The mere fact that the family of Endios is forced to acknowledge that Phile received some dowry probably means that there was undeniable evidence of the *engye* contract between Endios and Xenokles, and a dowry was explicitly included in it. However, if the family of Endios had acknowledged a dowry any higher than ten minae, they would have effectively acknowledged Phile's legitimacy. We should not take their claim as evidence that her dowry was only ten minae, and even if it was, this did not prove that Phile was illegitimate. If Xenokles had agreed to marry her with this dowry because, let's say, she was supremely attractive, this could not have impacted the legality of the *engye* in any way. The family of Endios is truly scraping the bottom of the barrel for evidence of illegitimacy.

110. Plangon may have been another Athenian woman who worked as a hetaira for some time. pressed by financial hardship (see the discussion ad loc., pp. 43–6).

111. Ναΐς Harp: Λαΐς codd.

112. See the discussion in Chapter 1, pp. 117–20, and also in Kapparis 2019a: 210–13.

113. Athen. 13.62.

114. See Ar. *Plu*. 302–15; Pl. Com. Fr. 65; Theopompos Fr. 5–6; Nicochares Fr. 4; Philyllios Fr. 22; D. 27.56, and also Totaro 2015: 163–79, with emphasis on the *Wealth* of Aristophanes.

115. See Chapter 1, pp. 36–9.

116. The literature on the artistic and literary representations of Phryne through the centuries is very extensive. For starters, it would be impossible to discuss Praxiteles without discussing his muse and patron, and the influence of the mythology of Phryne has taken so many forms and has exerted such vast influence upon artists, writers and scholars through the centuries that it could be easily the subject matter of several independent volumes. Here we must be content with a sensible reconstruction of the main facts surrounding her *asebeia* trial. For a representative selection of the literature on Phryne see Morales 2011: 71–104 (with emphasis on the functions of the ekphrasis in relation to the mythology surrounding Phryne); Keesling 2006: 59–76; Hoernes 2012: 55–70; Corso 1997: 123–50; 1997–8: 63–91; Corpataux 2009: 145–58; Chambet 207: 233–40; Papet 2007: 362–93; Davidson 2006: 29–51; Feldman and Gordon 2006; Lehoux and Siron 2016; among others.

117. See Kapparis 2018: 258–61; 2019a: 200–4; 2020: 69–72.

118. The most systematic and influential discussion of the fragments is that by Craig Cooper (1995: 303–18). Cooper evinced much scepticism about the trial as presented in these fragments, and his view that much of the evidence from later antiquity should not be taken at face value has now become a scholarly orthodoxy.

119. See for example Christine Havelock (1995: 3–4, 42–7), who believed that the case against Phryne is largely fictional; Jakub Filonik (2013: 11–96), who, in his

excellent study on impiety in Athenian law, wonders whether the trial of Phryne took place at all; Helen Morales (2011: 100), who has concluded that the trial of Phryne 'can be read allegorically, about the operations of art and ekphrasis'; among others.

120. Davidson 2006: 35
121. Anon. Seg. *Ars Rhet.* 215 Hammer. According to Hermippos the speech of Euthias was composed by Anaximenes (Harp. s.v. *Euthias*; Alciphr. 4.3–5, Hermippos Fr. 50 Müller = Athen. 13.60; Anaximenes *FGrH* 72 T 17a).
122. David Phillips (2013: 458) has argued that it was an *eisangelia*, but all sources speak about a *graphe asebeias* (e.g. Alciphron 4.3; Anon. Seg. *Ars Rhet.* 215; Chorikios 29.2.45, 76; Eustathios *Com. Il.* 4.579).
123. Hyp. Fr. 177 Jensen.
124. Athen. 13.59
125. Athen. 13.58–9; Quint. *Inst.* 2.15.9 .
126. E.g. O'Connell 2017: 1–2; Lehoux and Siron 2016.
127 Eidinow 2016;also 2010: 9–35.
128. Keesling 2006: 59–76; Hoernes 2012: 55–70; Corso 1997: 123–50; 1997–8: 63–91; Cavallini 2004: 231–8. For the *Nachleben* of Phryne's artistic image see Chambet 2007: 233–40; Lehoux and Siron 2016; Papet 2007: 362–93; Corpataux 2009: 145–58; Davidson 2006: 29–51; Feldman and Gordon 2006.
129. See for example Dinarchus, *In Demosthenem* 18, 24; D. 18.41, 47 al.
130. Quint. *Inst.* 1.5.61, 2.15.9; Messala Fr. 22.
131. Trans. Andrew Wolpert.
132. Morales 2011: 71–104; Cavallini 2004: 231–8; n.d.
133. It is quite possible that a cluster of the fictional letters of Alkiphron (4.3–5) echo passages from the speech. Of particular interest is the phrase in 4.5 quoted above in this section. This phrase may echo some accusations from the speech, but there is no certainty without external corroboration because often the information in Alciphron's letters may be an echo from secondary, later and unreliable sources, if not made up altogether.
134. Hermippus Fr. 68a1 Wehrli = Harp. s.v. Euthias.
135. See Suda α 3959; Sch. Ar. Lys. 645; Fauth 1984: 93–9; Papadimitriou 1959; Bevan 1987: 17–21; Crummy 2010: 37–93; Perlman 1989: 111–33; Petrovic 2010: 209–27; Walbank 1981: 276–81.
136. See also above, pp. 52–3, for the case about the daughter(s) of Aristophon attributed to Deinarchos.
137. See Apostolakis 2007: 179–92; Edwards 2017: 243–50; Wohl 2010: 33–70.
138. Trans. A. T. Murray.
139. If someone else had prosecuted and convicted Theoris, perhaps Demosthenes would have said who that person was. By referring to her conviction and execution as the direct will of the people he tactfully avoids naming himself as her prosecutor, and at the same time presents her punishment as the will of the people. On another level, this re-establishes that bond of mutual trust between the orator and his audience which had led to the successful prosecution of Theoris in the previous trial.

140. See And. 1, and the highly informative commentary by D. M. MacDowell on the speech.
141. Collins 2001: 477–93.
142. Eidinow 2016; also 2010: 9–35. See also Dillon 2002: 183–207.
143. Ach. Tat. 2.38.5: τὰ δὲ φιλήματα σοφίαν μὲν οὐκ ἔχει γυναικείαν, οὐδὲ μαγγανεύει τοῖς χείλεσι σινάμωρον ἀπάτην ('the kisses do not have a feminine wisdom, nor do they inflict with the lips a tricky deception').
144. D. 46.14, 48.56.
145. See Kapparis 2018: 441.
146. E.g. Arist. Fr. 320; Cratinus Fr. 316; Sud. o 169; Herodas 6.
147. Iuv. *Sat.* 6.117.
148. X. *Mem.* 3.11.

PART II

Women and the Athenian Justice System

CHAPTER 1

Women's Participation in the Athenian Justice System

WOMEN'S ACCESS TO THE VARIOUS LAYERS OF THE JUSTICE SYSTEM

The participation of women in the Athenian justice system has been a seriously understudied issue for one simple reason: it has been an almost universally accepted axiom that woman were totally excluded, and therefore there was nothing much to discuss. However, this assumption is based upon two faulty premises. The first sees participation as a black-and-white issue where someone is either totally in or totally out. The logic behind it runs as follows: women were excluded from public life and could not turn up in court to speak for themselves, either in their defence or to prosecute someone. But since in the Athenian justice system the individual citizen was the one to introduce lawsuits, and to personally defend himself if prosecuted, inevitably a woman had no access to Athenian justice. The second faulty premise has to do with a very simplistic perception of the Athenian justice system as a single-layer process with two citizens appearing in court in person as opposing litigants, speaking before a large jury and either winning or losing the case. In reality, the Athenian justice system was a complex machinery with several different layers, each allowing different levels and types of access. Only the top layer, the *dikasterion*, was limited to male participants, and even at this level the concept of two male litigants battling each other is simplistic, because it does not take into account the time, money and machinations involved in the backstage operation, routinely dominated by skilled advocates, legal advisors and shadow speechwriters. Even though women could not stand up and speak for themselves in the *dikasteria*, they certainly had indirect access through representatives and advocates speaking for them, and would be able to set up these mechanisms to work for their benefit.

Once we take a closer look, and also account for intersections with socio-economic circumstances, citizen status, race and immigration, and prevailing ideologies, the entire picture becomes much more nuanced and complex. The women of Attica were not equal to each other in legal, social or economic terms, and there was no clear-cut and linear correlation between inequalities and social stratification. For example, slave hetairai could be much better connected in the upper echelons of Athenian society than poor citizen women, and have the resources and support of powerful lovers if they got into trouble with the law, or free alien women could be much much better-off than poor Athenian widows. Factors such as these could seriously influence access to justice even in a legal system like that of the Athenian democracy, which was meticulously designed to make access to it as egalitarian as possible. In order to understand how these factors affected woman's access to the Athenian justice system, it will be necessary to present a brief outline of the justice system and the specific pathways available to different groups of the population.

The justice system as we know it from the court speeches of the classical period and the *Athenaion Politeia* attributed to Aristotle is a hodge-podge of successive developments, alterations and additions, which go back all the way to the aristocratic state in the seventh century.[1] However, even before the early years of the Athenian Empire responsibility was gradually shifting away from institutions which were seen as a representation of the aristocratic state, and the transformation was complete by 362, when Ephialtes substantially limited the powers of the Areopagos council. The magistrates of the state, even the formerly powerful nine archons, had become civil servants, each overseeing an important aspect of public life and exercising authority on behalf of the Athenian people (δῆμος). All these public officials, over 1,000 in number and mostly appointed by lot for one year, were on the front line of implementing justice in the Athenian state. Their duties were not limited to the effective processing of the state bureaucracy, but also included significant powers of decision-making. Their decisions did not always result in a definite dispute resolution, as there were statutory limits to the authority of magistrates, and moreover, angry litigants could always find ways to escalate matters through the courts. However, one would imagine that often the decision of a magistrate could settle a dispute at its initial stages, especially if it was a rather minor issue and the quarrelling parties were willing to accept the outcome and avoid the troubles and expenses of a court trial.

The *Athenaion Politeia* describes the steps towards a dispute resolution in the time of the orators as following:

Κληροῦσι δὲ καὶ <τοὺς> <τετταράκοντα>, τέτταρας ἐκ τῆς φυλῆς ἑκάστης, πρὸς οὓς τὰς ἄλλας δίκας λαγχάνουσιν. οἳ πρότερον μὲν ἦσαν τριάκοντα καὶ κατὰ δήμους περιιόντες ἐδίκαζον, μετὰ δὲ τὴν ἐπὶ τῶν τριάκοντα ὀλιγαρχίαν τετταράκοντα γεγόνασιν. καὶ τὰ μὲν μέχρι δέκα δραχμῶν αὐτοτελεῖς εἰσι δ[ικά]ζε[ι]ν, τὰ δ' ὑπὲρ τοῦτο τὸ τίμημα τοῖς διαιτηταῖς παραδιδόασιν· οἱ δὲ παραλαβόντες, [ἐ]ὰν μὴ δύνωνται διαλῦσαι, γιγνώσκουσι, κἂν μὲν ἀμφοτέροις ἀρέσκῃ τὰ γνωσθέντα καὶ ἐμμένωσιν, ἔχει τέλος ἡ δίκη. ἂν δ' ὁ ἕτερος ἐφῇ τῶν ἀντιδίκων εἰς τὸ δικαστήριον, ἐμβαλόντες τὰς μαρτυρίας καὶ τὰς προκλήσεις καὶ τοὺς νόμους εἰς ἐχίνους, χωρὶς μὲν τὰς τοῦ διώκοντος, χωρὶς δὲ τὰς τοῦ φεύγοντος, καὶ τούτους κατασημηνάμενοι, καὶ τὴν γνῶσιν τοῦ διαιτητοῦ γεγραμμένην ἐν γραμματείῳ προσαρτήσαντες, παραδιδόασι το[ῖ]ς δ' τοῖς τὴν φυλὴν τοῦ φεύγοντος δικάζουσιν. οἱ δὲ παραλαβόντες εἰσάγουσιν εἰς τὸ δικαστήριον, τὰ μὲν ἐντὸς χιλίων εἰς ἕνα καὶ διακοσίους, τὰ δ' ὑπὲρ χιλίας εἰς ἕνα καὶ τετρακοσίους. οὐκ ἔξεστι δ' οὔτε νόμοις οὔτε προκλήσεσι οὔτε μαρτυρίαις ἀλλ' ἢ ταῖς παρὰ τοῦ διαιτητοῦ χρῆσθαι ταῖς εἰς τοὺς ἐχίνους ἐμβεβλημέναις.[2]

They also elect by lot forty persons, four from each tribe, who are the court before which the other suits are brought; formerly they were thirty and went on circuit trying cases in each parish, but since the oligarchy of the Thirty their number has been raised to forty. They have summary jurisdiction in claims not exceeding ten drachmas, but suits above that value they pass on to the Arbitrators. These take over the cases, and if they are unable to effect a compromise, they give judgement, and if both parties are satisfied with their judgement and abide by it, that ends the suit. But if one of the two parties appeals to the Jury-court, they put the witnesses' evidence and the challenges and the laws concerned into deed-boxes, those of the prosecutor and those of the defendant separately, and seal them up, and attach to them a copy of the Arbitrator's verdict written on a tablet, and hand them over to the four judges taking the cases of the defendant's tribe. When these have received them they bring them before the Jury-court, claims within 1,000 drachmas before a court of two hundred and one jurymen, and claims above that before one of four hundred and one. The litigants are not permitted to put in laws or challenges or evidence other than those passed on by the Arbitrator, that have been put into the deed-boxes.

A woman could approach a magistrate directly to enter a claim, register a complaint, or initiate divorce proceedings without the need to be represented by her *kyrios*. One good example of this is provided in the speech *Against Pankleon*, where we are told that a woman appeared before the polemarch to enter a counterclaim on Pankleon, arguing that he had been a runaway slave of hers.[3] Her intention was seemingly to prevent Nikomedes, who was claiming that Pankleon was his own slave, from seizing him, and also stop Pankleon's brother from releasing him into freedom (ἀφαίρεσις εἰς ἐλευθερίαν). If that dispute ever came to court the unknown woman would have needed an advocate to speak on her behalf, but the law did not prevent her from laying the initial claim before the magistrate and thus directly influencing subsequent litigation. Another good example is the case where the wife of Alcibiades decides to appear before the archon to divorce her husband.[4] In this instance her presence was not optional. The law required that if the divorce had been initiated by the woman she had to appear in person before the archon and register her intention to leave her husband. From that moment onwards the divorce was official and the husband owed 18 per cent interest on her dowry, if he was not prepared to return it at once. The law of Athens empowered a woman not to stay in a marriage in which she did not want to be, and allowed her direct access to the magistrate responsible for social affairs, so that she could formally finalise her divorce. The men concerned – her former husband and the male relative from her natal family who would become her new *kyrios* – had no legal way to reverse her decision.[5] All that was left for them to do was to settle the ensuing property matters with the return of the dowry. A third example is attested in the speech *Against Makaratos*, where a woman who was laying claim to an inheritance was invited to appear in person before the magistrate as part of the official proceedings of the *diadikasia*, the process intended to decide who would win the inheritance contest. In this instance the woman was seen as the claimant and this is why her presence was requested. She could have chosen to appear in person, or she could have selected to be represented by a male relative or advocate. Although few such cases are attested by the Attic orators, they are sufficient to illustrate that women had full and direct access to the numerous magistrates of the city, and although in most instances men would act and talk on their behalf, it was possible for women themselves to appear before a magistrate and speak for themselves.

A fourth example, a fleeting reference in the *Frogs* of Aristophanes, is of particular significance because it confirms that the numerous free women who owned small businesses in Athens, citizen or metic, had direct access to the magistrates in charge of commercial disputes.[6] In the underworld when the innkeeper believes that she recognises Herakles, who had stolen from her and had eaten large amounts of food without paying, she goes to fetch Kleon, her protector (προστάτην), as she puts it, and then Aiakos, the magistrate to whom a complaint about the theft has been made, appears with the intention of pursuing the thief. This comic scene is indicative of the processes available to the female owner of a small business, if someone had tried to defraud her. Of course, she would need to enlist the help of a male *prostates* if a claim were to be pursued through the courts, but at the same time she has direct access to the magistrate with whom she has clearly lodged a complaint. Although a comic play is not the best source for our understanding of legal procedure,[7] and the scene is not even supposed to be taking place in Athens, still the outlined processes are helpful for a better understanding of the important but difficult question of how it would be possible for a free woman to run a business in an open-market economy without direct access to the legal system. This passage implies that women could have direct access to the magistrates responsible for commercial offences, and could ask for their help. Small disputes in the marketplace would rarely exceed the value of ten drachmas, and thus it would be within the competence of the Forty to resolve them without further steps. If, let's say, someone failed to compensate a working woman in the agora for goods or services worth less than ten drachmas, she could directly approach the Forty and have her case heard and decided. The assistance of a male representative might be preferable, but it was not required.

If the dispute was of a value greater than ten drachmas, the Forty would refer it by default to public arbitration. This applied to all private lawsuits.[8] The arbitrator's role was to conduct hearings and try to effect a resolution acceptable to both parties. As with modern arbitration, a compromise would often be sought, but if the parties could not agree to a settlement, then the arbitrator ruled in favour of one side. The losing side had the option to accept his verdict and move on, or appeal the decision to the heliastic courts. Alternatively, the two opposing sides in both public and private lawsuits could try to resolve their differences through private arbitration. They could choose one or more persons they trusted and ask them to resolve the dispute. As with public arbitration, efforts would be made to strike an acceptable compromise. If they failed to reach a settlement, the arbitrator(s) could find for one side, but in this instance the law did not allow an appeal; the ruling of the arbitrator(s) was final. MacDowell explains this difference as follows: 'In private arbitration both disputants agreed voluntarily to submit their dispute to an arbitrator selected by themselves, and so it was reasonable that they were then required by law to accept his judgment as final, having the same validity as a jury's verdict.'[9] Of course, unhappy litigants would always find ways to pursue the case farther, but the nature of private arbitration and the efforts of common friends to find a solution often produced a satisfactory and acceptable end to the dispute.[10]

Arbitration in many ways is truly the stage that resembles a modern trial by the bench. Unlike the staged speeches and arguments in the *dikasterion*, an arbitration did not have a rigid format. Questions could fly back and forth for as long as was deemed necessary to reach the truth, and typically an Athenian arbitration could last as much of the day as was necessary. A recess was allowed if one of the litigants requested it, and if one day was not sufficient to complete the process it could take several days or even longer, until both parties were satisfied that they had sufficiently explained their side of the story.[11] Witnesses in an arbitration did not simply confirm some stale statement, crafted for them by the litigant who summoned them. They actually spoke and answered questions by the opposing litigant as well as the arbitrator. Women had full and direct access to this stage of litigation too, and like male witnesses and litigants they could speak for themselves, answer questions and testify or take an oath, presenting before the arbitrator their version of the facts.

We have two very clear and informative examples of the direct access of women to arbitration proceedings. In a famous incident in the second speech *Against Boiotos* (D. 40; see also the discussion in Part I, pp. 43–6) Plangon, an Athenian woman who had been married to a man named Mantias, appeared before the arbitrator to give evidence about the paternity of her two sons. Her testimony was vital because Mantias did not recognise the boys as his own and she needed to convince him and the entire community that they were truly his sons. Plangon was summoned before the arbitrator, because as the mother of the children she should know who was the father. Mantias challenged her to take an oath before the arbitrator that the children were his own sons. According to Mantitheos, this was a set-up. She was supposed to refuse, and accept a secret bribe instead. We don't have to believe this, but it does not matter much because as a matter of fact Plangon accepted the challenge and swore that the two boys were his own sons. Mantias was compelled to recognise them and register them with his phratry and deme as his own legitimate sons. The testimony of Plangon before the arbitrator, and the oath she took, were the deciding factors for the outcome of this case.

Another interesting case where a woman's testimony before the arbitrator was critically important is that of Neaira, who testified in a private arbitration meeting in defence of her own freedom. The dispute had arisen when a former abusive lover, who had paid for her manumission, seized her and tried to hale her back into slavery. He had no legal right to do so, because there was no stipulation in her manumission contract allowing him to retain any control over her.[12] Her new lover, Stephanos, intervened in the belief that the actions of Phrynion were unlawful, provided sureties and removed her to freedom with *aphaeresis eis eleutherian*. A trial was to follow which would determine her status. Much was at stake for all three of the main participants, because one of the two men would be the loser in this possessive love triangle, and Neaira herself was fighting once again for her freedom. This is why private arbitration seemed to be the best way forwards. The three parties came together and Neaira appeared in person to plead her cause. The final ruling of the arbitrators seems to be bizarre. Neaira had her freedom recognised and guaranteed, but she had to share her life with each of the men in equal portions, and the three of them were to become friends. The arbitrators in their wisdom recognised that male ego was the true cause of this dispute, and came up with a settlement which, without antagonising the egos of the participants, allowed for time to cool the hot tempers and procure a resolution. Right enough, it seems that after a while one of the lovers dropped out of the picture and let the other two stay together. Neaira as a concerned party in these proceedings not only was present and spoke, but seems in the long run to have got everything she wanted out of this delicately and cleverly handled arbitration.

Only when arbitration failed to produce a resolution would a case come before a heliastic court. Historically the trial before the *dikasterion* was envisaged as a final appeal process before the *demos* (the people), of whom the large, randomly selected jury was a representative segment. In the classical period the *dikasterion* would have the final say when all other avenues of dispute resolution had failed. In a single day under tight rules the two opposing parties would have the opportunity to pitch their case before a large body of their peers, consisting of approximately 200 men (400 in large disputes, according to the *Athenaion Politeia*),[13] with carefully staged speeches. This was not a world for women, and even though there was no law explicitly barring them from speaking in court, a strong custom in place from time immemorial, and powerful social norms of respectability governing the lives of Athenian women, would not allow them to stand and address a large room full of strange men. When they needed to access the court in order to defend their interests, to pursue someone who had done them harm, or to answer for charges brought against them, they had to use a male representative, typically their *kyrios* or some other close family member, and on the few occasions when women were independently wealthy, as for example in the case of prominent hetairai, they actually could directly hire an advocate who was going to speak on their behalf. He was not supposed to speak for them because he was paid, but was to take the role of advocate because he had a strong personal connection with the woman; the same applied to advocates of male litigants. For example, when Hypereides stood up to speak on behalf of Phryne when she was prosecuted for impiety. in the opening sections he stressed his personal connection with the famous hetaira, informing the jury that he was one of her lovers. One of the reasons why he did so was because he did not want to allow suspicion that he was paid handsomely for her defence, even though in reality he probably had been paid well, because this would undermine his credibility in their eyes.

The court cases discussed in Part I of this volume were presented before *dikasteria*, in a rich variety of circumstances that brought women and their representatives before the heliastic courts as claimants, prosecutors or defendants. These cases also reveal a broad range of approaches in response to the needs of the case, with much attention to detail and what might work in court. Gender is a major factor in the construction of many of these cases. Gender stereotypes, social preconceptions, fears and anxieties about the 'other woman', as well as character and identity construction which often rivals, and sometimes even overtly imitates, that of the heroines of the dramatic stage, are manipulated and exploited as litigation tools. However, the construction of these cases is not some cartoonish assembly of gender stereotypes; it is an imaginative array of topics, which help create those images of female villains or heroes, in such a way that each is unique, believable and memorable. The orators have constructed the identities of these women in vivid colours; they are very different from each other, and even though these constructs may bear little resemblance to the real person, they still appear to be truthful and real.

It is clear that women had direct access to the two lower layers of the Athenian justice system. They could go to magistrates and enlist help in dealing with criminals that had defrauded them, they could appear before them to make a small financial claim, register a divorce decided on their own initiative, or take care of other business directly affecting them and their interests. With the exception of the divorce initiated by the woman, where her presence before the archon was required, in other cases woman did not have to appear in person, if they chose not to do so, but could act through male representatives. The second layer of the Athenian justice system consisting of public and private arbitration was also directly accessed by women, who could appear before the arbitrator and give evidence. It is only the third layer, the large heliastic courts, which were a male domain, and these could be accessed only through representatives speaking on behalf of the women.

REPRESENTATION VERSUS EXCLUSION

The *dikasteria* were at the heart of public life: men competed with each other and, according to some scholars, expressed their aggression in a channelled and more controlled manner through the courts of the democracy.[14] The men of Athens turned up in person to pursue enemies, or to fend off aggression from enemies, and in some extreme versions of this narrative the courts were not even implementing justice, but were rather functioning as a safety valve for releasing tensions.[15] In this narrative women do not feature at all, and there are no professional lawyers or advocates, but only amateur speakers tending their own affairs. In a previous study I have argued that this concept of the amateur Athenian litigator is a carefully cultivated illusion, which Athenian sources encourage, while the view of the Athenian courts as some kind of honourable antagonism to release some steam very seriously undermines their central function, not to mention the stiffness of their penalties, and the often harsh justice that they implemented. This was not a gentlemen's game in a club which excluded women; it was a system that was designed to give open and direct access to all free persons regardless of birth or wealth, because doing anything else would violate the spirit of the Athenian democracy, of which the *dikasterion* was the guardian and the voice. A closer look to some important principles of the Athenian justice system suggests that the courts of the democracy were designed and meant to be places where any free person would seek redress for wrongs done to them, or answer an accuser, with confidence in the democratic principles that defended the weak against the strong, when right was on their side.

In theory, the ordinary citizen of Athens could go to court to lay claim to a piece of property, to prosecute an enemy, or to defend himself or a member of his *oikos* without the need for professional lawyers. The law itself was intentionally kept relatively simple, composed in a language that the ordinary citizen could easily understand, rather than in technical jargon as happens with modern legal systems, and every law of the state was displayed in a public place so that any interested person could read it and make a copy of it.[16] In the fourth century there was even a central archive of the valid laws of the state kept in the Metroon, accessible to all.[17] This is what democracy meant, after all; one of its key concepts was *isonomia*, namely equality before the law, and the citizens of the Athenian democracy took this concept rather seriously. However, the reality is somewhat more complicated. The speakers in Athenian courts were no amateurs, and the hundred or so court speeches that we have from a fairly broad range of trials, and by many different hands,[18] prove this point beyond reasonable doubt. Most of these texts were composed by highly skilled, highly competent experts, whose rhetorical prowess and level of accomplishment we still admire. Moreover, these compositions do not seem to be amateurs' random pieces put together as they came; they are composed according to disciplined models and organised principles, with deep understanding of the law, the impulses, reactions and operating principles of juries, and uncanny perceptions of human emotions and instinctive reactions.

The Athenian litigant had a broad network of support to draw from when preparing for a trial. Of course his own research could and would be helpful but probably not enough, because even in a place where someone did not need the professional lawyer, there was still a considerable body of laws the knowledge of which was indeed a matter of practice, and especially in the fifth century, before efforts towards codification in the last decade brought some order to the chaos, these laws could be scattered all over Attica, inscribed outside temples and other public buildings. So familiarity with the law was an advantage which some possessed and could be of great value to someone preparing for a trial. And this was only the beginning, because it would be a very bold assumption to think that the majority of citizens in Athens had sufficient rhetorical prowess and confidence in speaking before large groups of people. Certainly many people did not have such skills, and thorough preparation would be of paramount importance. Someone who could write a speech for them, which they would memorise and deliver, was surely worth his weight in gold.

This is no great exaggeration. The skilled orators of classical Athens who functioned as shadow writers and legal advisors to persons preparing for a trial, like Lysias, Hypereides, Demosthenes, Isaios or Isocrates, were wealthy, because their skill was highly valued. Sometimes orators were hired to do even more than offer advice on the laws and compose a speech in the shadows. They could actually take over the entire prosecution or defence on someone's behalf, as the Roman advocate or the modern lawyer would do, with one very important difference. The law of Athens did not allow an advocate (*synegoros*) to be paid for his services, as advocates at least in appearances were to support a litigant because of friendship or family relationship.[19] Even when they were paid, and surely on many occasions they had been paid handsomely for their services, this would have happened under the table and was never to be admitted in court. Therefore, the question to ask is not whether Athenian litigants were amateurs turning up in court to speak for themselves when necessary, because this certainly was not the case; the question to ask is why, when a highly profitable backstage industry had developed to support Athenian litigants, which included fully fledged schools of rhetoric systematically teaching the tools of litigation, like that of Isocrates, a façade of friendship and amateurism still had to be maintained at all costs.

The answer to this question surely lies in the function of the *dikasteria* within the wider frame of the Athenian democracy, and in accordance with those precious principles of *isonomia* (equality before the law), *isegoria* (equal right of speech), *isopoliteia* (political equality) and *demokratia* (rule of the people). A legal system like that of the United States or other Western countries in our times, where money and privilege can very openly make a huge difference, would have been intolerable to the citizens of the Athenian democracy, because it would have been seen for what it was, as a force maintaining elitist privilege in direct violation of the main principles upon which the democratic constitution was established. This is why the intent to prevent this from happening is abundantly clear in the Athenian legal system. First, the officials operating the system, namely the introducing and presiding magistrates in court, like the nine archons or the Forty, were mostly random unpaid citizens appointed by lot (except the generals and some financial officers, who were elected). Their office was seen as a service to the city and the democracy, and not as a paid profession. But even those citizens who in large numbers had to devote about 200 full days of each year to serve as jurors were only compensated with three obols a day, a sum equal to the minimum wage of an unskilled worker; this was nothing more than a token reimbursement for the full day's work. These provisions unambiguously suggest that the state did not understand involvement with the justice system as a career option, or a job, but rather as voluntary service. In this context people who might be helping the litigants were not to be doing it for money either. Relatives were to help members of the family, as Apollodoros does when he appears as the *synegoros* of Theomnestos in the case against Neaira (59.16 ff.); friends were to help friends, as Demosthenes does when he appears as a *synegoros* in defence of his political ally Timarchos; and on occasion lovers could offer their support, as Hypereides supposedly did when he accepted the defence of Phryne. Such ties are prominently explained early on in a speech, even when they are superficial or fake, in order to shake off any suspicion of a conspiracy, bribery (especially in political trials) or elitist privilege.

A *synegoros* could be a family member, a political ally, a fellow public official (like an ambassador on the same embassy), on occasion a member from the same deme or tribe, or indeed, anyone at all willing to stand up and speak on someone's behalf who could be trusted by the litigant to help his case. It was the duty of family members to support one of their own in court, and a democratic and moral thing to do. This is why it does not surprise us to see women as well as men supported by their relatives through such proceedings. There was nothing unusual in asking a male relative or friend to give a helping hand, and this help could go as far as standing up in court and speaking on the litigant's behalf, delivering either all or part of the litigant's speech within the allocated time. The same rules on *synegoria* applied to men and women litigants in every other respect; the only difference between men and women was that while for the former *synegoria* was an optional tactic intended to enhance one's chances of winning, for women *synegoria* was the only available option in the *dikasteria*.

Representation by an advocate or legal advisor in court has been the cornerstone upon which most legal systems have been built throughout history. The Athenian legal system, which was built around the concept of the citizen representing himself, was the exception rather than the rule, and as mentioned above even in the Athenian system representation and support by an advocate, a shadow speechwriter, or someone skilled in the laws and experienced in public life, was common. Representation has never been tantamount to exclusion from a legal system; on the contrary, almost universally in our times and more often than not in past times representation has been the standard avenue through which an individual accesses the legal system. This is why we should not interpret the necessity of Athenian women to be represented in the *dikasteria* as a form of exclusion, but rather as an alternative avenue by which to pursue claims, prosecute persons that had injured their person, property or interests, or defend themselves and their interests against attacks. The law of democratic Athens considered individuals regardless of gender or social status to be personally responsible for their conduct. The law did not hold a woman's *kyrios* accountable for her conduct, nor would it fine, imprison or punish the *kyrios* or any other person for transgressions committed by the woman herself. An adult woman was always responsible for her actions before the law, and the logical consequence of this principle is that she was to be able to to defend herself. Likewise, when a woman had been the victim of criminal behaviour the law recognised the need for her to seek redress through her legal representative.

Property law was more complex, because although the right of an individual to own property and dispose of it in any way he or she wished was firmly established in classical Athenian law, inheritance law itself had been largely developed in the archaic period and rather had in mind a form of collective ownership of property within the *oikos*, since it was the *oikos* itself with all the property it contained that was transferred from one generation to the next. Somehow, classical Athenian law had successfully incorporated the Solonean laws on family life and inheritance, and had struck a working balance between the rights of the individual to own property, and ownership within the *oikos*.[20] Women were caught up in the middle. While so much of the legislation which protected their property rights and vital interests had been introduced by Solon and viewed these rights within the context of the *oikos*, the women of classical Athens, as time went by, quietly and steadily asserted their right to own property individually, at first perhaps in the form of valuable items included in their dowry, such as jewellery or golden or silver cups and bowls, and by the fourth century fully as the heiress to whom the property of her natal family went, in the absence of male siblings or their descendants. The law had not changed but social attitudes had, and fourth-century Athenians were more willing to see the woman as the true owner of the property of her father than their ancestors two or three centuries before.[21]

It is within this context that we need to interpret numerous lawsuits brought on behalf of women, of which we have fragments. The question 'Who was the owner of the property?' has no easy answer, because as mentioned above the property belonged to the *oikos* and went along with the woman, but of course an *oikos* is an abstract concept, an institution, and abstract concepts do not own property in any other sense except in legal documents. There is always a person who ultimately benefits from the ownership of a certain property, and that person was the woman herself, with her husband and her children. Increasingly this concept of the rich wife became more entrenched in Athenian life and legal procedure, and by the time we get to the age of Deinarchos, on the cusp of the Hellenistic period, we encounter a type of lawsuit that doesn't appear in earlier periods, a *synegoria* for an *epikleros*, a woman identified, as custom dictated, by her father's name.[22] This terminology makes sense only if the *epikleros* was no longer perceived as the vessel through which the property of the *oikos* could be passed on, but as the actual contestant, the potential owner of the property, directly engaged in a dispute with her opponent and supported by a *synegoros* on comparable terms with those of a male litigant. It appears that by the time of Deinarchos the evolution was complete and the woman could be seen as the owner of her family's property. In the plays of New Comedy, which come from the same period or slightly later, and their Latin adaptations, wealthy women in full possession of their property, like the bossy *epikleros* Artemona in Plautus' *Asinaria*, are no longer a radical concept (although the humour is often built on the power to dominate others which their wealth offers them). In this sociocultural context it is not surprising to see women perceived as claimants in litigation concerning the property which they have inherited.[23]

Women had access to the *dikasteria* with the assistance of a male representative, typically their *kyrios* or another family member of their choosing.[24] That man in turn could use the services of a *logographos* or a *synegoros*, if he felt that he needed them to win the case. Those women who were independently wealthy, like the numerous hetairai living and working in Athens, had additional options, like hiring an advocate who would serve as a *synegoros* and handle the entire case on their behalf, as Phryne seems to have done. In addition, I have argued that a subtle evolutionary process slowly unfolded in the classical period, with women being perceived gradually as the claimants and masters of their own property. These procedural realities had their own limitations, especially in those cases where women needed to give evidence. Having to go through a male representative offered no guarantees that their words would be reported accurately; the man in question could say whatever he wanted with little chance of facing real-life consequences if he lied or misrepresented the words which he was supposed to carry to the courtroom. Such limitations notwithstanding, and while we could never claim that women had equal access to the justice system with men, we are bound to conclude that far from being excluded they had sufficient access to enable them to protect themselves and their interests.

NOT ALL WOMEN ARE THE SAME

Sometimes the women of Athens are treated as a single group in the population, and this, however convenient, is methodologically indefensible. The slave or poor metic women of Attica had very little in common with affluent upper-class citizen women, and their experience of involvement in the life of the community was vastly different. Wealth also created different dynamics in the level and form of access of the legal system, even when Athenian democratic discourse was propagating that the purpose of the law was to be equal for all and to defend the weak against the strong.[25] Let's say a wealthy alien hetaira, like Phryne, had the resources to hire Hypereides, one of the most expensive and sophisticated litigators in the city, when she faced a court case, while the poor alien woman scraping a living from making cloth and selling it in the marketplace might not have a male acquaintance willing to step in and defend her and her interests, which placed her in a very vulnerable position. On account of such differentials it is important to examine how citizen status, wealth, family connections and the willingness of male relatives to put themselves to considerable trouble in order to represent their womenfolk in court influenced women's access to the legal system, and their ability to seek justice.

On occasion the argument has been made that status differences should be unimportant because all women were treated as legal minors, and therefore in need of representation. However, a closer look indicates that the picture is more complicated. First, while free women had access to the two lower layers of the justice system, namely magistrates and arbitrators, and were only required to have a representative or advocate at the top level, the *dikasteria*, slave women had no access at all. Athenian magistrates did not accept complaints from slaves, and their testimony either before an arbitrator or in the *dikasterion* was only acceptable if it had been extracted under torture (*basanos*). Slaves had no authority to prosecute anyone, or bring anyone before the *dikasterion*; they could not enter claims, and they did not have an inherent right to a fair trial when accused of serious offences. In the few instances that we get to hear about where a slave has committed a serious crime, summary procedures were followed.[26] It seems that no one would waste the court's time trying to prove the innocence or guilt of a slave.

Free women, like free men, were protected from torture by a decree which had been passed in the archonship of Skamandrios,[27] and they could access the two lower tiers of the Athenian justice system. However, even among them not everything was equal. Citizen women could normally rely on a relative, such as their father, brother, son or husband, to represent and protect them, and look after their interests. If he was not up to the task, he could ask for help, and even if he came from a poor family, he could still rely on the help of other citizens, friends or family. In this respect, there was a safety net in place to protect and support the citizen woman if she found herself on the wrong side of the law, and to advance her interests as well as those of the family before magistrates, arbitrators and judges. For example, when the stepmother was prosecuted by her stepson for the murder of her husband in Antiphon 1, her own biological son, the half-brother of the prosecutor, stepped in to defend her; and if the priestess Ninos was indeed put to death after her conviction she found an avenger in her son, who in turn prosecuted Menekles, her prosecutor. Another citizen woman prosecuted for impiety, the sister of Lakedaimonios, was acquitted thanks undoubtedly to the support of her family and their political friends. Outside criminal justice, there are numerous examples of family members supporting the claim of female relatives to property, like Xenokles, the husband of Phile in Isaios 3, *On the Estate of Pyrrhos*, who engaged in protracted litigation with the family of Endios on her behalf. Of course, in such cases altruism and familial duty were not the only motives, as a successful claim to an inheritance would benefit the entire family, and primarily the husband as the manager of the property.

Metic women could be more of a mixed bag. Affluent metic women like Archippe, the wife of Pasion before his naturalisation, or the unnamed wife of Kephalos and mother of Lysias, might have a wealthy and powerful family and skilled orators to look after their interests when needed, but the poor innkeeper in Aristophanes' *Frogs* needs to rely on a stranger like Kleon to protect her interests. How vulnerable poor metic women could be becomes apparent in the episode involving Zobia in the speech *Against Aristogeiton*.[28] She was a person of modest means, but apparently generous to a fault towards Aristogeiton. She had offered him shelter and money when he had escaped from prison and was pursued by the

Eleven. When he became a powerful and affluent political figure she was pestering him for money. He refused, assaulted her and threw her out of the house. As she was persistent, he seized her and dragged her to the auction house, accusing her of having failed to meet her obligations as a metic, and therefore demanding that she should be sold as a slave, as the law required for delinquent metics. Fortunately for her, Zobia had paid the *metoikion*,[29] which officially proved that she was a free person and a metic in good standing with the city. An unnamed *prostates*, a male protector of Zobia, is mentioned in the proceedings, who spoke and acted on her behalf and secured her freedom. If Zobia was indeed a sex worker, then it is quite likely he was her procurer. It seems clear that the case never went to trial, because the payment of the *metoikion* offered formal proof that Zobia was a properly registered metic. Aristogeiton was employing intimidation tactics in order to force Zobia to step back and let go.

Even low-class prostitutes had some protection provided by their procurer on account of their value as assets. The second mime of Herodas contains a fictional scenario where the pimp of a low-class brothel has taken to court a sailor who assaulted and injured one of the women. The pimp is asking for compensation, and he is angry not because the sailor had injured the woman, but because he did not pay for it. Undoubtedly real cases like this one ended up in court quite often, given the number of prostitutes working in Attica and the volatile nature of their clients under the influence of alcohol. More expensive free sex workers had greater capacity in buying protection and representation. They could routinely offer money and favours to someone who would speak on their behalf and take care of their business with the law at all times. This seems to be the case with the hetaira Nais. Athenaios, actually quoting from a speech attributed to Lysias, attests that her *kyrios* was a man named Archias, and she had a friend (ἐπιτήδειος) named Hymenaios, which sounds like the typical name of a procurer.[30] The precise meaning of *kyrios* is difficult to determine in this case, unless we assume that she had a family which was complicit with her practices as a prostitute. That would be untypical, as most free women in prostitution, Athenian or foreign, seem to come from broken homes and have no living male relatives. However, it would not be impossible. When Epainetos accused Stephanos and Neaira of entrapping him, he claimed that the house of Stephanos was like a brothel, and they had turned the sale of sex into a very profitable business. Most likely Apollodoros is misrepresenting these events, but still he could not have made such claims in court with any degree of credibility if there were not some houses around the city from which prostitution was practised with the connivance of the *kyrios* of the house. Nonetheless, this interpretation is not inevitable in the case of Nais. An alternative, and perhaps more convincing possibility would be that Archias was a hired man acting on behalf of Nais, in the same manner that Pythodoros, an Athenian man, was taking care of all the legal affairs (ἅπαντα καὶ λέγει καὶ πράττει) of Pasion before the latter was offered citizenship.[31] Hymenaios may have been her procurer; this rather poetic name must have sounded exotic in classical Athens (although inscriptions suggest that it became commoner in later times),[32] and the word *epitedeios* sounds like a euphemism employed by the defender of Nais, who seemingly did not wish to use a harsher word.

CONCLUSIONS

There are two sides to the Athenian justice system. On the one side, the democratic constitution with its mighty principles of equality, fairness and inclusivity dictated that access to justice should be open to all free persons, including people from other Greek cities or other parts of the world who might need to go to the Athenian courts to defend their interests. In order to achieve this the corpus of Athenian law remained small, it was written in language accessible to all, and it was prominently displayed in public places so that every citizen could easily find out what the law dictated on any particular issue. The actual implementation of justice did not require professionals either, because in theory every free person could appear before a magistrate or an arbitrator and seek justice or defend themselves, and every free man could appear in court without the need of professional lawyers to take care of his business. Through these measures the Athenian democracy tried to make sure that the principle of equality before the law (*isonomia*) was not just a hollow ideal, but a standard feature of public life.

However, once we view things from the other side, that of a litigant who was fighting for an inheritance, was engaged in a dispute involving a large sum of money, or more seriously was fighting for his citizen rights, for his chance to avoid permanent exile, or for his or her life, then the picture looks very different. From such a position of fear and anxiety over the outcome of litigation,[33] we can understand why the lofty principles of democratic justice would not sound very comforting, and if someone could secure any kind of practical help, that would be most welcome. Sometimes that help came from family, friends, relatives or political allies and did not have a monetary price tag attached to it, but on other occasions help came from professional speechwriters, legal advisors and advocates operating in the shadows to prepare the litigant, and this type of assistance came with a hefty price. In time, as legal support became more effective and sophisticated, its prominent practitioners became wealthy professionals in the business of assisting litigants with their court cases. Women could access the legal system under somewhat different terms from men, but nonetheless they were not immune to the forces which, in parallel and in opposition to the democratic principles of *isonomia* and *isopoliteia*, allowed a robust for-profit legal support system to flourish in the shadows. Their status in society, their financial capacity and the connections of the family in public life would make a very big difference, perhaps as much as the difference between life and death, if we understand that the poor, lone, alien woman Theoris of Lemnos lost at her trial and was executed, while the affluent citizen woman, the sister of Lakedaimonios, was acquitted because of her family's money, support and political affiliations.

NOTES

1. Important studies on the Athenian justice system are MacDowell 1978; Todd 1993; Harrison 1968; 1971. For the intersection of law and society see Just 1989 and Kapparis 2019a. For the Solonean legislation see Leão and Rhodes 2015, the classic work of Eberhard Ruschenbusch 1966, and more recently the excellent chapter by Werner Riess as well as several other studies on Drakon and Solon in Riess 2018b. From the older scholarship, Lipsius 1905 and Gernet 1955 remain relevant for numerous issues. An excellent source book with brief, well-informed discussion is Phillips 2013.
2. Arist. *Ath.* 53.1–4; trans. H. Rackham.
3. Lys. 23.10–11.
4. And. 4.14; see also D. 30.26, Is. 3.78, and the discussion in Kapparis 2019a: 185–9; Mélèze-Modrzejewski 1981: 258–60; Cohn-Haft 1995: 1–14.
5. However, a powerful man like Alcibiades did not rely on legal means to prevent his wife from divorcing him. He seized her on her way to the magistrate and brought her home by force, and no one tried to stop him. Her brother, who would be her new *kyrios* after the divorce and had the legal right and obligation to protect her, clearly shied away from a confrontation with Alcibiades. This underlines the fact that, even though the law empowered a woman to walk away from a bad marriage by directly registering the divorce with the archon, the reality of the situation was more complicated.
6. Ar. *Ra.* 549 ff.
7. See Wohl 2010: 33–70; Apostolakis 2007: 179–92; Scafuro 1997.
8. All Athenian men in their fifty-ninth year of age, the last year when they were eligible for military service, were appointed as public arbitrators. The *Athenaion Politeia* (53.4–7) defines public arbitration as follows: διαιτηταὶ δ' εἰσὶν οἷς ἂν ἑξηκοστὸν ἔτος ᾖ. . . . καὶ ἀναγκαῖον ἃς ἂν ἕκαστος λάχῃ διαίτας ἐκδιαιτᾶν. ὁ γὰρ νόμος, ἄν τις μὴ γένηται διαιτητὴς τῆς ἡλικίας αὐτῷ καθηκούσης, ἄτιμον εἶναι κελεύει, πλὴν ἐὰν τύχῃ ἀρχὴν ἄρχων τι[ν]ὰ ἐν ἐκείνῳ τῷ ἐνιαυτῷ ἢ ἀποδημῶν· οὗτοι δ' ἀτελεῖς εἰσὶ μόνοι. ἔστιν δὲ καὶ εἰσαγγέλλειν εἰς τοὺς διαιτητάς, ἐάν τις ἀδικηθῇ ὑπὸ τοῦ διαιτητοῦ, κἄν τινος καταγνῶσιν, ἀτιμοῦσθαι κελεύουσιν οἱ νόμοι. ἔφεσις δ' ἔστι καὶ τούτοις. 'Persons fifty-nine years of age may serve as Arbitrators, . . .; and it is compulsory for each of them to complete the arbitration of the cases allotted to him, for the law enacts the disfranchisement of anybody who does not become Arbitrator when of the proper age, unless he happens to hold some office in that year or to be abroad, these being the only grounds of exemption. Anybody unjustly dealt with by the Arbitrator may indict him before the Arbitrators, and the laws prescribe the

penalty of disfranchisement for an Arbitrator found guilty; but the Arbitrators also have an appeal' (trans. H. Rackham). As Rhodes (1981: 591) clarifies, ἑξηκοστὸν ἔτος ᾗ means the year in which they had their sixtieth birthday, not the year after they had reached their sixtieth birthday. This way of calculating one's age holds in Greek tradition to the present day.

9. MacDowell 1978: 209.
10. The law on private arbitration is preserved in D. 21.94. Initially Douglas MacDowell reached the conclusion that this document was not authentic (1978: 204), but later (1991: com. ad loc.) he refined his views, rightly arguing that the document cited here is the authentic law on private arbitration incorrectly inserted instead of the law on public arbitration. Whoever inserted this document in the manuscript of Demosthenes fetched the wrong law. Edward Harris, on the other hand, has disputed the authenticity of the law, in my opinion incorrectly (apud Canevaro 2013: 209–36; see also my 2015 review of the book). On arbitration see also Kapparis 2019a: 225–7; Hammond 1985: 188–90; King and LeForestier 1994: 38–46; Miyazaki 1996: 73–83; Roebuck 2001.
11. We know at least one instance (D. 21.84–95) where a hasty arbitrator closed the proceedings refusing to give any further extension to one of the litigants, and he was punished for that with permanent disenfranchisement.
12. The only stipulation in the contract was what could be seen as the opposite of a *paramone* condition; her former masters actually did not want her to be working as a prostitute in Corinth where they lived, and stipulated that she could no longer practise prostitution in the city (D. 59.32).
13. Arist. *Ath.* 53. 4; the issue is more complicated, but this discussion is not important for our purposes. See McCannon 2011: 106–21; Rhodes 1981: 728–30.
14. This is a much larger discussion, but not centrally important for our purposes; see the relevant discussions in Herman 2006; Cohen 1995; Riess 2012; Alwine 2015; Lanni 2016.
15. Thus Cohen 1995; Berent 2000: 2–34; Christ 1998; Hunter 1994; and to some extent Lanni 2016 (Lanni's account is more cautious and nuanced; it emphasises the preventative effect of law within the Athenian legal system, which encouraged law-abiding behaviour).
16. Kapparis 2019a: 60–1, 309–14.
17. Lyc. 1.66; Athen. 5.53; Shear 1995: 157–90; Sickinger 1999; also 2002: 147–69; 1994: 186–296; 2004: 93–109.
18. Many of the extant speeches attributed to the ten canonical orators were composed by different authors. Sometimes, as with the seven speeches of Apollodoros (D. 46, 47, 49, 50, 52, 53, 59), we can confidently identify the true author, but more often we cannot and, somewhat unfairly, we refer to the author as Pseudo-Lysias, or Pseudo-Demosthenes.
19. D. 46.26, law quoted by Apollodoros: . . . ἢ συνήγορος ὢν λαμβάνῃ χρήματα ἐπὶ ταῖς δίκαις ταῖς ἰδίαις ἢ δημοσίαις, τούτων εἶναι τὰς γραφὰς πρὸς τοὺς θεσμοθέτας ('or if someone serving as a *synegoros* accepts money, either for a public or a private trial, he is to be indicted to the *thesmothetai* [for bribery]').
20. This was probably not uncommon in archaic Greece. For example, in archaic and early classical Sparta the family lot (*klaros*) was passed on to the eldest son undivided,

while younger sons had to marry the daughters of men who had no sons to inherit the *klaros* of their father-in-law. In this system women could not own land. The system worked for some time, because it effectively discouraged a high birth rate, but one could imagine a whole array of different circumstances which could have easily derailed it. Perhaps such anxieties motivated the *rhetra* of Epitadeus in the fifth century, which changed the rules by effectively sanctioning individual ownership, while in theory still maintaining the transfer of the *klaros* from family to family. As a result of this, a century later 40 per cent of Spartan land was owned by women.

21. I am aware that some scholars might disagree with this evolutionary pattern of women's property rights. The excellent monograph by David Schaps (1979) is still valuable. In fourth-century sources we often encounter expressions which betray a concept of women as the owners of their property; see for example D. 27.56, 43.7, 47.57; Is. 3.62, 10.12; Isoc. 6.32; Amphis Fr. 23 al. See also Schaps 1975: 53–7; Griffith-Williams 2016: 111–16; 2012: 145–62; Cox 1998; Foxhall 1989: 22–44; Sainte Croix 1970: 273–8.

22. E.g. Din. Fr. 57 *Synegoria to Hegelochos, for the Epikleros*. As stated above, pp. 51–2, the exact title is disputed among ancient sources, but in at least one version of the title where Hegelochos is unambiguously the opposing litigant, the person who delivers a speech has no difficulty presenting himself as the *synegoros* of the *epikleros*.

23. On this subject see the recent discussion by Brenda Griffith-Williams (2019: 375–88) and also her earlier study (2012: 145–62). See also Schaps 1975: 53–; 1979.

24. The daughter of Diogeiton in Lys. 32 is not represented by her second husband, who was her *kyrios* at the time when she enacted litigation against her father for the inheritance of her children, clearly because he was unwilling to pursue the matter. Instead, she is represented by her son-in-law. This case makes clear that the law did not insist that her *kyrios* ought to represent her. She could choose another man if she so wished, without further ado.

25. E.g. D. 15.29, 21.45; Pl. *Grg.* 483 b.

26. For example, the slave woman in Antiphon 1, *Against the Stepmother*, who was responsible for the death of her partner Philoneos and the father of the speaker, was simply tortured and put to death without a trial.

27. See And. 1.43 and MacDowell 1962: com. ad loc.

28. D. 25.56–8. Zobia may have been a prostitute, but Demosthenes does not say that she was.

29. Metic tax of twelve drachmas a year for a man with a family, or six drachmas a year for an independent woman. See Kapparis 2019a: 100–15, with sources and previous scholarship.

30. Athen. 13.62 = Lys.s Fr. 299 Carey. See also the discussion in Kapparis 2018: 210–13.

31. Isoc. 5.33.

32. E.g. *IG* ii^2 2021 (twice), 2086, 2094, all second century.

33. The curse tablets used to bind the opposing litigant offer good testimony of the anxieties and state of mind of litigants before a trial. See several articles on the subject in Riess 2018b.

CHAPTER 2

Judicial Procedures Involving Women

AN OVERVIEW OF PROCESSES IN THE ATHENIAN JUSTICE SYSTEM

From the time of Solon judicial processes in Athens were divided into public and private. In theory, public procedures would deal with matters affecting the life of the community, and private procedures would deal with the affairs of individual citizens. So it should be easy to separate procedures that involved women from those which did not, since the traditional wisdom has been that women did not participate in public life. However, the reality was more complicated, since public procedures often directly concerned one particular individual under a thin veil of public interest. For example, a prosecution for impiety (*graphe asebeias*) was understood to be a public procedure because an individual's intentional offences against the gods and traditional religion could affect the entire community by inviting the wrath of some god or goddess. When Alcibiades[1] and his friends were accused of ridiculing the Eleusinean Mysteries their behaviour was thought to be a matter of grave concern for the city, because the anger of the Two Goddesses could be directed at the entire community, if it failed to punish the offenders.[2] However, the actual lawsuit, if it were brought to court, would be directed against Alcibiades as an individual citizen, and in this respect a public lawsuit could be brought against an individual citizen for something that he did in a private space.[3] On account of such flexible and subjective boundaries it is not always easy to separate public from private procedures.

Remarkably, litigation for homicide always remained a private procedure which would need to be initiated by a relative of the victim, although we would expect it to be a matter concerning the entire community, not least because even in the classical period it retained strong religious connotations and the prevailing belief that deadly supernatural pollution from a killer (*miasma*) could infect everyone. This probably has to do with the fact that homicide law was developed in the seventh century by Drakon, and precisely because of its religious connotations it always remained a very conservative part of Athenian law, tied to legal concepts such as family responsibility, which in any other context would be out of sync with classical Athenian law. Such peculiarities and conceptual inconsistencies need to be explained as the result of the long evolutionary processes of Athenian law from the time of Drakon to the radical democracy of the classical period, and it is outside our purposes to discuss them here in detail. Suffice to say that precise understanding of Athenian law is our only way of knowing which procedures were public and which private and why.

As stated above, what made a case public in the eyes of the lawgiver who instituted a specific law, and established procedures for violations of the law, was the perceived involvement of the entire community in this particular area. For example, most immigration and citizenship violations needed to be pursued through public lawsuits, because in the eyes of the law the entire community had a stake in this matter.[4] However, one of them was a private lawsuit (*dike apostasiou*). The purpose of it is not very clear in the sources. Stephen Todd has argued that through this lawsuit a former master was trying to extend his or her control over a former slave, and since this was only a matter which concerned these two parties the law understood this to be a private matter.[5]

Public lawsuits included matters affecting the state and its affairs, like the indictments for introducing a law or a decree, which contradicted an existing law (*nomon me epitedeion theinai, graphe paranomon*), a denunciation for subversive activity against the state and democratic constitution (*eisangelia*), or intentionally offensive behaviour towards the gods and the religious practices of the polis (*graphe asebeias*). A series of lawsuits dealing with seriously criminal behaviour by means of allowing summary arrest (*apagoge*), or indictment to the appropriate magistrate (*endeixis, ephegesis*), were also public lawsuits, as were procedures dealing with fraud or theft of public money (*phasis, apographe*) or property belonging to a sanctuary (*hierosylia*). As stated above, all offences related to citizenship and immigration, except the *dike apostasiou*, were also public procedures. What all of them had in common was the fact that any free man could introduce these procedures. Immigration offences (e.g. D. 59.16) and a few other procedures narrowly focusing on affairs of the polis, as for example a statute not allowing the introduction of a new law which is contrary to an existing one before the old law is abolished (D. 24.33), could only be introduced by an Athenian citizen – understandably so, because the city could not accept interference from any outsider on these matters. It is clear that non-citizens could and sometimes did introduce such lawsuits, as for example Lysias did when he pursued people who under the Thirty had been responsible for the deaths of members of his family and other citizens, through the process of *euthyna*.[6]

Public lawsuits could differ significantly from one another in terms of scope, procedure and goals. The most common and less involved type were single-tier (*graphe*) lawsuits submitted in writing to the appropriate magistrate. Some time later, which could be years,[7] the prosecutor needed to turn up to the preliminary hearing (*anakrisis*) and then appear at the trial to pursue the case. Understandably there was potential for abuse of such cases, as well as the possibility that after some time a prosecutor might forget about them and move on, and this is why the law ordered that the prosecutor who did not turn up for the trial or failed to secure one fifth of the votes had to pay the massive fine of 1,000 drachmas. Other procedures, like the *eisangelia* and the *probole*, were more involved to start with, but also risk free. These were two-tier processes, where the first tier was designed to stop frivolous lawsuits from advancing any further. Typically in the first tier one needed to secure the approval of the assembly or the *Boule* of the Five Hundred before being able to proceed to the second and bring the case to the *dikasterion*. The first tier was seen as a safety valve to prevent the misuse of these procedures to settle personal or political scores, but it is clear that it proved insufficient to stop abuses of the *eisangelia* in the fourth century. It seems that politicians with influence both in the assembly and in the *boule* were able to push through numerous cases, and this led to a change in the law around 330. Under the new provisions the *eisangelia* in public life was no longer going to be risk-free, but would carry the same risk of 1,000-drachma fine as the *graphe*.[8]

Public lawsuits were not sent to arbitration by default, as private lawsuits were, but litigants always had the option to drop formal proceedings and entrust the case to private arbitration.[9] The trial in public lawsuits lasted an entire day. Each litigant had one lengthy speech at his disposal (approximately two and a half hours).[10] The possibility that the audience would get too tired or bored to listen to the litigant go on for so long was very real, and this is why *synegoria* was more important in public lawsuits, as alternating speakers could break the monotony. Additional measures to keep the attention of the audience alive, like citations from poetry and drama, were also employed frequently by litigants.[11] After hearing both sides the jury voted, and if the defendant was convicted and the law did not set the penalty, each litigant would be given a short speech of approximately half an hour to argue on the penalty. It was to be expected that the prosecutor would argue for a more severe penalty and the defendant for a more lenient one. This procedure is well described in the *Apology* of Plato, where Anytos proposed the death penalty for Socrates, and Socrates first proposed that he should receive free dinners at the Prytaneion, and in the end he proposed a fine of thirty minae, which his friends would pay. The text of the *Apology* makes clear that both sides were to take this step very seriously because in the end the jury would need to be convinced that the penalty was appropriate for the offence. Whether fixed by the law or left to the jury, the sentences in public lawsuits tended to be more severe, partly because these lawsuits dealt with matters important to the whole community and therefore more serious, and partly because successful prosecutors would seek very severe penalties and often succeed, considering that the penalty was decided by exactly the same jury which had voted in their favour less than an hour earlier. This is why it was always in the best interests of the convicted defendant to try and negotiate the penalty directly with the prosecutor, and if they reached an agreement (συγχωρεῖν), the speeches were skipped and the agreed sentence was accepted by the court.[12]

Most private lawsuits were very similar to each other in terms of procedures and outcomes. Although the orators and later grammarians and lexicographers use different names for them (e.g. *dike aikeias* for battery, *dike pseudomartyrion* for false witness, *dike biaion* for an illegal seizure or sexual assault, etc.), the procedure was the same in all of them. One needed to submit a lawsuit to the Forty (δίκην λαγχάνειν), the case would automatically be referred to public arbitration, and only if one of the litigants did not accept the ruling of the public arbitration would the case come to court. In court each side had two fairly short speeches, in the order prosecution, defence, prosecution, defence. This format was more suitable for private lawsuits, which often involved financial affairs, so as to give each side a better chance to check and dispute the facts and figures of the other side. In the end the court decided for one side, and that decision was final. Typically compensation would be awarded to the successful litigant, while the loser, in addition to compensation and any fine that he had to pay, also needed to carry the cost of the modest initiation fee (πρυτανεῖα) paid by the prosecutor when the lawsuit was initially submitted. Some private lawsuits, like the *paragraphe*, the purpose of which was to block any legally submitted lawsuit by the opposing litigant, did not include a monetary reward, because their primary purpose was not to assign guilt or punishment, but to clarify procedural matters.

Homicide was very different from other private lawsuits in terms of both procedure and penalties. The homicide courts operated in ways that seem alien within the democratic constitution of the classical period. First, there were some terrifying exchanges of oaths and curses for litigants who did not tell the truth, which culturally and in terms of legal procedure firmly belonged to the archaic period, when homicide law was first established by Drakon (621 BC). Then the legal concepts of collective responsibility affecting entire families, as well as individuals, again belonged to the archaic period. And finally, there was a requirement that the litigants stick to the point, which might have been taken somewhat more seriously than it would have been in ordinary courts. The courts themselves were not manned by ordinary jurors, but by members of the Areopagos council. It seems that the entire council heard trials for intentional homicide of Athenian citizens, and sections of it consisting of fifty-one men, called Ephetai, heard cases of justified homicide at the Delphinion, cases involving the killing of aliens or slaves at the Palladion, or cases of homicide involving persons who had not been living in Attica at the sea-front court of Phreatto (the defendant was not allowed to disembark unless acquitted). Once the trial started the procedure was similar to other private lawsuits with two speeches for each side, with one more difference: after the first set of speeches the defendant had the opportunity to leave Attica permanently, rather than face certain death, which was the penalty for the homicide of a citizen. The reason for this peculiarity was again history and tradition.[13]

Free adult men could appear as witnesses in public or private lawsuits regardless of citizen status. Slaves, on the other hand, could not give evidence unless it was extracted under torture, and since torture has never been a reliable way of securing evidence, because someone under torture would say anything to make it stop,[14] there is no known case where the testimony of the slave was directly admitted. Litigants often argued that a slave knew the truth, but of course these were their own words, which an individual dikast might choose to believe or not, and certainly did not carry the same weight as a properly presented testimony in court. Witnesses in the time of the orators were simply summoned to confirm or deny the testimony composed by the litigant who summoned them, and this is why they were often supportive of the litigant.[15] What the witnesses said in court could be challenged through a *dike pseudomartyrion*, a lawsuit for false witness, and if the challenge was successful the witness was punished and the outcome of the initial lawsuit was ignored.[16]

Unlike slaves or children, free women were not considered legal minors, unable to testify. They were free adults, and their testimony was treated as such. It did not need to be extracted under certain conditions, like that of a slave, and it was not weightless, like that of a child. It was not the law that kept women away from appearing as witnesses in the courts, but rather custom and social convention, and this is why in less pressurised environments, where a woman's sense of respectability would not be compromised in a small circle of people, her testimony was acceptable. A woman could not give evidence in court, but she could give evidence before a magistrate, and also before an arbitrator. This meant that in a private lawsuit what the woman said before the arbitrator would be noted and sealed (σημαίνειν) along with other documentary evidence, to be presented in the appeal trial before the court if necessary.[17] Thus, in private lawsuits if a woman had appeared before the arbitrator, her testimony would be directly available to the judges during the trial, and this explains why Mantias felt that he had no other choice but to back down and accept the two sons of Plangon, namely Boiotos (aka Mantitheos) and Pamphilos, as his own. If he had not, and had chosen to take the case to court, the weighty testimony of the mother of the children, offered in the form of an accepted challenge to an oath, would have been available to the judges, and could have counted decisively against him. However, there was one significant difference between male and female witnesses. While men could appear in person during the trial to confirm or deny their testimony, and needed to do so if summoned, women could not appear in person and needed to rely on male representatives, who were under no obligation to convey their words accurately. This is why male witnesses were legally responsible for the testimony they gave and could be prosecuted with a *dike pseudomartyrion*, while women could not be held accountable for words others said or did not say on their behalf, and therefore could not be prosecuted for false witness.

WOMEN AND POLITICS

This may seem like an oxymoron to generations of classical scholars who have been brought up in the firm and justified belief that the women of Athens played no role in the political life of the city. And yet it was an established topos that all sacrifices at war and in public life were made for the benefit of women and children.[18] Perhaps there was something more to it than mere rhetoric, as this topos underlines the fact that the domain of public life was not hermetically sealed off from that of home and private life. And this was not always for the best. Often in history women were collateral damage in the public fights of men. A distant historical parallel from the Roman Republic of the first century BC amply illustrates how the five wives of Pompey, the four wives of Mark Antony and the three wives of Caesar were mere pawns in the high-stakes political games, alliances and conflicts of those turbulent times, and although they themselves had no formal say in the running of the Republic their lives, marriages and divorces were inextricably linked to its public affairs.[19] The Athenian democracy of the classical period was not at the mercy of strongmen as the dying Roman Republic was, but still the squabbling politicians of the *demos* often drew women into their affairs, and like their Roman counterparts these women were caught up in the political games, alliances and bargaining, even though they had no say in these matters.

The prosecution of Aspasia for impiety in the fifth century could be read as a good example of this unfortunate mix of public and private life. While it could be argued that Aspasia already had a big bull's-eye on her back, because in so many ways she was an unconventional woman for her time – a scholar, an intellectual and someone who questioned established orthodoxies – there can be no doubt that her prosecution was largely associated with her relationship with Pericles, the most powerful man in Athens. Plutarch's narrative, which attests the incident quoting the student of Aspasia, the philosopher Aeschines Socraticus, cites both her unorthodox views and her association with Pericles as the reasons behind her prosecution, and explicitly states that the primary purpose of her accusers was to injure her partner. In Plutarch's narrative a tearful Pericles begs the jury to give him back Aspasia, and it is clearly suggested that it was his powerful oratory and influence with the people that secured her acquittal.[20]

A century later the trial of Neaira for allegedly breaking the law which prohibited aliens such as herself to live in marriage with an Athenian citizen bears some striking similarities with the trial of Aspasia. The case against Neaira was built on the assumption that her non-Athenian family, which included four children (three boys and one girl), had been fraudulently presented as a citizen family, because the sons were registered as Athenian citizens, and the daughter of the family was given twice in marriage to Athenian men on the assumption that she was an Athenian woman. All these charges were made up; Neaira had been a famous hetaira in her youth, and was certainly an alien woman, and the defence agreed with all this. However, the four children of the family were not her biological offspring but the children of her Athenian partner Stephanos from his first marriage to an unknown Athenian woman. When Neaira was prosecuted the children of the family were in their thirties, and one of the boys had already died. The question is why anyone would go to great lengths to build up a risky public case with obviously false allegations, and face a fine of 1,000 drachmas if he lost with less than one fifth of the votes, against an elderly woman he had never met in his life, who had given up prostitution thirty years before and had faded into respectable anonymity as the concubine of an Athenian man. The short answer is that Neaira was collateral damage in the political fights of men around her, in which she had played no part.

Apollodoros, her real prosecutor, acting as the *synegoros* of his brother and son-in-law Theomnestos, was not going after Neaira but after Stephanos, and he saw her as the soft underbelly. Stephanos had powerful connections and was supported by a large section of Athenian public opinion that did not want to go to war with Philip. But in the late 340s a new consensus was building among leading Athenian politicians that Philip was a grave threat to the interests of the city, and a proper response to his expansive plans was a matter of the utmost urgency. The leaders of this new consensus, which of course included Demosthenes but also Euboulos, his former political foe and determined proponent of a non-aggressive foreign policy, were certainly aware of the fact that there were still determined defenders of a peaceful accommodation with Philip which could derail the process. The case against Neaira must be seen as an attempt to eliminate one of those hardliners, her partner Stephanos. He had successfully derailed attempts to transfer resources into the war chest of the city, the stratiotic fund, in the earlier part of the decade, and could still pose a threat to the plans of those who were fanning the flames of war. A direct assault on Stephanos might have backfired because, although Philip's plans and provocations had become serious enough not to be missed by anyone who was looking, shifting the majority of the Athenians towards favouring war would take much effort. With the hindsight of history we know that it actually took the siege of Byzantium (340–339), a city vital for the trade and foreign policy of Athens, to galvanise the assembly into action. This lawsuit came a year or two before that and was part of a larger plan to prepare the assembly for the great challenges lying ahead in an all-out war with Philip.

With so much at stake no one stopped to consider the grave injustice of putting an elderly woman on trial for an offence she had not committed, just to get at her partner. But much was to be gained by the opponents of Stephanos, if she was convicted. First, Neaira would be sold into slavery, and if Stephanos wanted to buy back her freedom he would need to spend a considerable amount of the family's assets on this. Second, the assets of Neaira, probably including four family slaves who belonged to her (Thratta, Kokkaline, Drosis, Xenis), could be confiscated through an *apographe* and the family might need extra resources to buy these women back, since at least two of them had been with Neaira for more than thirty years. Then, Stephanos' credibility in public life could be seriously diminished, because many ordinary citizens would be shocked to hear that he had deceived the city by repeatedly introducing the children of an alien hetaira as his own. Fourth, the status of his own children would come into question in a very public manner, and this would create some very uncomfortable and scary family situations, which would seemingly gratify his sworn enemy Apollodoros. Stephanos, in addition to all these expenses, would need to pay a large fine of 1,000 drachmas to the city, and if he failed to do so, which seems the most likely scenario under the circumstances, he would be disenfranchised and thus effectively removed from public life. This was the ultimate goal of the political figures behind the prosecution of Neaira. By overwhelming her partner with massive expenses and making him a debtor to the state, they could have removed a persistent and dangerous opponent of their plans from public life, probably forever. The callousness of having an innocent elderly woman sold into slavery because it suited their political ends has provoked an emotional reaction even from the usually restrained Friedrich Blass, who expressed the sentiments of countless readers of the speech through the centuries in the phrase 'Dass der Racheact der beiden gelang, und Neaira verkauft wurde, möchte ich nicht glauben.'[21]

It is likely that political motives could be traced in other public lawsuits against women, like several prosecutions on religious grounds, which somehow do not make good sense as cases motivated by piety alone. We should not be surprised if some of them were part of larger political games since, as Jakub Filonik has convincingly demonstrated, the *graphe asebeias* as a procedure was typically entangled with politics.[22] Unfortunately the fact that we only have a few fragments, all very limited in scope, does not allow us to see the bigger picture behind the prosecutions of Phryne, Ninos, Theoris or the sister of Lakedaimonios, and we can only broadly speculate about the motives.[23]

CITIZENSHIP AND IMMIGRATION VIOLATIONS

The primary procedure used against aliens who pretended to be citizens in Attica, the *graphe xenias*, was never used against a woman as far as we can tell, and there is probably a good reason for this. The *graphe xenias* was tailored to the needs of public life and targeted alien men who participated in politics, the assembly, the courts and public offices, under the pretence that they were citizens. Women were prosecuted for other citizenship and immigration violations in the fourth century, such as an illegal marriage to a citizen, failure to meet their legal obligations as metics (*graphe aprostasiou*) or failure to meet their legal obligations to their former master (*dike apostasiou*). Such cases need to be explored as part of broader patterns and currents in contemporary Athenian society, and were often fuelled by personal motives. Although the number of women immigrants in Athens in the fifth century at the height of empire was certainly high, all the cases of women indicted for immigration violations known to us come from the fourth century, and as I explain in Chapter 4, I am convinced that there was much more to this than an accident of transmission.

In 403 a decree by Aristophon and Nikomenes brought back into force the Periclean citizenship law of 451, which had fallen into disuse in the years of the Peloponnesian war. Persons born after that date could only be Athenian citizens if they were born of two Athenian parents. For free persons who did not belong to the citizenry but were living in Attica, legal arrangements on metics established in the fifth century were still in place. According to these, all metics had to register with the polemarch and pay a modest tax called the *metoikion*, which was set at twelve drachmas a year for a man and his family, and six drachmas for an independent woman. Although the *metoikion* seems to be an additional obligation, in fact it was also an important safeguard, because its regular payment constituted undeniable proof of lawful status, and it could be used to verify that someone was a free person in good standing with the Athenian polis.[24]

It is interesting to see that unless a metic woman was living independently and providing for herself, she did not have to register individually. Metic women living in families were invisible to the Athenian state, because their *kyrios* registered and paid for the entire family. We do not know for sure whether he had to record in the register every single member of his family, but chances are that he did not, because if he simply registered himself and paid the fee for himself and his family, the state had received the tax that was due, and had no particular incentive to get further involved. The Athenians did not keep registers of births, marriages or deaths for their own citizens, so why would they keep detailed registers for the alien families in their land beyond what was necessary for the purposes of taxation of the metic population? This observation has led me to believe that mixed families, where free non-Athenian women were living under the protection of an Athenian *kyrios*, as concubines or illegitimate daughters, sisters or other relatives, fell into a grey area of Athenian immigration law. Surely the Athenian *kyrios* would not be expected to pay a foreign tax for members of his household, and since the non-Athenian women in it were not independent, but were part of an Athenian *oikos*, they did not have to register as independent metics.[25] The fact that there is not a single reference to a scenario where an Athenian man needed to pay the *metoikion* on behalf of a non-citizen family member should confirm our suspicion that such a prospect was inconceivable.

This observation could help explain why several alien women seem to have fallen foul of the immigration law, and got into trouble. Let us take Aristagora as an example.[26] Let us assume that Idomeneus' information, that in her prime she was a prominent hetaira and then she became Hypereides' concubine, is accurate. The subsequent existence of two vicious lawsuits against her initiated by her former lover implies that at some point they fell out and she left his household, and legal protection, probably to make a living as an independent hetaira. While Aristagora was Hypereides' concubine and a member of his *oikos*, neither she nor her *kyrios* owed the *metoikion*. However, after the separation, when she no was longer a member of an Athenian *oikos*, she should have registered as an independent metic paying the *metoikion* of six drachmas a year, which for a pricey hetaira like herself should have been a mere trifle. So, why didn't she, to be safe with the law? One can think of two possible reasons. First, she might be hoping to find another lover very soon, and as a member of his household she would not need to register and pay the foreign tax. Second, a passage by Aeschines on the prostitution tax (*pornikon telos*)[27] suggests that once someone was registered on those lists for the purpose of taxation, he or she would be expected to keep up with payments, and we do not even know if there was a mechanism for a woman to stop paying and be removed from the list if she became the concubine of an Athenian citizen. One can imagine that there would be a reluctance to be included in the list if there was the possibility of finding another lover very soon, because once she was on the list, it would be difficult to get off it. The women who got into trouble with the law were probably in this legal grey area at the time, and this made them vulnerable to the vengeful instincts of previous lovers and the whims of procurers or other persons ready to take advantage of the situation. This indeed seems to have happened to Aristagora. After the separation she was not fast enough to register as an independent metic, and she found herself vulnerable. Her former lover took advantage of this and proceeded with two angry lawsuits, one after another, with the sole objective of having his former mistress sold into slavery. We do not know much about the two women prosecuted with *graphe apostasiou*, Demetria and Hedyle, but both seem to be hetairai liberated on certain conditions, which they had seemingly breached. Perhaps they had been required by their manumission contract to offer part of their earnings to their former master and procurer, and were accused of failing to do so.

Passion and vengeance were the motives behind the legal quarrel between Phrynion of Paiania and Neaira, supported by her lover Stephanos.[28] Phrynion was a former lover who had paid for Neaira's liberation and represented her in the contract of her manumission. After that she had followed him to Athens as his lover for some time. During that period Neaira did not have to register as a metic because she belonged to the *oikos* of Phrynion as his concubine. However, Apollodoros provides some grisly details of his abusive behaviour towards her, and empathises with her decision to flee to Megara, where she tried to make a living as an independent hetaira. A couple of years later she was happy to return to Athens with a new lover, Stephanos of Eroiadai, seemingly a widower with four small children. Phrynion was livid and staged an abduction from Stephanos' house, alleging that Neaira was his slave. Although he knew very well that this was not true, he took advantage of Neaira's vulnerability at this stage, because unless someone else stood up for her, challenged him, and removed her to freedom, he could have actually pulled it off and turned her into his slave, against the law and in violation of the contract of her liberation, which he himself had agreed with her former masters. But Stephanos was not going to let go as easily as that. He provided some sureties that Neaira was not going to flee and she was going to stand trial to determine her status. At that point Phrynion was legally obliged to let her go back to Stephanos (*aphairesis eis eleutherian*). In the end, given what was at stake for everyone, both men were persuaded by common friends to allow the matter to be decided through private arbitration. The arbitrators succeeded in defusing tensions and appeasing male egos, while at the same time they reaffirmed that Neaira was a free person.

Throughout all this dispute there was a question mark over Neaira's status, no doubt because the one person who could testify that he was present and represented her in her manumission contract was the same person who was trying to hale her back into slavery. Neaira never had to register as a metic, because in her first long-term stay in Athens she belonged to the *oikos* of Phrynion, and then she came back as a member of the household of Stephanos. But in a situation like this we can appreciate the importance of the register of metics, because if she had ever been registered as a metic and paid taxes it would be much easier to provide official proof of her status as a free person, as happened with a metic woman named Zobia in a similar situation, where a vengeful former lover was trying to hale her into slavery.[29] The fact that Neaira had never been registered as a metic, because she had never lived independently in Athens for any length of time, made her extremely vulnerable to attempts at enslavement, and it took the resources, connections and protection of her devoted lover and partner to rescue her from this dire fate.

It appears that alien hetairai were particularly vulnerable to prosecutions for violation of the immigration laws of the city. New Comedy and its Roman heirs suggest that this was indeed a hot issue. The basic plot in which a young Athenian man is in love with an alien hetaira, whom he cannot marry because of their difference in status, is very common and allows for many twists and different dramatic outcomes. Sometimes the foolish young man is lucky to escape since the law stands as an impenetrable firewall guarding against an improper marriage, but sometimes a recognition plot is used whereby a likeable and good-natured mistress is recognised as an Athenian who had been separated from her family, and after that she can marry her beloved.[30]

The law cited by Apollodoros in *Against Neaira*, which prohibited lawful marriage between citizens and non-citizens, was introduced in the early decades of the fourth century precisely in order to deal with situations such as those described in the plays of New Comedy, where attractive alien hetairai could seduce citizen men into unsuitable marriages.[31] Apollodoros says as much in his discussion of the law in the argumentation of the speech.[32] He warns the jury that if attractive hetairai are allowed to become the wives of Athenian men, then Athenian women who would be left without husbands could turn to prostitution. This kind of scaremongering may well have been one of the reasons why this law was introduced, but perhaps not the only reason. Its introduction not only closed all avenues of marriage between citizens and non-citizens, but also eliminated all possible scenarios of pretended marriage. This law reveals the firm determination of the Athenian state to keep lawful marriage and the birth of legitimate children within it limited to citizens.

Since the marriage between an Athenian and an alien would be pointless in the first place, because it could no longer produce legitimate heirs following the reinstatement of the Periclean citizenship law in 403, the real target of this law was the pretence of lawful marriage. When an alien and an Athenian acted as if they were married in order to secure for themselves and their offspring the rights and privileges of married Athenian citizens, they were subject to its provisions. The penalty for the citizen was a severe fine of 1,000 drachmas, while the alien spouse faced confiscation of property and being sold into slavery. With penalties so severe, the law intended to end the practice of mixed marriages once and for all and firmly discourage situations where couples acted as if they were legally married. Situations of a pretended marriage would not be too difficult in a society where one did not need to register a marriage in a central archive. Any couple could say that they were married, but from the moment that they started claiming the benefits and privileges of legally married citizen couples they had fallen foul of this law.

New Comedy and its heirs have preserved the memory of the actual social impact of this law. A couple of examples should suffice: in one of Lucian's *Dialogues of Courtesans*,[33] Doris, an alien hetaira eight months pregnant with the child of a man named Pamphilos, is expressing her frustration because she thinks that her boyfriend is getting married. His response is interesting: while he assures his lover that he is not getting married and confesses his love for her, he does not exclude the possibility of marriage to a citizen woman altogether. He simply says that if he decided to get married to a citizen woman, he would choose another one who was richer and better looking than the one his mistress thought that he was going to marry. It appears that both Doris and her lover have acquiesced in the reality of their situation – that is, they can never be married – and that the best Doris can hope for is an assurance of love and support for her and her unborn child, while she needs to accept the fact that one day her lover is going to take a citizen wife and have legitimate children with her.

In Terence's *Heautontimorumenos* the *bona meretrix* Bacchis contrasts a hetaira's way of life with that of a citizen wife:

> quippe forma inpulsi nostra nos amatores colunt;
> haec ubi immutata est, illi suom animum alio conferunt:
> nisi si prospectum interea aliquid est, desertae vivimus.
> vobis cum uno semel ubi aetatem agere decretumst viro,
> quoi(u)s mos maxumest consimili' vostrum, [h]î se ad vos adplicant.
> hoc beneficio utrique ab utrisque vero devincimini,
> ut numquam ulla amori vostro incidere possit calamitas.[34]

> For our lovers, allured merely by our beauty, court us for that; when that has faded, they transfer their affections elsewhere; and unless we have made provision in the mean time for the future, we live in destitution. Now with you, when you have once resolved to pass your life with one man whose manners are especially kindred to your own, those persons become attached to you. By this kindly feeling, you are truly devoted to each other; and no calamity can ever possibly interrupt your love.

The alien hetaira Bacchis outlines her expectations of life compared to those of Antiphila, the citizen wife to be. While Antiphila can expect to find love, devotion and lifelong safety in her marriage, Bacchis only hopes that she will be prudent enough to make sufficient provisions in her good years so as not to face destitution when her looks fade. Seductive alien hetairai, like her, were perceived as a particular menace, because with their looks and skills they could induce Athenian men to shun citizen women, especially the less attractive (D. 59.113: ἂν καὶ ὁπωστιοῦν μετρίαν ἡ φύσις ὄψιν ἀποδῷ), or poor ones (D. 59.113: κἂν ἀπορηθῇ τις), and marry the hetairai instead.

It is within this cultural context that we need to see the prosecutions of alien hetairai for immigration offences. There is always more than meets the eye in such procedures, because taking the risk of a large fine just to bring to court some alien woman who was trying to make a living through prostitution never seems to be a good enough reason. We can be certain that there were always additional, personal, cultural and often other compelling reasons behind such cases, which will be explored further in Chapter 4.

PROSECUTIONS FOR RELIGIOUS OFFENCES

When considering the demographics of people who were prosecuted for religious offences we immediately notice that the list is disproportionately populated by women, compared to other offences. Why woman feature heavily in this particular list has been a matter of intense speculation in a number of studies, and this discussion has demonstrated how elusive a clear and convincing answer to this question can be.[35] If classical Athens were a theocratic society we would be able to understand which sensibilities and norms of their contemporaries these women offended, and if it were a monotheistic society we should be able to surmise that these women did not tow the line on acceptable religious beliefs and practices. But here lies a mystery: classical Athens, especially in the fourth century, was a polytheistic amalgam of a wide variety of beliefs and religious practices, and it was a society which did not have a holy book of unchallengeable authority; the nature of the gods, religious practice and concepts of belief and rite were matters open to interpretation, debate and speculation, and most of the priests and priestesses did not even need to be particularly religious;[36] they were public servants appointed by lot, and subject to a *dokimasia* and an *euthyna*,[37] like all other magistrates of the state. In this religious and moral diversity, how and why some women were prosecuted for impiety remains a puzzle. What makes our task less hopeless is the fact that, as stated above, classical Athens was not a society obsessed with religious righteousness, so there were always additional motives behind such prosecutions, and these motives were typically stronger and more central to the case than religious righteousness, which was a peripheral factor at best. This is why, if we can detect those external but decisive factors in the attested cases, we can reach a better understanding of the circumstances and true reasons behind such prosecutions.

The *graphe asebeias* was the primary procedure followed for intentional violations of religious rite, or other actions deliberately offensive to the gods. Several cases, which I have discussed in more detail in a previous study,[38] strongly suggest that the alleged impious behaviour needed to be intentional, understandably so because if the person was convicted the vengeful prosecutor could ask for the death penalty. The severity of the consequences demanded that the accusations were not made for behaviour which may have seemed offensive to the gods and people's religious sensibilities but in reality was accidental, innocent, or the result of ignorance rather than purpose. Perhaps the most famous example of this was Andocides, when he placed a suppliant's bough on the altar of the Eleusinium during the Mysteries, not knowing that this was forbidden by some ancient sacred rule under penalty of death.[39] However, because he had done it without knowing about that rule he was acquitted. This is why it is important to keep in mind that the women who were accused of violations of religious rites and offences against the gods were presented by their prosecutors as villains who had intentionally perpetrated acts offensive to the gods, and not innocent victims of misunderstanding or ignorance.

The trial of Aspasia for impiety may be the first in a series of several prosecutions of women through a *graphe asebeias*.[40] If Plutarch is reflecting the charges accurately, they are similar to those brought against Socrates.[41] Aspasia was accused of questioning the traditional order of things and the gods themselves in her intellectual circle, and also of having a corrupting influence upon the women of Athens. We do not need to be tied down by the specifics of this accusation, namely that Aspasia was procuring married women for Pericles. This could be a later antique rationalisation of the charges of Aspasia's corrupting influence upon the women of Athens, or indeed, if we accept that she had been a procuress, as Aristophanes joked in *Acharnians*, this could be a reflection of rumours in Plutarch's sources. Either way, we can recognise in the charges against Aspasia similar accusations to those levelled against Socrates, that he wanted to replace the traditional gods and that he had a corrupting influence upon the young men of Athens, and also against Phryne, that she wanted to introduce a new deity, the barbaric god Isodaites, and that she was a bad influence on young men. In all these three prominent cases of a *graphe asebeias* the basic ingredients seem to be the same, and perhaps we can even see the same recipe behind the prosecution of Theoris. The accusation that she was using strange potions, spells and incantations could be interpreted as a threat to the traditional religion of Athens, and the belief that she was having a corrupting influence by teaching slaves to deceive their masters sounds familiar. It looks as if a formula was used in impiety cases, which, with some variations related to the specifics of each case, presented the accused as a threat to the established order of things and the gods, and also as a bad influence upon a vulnerable group of the population.

The most notorious prosecution against a woman with a *graphe asebeias*, the trial of Phryne,[42] was certainly motivated by factors other than religious correctness. If anything, the religious element in this case was so thin that later antiquity had to come up with a fake story about the reasons why Phryne was prosecuted. According to a story told by later authors, Phryne was prosecuted because she went into the sea naked at the sanctuary of Eleusis during the festival of Poseidon, in full view of the believers.[43] The actual charges against Phryne are preserved in a fragment from the prosecution speech of Euthias, probably from the closing section.[44] They were intentionally modelled on the trial of Socrates and the successful tactics of his prosecutors. The first of these challenges was that Phryne was partying at the Lycaeum. This was a place of study frequented by youths, and we should understand this accusation as an attempt to persuade the jury that Phryne posed a danger for the young men of Athens and was a corrupting influence on them. A similar accusation had probably been the most detrimental in the case of Socrates. His prosecutors successfully made the case that some men who were deeply hated and mistrusted at the time of his trial, like Critias, Alcibiades and the historian Xenophon, had been corrupted by the bad influence of Socrates. The second of the accusations was that Phryne had introduced a new deity, probably a minor one from Asia Minor named Isodaites, a deity of the sympotic space, and in this capacity a favourite of hetairai. This accusation was also modelled on the trial of Socrates. His prosecutors had successfully argued that he intended to abolish the traditional Athenian religion, just as the fictional Socrates does in Aristophanes' *Clouds* when he seeks to replace the Olympian gods with the Clouds. Undoubtedly Phryne's prosecutor had amplified this introduction of a minor cult popular among prostitutes into a serious attack against traditional religion.

The third accusation, that she had assembled illicit religious associations of men and women, was most likely related to the second, and was presented as a part of the subversive activity against traditional religion, which had seemingly involved a number of women and men around the city. Phryne, like Socrates, had been presented as a detrimental presence in the city, and one needing to be removed for the greater good. Like Socrates' prosecutors, Phryne's accuser had tried to turn her into a symbol of what had gone wrong in Athenian society in his time. It would have been helpful to know exactly when the prosecution of Phryne took place, as it might have given us a more precise understanding of the forces behind it. Unfortunately our only point of reference is the life of Hypereides, which ended in 322. The trial of Phryne could be placed in those times of intense turmoil following Chaironeia and the end of the independent Greek polis. Could Phryne be turned into a scapegoat, a symbol of all the dysfunctions in Athenian society which brought about the end of the polis, as Socrates had been made the scapegoat for the defeat and sufferings of the city at the end of the Peloponnesian war and under the tyranny of the Thirty that followed? Jakub Filonik insightfully places *graphai asebeias* on critical fault lines of Athenian history, moments when major changes had occurred or were under way. Perhaps we can place the trial of Phryne on one of those fault lines, when the polis was ending and the Hellenistic world was arising, and the hetaira's unusual worldview and lifestyle were seen as a sign of what had gone wrong with the old polis.

We cannot safely make such a determination on the basis of the slim evidence available to us, but I am inclined to think that a dark force greater than envy for the shining hetaira must have been at work. Envy has been considered to be the main reason behind the prosecution of Phryne by the majority of scholars, and it is certainly the prime suspect in this case.[45] Phryne came from a poor immigrant community, and if a passage of Athenaios saying that the young Phryne was trying to scrape a living from picking and selling capers is a true reflection of her early life, her origins were very humble.[46] The Thespians were expelled in 371 BC, after the destruction of their city by Thebes, and most of them found refuge in Athens. And yet this destitute foreigner succeeded in becoming a very wealthy woman in her own right.[47] With her pale skin and flawless physique she was very successful as a top-of-the-range hetaira not only because she was exquisitely attractive, but also because she was a highly effective self-promotion machine. She was the muse of Praxiteles, perhaps the most highly accomplished sculptor of her time, and the model for and patron of some of the most famous artworks in the ancient world, like the Thespian triad of herself, Aphrodite and Eros, standing among images of kings and heroes at Delphi.[48] She was a fiercely independent woman who could not resist taking a dig at the old enemy, Thebes, when it had been humbled by Alexander, by offering to rebuild the walls of Thebes with her own money, if an inscription were to be placed on them saying that Alexander destroyed the walls and Phryne the hetaira restored them. Surely such actions and words invited envy, and classical Athens had put many people in their place when they appeared to have grown too big for their boots.[49]

For a fourth-century woman Phryne was extraordinary in some important aspects. Her wealth and ability to spend it as she pleased, without having to depend on any man for her extravagant tastes, set her apart from most other women in Athens. Even high-born citizen women, daughters of some of the wealthiest and most prominent families in the city, like Hipparete, the daughter of Hipponikos, sister of Kallias and wife of Alcibiades, did not enjoy this level of control over their properties, lives and fate. There were other wealthy, independent and strong-minded hetairai in fourth-century Athens. Several of them have become legends in their own right, were immortalised in the plays of Middle and New Comedy and had famous monuments built in their honour by lovers, like Glykera, Sinope, Pythionike, Lamia and others. And yet none of these extraordinary women seems to come near the heights of publicity and attention which Phryne has received through the centuries. A self-marketing machine, who trampled on all convention, lived exactly as she liked, and from very humble origins became one of the wealthiest and most talked-about women in the Greek world of her time, would surely be the object of envy, and sometimes outright resentment.

A woman who pushed hard against boundaries and traditional restrictions should perhaps have expected a pushback from more traditional elements in Athenian society. The boundaries that Phryne was pushing up against were not trivial; they were not customary follies and vanities. They were powerful traditions which had imposed serious restrictions upon the lives of women for as long as anyone could remember. In the statute books of Athens there was still an ancient Solonean law which restricted the ability of women to perform transactions larger than a week's household expenses.[50] This law had fallen into disuse many years before Phryne's time, but its presence on the statute books and the fact that it is invoked by an orator in the courtroom are stark reminders of how dependent Athenian women were for the management of their own money and property on male relatives. Phryne, and other wealthy hetairai of her time, shattered the glass ceiling in this matter. They had acquired substantial wealth and were willing to spend it as they pleased, without the consent or mediation of any man. Among them Phryne, more than any other, spent her wealth lavishly in ways that were bound to attract much public attention. But more importantly,

Phryne and other women of her time were setting in operation a new model for how a woman could live, safely and contentedly, outside the restrictions of the *oikos*. Although this was not the only factor contributing to the dissipation in later antiquity of the *oikos* as the fundamental unit upon which the life and laws of the city were built, it certainly played a major role by showing that it was possible for women to live and prosper outside the protective umbrella of this ancient unit. A pioneering figure who went up against such powerful traditional norms could be expected to become an object of resentment, perhaps even fear.

The prosecution and trial of Phryne for impiety had little to do with strait-laced piety and much more to do with the insecurities, anxieties and emotional reactions of Athenian society towards the end of an era, the end of the traditional Greek polis and its institutions, and the dangers coming with such changes, which Phryne symbolised and was probably considered responsible for, with her provocative rejection of traditional models of feminine behaviour. Like Socrates, Phryne probably found herself blamed for the failings of her times, and in her acquittal it is difficult to see whether the jury saw through the mirage and truthfully reached the honest conclusion that the prominent hetaira was not to be blamed for all the ills of her time, or simply fell for the highly skilled rhetoric and the tricks of her experienced defender. Perhaps it was a mixture of both, but whatever the case, her prosecution proves that any changes in the status of women in the fourth century, before the law and inside the *oikos*, did not happen effortlessly or painlessly.

Even more puzzling seems to be the prosecution of Theoris of Lemnos for impiety. We can surmise the three prongs of her prosecution from our sources. Theoris was prosecuted, it seems, for being a *pharmakis*, namely an expert in strange potions with supernatural powers which had the ability to make a man fall in love against his wishes, or deceived him in some other way. She also had spells that went along with these potions and philtres to a similar effect. It seems that the prosecutor successfully presented her as a dangerous woman who had the skill and the means to deceive people and force them into detrimental situations against their true wishes. The second prong was that she had engaged extensively in conspiratorial activities, and even taught slaves how to deceive and defy their masters. We can envisage how a skilled prosecutor like Demosthenes presented this activity as a threat to the security of the state. The third prong was that she was an oracle, and while this in itself would not be against the law, pretending to be an oracle and usurping the rituals of respected and established oracles would definitely not only be against the law, but would probably have the same gravity as an offence as the mocking of the Mysteries by Alcibiades and his friends in 415. Intriguingly, the case against Theoris also began with a denunciation by her maid. Perhaps we can see some similarities with the hysteria of 415, and understand why Theoris and her entire family were convicted and put to death. As stated in Part I, her conviction and execution may have been the result of an intense emotional reaction to the denunciations made by her maid.

We are almost in the dark when it comes to the prosecution of the priestess Ninos for impiety. Ninos by the look of it was a citizen woman, because she is never referred to by any other designation except ἱέρεια (priestess), the title which properly belonged to a citizen woman in the service of some deity, and was only improperly used for alien women serving in cultic roles. This prosecution too resulted in conviction, and probably the death penalty. Some later sources seem to imply that Ninos was prosecuted because she had introduced a new god, but this evidence is not reliable.[51] While we are totally in the dark about the actual accusations against Ninos, in this case we are somewhat better informed about the context. We know that her prosecutor, a minor political figure called Menekles, was a run-of-the-mill sycophant, who would blackmail affluent people and if they did not agree to his demands could put them in danger through the courts. If the narrative of Mantitheos in D. 40, *To Boiotos on his Mother's Dowry*, presents the facts accurately, his father Mantias was threatened, blackmailed and pushed into a corner by Menekles, in cahoots with his half-brothers, in order to get them recognised by Mantias as his own sons and take a big slice out of his prosperous *oikos*. This presentation by Ninos' prosecutor may be able to supply a motive. Ninos could have fallen victim to a vile and aggressive sycophant for reasons that might not even directly concern her. Conceivably she, like Neaira, found herself in the middle of ugly political games played by men. A fragment attributed to Dinarchos (Fr. 33 Conomis), where Ninos' son is prosecuting Menekles, may lend further credence to the suggestion that she was an innocent victim of male disputes and power games, and perhaps this is why we never get to hear the reasons for which she was convicted. If they were trivial and unimportant matters amplified and weaponised by a skilled sycophant, we can understand why later centuries completely ignored them.

The fourth woman to be prosecuted with a *graphe asebeias* around that time, a citizen known as the sister of Lakedaimonios, was acquitted. Like Ninos' prosecutor Menekles, Euboulides, the man who accused the sister of Lakedaimonios of impiety, was perhaps a meddlesome and ruthless minor political figure, who succeeded in having the citizenship of a man named Euxitheos revoked during the *diapsiphesis* of 346, in order to settle personal scores. This kind of man could quite possibly have used the sister of Lakedaimonios as a weapon against her brother.

We do not have the whole story when it comes to the prosecution of several women for impiety around the same time, namely in the third quarter of the fourth century, but as far as we can tell, at no other point in Athenian history is there such a concentration of impiety prosecutions brought against women. It does appear remarkable and may seem like a witch-hunt, but I am more inclined to agree with

Jakub Filonik that these prosecutions for impiety tend to fall in times of trauma and change in Athenian society. Whether contemporary Athenians realised it or not, the changes brought about by the defeat at Chaironeia and the subsequent willy-nilly unification of the Greek world under the Macedonian banner were much deeper and more lasting than the consequences of the Peloponnesian war for Athenian society. Athens survived the latter as an independent state, and was soon able to rebuild and regain much of what was lost. However, after Chaironeia there was no turning back; the world had changed forever. It is in those turbulent and historically consequential years that we find a high concentration of prosecutions of women for impiety. It is tempting to extend Filonik's argument to these cases and consider them a sign of their times.

Classical Athens was as remote from a theocracy as it ever gets, and yet religion was weaponised to serve other interests. This would not seem untypical or strange to us, since religion is so often weaponised in our own political discourse, to serve more pragmatic purposes. Probably this happened in fourth-century Athens too. In that critical junction of history, where so much was at stake, these prosecutions of women for impiety were motivated by larger political and ideological currents and conflicts.

ECONOMIC DISPUTES

The women of Athens were caught up in a legislative paradox in the classical period. While society had progressed in many significant ways from the archaic period, the laws regulating family life, succession, inheritance and property rights were almost in their entirety Solonean. It is certainly an astonishing phenomenon to observe that some of the primary laws regulating economic activity did not even mention sums in drachmas, but used older monetary standards which had preceded the introduction of coinage. For example, as we have seen, the primary law which regulated the economic activities of women set a ceiling for the amount of a transaction which a woman was entitled to complete at one *medimnos* of barley.[52] It is highly doubtful whether this would have meant anything to families in the classical period, but it is certain that the law had not been updated to reflect the sum in drachmas because it had fallen into disuse well before the time of the Athenian Empire. The Solonean laws on family, property and inheritance were archaic in spirit and clearly motivated by one primary concern: to maintain the *oikos* and keep the property within it. In order to accomplish this goal the laws run different scenarios of the appropriate course of action depending on the actual circumstances of a family, such as the existence or absence of legitimate sons, adoption, inheritance by legitimate daughters married with children or by daughters who were still childless (*epikleroi*), and finally inheritance by lateral relatives.

The logic of the order of inheritance was simple: legitimate descendants, natural or adopted, had priority over lateral relatives, and among relatives of the same degree preference was given to the agnatic line, but not to the exclusion of the enatic line. Consequently, among siblings the bulk of the family property would go to sons in equal portions, while daughters were entitled to a smaller portion of the family property in the form of a dowry. However, since women never acquired inheritance rights in their husband's *oikos*, and always retained inheritance rights in their native *oikos*, in the absence of a male heir with a stronger claim their claim to the property of their natal *oikos* became dominant and took priority over the claims of lateral relatives. The law's objective of keeping the family property within the *oikos* sometimes resulted in absurd arrangements like that of an *epikleros*, namely a woman with no male siblings who became an heiress to the property of her father or her brother having to marry her father's closest male relative. From our perspective a law which removed from a woman her right to have any say at all in who she was going to share her life with, and forced her to marry the closest and oldest male relative of her father, seems ridiculous.[53] Yet it is clear that the Athenians did not find this law bizarre, and the fact that they stuck by it for centuries probably means that they thought of it as a good guide for the passage of property from generation to generation. The law on the family lines (*anchisteia*) is quoted in the speech *Against Makaratos*.[54]

The order of succession as stated in the law was very clear, but this did not end inheritance disputes. In a society which did not keep exact records of marriages, births and deaths, deciding who had the better claim in accordance with the law was not always a straightforward matter, especially when there were no obvious heirs, like legitimate sons and daughters, and more distant relatives had to fight each other. The difficulties of the system are the primary reason for some awkward rules, like the one where essentially the Athenian state through its chief magistrate on domestic affairs, the archon, sanctioned, and often even decided, who the husband of the *epikleros* would be. There was a very clear reason behind this. The state recognised that a lone woman who did not have an immediate male relative to fight her corner was particularly vulnerable to the rapacious appetites of relatives who had set their eyes on her property. This inherent vulnerability was exacerbated if the woman was too young to understand what was happening, too rich or too poor, too attractive or too unattractive, and the state simply did not trust families to do the right thing. What confirms for us that this was truly the intention of the law is the fact that even in those cases where there was no dispute, the archon still needed to give the green light before a relative could claim the *epikleros* and her property. This 'no exceptions' policy was born out of insecurity and mistrust of the woman's relatives and their intentions.

The commonest way to claim an *epikleros* and her inheritance was through a *diadikasia*, where all competing relatives needed to explain before the court why their claim was the best, and the court decided who should marry her (*epidikasia*). Sometimes relatives who were already married and unwilling to divorce their wives, or were too old or simply not interested in the *epikleros* themselves, could step aside in favour of their son or another relative. The *diadikasia* was also the appropriate procedure for claiming an inheritance directly, when the claimants were male relatives, or married female relatives with children, and therefore not *epikleroi*. Other types of private lawsuits (*dikai*) were also used as alternative legal avenues intended either to undermine and in essence reverse the result of a *diadikasia*,[55] or as pre-emptive strikes intended to weaken someone's claim.[56]

In a process of *epidikasia* the *epikleros* had no say over the proceedings. She was simply informed at the end of the process who was going to be her husband. In other property disputes women did have a say, especially older women with precise knowledge of the family affairs. As stated in the previous chapter, they always had the option of appearing as witnesses before an arbitrator, in the obligatory public arbitration for all *dikai*. This rarely happens in the extant corpus of the Attic orators, but this image may not be accurate because the cases that we have were the ones that were not resolved before the arbitrator and went to court, which was the exclusive domain of male litigants. It is quite possible that in a large number of lawsuits that never made it to the courts, but were settled at the level of arbitration, women had a greater role and a greater say in the proceedings.

For those cases that went to court, women were represented by male relatives, who were supposed to defend their interests and relate to the court the women's point of view and support their claim. To what extent they conveyed what women had said is impossible to tell, but one would imagine that the voice of a savvy woman with privileged knowledge of the family affairs and a firm grasp of the economics of the household would come through loud and clear, not least because it was in the best interests of the men who were representing her to convey her voice to the courtroom. For example, the forceful words which Lysias puts in the mouth of Diodotos' wife in the speech *Against Diogeiton* could be a reflection of her actual words, since of all people she knew the family finances best.

Among extant speeches the property dispute presented in Isaios *On the Estate of Pyrrhos* is of particular interest, because it underlines with great clarity how vulnerable the female heirs could be even when there was no good reason to doubt their legitimate birth or family relation to the deceased.[57] Phile's claim to the estate of Pyrrhos should have been without a challenge. No one disputed that she was the daughter of Pyrrhos, and no one should have had any reasonable doubt about her legitimacy. She was the only biological child of Pyrrhos by an Athenian wife, whom he had married in the presence of no fewer than four witnesses. In the absence of a legitimate son he adopted a close male relative, his nephew Endios, his sister's son, who by the look of it proved worthy of his uncle's trust and managed the affairs of the family equitably and appropriately. At some point after her father's death, Phile was betrothed by her adopted brother, as expected, to Xenokles, an Athenian man, and she had children with him, who at the time of the dispute would undoubtedly have been considered to be Athenian citizens. These facts perfectly match the profile of a typical Athenian woman.

When Endios died childless Phile had priority over any other relative to her father's estate, as Pyrrhos' only direct descendant. But then the mother and brother of Endios decided to register a claim of their own. From a legal perspective they had no standing, but what they lacked in legal rights they made up for in ingenuity and ruthless determination. First, they hired Isaios, an expensive and effective litigator. Undoubtedly they were advised that the only way for them to inherit would be if Phile were out of the picture. This could only happen in one possible way: they needed to convince the jury that she was illegitimate. But this should have been near impossible. There were witnesses to the marriage of her father with her mother, witnesses to her own marriage to Xenokles, with whom she undoubtedly had legitimately born citizen children,[58] and her husband was right there pursuing the claim on her behalf. No jury would have accepted that she was illegitimate in the presence of all these witnesses attesting to the opposite.

So the strategy of Pyrrhos sister and her son first needed to focus upon the weakening of Phile's case by depriving her of some key witnesses. If they succeeded in those first vital steps of their plan, the chances of prevailing in the main procedure that would award them the property was significantly higher. First a *diamartyria*, and then a *graphe pseudomartyrion* were intended to do just that, namely to strip Phile of important witnesses, and force her to withdraw the claim, or at least fight for it from a much weakened position.[59] The strategy was certainly ingenious but on its own it could not have worked, because even then Phile was by default the natural heiress. Something more was needed so as to bypass her, and Endios' mother and brother came up with the story that Phile could not have been legitimate because she was the daughter of a hetaira. As evidence for that, they provided witnesses who seemingly attested that they had been her lovers and that there were rowdy parties at Pyrrhos' house. As stated in Part I, this assumption is based upon a false dichotomy between the hetaira and the wife. Is it possible that the wife of Pyrrhos, who, according to proper etiquette for a citizen woman, is never mentioned by her first name, was truly a hetaira before she married Pyrrhos? This would not make her any less of a wife, if a proper *engye* in the presence of witnesses had taken place, which absolutely seems to be the case here. The other false dichotomy upon which the case is based is that between the alien and the Athenian woman. By assuming that Phile's mother was a hetaira, Endios' mother and brother assumed that she must also be alien, even though she was clearly an Athenian woman with Athenian relatives. Again, even if she had been a hetaira in her younger days, this did not make her an alien. The case against Phile should never have happened, but it did, because skilled litigators and ruthless relatives went after her property and were willing to strategise and to do what it took, playing dirty, and exploiting the prejudices of the jury.

Surely Phile was not the only woman in Athens who had to fight an uneven battle to defend what was rightfully hers. At least some of the lawsuits that we have in fragmentary form may have been cases like this where ruthless relatives, sensing weakness, attempted to get their hands on the property of the lone woman who had been left without her natural protectors. As far as we can see from the scant fragments of the speech, the case regarding the daughter(s) of Antiphon was another such dispute. The woman was left with no male relatives after the flight and subsequent death of her father under the Thirty, and she had some powerful and rapacious members of the regime going after her property. Sometimes we admire the inventiveness of the tactics used in such disputes. Phile, it seems, was not the only victim of master tacticians. The daughter (or daughters) of Aristophon may have found herself (or themselves) faced with a similar conundrum. Assuming it was only one woman that was involved, it seems that someone who had set his eyes on her property tried to claim her as an *epikleros*, although by the look of it she was already married with children and therefore not an *epikleros*. Even though such a case should never have happened, it did, and the woman with her *kyrios* needed to prove before a jury that she was not subject to *epidikasia*, and therefore the property of her father belonged to her and her descendants. However, vulnerability should not be taken as absence of a fighting spirit. In all these cases we see women fighting back hard, through their *kyrioi*, and at least in one intriguing case, that of Hegelochos, quite possibly with a hired advocate.

Much was at stake in these cases, as the properties in dispute were often large, and we can understand why claimants would fight fiercely for them using every trick in the book. What we cannot quite understand is the reason why, given the difficulties of keeping tabs on property ownership and rightful succession, the Athenian state or the local demes did not venture at some point to form centrally held registers of families, which would have made a great deal of difference in deciding the right order of succession. The answer to this question probably has to do with the fact that Athenian family law changed at a very slow pace. It seems that while the Athenians saw public life as dynamic, ever-changing and shifting, and frequently changed their laws to match political and military developments, they preferred to see family life as something serene, immutable and tethered to time-honoured certainties.[60]

VIOLENT CRIME

The audiences of the tragic stage were accustomed to women performing atrocious acts of violence, sometimes with cold-blooded deliberation, like Klytemestra or Phaedra, sometimes accidentally, like the distraught Dieaneira, or in the grip of madness, like Agave and the other Bacchants, or as an act of self-harm, like Jocasta or Antigone.[61] Granted that these were extraordinary women in extraordinary circumstances, and that, as Victoria Wohl has emphasised,[62] fictional characters are not always our best guide to a better understanding of legal matters and historical realities, still the presence of these fictional characters on the tragic stage is informative in some important ways. First of all it suggests that Athenian audiences considered women just as capable as men of extreme acts of cruelty and violence towards others and themselves. Second, it suggests that audiences were accustomed to the concept of personal responsibility, where these women were personally held responsible for their actions, and suffered the consequences, whether their motives were sinister on not. Finally, the audiences expected punishment and retribution for wrongdoings perpetrated by women, just as they would have expected if these wrongdoings had been perpetrated by men, and it was only through this punishment that the catharsis eventually came. These underlying concepts of justice and retribution acquire particular significance in those few cases of violent crime involving women known to us.

The speech of Antiphon *Against the Stepmother* is the only extant example of Attic oratory where a woman is accused of a violent crime, and the presentation of this particular case may have something important to tell us about women and violence. A man is accusing his stepmother of the murder of his father, which allegedly she committed several years ago while the man was still a minor. An Athenian homicide court would not have been surprised to hear that all these years had to go by before the stepmother was prosecuted for homicide. This duty fell upon close male relatives of the deceased, and the man's half-brother, the biological son of the stepmother, was defending her innocence. Under these circumstances the speaker had to wait until he came of age before he could avenge his father, and this is what he is trying to do through this prosecution. He presents no concrete evidence implicating the stepmother in the death of his father. Instead, the case relies heavily on *ethopoeia*.

His portrayal of the stepmother as another Klytemestra is designed to carry the case for the prosecution. His only chance of success, essentially without any evidence, rests squarely upon being able to convince the jury through such associations that the stepmother was just as sinister and ruthless as the tragic heroine. However, some of the differences from the tragic heroine are particularly significant, and it is likely that they are so by design. Unlike Klytemestra, who stabs her husband in his bath, with her own hands drenched in his blood, the stepmother does not stain her hands. Instead, she does something which the ancient jury might consider a very womanly thing to do: she kills from a safe distance and without the need to get her hands dirty, with lethal cunning and efficiency. The stepmother is ingeniously portrayed as the hidden danger, invisible to the victim until it is too late, and this is what makes her more dangerous, and more frightening. This portrayal plays with the fears of the male jury about the hidden dangers from women like the stepmother, who would not assault and kill a man in a direct confrontation, but would do so secretly, surreptitiously and in a manner that would prevent the hapless victim from facing danger head on. It would be interesting to think that this portrayal was intentional because it had a higher chance of success when presenting a violent woman not so much like Klytemestra, as a killer drenched in blood, but like Phaedra, as the devious and wicked brain behind the entire operation.

PERSONAL RESPONSIBILITY BEFORE THE LAW

Adriaan Lanni in a dedicated study on the subject has reached the conclusion that the Athenians sometimes imposed collective sanctions on groups of people.[63] Lanni mentions three areas where collective punishments could be assigned: disenfranchisement for debts to the state, punishment for treason, and collective responsibility of boards. Lene Rubinstein and J. Fournier (response to Rubinstein) have also discussed the issue of collective responsibility of boards of magistrates.[64] However, a closer look indicates that a more cautious approach is needed. The first sanction, namely disenfranchisement for debts to the state, should not be viewed as an issue of collective punishment, because it was not. From a legal point of view, only the debtor was punished. The debt and consequently the disenfranchisement would roll on to the next generation after the death of the debtor, simply because the son(s) or the deceased debtor automatically inhertited their father's assets and liabilites. While the debtor was alive, his son remained fully enfranchised, and if he was outlived by his father, he never became *atimos*. The third category probably should not be treated as an issue of collective punishment either. If we look more carefully into the language of such sanctions, in the event that a board was found to be deficient in the performance of its duties, it was sanctioned as one body (typically in the form of a mild administrative rebuke, as Lanni correctly points out). Let's say, if the assembly refused to crown the outgoing *boule* because of serious shortcomings in its conduct, it was penalising not 500 individual members (τοὺς βουλευτὰς or τοὺς βουλεύοντας), but the council as a single concept (τὴν βουλήν).[65] Individual members of such boards accused of serious offences, such as treasonous conduct, bribery or antidemocratic activities, could always be prosecuted individually, as Lanni points out. The second case, where *atimia* was imposed as a sentence on someone and his descendants for treason or an offence of comparable gravity, was a genuine issue of collective responsibility, a vestige of archaic justice.

Overall, it seems that the traditional view, that the laws of the Athenian democracy sanctioned individuals and not entire familes for their transgressions, is broadly correct. However, I agree with Lanni that classical Athenian law contained archaic concepts of justice which occasionally sanctioned groups. In the course of the classical period there was a decisive shift away from models of collective responsibility, but since democratic Athenian law contained large segments which had been developed by Drakon or Solon in the archaic period (homicide, family and inheritance law, almost in their entirety), and never carefully revised, it is inevitable that some vestiges of those times, with different concepts of guilt, punishment and justice, would still be traceable in the classical period. While in public life these vestiges can only be observed in a small number of legal provisions covering crimes which threatened the state and the democratic constitution, in private life the vestiges of archaic collective responsibility are more far-reaching, as most of the laws on private life had been introduced in the archaic period.

The conceptual underpinning of Solonean law recognised families in most areas of private life and was one of collective responsibility, where the law was dealing with the *kyrios*, and the woman herself was essentially invisible to the criminal justice system. A very good example of this would be the Solonean adultery laws, which viewed adultery as an offence of one man against another, and imposed severe sanctions against the man who had invaded another man's *oikos*, but left the equally guilty female party out of the picture. It was not before the mid-fifth century and the introduction of the Periclean citizenship law, which made the woman an essential vessel for the transmission of citizenship, that she was penalised, and even then the punishment did not involve court cases or formal prosecution, but only public humiliation if she did not observe the legal requirement of abstention from public temples. Only for some very serious offences such as homicide was a woman held personally responsible in archaic Athens.

With the establishment of the democratic constitution and the empowerment of the individual citizen, the concept of personal responsibility before the law became more central, and this affected women too. The laws of the classical period typically do not distinguish along lines of gender. Someone who broke the law needed to be punished, regardless of gender. But since the legislation valid in the fifth and fourth century was a blend of old Solonean laws with legislation introduced under the democratic constitution, we encounter some apparent contradictions when it comes to the concept of personal responsibility before the law as it applied in the case of Athenian women. As mentioned above, for some offences a woman was shielded behind the protective cover of the *oikos*, but for other offences, like homicide, immigration violations, impiety or violent crime, a woman would be held personally responsible, and the duty of her *kyrios* was to represent her, but not to face any form of punishment himself for her actions. While Athenian law was willing to recognise the *oikos* as a safe space under the protective authority of the *kyrios*, on the other hand, it did not consider one person responsible for the crimes of another, and if women committed crimes, they were the ones who had to face the consequences of the law on the same footing as men. This is the main difficulty which we face when we try to understand the extent of women's responsibility before the law. On the one hand we can see that so often they were shielded behind the *oikos*, and the *kyrios* was dealing with the law on their behalf, but at the same time we can see a clearly defined sense of personal liability. This apparent contradiction needs to be interpreted as part of the historical evolution of Athenian law, and how collective responsibility and personal liability were balanced in each particular case needs to be assessed on a case-by-case basis, taking into account the specific circumstances and objectives of both prosecution and defence.

NOTES

1. The literature on this charismatic Athenian is vast. Some representative publications include the recent book by David Stuttard (2018); Rhodes 2011; McBrayer 2017: 75–90; Helfer 2017; Fulkerson 2013: 269–98; Faulkner 2007; Vickers 2008.
2. How the Athenians understood these concepts of communal punishment by the gods can be amply illustrated by the fate of Oedipus in Sophocles' masterpiece, *Oedipus Rex*. Oedipus has unknowingly killed his father, albeit in self-defence, and because he remains unpunished the entire city is suffering from hunger and disease in the opening scenes. The only remedy to the situation is to find and punish the killer. Outside fictional literature, the perils of the deadly *miasma* (supernatural pollution) are outlined with equal vividness and imagination in Antiphon's speech *On the Murder of Herodes* (5.82–5), where the fact that the boat on which he was sailing did not sink is used as evidence by the speaker that he was not a killer.
3. On the violations of the Eleusinian Mysteries and the ensuing scandal see And. 1, with MacDowell's still valuable commentary.
4. See Kapparis 2019a: 202–7.
5. Todd 1993: 190–2; I have argued that the mechanism through which the former master was seeking to extend his or her control was the enforcement of a *paramone* condition in the manumission contract; see Kapparis 2019a: 90–1; see also the discussion in Part I, pp. 46–7.
6. E.g. Lys. 12 and 13. The standard study on *euthyna* is Efstathiou 2007: 113–35; see also Oranges 2016: 81–97.
7. As long as six years in the case *On the Crown* (D. 18 versus Aesch. 3).
8. The *probole* faired better because it was much more restricted to start with, and could only be introduced twice a year, once in March for religious violations during the festivals, and once in the summer for sycophantic activities. See D. 21.8–9; Arist. *Ath.* 43.5; Kapparis 2019a: 257–68. Important studies on *eisangelia* in public life are Hansen 1975; 1980: 89–95; Carawan 1987: 167–208; 1985: 115–40; Pecorella Longo 2002: 222–8; Piccirilli 1983: 333–63; Rhodes 1979: 103–14; Sealey 1981: 125–34.
9. See for example D. 59.46–8 (immigration status dispute) and 67–71 (a *graphe* for illegal entrapment under false allegations of adultery).
10. Aesch. 3.197; MacDowell 2000: 536–8; Worthington 2003: 364–71; Rhodes 1981: 726–7.

11. E.g. Aesch. 1.132 ff.; D. 19.245 ff.
12. See one such instance in D. 53.18.
13. Important studies on homicide include MacDowell 1963; Carawan 1998; also 1991: 1–16; Gagarin 1981; also 1979b: 111–20; 1979a: 301–23; 1990: 81–99; 2000: 569–79; Phillips 2008; Wallace 1989; Stroud 1979; Tulin 1996; Riess 2008: 49–94; Hansen 1976.
14. A clear point on the awareness that torture can never provide reliable evidence is found in Ant. 5.29–35. On such challenges see the discussion in Tulin 1999: 21–4 and pp. 43–6 above.
15. Sometimes, however, hostile witnesses do appear, for example Deinias, the father-in-law of Apollodoros, who refuses to confirm the testimony which Apollodoros had prepared for him (D. 45.55), or the reluctant Hipparchos in D. 59.28 or Misgolas in Aesch. 1.45–50. Aeschines capitalises on the fact that sometimes witnesses refuse to give evidence for their own reasons, and tries to explain the complete lack of evidence in the speech *Against Timarchos* (45–50) as a result of this reluctance.
16. On witnesses and their role see Mirhady 2002: 255–74; Thür 2005: 146–69; Carey 1995: 114–19; Spatharas 2008: 177–91.
17. E.g. D. 45.8, 17; Arist. *Ath.* 53.2.
18. E.g. Isoc. 11.168; Din. 4.65, 66; Lyc. 1.2.
19. See Haley 1985: 49–59; Dixon 1983: 91–112; Mulhern 2016: 432–59.
20. See the discussion in Part I, pp. 39–43.
21. Blass 1893: 539. 'I do not want to believe that the act of vengeance of those two [Apollodoros and Theomnestos] succeeded and Neaira was sold.'
22. Filonik 2013: 11–96; 2016: 125–40.
23. See Eidinow 2016.
24. On metics see also the discussion in Part I, pp. 33–4.
25. See also Kapparis 2019a: 89–91.
26. For sources and the details of the case see the relevant entry in Part I, pp. 29–36.
27. Aesch. 1.119; Kapparis 2018: 267–71; Glazebrook 2011: 46–9; Fisher 2001: 258–9.
28. D. 59.27–48.
29. D. 25.56–8 and also the discussion in Chapter 1, pp. 91–2.
30. As for example happens with Glykera in Menander's *Perikeiromene* and Palaestra in Plautus' *Rudens*. For a more thorough discussion see Henry 1984; Kapparis 2018: 179–82.
31. D. 59.16; see also my discussion in Kapparis 1999: ad loc.
32. D. 59.107–25.
33. Luc. *DMeretr.* 2.
34. Terence, *Heautontimorumenos* 389–95; trans. H. T. Riley.
35. E.g. Eidinow 2016; also 2010: 9–35; Dillon 2002: 183–208; Filonik 2013: 11–96; 2016: 125–40.
36. On Greek priestesses see Connelly 2007; Skov 1975: 136–47; Cole 2004; Goff 2004; Dillon 2002.
37. The δοκιμασία was a scrutiny during someone's entry into office, typically limited to a few standard questions intended to make sure that the appointee was

a citizen of good standing in the polis. The εὔθυνα at the end of someone's term of office was a more serious affair consisting of two stages, one which checked the financial affairs of the exiting magistrate, and one which checked more generally the magistrate's conduct in office. Any citizen had the right to approach the board of the magistrates conducting the εὔθυνα (εὔθυνοι) and make a complaint, and if they thought that it was well founded they could refer the case to court. See the δοκιμασία speeches of Lysias (16, 25, 26, 31) and Weißenberger 1987; Wolpert and Kapparis 2011: 52–8; Feyel 2009; Lepri Sorge 1987: 427–34; Adeleye 1983: 295–306; Todd 2010: 73–108, with response by Gagliardi. On the εὔθυνα see Efstathiou 2007: 113–35; Oranges 2016: 81–97.

38. Kapparis 2019a: 257–67. The best study on impiety trials is Filonik 2013: 11–96. See also Filonik 2016: 125–40; Delli Pizzi 2011: 59–76; O'Sullivan 1997: 136–52; Cohen 1989b: 99–107; Jenks 2004: 193–210; Burnyeat 1997: 1–12; Lännström 2013: 31–48; Muir 2018: 387–403; among others.
39. And. 1.110 ff.
40. See also the discussion in Part I, pp. 76–82.
41. The literature on the trial of Socrates is large, and beyond our purposes to discuss in detail. For a representative selection see Brickhouseand Smith 1988; 2002; Connor 1991: 49–56; Hansen 1996: 137–70; 2002: 150–8; Stone 1988; Waterfield 2012: 269–305.
42. See also the discussion in Part I, pp. 76–82.
43. Athen. 13.59.
44. Anon. Seg. *Ars Rhet.* 215 Hammer.
45. See Eidinow 2016 for the discussion on envy, and also the important studies on the subject by Sanders (2014) and Walcot (1978).
46. Timokles, *Neaira* Fr. 23 = Athen. 13.22. See also the discussion in Apostolakis 2019: 196–202.
47. Athen. 13.60: ἐπλούτει δὲ σφόδρα ἡ Φρύνη.
48. See the discussion in Kapparis 2018: 320–5; Corso 1997: 123–50; and the discussion in Part I, pp. 76–82.
49. The policy of ostracism in the first half of the fifth century is an excellent example of this. A prominent Athenian was sent into exile for ten years when he appeared to be too powerful to be controlled and a danger for the democratic constitution. The fate of Alcibiades, one of the most charismatic men in Athenian history, is another excellent example. He was removed from the command of the most ambitious expedition in Athenian history, which he had inspired and promoted, primarily because his fellow citizens feared his popularity. Many more examples like this can be found in the course of Athenian history.
50. The law cited in Is. 10.10 states that a woman did not have the ability to perform transactions larger than one *medimnos* of barley, which would be roughly equal to the expenses of a household for a week. The fact that the sum is not given in drachmas means that the law fell into disuse in the archaic period and was never revised or revived in any form or shape.
51. See the discussion in Part I, pp. 69–73.
52. Is. 10.10.

53. See also the discussion in Part I, pp. 46–8.
54. D. 43.51; see pp. 235–7.
55. D. 48 *Against Olympiodoros* is a good example of this. The husband of the sister of Olympiodoros, acting on her behalf, is bringing a lawsuit against her brother, after he won an inheritance dispute.
56. Is. 3. *On the Estate of Pyrrhos* is a *dike pseudomartyrion* (indictment for false testimony) the primary purpose of which is to deprive Phile, the daughter of Pyrrhos, of a key witness and make a claim to her inheritance easier for the relatives of her adopted brother.
57. See also the discussion in Part I, pp. 73–5.
58. If Phile had had no children, a male relative of her father might have been able to claim her and the property as an *epikleros*. The fact that the possibility is never raised means that she had children and that she could not be removed from her marriage to Xenokles and claimed as an *epikleros*. Then, if these children were not believed to be Athenian, this would have been the best and strongest argument in favour of the brother of Endios. However, the silence here is pregnant: these children were understood by everyone to be legitimately born and Athenian citizens, born properly in marriage from two Athenian parents.
59. The *diamartyria* (presenting a counter-witness) was an old process by which if someone disputed the legality of the proceedings he could present a witness who would give evidence on this issue. By doing so the litigant blocked the initial lawsuit, and his opponent could only proceed with it if he first won the *diamartyria* trial. The *dike pseudomartyriou* was a lawsuit by which someone could attempt either to cancel the result of the previous *dike* on the grounds that his opponent had won because some witness lied, or in a pre-emptive strike to trying to eliminate a key witness of his opponent.
60. For further discussion on the inheritance rights of women see Schaps 1979; 1975: 53–7; Just 1989: 53–73; Craik 1984: 6–29; Griffith-Williams 2012: 145–62; 2016: 111–16; Karnezis 1972; Katz 1992: 692–708.
61. See e.g. McHardy 2005: 129–50.
62. Wohl 2010: 33–70; see also Scafuro 2003.
63. Lanni 2017: 9–31.
64. Rubinstein 2012: 329–64.
65. E.g. D. 22.37; Aesch. 1. 112.

CHAPTER 3

Gender as a Factor in the Construction of the Argument

GENDER STEREOTYPES AS A FACTOR IN TRIALS INVOLVING BOTH MEN AND WOMEN: AN INTRODUCTION

Male litigants tried to curry favour with juries by pointing out that they had been exemplary citizens with impeccable democratic credentials, they had performed liturgies, participated in military campaigns, served in public office, were protective of their families and had looked after their parents.[1] In doing so they were employing positive norms of what society considered to be laudable behaviour for a man, and through the use of these stereotypes they were trying to communicate to their peers sitting in the jury that they deserved their favour. On the other hand, litigants often communicated to the jury that their opponent had engaged in activities which were harmful to the democratic constitution and the city as a whole, that they had evaded military service and other duties to the city, that they mistreated their parents and friends, wasted their patrimony, and had lived a life of excesses and unbridled passions. By doing so, they employed negative norms and stereotypes to vituperate their opponent in court and turn the jury against him. For women litigants most of these stereotypes would not apply. Although they were perceived to be citizens in law and custom, their citizenship was understood very differently from that of male litigants, and the positive or negative stereotypes about what constituted feminine virtue or vice were significantly different. This is why the build-up of the case involving a female litigant or person of interest needed to be substantially different from that involving a male litigant. While the basic skills and techniques of truths, half-truths and lies, praise or blame, skilful manipulation of the evidence or emotional influencing of the judges, remained the same, the ingredients for a successful speech needed to be different.

The relatively small number of extant speeches available to us where one of the litigants, or a significant actor in the development of the case, was a woman is barely sufficient to provide us with enough information to build a frame of reference for a better understanding of fragmentary evidence from speeches which have not survived intact. Nonetheless, they allow us some glimpses into positive or negative gender stereotypes about Athenian women, and the ways the orators put them to good use in court. They tell us what techniques the orators used, what they were trying to accomplish, and what kind of ingredients they considered necessary to build up a successful case involving a woman. The unambiguously positive portrayal of his mother by Demosthenes in the epitropic speeches, the spirited widow of Diodotos (Lys. 32), the prudent wife of Polueuktos (D. 41), the loyal wife of Menekles (Is. 2), the trustworthy wife of Euphiletos before her fall from grace (Lys. 1), the proud, dignified wife of Alcibiades (And. 4), the faithful old servant who pays for her loyalty with her life (D. 47), or the virtuous Olynthian woman (D. 19, Aesch. 2 and Dinarchus, *In Demosthenem*) all provide strong, positive examples of feminine virtue in a broad array of settings, and inform us about positive social norms and paradigms which an orator could safely use in a public forum such as the court if he wished to build a positive portrayal of a woman. Conversely, memorable villains like Neaira, or her alleged daughter Phano (D. 59), the ruthless and devious Plangon (D. 39 and 40), the murderous stepmother (Ant. 1), the frightening witch Theoris (D. 25), the crafty and deceitful Antigona, ever ready to take advantage of a man blinded by erotic passion (Hyp. *Against Athenogenes*), or the fickle prostitute/concubine in the middle of the quarrel in Lysias 4 allow us insight into those negative characteristics which were expected to prejudice a jury against a woman.

These insights can be enriched by images of women in other literary genres, as well as artistic representations of women in contemporary vase iconography. The ideal wife of Ischomachos in Xenophon's *Oeconomicus* is a prime example of what Athenian society considered to be the perfect wife, as her character and identity have been constructed with all the virtues vested by society in the model wife and mother. The real woman behind her was as flawed as any human being, if not actually more than average, as the text of Andocides indicates.[2] However, the fictional wife comes across as that living, breathing incarnation of the ideal woman, and even when she has some flaws, like feminine vanity, these are venial and not unexpected of her sex. The heroines of the dramatic stage also offer lucid paradigms of feminine virtue and vice, and even when the characters of heroines are constructed with considerable ambiguity, the audience should still have been able to identify their positive and negative traits. Speculating whether an Athenian audience would consider the stubborn resistance to authority and unyielding determination of Antigone to be a positive or negative trait is impossible to answer conclusively, and certainly beyond our purposes here, but we can cross-reference social norms and attitudes as expressed in the play with those expressed in the works of the Attic orators, and perhaps reach some useful conclusions on what an average Athenian audience was willing to accept as proper feminine behaviour. Of course, extreme caution is required when we propose that fictional standards and stereotypes are reflections of true social norms. Antigone, Andromache, Alcestis or Lysistrata may have some traits of real Athenian women, but they are not and could never be real, because real people are far more complex, random and unpredictable in their behavioural patterns than schematic literary constructs. Nonetheless, such comparisons can be informative and enriching for our understanding of the building materials which the orators were employing in order to construct the identities and characters of the women featuring in their speeches.

Likewise, artistic representations of women pose their own challenges, and typically interpretations of images rely on context provided by literary sources.[3] All the same, the immediate message of an image has an inherent value of its own. For example, we do know from literary sources that for women religion was the primary area which allowed them to express their identity as citizens and members of society, and this is why it was important to them, and their role in state religion was extensive and significant. However, when we see countless images in Attic vase iconography depicting women engaging in cultic roles and rituals, these images drive the message home, unambiguously stating that Athenian society understood the involvement of women in religious affairs to be of great importance and an inextricable part of their identity as citizens, wives, mothers and daughters.[4] Thus, we should not be surprised to see that the number of women prosecuted for religious offences is disproportionately high, when compared with the overall number of other prosecutions of women.

Constructing social norms on the basis of literary and material evidence would be a massive task which far exceeds our purposes here. Our goal is much more modest: we must try to understand why the orators used certain building materials in the construction of the characters and identities of the women appearing in their speeches, what they were trying to do with these materials, and how they believed that they could influence the vote of the jury by doing so. In order to accomplish this we need to consult the extant speeches and other literary and material resources, so as to be able to form a clearer idea of the function of these elements in speeches involving women and the tools employed by the orators, and, on the whole, of the processes behind the building of cases involving female litigants.[5]

THE DUTIFUL WIFE AND MOTHER

The central importance of the perception of women as wives and mothers is affirmed in several speeches and numerous other sources. It is no surprise that Athenian society perceived the primary duty of women to be their role as wives and mothers. However, what is rather surprising is how Athenian society understood that this important function is best fulfilled. The literature of the 1980s portrayed Athenian women as victims of history, silenced, muted and pushed away into the margins of society, in dark, secluded quarters (γυναικωνῖτις), to lead an uninteresting existence marked, in an apparent contradiction, simultaneously by a mighty sense of duty and a distinct lack of a higher purpose in life, all at the same time. For generations of scholars educated to believe in this muted and marginalised role for Athenian women, it may come as a surprise to see that positive characters of Athenian mothers and wives in the speeches of the Attic orators tend to be anything but muted and compliant. Quite the opposite: these women are portrayed as strong characters, with an unyielding sense of duty and responsibility towards children, family and property, stamina and courage, intelligence, loyalty, proud dignity, zeal and ability in the performance of their duties, and the determination not only to stand as a faithful guardian of the affairs and fortunes of the household, but more importantly to stand up and fight for what was right, sometimes with the ferocity of a lioness protecting her cubs. More to the point, it appears that other literary genres actually support this perception with plentiful examples.

The quintessential paradigm of a fierce wife and mother fighting for the rights and well-being of her children is the daughter of Diogeiton in Lysias 32.[6] Her relationship with the man against whom she is fighting with such resolve is complex, because he is her own father, and also the brother of her husband, while the children whom Diogeiton was allegedly depriving of their inheritance were at the same time his own grandchildren and also his nephews and nieces. The family history briefly is that Diogeiton gave his only daughter as a wife to his brother Diodotos, and the wealth of the latter from successful business investments may have had something to do with this arrangement. Diodotos before going away on a military campaign made a will, leaving large amounts of money to his family, and appointing his brother as the guardian of the children, if he happened to be killed in battle. When Diodotos did not return Diogeiton took over the property and years later he told the elder son of Diodotos, who had reached adulthood, that their father had left a very modest sum of money for them.[7] The distraught children of Diodotos turned to their mother and asked her to intervene and safeguard their property rights. Her reaction was explosively confrontational, as well as methodical, and Kenneth Walters has rightly interpreted it as evidence of the power women could have within the household.[8] She did not beg, plead and have a quiet word with her father; instead, she set out to expose and embarrass him before the entire wider family. She called a family council, where we are told that she addressed her father with great eloquence, quoted facts and figures, and accused him openly of putting money above family.[9]

The daughter of Diogeiton courageously challenged her father on the basis of facts and numbers. There was no response to her compelling speech; only stony silence, as family members clearly did not want a direct confrontation with

Diogeiton during the meeting, but were also taken aback by the allegations. It is interesting to see that the second husband of the spirited widow stayed aloof throughout all this. Maybe he disagreed with his wife's strategy or, more likely, he did not wish to get into the midst of an angry fight between Diogeiton and his daughter for a matter that did not concern him directly. Either way, it is clear that his wife acted on her own accord, and possibly against his wishes, in order to defend the financial interests of her children. The fact that he was not involved in subsequent litigation and stood aside, leaving it to the husband of Diodotos' daughter to take over the case and bring it to court, probably indicates that he was not supportive of the actions of his wife. But we get the impression that no one or nothing could stop the daughter of Diogeiton from holding her father accountable, not even her husband's disapproval and refusal to get involved. What is more interesting is that this disobedient, relentless, fierce woman is portrayed as an unambiguously positive character, a steadfastly virtuous wife and mother who can only be praised for doing the right thing for her family regardless of the cost.

Equally steadfast in her resolve to defend the best interests of her children but less confrontational in her approach was Kleoboule, the mother of Demosthenes. As with the widow of Diodotos, we are repeatedly told that she enjoyed the complete trust of her husband, she was made privy to all arrangements he made in his final days, and she had full and complete knowledge of the finances of the family.[10] Armed with this knowledge she was able to stand up for her children in a series of family meetings and discussions about the proper course of action for the recovery of the estate of Demosthenes senior. Her resolve to protect her children's welfare above all else is praised by her son with the remark that she never remarried but chose lifelong widowhood for the sake of her children.[11] Kleoboule's positive portrayal as a model widow and mother relies on two interwoven concepts: her willingness to put her children above everyone else, even above herself and her own happiness, and her sagacity and prudent understanding of the finances and affairs of the family. In this respect, her portrayal as a positive model of an Athenian woman moves along the same lines as the portrayal of the widow of Diodotos, even if the style of the two women when they act to defend the interests of their children may be significantly different.

Prudent management of the assets of the household and the ability to keep exact records, and earn the trust of the entire family, are also attributed to another remarkable Athenian wife and mother, the wife of Polyeuktos.[12] While her husband was alive, we are told that she enjoyed his complete trust, and that her mere presence was enough for her husband to perform financial transactions without the need for any other witnesses.[13] The two daughters of the family had been given in marriage during the lifetime of their father with *engye*, and clearly had children by the time of his death, so they never became *epikleroi*. Each was offered a generous dowry when she married, and the remainder of the estate, probably the bulk of it, stayed in their father's possession. After his death the widow of Polyeuktos became the effective manager of the family property. She kept exact records of all transactions and, in a move which seems to be ahead of her time, she wrote down everything, especially when she lent money to her sons-in-law. It also seems that loans to her sons-in-law were not interest-free. The meticulous and thorough widow wrote down everything, so that when the time came after her death to distribute the remainder of the estate between the two families, all debts to the estate would have been noted down, and the distribution of the assets would be fair and equitable. If what this savvy woman was trying to accomplish by leaving behind exact written records of all the loans from the estate was to prevent family quarrels, then she seriously underestimated the pettiness and greed of her children and their husbands. The two families ended up in court with disputes which ranged from one's share to funeral expenses to a claim over an entire house. The speaker's unreservedly positive portrayal of the widow is built upon her formidable skills as a manager of the assets of the household, her sense of justice and steadfast refusal to favour one of her children at the expense of the other.

Prudent household management is also the quality for which Euphiletos praises his wife, and explains why he came to trust her with all domestic affairs and relax his careful supervision of her.[14] If there is any truth in his claim that she had an adulterous affair with Eratosthenes, after a persistent pursuit by the latter, surely she had other attractive and endearing qualities about her, to which her rigid and severe husband seems oblivious. He only praises her thriftiness and skill in looking after the household,[15] and for this reason he says that he considered her to be the best wife on earth. This is significant, especially if we take into account how tightly the character of Euphiletos is constructed by Lysias. We can detect certain objectives behind this: Euphiletos is presented as an upright citizen in full control of his intellect, and not subject to passions or emotional manipulation by women. This definition of a good wife by an upright Athenian male would be consonant with the famous expression of Apollodoros that 'we have wives to give us legitimate children and to stand as faithful guardians of our household'.[16] The *Oeconomicus* of Xenophon, which provides a detailed list of the duties and responsibilities of the ideal Athenian wife, also confirms this perception of her as the guardian and manager of the household and its assets.[17] The theme appears too on numerous occasions in Attic drama and is exploited for its plots in many imaginative ways. In the *Ecclesiazusai* such skills are the reason why it is best to entrust the administration of the cash-strapped city to women.[18] Even Klytemestra, before the heinous murder of her husband, puts herself in the role of the faithful and dutiful wife, loyal like a fierce guardian dog (δωμάτων κύνα) in her husband's household, and careful keeper of his property despite the passage of a long period of time since his departure.[19]

Unconditional devotion to her husband, even when he is too old and impotent, and unable to have children, is presented as praiseworthy virtue in the speech of

Isaios 2 *On the Estate of Aristarchos* (6–10). The devoted wife of Menekles is childless, and her husband is well aware that it is his fault. Menekles is presented as a caring husband who loves his wife and wants the best for her. This is why, on his own initiative, he proposes to her brothers that she should be given in marriage to another man with his blessing. They defer the decision to the woman herself, who in the beginning is adamant that she does not wish to leave her husband. It took a while, we are told, and some pressure before she agreed to the divorce and another marriage. In order to make clear to the community that his wife was not to blame for the divorce, Menekles not only participated in her betrothal to her new husband,[20] but also added to her dowry and adopted one of her brothers as his heir. Devotion to the family and a desire to protect the assets of the *oikos* cost the faithful old servant of an Athenian household her life. In a dramatic incident narrated by the speaker in *Against Euergos and Mnesiboulos for False Witness*,[21] two men invaded the house of the speaker to collect a debt, and started taking stuff away and damaging household items. An old servant of the family hid in her bosom a cheap cup from which she was drinking to protect it. As they assaulted her trying to take away the cup, she suffered injuries and died. The speaker praises her for her devotion to the family, which she died trying to protect.

A clear pattern is emerging from such descriptions of women's role in public discourse. Whether citizens or not, the good women of Athens are not praised by their husbands or *kyrioi* for their charm, attractiveness, intelligence, social skills or other such qualities which would be valued in our times, nor for their gentleness, domesticity and meek disposition, but for their ability to be loyal and competent managers of the household and its assets, vigilant watchdogs of the *oikos*, and indomitable defenders of their children, family and interests. Interestingly, nowhere in these positive representations of Athenian women do we encounter praise of women faithful to their husbands, models of modesty, delicate or fragile. Since being faithful to her husband would be an essential condition for the marriage of an Athenian woman to continue, and adulterous liaisons carried severe penalties in the classical period, we can easily understand that marital fidelity was not considered to be an extraordinary virtue to be proud of, but a self-evident and necessary condition for all married women in Athens. However, the rest of the qualities of modesty, fragility and a delicate and timid disposition, which past societies often idealised as the quintessential qualities of feminine virtue, and the literature of the 1980s readily identified with the norm for Athenian women too, were clearly not as valued as one might think. The positive role models of feminine virtue in the Attic orators are all women of action, intelligent, energetic and fiercely protective of their household, children and families.

Respectability was certainly a highly valued quality in a woman, closely entwined with her self-esteem and place in society. However, here again the portrayal of respectable women in the Attic orators has some surprises for us. Of course, the women mentioned above were all very respectable wives and mothers, each one in her own way, but we can see more clearly how respectability was to be understood in those few instances where it was challenged. A very good example of this is a description in the speech *Against Alcibiades*[22] about the reaction of his wife to the mistresses that he was bringing into the family home.[23] The haughty Hipparete was the daughter of Hipponikos, the richest man in Greece, and had been given in marriage to Alcibiades with the massive dowry of ten talents. She was certainly not going to put up with such effrontery. Athenian wives might not have been able to stop their husbands from sleeping around, but they were certainly not expected to put up with such impertinent behaviour as bringing a mistress into the family home. Athenaios points out a sharp difference between oriental cultures, where a wife is expected to put up with her husband's other wives and concubines, and the Greek world, where no wife would put up with this.[24] The conflict which would be created if the husband brought his mistress in the marital home is central to the plot of Sophocles' *Trachiniai*, where the distraught Dieaneira tries to gain back her husband's love with what she believes to be a love-philtre, and, in a scenario which reminds us of the speech of Antiphon *Against the Stepmother*, ends up unwittingly causing the death of Herakles. Hipparete did not try to gain back her husband's love; instead she was determined to divorce him. She abandoned the marital home, heading for the archon to register the divorce, as the law required, but before she got there she was intercepted and taken back home by force. Without the support of her natal family she was running out of options at this point. Regardless of the outcome of her spirited and desperate attempt to divorce the most powerful man in Athens, Hipparete is praised not because she patiently and obediently put up with her husband's indiscretions,[25] but for the exact opposite reason, namely because she had enough self-respect and the courage to walk away from her marriage.

Spirited and courageous also was the reaction of a respectable Olynthian woman to an attempted rape, in an incident which gained Panhellenic notoriety and was discussed for years in assemblies and public fora.[26] The incident took place in Macedonia after the fall of Olynthus and the enslavement of its population by Philip. According to the narrative of several sources, an attractive Olynthian woman was brought into a party, clearly against her wishes, as this alone was compromising her, because according to Greek custom only women of ill repute took part in symposia with men. Aware of her dire circumstances, the unnamed woman was sitting in the corner by herself eating quietly until someone demanded sexual favours. When she refused, she was whipped, and even then she would not compromise her respectability. Instead, she fell at the feet of one of the guests as a suppliant begging for his help, and he removed her from the room. The incident struck a chord with many in the Greek world, and exposed the stark realities of Macedonian power. It underlined the abusive treatment of a Greek city and its population at the hands of Philip, and was undoubtedly a public relations disaster for a savvy political mind who had achieved much in the Greek world not only by force of arms, but equally, if not more, by his skilful diplomatic moves. In Athens the incident about the respectable Olynthian woman was used for political capital in the angry quarrel between Demosthenes and Aeschines over the embassy to Philip. The Olynthian woman is praised for her self-respect and courage in standing up and resisting her rapists, even in the face of relentless whipping and imminent danger to her life. Again, as above, it is not obedience, modesty, feminine impotence and fragility that are idealised, but their exact opposites: strength, integrity, defiance and courageous self-respect.

In the light of this discussion it is unfortunate that we only have so few extant speeches featuring a woman as one of the litigants. Even in those we sometimes have serious challenges, like our attempts to understand how and why such powerful positive stereotypes are centrally important for the build-up of the identity and character of Neaira, while reason alone suggests that they should never have been employed extensively in a prosecution speech. I have noted in a previous study that the portrayal of Neaira is intentionally ambiguous.[27] She is consistently portrayed as a caring mother and grandmother who would not hesitate to go to great lengths in order to protect those she loves, and as a loyal and lovable partner,[28] while at the same time she lacks some of the distinctive qualities which would characterise the negative portrayal of a fourth-century hetaira, like the deceitful treatment of lovers, a money-grabbing and perfidious attitude towards erotic relations and a fickle character. Initially I was convinced that this was accidental, that Apollodoros miscalculated and created a profile which was fundamentally flawed and inconsistent.[29] On second thoughts, in a more recent publication I have argued that this portrayal of Neaira was very much deliberate and calculated for a very specific reason. Apollodoros was not trying to create the image of a ruthless, perfidious hetaira; his tactics were much more refined. The character he was trying to portray was a subtler one, of a woman who was not fundamentally bad, but on the contrary, was a caring mother and, like other positive female characters in the Attic orators, was prepared to do anything necessary to protect her children and family. This was a much more convincing character and explained why this harmless elderly woman who was sitting in the court on that day had broken some important laws of the Athenian state. She had not done it for herself, but for her family, like any good mother. This was the narrative which Apollodoros was pushing, and for this purpose a more ambiguous, if not outright sympathetic portrayal of Neaira was more expedient.

If anything, it is difficult to find negative attributes in the character of Neaira once we accept that even her bad deeds, illegal actions, conspiracies and blackmail were not done out of wickedness, not even out of selfishness, but out of a need to do what was best for her family. This strategy of Apollodoros was certainly bold, and largely responsible for the popularity of the speech through the centuries. By successfully building the identity of a sympathetic woman acting out of desperation, he created a memorable and convincing character which was more likely to be believed. And if the jury believed that this elderly woman before them had done these bad things, it would be much easier to cast a ballot for conviction. Apollodoros suggests that Neaira was a danger to the city, its laws, its institutions and its women not because she was a bad person, but because she was desperate. With this bold and crafty characterisation a positive portrayal was meant to achieve a damning verdict.

THE INDECENT WOMEN OF ATHENS

The Attic orators' works contain several memorable villains, whose characters have been built on a heap of negative stereotypes about women. Neaira's portrait, surprisingly, has been built with relatively few negative stereotypes, as mentioned above, and once we get past the fact that she was a hetaira, and accept that certain behaviours, like taking lovers, partying and dining with strange men, and earning a living with her body, were simply part of the job, there is little else left which would portray her in a bad light. Her alleged daughter Phano is treated much more savagely at the hands of the prosecutor. As soon as the prosecutor comes to her, his first words are an assault on her modesty, propriety and decency as a wife. We are told that she was not well behaved (51: οὔτε κοσμίαν οὖσαν), that she was argumentative and disobedient (51: οὔτ' ἐθέλουσαν αὐτοῦ ἀκροᾶσθαι), extravagant and unaccustomed to good household economy (50: ὡς δ' ἦλθεν ὡς τὸν Φράστορα, ἄνδρα ἐργάτην καὶ ἀκριβῶς τὸν βίον συνειλεγμένον, οὐκ ἠπίστατο τοῖς τοῦ Φράστορος τρόποις ἀρέσκειν), while her morals were questionable and more fitting for a hetaira, like her (alleged) mother's (50: ἀλλ' ἐζήτει τὰ τῆς μητρὸς ἔθη καὶ τὴν παρ' αὐτῇ ἀκολασίαν, ἐν τοιαύτῃ οἶμαι ἐξουσίᾳ τεθραμμένη). After this damning account the listener should not be surprised to hear that her husband divorced her, and moreover, he did so while she was pregnant. Of course, it is possible that he did not know about the pregnancy when he divorced her. This and many other facts in the prosecutor's account are highly questionable, but this is beside the point. An Athenian jury was expected to understand that her husband divorced Phano while she was pregnant, among other things, on account of her many negative traits, and this helps us understand which behaviours Athenian public opinion considered to be inappropriate and unacceptable for a married woman.

What follows about Phano is much worse: not only does Apollodoros accuse her of being an unsuitable wife, but he also alleges that she engaged in actions which Athenian society would find utterly inexcusable for any woman. First, she manipulated her former husband to acknowledge the son that she had borne, taking advantage of her husband's infirmity when he was seriously ill. Thus an act of kindness, in which Phano and Neaira went out of their way to nurse back to health a man who had treated Phano very badly, is distorted into a wicked plot, intended to manipulate an upright, but currently vulnerable, Athenian citizen into acknowledging an alien child as his own legitimate son. That this was not the case, and that Phrastor cared for his son and was prepared to go to any lengths to defend his legitimacy, was proven by subsequent litigation.[30] But even more was to come in this salacious tale of adultery, prostitution, deceit, entrapment and blackmail, and Phano and her family are presented as guilty of all these grave offences.

Apollodoros does not seem to have any particular difficulty with glaring contradictions, if the objective of portraying Phano in a very negative light can be handily achieved. He does not hesitate to imply that Phano was both a prostitute and an adulteress, and that she should be punished as an adulteress,[31] even though he quotes the law which clearly excluded prostitutes from the force of the adultery laws.[32] On the one hand, he maintains that her family was prostituting her, but on the other hand he invokes the adultery laws, suggesting that this unhappy divorcee consented to the lavish attentions of an older man. But these two were mutually exclusive in Athenian law. A woman who was prostituted was automatically excluded from the force of the adultery laws (*moicheia*), even if she had consented to the affair. Apollodoros wants to have it both ways; he wants to heap upon the unfortunate woman every negative stereotype he can think, and if the two worse things one can say in order to demean a woman are that she was a whore and an adulteress, he has no qualms about using both with no regard for conceptual contradictions or legal impediments.

Similar building blocks have been used for the profoundly unflattering portrait of another famous villain in the world of the Attic orators, that of Plangon the daughter of Pamphilos.[33] She features in two speeches delivered by Manthitheos, the son of her former husband Mantias with another woman, against her own son by Mantias, also called Mantitheos or Boiotos (D. 39 and 40). She is only mentioned in a cursory manner in the first speech, where the centre of attention is her elder son. His half-brother is arguing that the original name of the elder son of Plangon was Boiotos, not Mantitheos, but of course this is a deceptively simplistic presentation of the dispute. The angry and protracted quarrel among the sons of Mantias was very much about property, inheritance and legitimacy, and this becomes much clearer in the second speech (D. 40), the one concerning the return of Plangon's dowry. It appears that after the failure of the first speech in court, Mantitheos hired another speechwriter who was far less delicate towards the mother of his opponent. The writer of the second speech uses very different tactics: he makes Plangon the centrepiece of the entire speech, and presents her in the most unflattering manner, disrespectfully calling her by her first name eight times, which in itself would be inappropriate for an elderly, respectable Athenian woman, but suitable for a hetaira. Although he stops short of calling her a whore, he attributes to her behaviours which an Athenian jury would readily identify with a hetaira, such as extravagance, haughtiness, lustful conduct, hedonism, a series of relationships with other men, argumentative behaviour, untrustworthiness, ruthlessness and selfishness.

The message which Mantitheos tries to convey to the jury is unmistakable: Plangon had used her exquisite looks to manipulate his father, she used sex as a weapon to entrap him and squeeze as much money as she could out of him, and in the end she succeeded in her ploy to pass off her illegitimate brood as his own children, and by publicly shaming and blackmailing him she compelled him to recognise them as his own sons. This was typical behaviour for a hetaira, but certainly not for a respectable Athenian woman. Mantitheos' strategy may be even more underhanded, and quite possibly he was deliberately trying to create a confusion of identities with the famous contemporary hetaira Plangon of Miletus. Members of the jury who might have heard stories about the famous hetaira, but did not know who she was, could have confused her with Plangon the daughter of Pamphilos, and readily accepted the supposition of Mantitheos that she was a hetaira.

In the case of Plangon, gender stereotypes are used as a weapon to tarnish the reputation of a woman who was instrumental for the understanding of the entire dispute. If the underhanded tactics of Mantitheos proved successful, and he effectively implanted in the minds of the judges the image of Plangon the hetaira, his path to victory would be open. His argument that Plangon did not bring a dowry with her would be won by default, because hetairai did not get married with dowries as respectable women did.

We cannot tell for sure whether there is any substance behind such allegations. In a previous publication I have argued that Plangon matches the profile of a citizen woman who may have taken lovers.[34] She was very attractive, brought up in an affluent household and accustomed to a certain lifestyle, and if there is any truth in Mantitheos' description, she was spirited and sufficiently assertive to do something about her changed circumstances, when she found herself divorced and penniless, living with her impoverished brothers after the confiscation of her father's estate, and saddled with two young children whose father did not even want to recognise them as his own. The lifestyle changes which Plangon would need to face after her divorce from Mantias and the bankruptcy of her own family would be rather extreme, and we can understand why she might be pushed by circumstances to capitalise on the only marketable commodity which could provide for her entire family, namely her looks. This is a possibility but there is no certainty, and regardless of the actions of the real Plangon, her accuser has employed an array of negative gender stereotypes in order to win a property dispute which otherwise might have been very difficult to win on its merits.

It seems very likely that Plangon had at some point married Mantias, and if any witnesses to the *engye* were still alive and prepared to testify, Mantitheos would have had an uphill task trying to prove that the daughter of a rich Athenian man, as

Plangon was at the time of her marriage to Mantias, came into his affluent household without a dowry. Mantitheos is aware of the huge difficulties he is facing, and chooses a strategy which does not involve a direct confrontation on the merits of the case with his half-brothers. Instead, by trying to discredit their mother through the employment of negative gender stereotypes, and establish for her the identity of an Athenian hetaira, he hopes to win by default. If the jury believed Mantitheos and accepted that Plangon was a hetaira, then it would be much easier to believe that she had come to his father without a dowry as an *eromene*, a paramour in a relationship based on lust.

A similar strategy appears to be followed by Hypereides in the second speech against Aristagora, if my understanding of her case is correct. I believe that Hypereides, after an unsuccessful attempt to secure a conviction for immigration offences, reopened the case against her using the *graphe doroxenias*, namely alleging that she had been acquitted in the first trial through bribery.[35] His ultimate objective was to exact vengeance on a former mistress after their relationship went sour, and this is why he did not hesitate to use any means necessary to secure her conviction in the second trial. A few citations from the two speeches in later grammarians and lexicographers are all that remain. They suggest two vectors of assault, both directly related to the gender of the accused. Clearly the fact that she had been a hetaira played a very important role in her prosecution. We have evidence of nostalgic references to past beauties, famous hetairai who had reached their floruit at the turn of the century. These past beauties were seemingly contrasted with contemporaries of Aristagora. The argument appears to be that unlike those legendary women of the past, Aristagora and her cronies were down-market, disreputable and disgusting. We have the testimony of Athenaios that Hypereides used slanderous language (κακηγορεῖν) against these women. He plausibly staged an attack reminiscent of the assault against Plangon, using negative gender stereotypes, evoking unflattering images of prostitution, and warning of the dangers for men who associated with such women.

More explicit and distasteful in the eyes of rhetoricians and lexicographers of later antiquity were the references to low-end prostitution which Hypereides employed in the speech *To Timandra*. An orator who has been much admired through the ages for his elegance and refined style surely did not need to resort to such tactics unless he believed that they were brutally effective. The shock factor from references to items which most members of the jury would recognise as paraphernalia commonly found in brothels, such as the cheap straw mat covers which could be changed after each client (ψίεθος), or the small washing basins which could be used for localised clean-ups before or after intercourse (λεκανίς), would greatly contribute towards capturing the attention of a jury. Even less ambiguous references to dildos, undoubtedly beyond the pale of polite discourse, were intended to provoke a reaction and generate strong emotional responses towards the accused, even if their actual connection to the charges at hand were at best tenuous. We can be certain that Hypereides did not parade such explicit and distasteful images before the eyes of the judges because they were central to the argument; he did so because by shocking the judges he expected that he could strongly prejudice them against the filthy woman that was standing before them.

Degrading images of prostitution intended to generate prejudice and hostility towards defendants who had been hetairai in their youth, even if this was thirty or forty years in the past, are also attested elsewhere in the Attic orators. In Lysias 4 it appears that part of the strategy was to generate hostility towards the woman who was at the centre of the quarrel between the two litigants. This ugly quarrel ended up in court under the serious charges of deliberate wounding (*trauma ek pronoias*), which could result in permanent exile for the defendant. His core strategy was to reduce the woman in question to a mere sex toy, a commodity worthy of some money, but no respect or affection. In reality, she was probably an expensive hetaira, whom the two men had shared, each paying half the price for her, as Eukrates and Timanoridas had shared Neaira. However, while Neaira's lovers succeeded in keeping the entire affair amicable and parted on good terms, the two unnamed men in Lysias 4 fought over the woman, and the one who lost in love seemingly attacked his rival and injured him. Instead of responding to the charges directly, and maybe turning his attention to his rival, he focuses upon the woman, pinning the entire quarrel on her, disparaging her as an unworthy sexual commodity, eventually calling her 'a slave and a whore' (πόρνην καὶ δούλην ἄνθρωπον). The alien female prostitute was a much easier victim than a rival male citizen, and easy prey for disparaging comments intended to create a negative portrait , shift the blame away from the attacker to the woman at the heart of the rivalry, and secure the acquittal of the defendant. He was hoping that the judges would share his opinion that a lowly slave whore was not worth the exile of a citizen man.

The speech *Against Neaira* goes even further with degrading images of the two women, Neaira and her alleged daughter, and contains several scandalising descriptions of explicit and unbridled sexuality, which is used as a weapon of character assassination. The cryptic language which Apollodoros is using in order to convey the idea that an underage Neaira, not much older than twelve or thirteen, was offering anal intercourse to clients is echoed with fewer restraints in the narrative of Procopius about an underage Theodora.[36] Procopius also exaggerates to a level of absurdity another famous incident where Apollodoros first says that Neaira was forced to have intercourse with her lover Phrynion in public with his friends watching, and then that in a state of semi-consciousness she was raped by a number of men including some servants.[37] As if this were not bad enough, Procopius augments the story, echoing the passage in the *Anecdota* with his Theodora in the starring role. Only his Theodora is not the drunken victim of a rape scene; she is an aggressive sexual predator who not only consents to but also actively pursues sex with large numbers of robust young men. Sophronios of Jerusalem pushes the, by his time, thousand-year-old motif of the sexually insatiable woman, which Apollodoros started, to further absurdity in his *Vita of St. Mary of Egypt* (18–21), with Mary aggressively having intercourse with an entire boatload of sailors.

The sexual indiscretions of Neaira are brought to a climax in the brief argumentation of the speech, where the jury is told that she had plied her trade in every corner of the Greek world with a large number of men. This is where I have argued that we should reinstate in the text the phrase 'she was working with her body from three holes', which later antique rhetoricians found so offensive that they deleted it from the text, leaving Hermogenes as the only witness to its presence. It is unlikely that Hermogenes would have invented something so explicit and specific if it had not been there in the first place, while it is more believable that such a shocking phrase would have been intentionally omitted. An explicit reference to a prostitute who would offer her clients vaginal, oral and anal sex was a fitting climax to the sordid tale that Apollodoros had been telling the judges that afternoon, and probably startled the members of the jury, leaving a lasting impression and a vivid memory of the distasteful deeds of the accused in her younger days.[38]

Even though the story of Neaira has shocked and titillated audiences through the centuries, such distasteful tales of sexual depravity were by no means rare in Athenian trials. John Tzetzes reports that Dionysios of Halicarnassus mentioned a speech of Lysias, where it was said that the hetaira Antiope had intercourse with her clients from two holes (vaginal and anal).[39] An epigram in the Palatine anthology also preserves a memory of that literary theme.[40] Such references suggest that more shockingly explicit passages could be found in the works of the Attic orators. Dionysios Halicarnasseus in fact mentions that he had written an entire study containing such distasteful constructions (ἀηδεῖς κατασκευαί), of which no trace has survived.[41] The purpose of such themes was to influence the judgement of juries through the deployment of stereotypes. While it is widely understood that stereotypes are inaccurate indicators in almost any situation, yet they form a universal language which all members of a certain community can easily understand. The stereotypes of the unfaithful woman, the filthy whore or the lustful female with insatiable appetites were shared concepts among the members of the jury; the judges understood such categories and formed their opinions accordingly when prompted by skilled orators to think along these lines.

THE POISONER AND THE WITCH

The assault against Aristagora contained another vector of attack which we also encounter in the prosecution of Theoris of Lemnos, and quite possibly of other women accused of religious offences. The theme of mysterious and magical powers in the hands of women, who had the ability to do miraculous deeds, and also inflict a great deal of damage and pain on unsuspecting men, had been repeatedly dramatised on the Attic stage in plays like the *Medea* and the *Bacchae* of Euripides or the *Trachiniai* of Sophocles. Women had the power to set their enemies on fire with an object like a dress cursed with magical powers, as Medea does with Kreon and his daughter Kreousa. They also had the potential to inflict enormous suffering on the unfortunate men with whom they were in love, sometimes on purpose, as Medea does with Jason, and sometimes unwittingly, as Dieaneira does with Herakles. Crafty orators like Demosthenes and Hypereides had transformed the fantasy of the plays into credible, realistic narratives in court settings aimed at women who were supposed to possess apocryphal and dangerous skills with philtres, potions and magic spells. From the early days of Attic oratory, Antiphon had built on the theme of the poisonous love-philtre which killed the father of the speaker and his friend Philoneos in the speech *Against the Stepmother*, and presented the stepmother as a plotting Klytemestra who used sneaky tactics and poisons to kill her husband. Although the extant references to the magical skills of Aristagora, especially her ability with poisons and philtres (φάρμακα), amount to nothing more than a couple of sentences, they are sufficient to paint part of the picture. The prosecutor of Aristagora alleged that she was an expert in love-philtres, and that she was harvesting the venom of spiders for her poisons. We do not know whether there was any truth in such allegations about expert pharmacological knowledge, but we can understand that regardless of any truth a very distorted image of Aristagora's mysterious powers and skills was presented in court. Very probably her prosecutor tried to present her as a dangerous woman, a killer and seducer of men who could not defend themselves against the invisible dangers from her evil and sneaky crafts.

Demosthenes implies that he used similar arguments in his prosecution of Theoris of Lemnos. Although the references to the case are very limited, it appears that the prosecutor of Theoris painted a dangerous woman in many aspects. First, he presented her as a fake healer who made false promises to persons suffering from epilepsy that she could heal them with spells and magic. Theoris seemingly had a large arsenal of philtres, drugs and potions, which after her execution were passed on by her maid to the twin brother of Aristoteiton, and he continued her work. Then, we are told that she engaged in subversive activities, teaching slaves how to deceive their masters. Although the evidence in our hands is limited we can extrapolate that the prosecutor of Theoris successfully painted the portrait of a very dangerous woman, expert in deceit, willing to take advantage of vulnerable people, capable of causing much harm through her potions and philtres, quite possibly someone in possession of arcane skills, and also someone with no respect for established social norms. Esther Eidinow is correct in her assessment that Theoris was not prosecuted as a witch, as we would understand such prosecutions in the Christian era.[42] She was portrayed as a danger to society in more than one ways, a living, breathing Medea.

If she had been a medical man or a trained midwife tending to a broad array of female healthcare needs, it would have been much harder to mount an assault on her on account of her craft. The Greeks respected their health professionals, male and female, and were prepared to submit to their sometimes strange, painful and bizarre treatments. Theoris' vulnerability has more to do with the fact that she was moving in a grey area beyond the boundaries of established medical practice. She was a healer in a much broader sense and this allowed her craft and practices to be interpreted as dangerous witchcraft of the kind that can surreptitiously cause harm to unsuspecting victims, while her *pharmaka* would be presented not as healing and life-giving potions but as malicious, harmful and sometimes even life-taking venoms. Ultimately Theoris was punished not because she lacked the skills of a healer, but because the jury believed her accuser when he argued that her skills with *pharmaka* were used to serve destructive purposes. It may be noteworthy that there was a healthy market for her treatments and cures even after her death, taken over by the twin brother of Aristogeiton, which may suggest that her contemporaries were upset with the woman herself and her overall conduct, and not necessarily with her treatments. We have insufficient evidence to pursue this point further, but perhaps in this instance misogyny did play a major part in her conviction.

The successful prosecution of the priestess Ninos introduced by Menekles is more of a puzzle. The scholiast of Demosthenes suggests that she was also accused of witchcraft, but there is a strong possibility hat this note was composed with the case of Theoris in mind.[43] Unlike the latter, Ninos was a citizen woman, and we have no evidence linking her with any form of magic, witchcraft or unorthodox religious practices. We do, however, have reliable evidence suggesting that Ninos, like Neaira, found herself caught up in the angry quarrels and sycophantic activities of men close to her. On the one hand we have the prosecutor of Ninos, Menekles, a low-ranking sycophant ready to spread lies and misinformation for profit, and on the other hand we have the son of Ninos prosecuting Menekles, probably as an act of revenge for the conviction of his mother. It is quite possible that Ninos had been caught up in some angry quarrel between the two men, as Neaira was caught up in the quarrel between Stephanos and Apollodoros. If this was the case, then Ninos, like Neaira, faced mortal danger on trumped-up charges, and unfortunately for her, she was convicted. How this could happen and what Menekles said against her is unclear, but the possibility that he used similar arguments to those used against other women accused of impiety, namely that she was a dangerous woman with potent arcane skills, and that she was subverting the religion of the Olympian gods with her practices, remains distinct.

Contrary to the widespread belief that the Greeks understood their women as more vulnerable and more fragile than men, and that in fact they idealised that fragility, these images suggest that stereotypes of strong, intimidating women and vulnerable, fragile men were sufficiently prevalent and widespread to convince juries that some women posed a mortal danger not only to the men who came in contact with them but to the entire city and its institutions. It could be argued that these women were exceptional, oddities in the order of things, and this is why they were put to death. However, unless they embodied the fears and anxieties of an entire society about the secret weapons and mystic powers of women and their ability to harm men, they would probably have escaped conviction, because the evidence against these women, by the look of it, was typically exaggerated and largely fictional. The question was not whether these women had upset the often arcane and inconsistent rules of traditional Greek religion, but whether they could be represented as a threat to society on account of this. In order to accomplish this, prosecutors stoked up fears and anxieties about the apocryphal powers of these women and suggested to their audiences that they could actually harm them.

IMAGES OF THE BODY AND SEXUALITY

Body images employed for the purposes of persuasion are not uncommon in the Attic orators.[44] The speech *Against Timarchos* contains some shocking body images through which Aeschines is trying to drive through the point that the young Timarchos abused the fabulous looks of his youth, while the body of the ageing Timarchos looked disgusting from many years of excesses. Nudity is mentioned in several episodes from the speech, such as an incident where Timarchos dropped (partially) his garment while giving an animated speech in the assembly, revealing the deterioration of his physical condition due to chronic abuse of drink and other excesses, or the episode where Pittalakos after a physical assault took refuge naked at the altar of the Twelve Gods. While the middle-aged Timarchos was criticised for the deterioration of his body, Lykophron was criticised by Lykourgos, in the *eisangelia* which Ariston brought against him, for exactly the opposite reason, namely because in his fifties he was still in splendid physical form, and still capable of seducing scores of women, according to his accusers.[45] It seems that one could not win; a determined prosecutor would find fault with a fit or an unfit body, as suited his purposes. The seductive appearance of the young Eratosthenes is presented as proof that he was a serial seducer of women, but Mantitheos takes pride in his great physique and clean lifestyle. What these images have in common is that they are memorable. The purpose of this ἐνάργεια is to establish carefully selected scenes and episodes firmly in the minds of the judges, to eroticise the events and evoke subconscious emotional responses.

GENDER AS A FACTOR IN THE CONSTRUCTION OF THE ARGUMENT 173

Sexuality always carries a charge of its own, and the Attic orators expertly put it to work for them.

Images of the body are particularly prevalent in cases involving women, undoubtedly because of their powerful potential for lasting impact upon members of the jury. The most memorable is certainly the narrative reported in later antique authors where the hetaira Phryne was paraded nude in front of a jury in an attempt to save her life when her defender Hypereides sensed that she was about to be convicted and sentenced to death. The details and controversy surrounding this episode are discussed elsewhere in this volume, but the possibility of a defendant stripped naked in court, however remote, is intriguing.[46] Such a direct and unexpected visual stunt, intended to shock, surprise and maybe even upset the judges, rather than arouse pity and sympathy, as some of our sources claim, could have succeeded on account of the fact that it was unprecedented, but certainly it was not the kind of behaviour that could be replicated often before Athenian juries, for if it had been we would certainly have known about it from many classical sources. We should therefore consider the Phryne episode, if it ever happened, to be nothing more than an aggressive and surprising tactic.

Images of the female body, on the other hand, were routinely evoked in the narratives of Athenian litigants. Even in cases where we would not expect to find lewd images of female sexuality, as for example the murder trial of the stepmother in Antiphon 1, there are some overt references to sexual desire and love-philtres intended to enhance it: the easy availability of the body of the slave concubine to her master, brothels and the low end of the sex markets. Finally there is a vivid image of the body of the slave concubine being tortured before she was handed over to the executioner. The speech *Against Neaira* also contains some very explicit images of the female body and sexuality. Almost from the outset of the narrative we have circumspect language implying, as I have suggested elsewhere, that a twelve-year-old Neaira was having anal intercourse with paying customers, under the watchful eye of her procuress Nikarete, thus making her body available before she was mature enough to take clients of her own.[47] The shocking image of an underage child violated by a succession of lustful men would surely have left a very strong impression upon the jury.

The saga continues with references to several rich and influential men who paid for the privilege of enjoying Neaira's body. Even when they are portrayed as thoughtful and caring, like Eukrates and Timanoridas, the two men who bought Neaira from Nikarete and then allowed her to gain her freedom, they still treat her body as a commodity to be shared for pleasure. So did the two men who seemingly loved Neaira, Phrynion and Stephanos. While it is clear that both men had strong feelings for her, it is also implied that to them she was a trophy to be possessed at a high price. Apollodoros argues that Stephanos continued to view her as an asset and a moneymaker for the whole family through the work of her body, but this is probably untrue. The facts of the case suggest that once the quarrel with Phrynion was over, the couple went on to live together in a devoted relationship for the next thirty years until the time of the trial. The most shocking episode in the entire speech is the gang rape of Neaira at a party, first by Phrynion, who has intercourse with her while the guests are watching, we are told, as a demonstration of his power over her. Then, while drunk and incapacitated, she is raped by several of the guests and even some of the servants. The entire sleazy episode, as narrated by Apollodoros, was adapted and repeated by other authors in later centuries, giving rise to a literary theme of unbridled female sexuality with a lifespan of over a thousand years.[48]

Fragmentary speeches also suggest a similar pattern, even though the actual evidence is scant. The obvious candidate, the case against Phryne, actually offers no solid evidence that either Euthias, the prosecutor, or Hypereides, her defender, made any references to her body in their speeches. The evidence that we have about her undressing in court is much later, and could be unreliable. The fact remains that in the actual fragments from the speeches of Euthias and Hypereides, as these are preserved by later grammarians and rhetoricians, there are no references to her body or nudity, and the most salacious allegations in these extracts are that she held a party at the Lycaeum, and that she was a bad influence on young men. The speeches against Aristagora also do not yield any direct clues that her prosecutor used body images, to shock, shame and vituperate, but we do have some peripheral references which may suggest the presence of the theme. First there is mention of two sisters, both hetairai, who had been nicknamed Aphyai (the Sardines) because of their appearance. We're told that they were skinny and pale with large dark eyes, hence the nickname. These women were contemporaries of Aristagora, and the unflattering reference suggests that they were body-shamed for their appearance and, as suggested above, contrasted with true beauties of the past like Lais, Okimon and Metaneira. A logical extrapolation of these observations would be to assume that Hypereides was body-shaming Aristagora too, along with the other women, perhaps arguing that her skills with drugs and potions were compensating for her lack of true beauty, and that she was a dangerous woman because she did not really attract lovers with her grace, but entrapped them with her drugs. The theme of past beauties also appeared in the speech of Lysias *To Lais*, where we are told that several famous hetairai who flourished around the turn of the century gave up prostitution at a young age. Conceivably the orator was contrasting them with Lais, who, if we believe that there is some truth in an obviously exaggerated joke by Philetairos, continued to practise prostitution down to her old age.[49]

The seductive appearance of Plangon in the second speech *To Boiotos* (D. 40) is used as a weapon against her. By emphasising how attractive she was, and how she made his father fall madly in love with her, Mantitheos successfully builds the portrait of a hetaira without actually risking the use of the word for his opponent's mother, as this might backfire. If he could subliminally suggest to the jury that Plangon was a hetaira, and consequently she could not be a wife, then the whole issue of her dowry, which is at the centre of the lawsuit, would be rendered meaningless.

The speech *To Timandra* also suggests that the theme of female bodies and sexuality was exploited in a series of images of brothel sex on cheap straw mats, with objects like dildos and washing bowls lying about. Refined establishments like that of Theodote in Xenophon's *Memorabilia* would never leave such objects lying about in public view.[50] This passage suggests that all this filthy talk about prostitutes (δυσφημία ἑταιρῶν) in the courtroom was sufficiently sensational to attract the attention of Demetrius, and could have had a substantial impact upon the jury.[51]

Images of female bodies and overt sexuality are included in speeches involving female litigants with sufficient frequency to suggest intent. An obvious purpose would be to excite and titillate male juries, and by doing so to grab the attention and keep the interest of the judges. One could imagine that vivid images like the ones bringing to life low-end brothels, with which most members of the jury would have been familiar at least in their younger days, could be burned into the minds of jurors, and have a more lasting impact upon their final decision to vote for acquittal or conviction than any rational argument presented before them. Such images of raw sexuality can leave a lasting impression and pass subliminal messages, like an association of a high-end hetaira like Timandra with cheap brothels. We do not have enough context for this passage to be able to say what exactly was said in this instance, but if indeed such references were directly related to Timandra, the orator was conceivably trying to say that she was nothing more than a common whore making her body available to anyone for a small fee, just as Apollodoros says about Neaira in his argumentation. If indeed this was his purpose those images would have done the job effectively, making it difficult for the defender of Timandra to counter them, especially because he would not have been responding to arguments and words, but instead trying to counter and erase entrenched subliminal messages, assuming that he was savvy enough to detect the sneaky tricks and tactics of the opposition. How does one counter subliminal images of brothels and cheap prostitutes? Rhetoric manuals in circulation in the fourth century would have left someone unprepared to counter such tactics, and the skilled litigators who composed these speeches were aware of the power and lasting effects of sexual imagery.

A WOMAN WITH A PAST

If we studied the formal accusations and the content of the speeches in most cases involving women we would easily notice remarkable digressions. On many occasions it is as if the speeches are not explaining or answering the charges, but are talking about other, irrelevant topics, and frequently about events which took place many years before the trial. Some scholars have considered such arguments to be irrelevant and extrajudicial, but others have argued that they form an integral part of the presentation of the case.[52] A full discussion of this subject far exceeds our purposes here, but I am convinced that the orators were building up their cases along these lines because it was expedient and helped them win trials. Justice systems around the world in our times take into account the criminal record of defendants and judge them on the basis of past as well as present infractions, because it is thought that past behavioural patterns can be relevant for understanding the facts of the case.[53] The Athenians did not keep criminal records, but nonetheless considered someone's past conduct to be relevant, and relied on memory, individual and collective, to furnish them with the necessary evidence about someone's past behaviour. This would make it easier to gather relevant material for men, who had a continuous presence in public life, but very difficult for ordinary women, who had a limited footprint outside the bounds of their home and immediate community.

It seems that when it comes to the past conduct of respectable Athenian women any evidence tends to come from family members, and it is much more controlled than it would have been if it came from third parties. For example, all we know about the past conduct of the wife of Euphiletos comes from her former husband, and without a doubt he only shares information which serves his purposes. When he informs us that she possessed formidable housekeeping skills, he does not do so in order to praise her, but in order to explain his own conduct, namely the reasons why he was not keeping a closer eye on her actions. Another good example would be the praise which the speaker heaps upon the smart, dutiful and competent wife of Polyeuktos. By explaining in some detail how in the past and for a long time she had been the most vigilant and trustworthy guardian of the finances of the household, the speaker only wants to strengthen his own claims on part of the estate.

On the other hand, in the one instance where we would have expected to hear about someone's past conduct and behaviours that led them to homicide, the silence of the prosecutor is deafening. There is absolutely no mention of the past of the stepmother in Antiphon's speech, no reference to her relationship with the husband she had allegedly killed, no mention of past behaviours which would justify such actions, no attempt to build the portrait of a cold-blooded, manipulative killer through her past. Could it be because in those earlier days in the fifth century, when the speech was delivered, the demand in homicide trials not to deviate from the topic was taken more seriously? This is possible but, on the other hand, the speech of Antiphon *On the Chorister* provides the full background of the events which led to the accidental death of the choir boy, and if this was possible and acceptable in this case, it should have been acceptable in the case against the stepmother too. The reasons why the speaker did not even attempt to provide a background shedding some light on the motives of the stepmother are difficult to ascertain, but by not making reference to past behaviours, patterns or incidents which might be relevant for this case, the prosecutor of the stepmother has failed to provide any motive for the alleged murder.

The past of women who were widely known outside their homes because they were not restrained by the same bounds of respectability as ordinary Athenian women, the numerous hetairai and other prostitutes who associated with men in public and private places, would be easier to trace, and in fact some of these women were legendary figures. The difficulty in their case would be not so much to gather stories about their past as to distinguish between reality and the tales, and separate the real woman from the legend. But litigants often don't seem to be deterred by such challenges, for the stories they present in court are the ones which suit their purposes, and not necessarily truthful. When, for example, Apollodoros digs fifty years into Neaira's past to the time that she was a small slave girl bought by a ruthless Corinthian pimp, he surely does not feel constrained by any obligation to tell the truth and nothing but the truth. So long as the stories that he can conjure about Neaira's past sound believable – and maybe some of them were part of the story about the legendary hetaira still in circulation – he stands on safe ground. This is what makes so perilous the prosecutions of women who had a public persona: tales were in circulation about them and their past, true or false. It was easy to conjure up a past which explained, illustrated and enhanced the story told by the prosecutor and to manipulate preposterous and mostly untrue tales, gossip and rumour in ways that served the purposes of a malicious prosecutor. This is a stable pattern in all these instances where women with a public persona stood before a court, and even in the cases where we have the entire speech, it is still very difficult to separate fact from fiction.

In the case of Neaira, where we have the entire speech, it is easy to observe that her past played a disproportionate role in building the prosecution, since one quarter of the speech is dedicated to events that, truly or allegedly, happened in Neaira's life more than a quarter of a century ago, and another quarter is dedicated to the past of her alleged daughter Phano and events that happened more than a decade before the trial. None of these events has a bearing on the case, even though Apollodoros is trying very hard to establish some tenuous connections. When he parades the career of the young Neaira as a prominent hetaira before the eyes of the judges, he is arguing that because she was an alien hetaira she could not be the wife of an Athenian man. But he did not need to state the obvious in so many words, because the defence was not disputing that; they agreed that she was an alien hetaira and that she was merely the concubine and not the wife of Stephanos. One would think that Apollodoros was wasting his breath and his time, and most scholars in the past have thought that this failure was the result of incompetent speechwriting. But Apollodoros at the time of this trial was a very experienced litigator with thirty years of frequent court appearances on his record; he knew better than to engage in a profligate waste of time. What he did, he did with intent. He knew that there was no evidence about the non-existent marriage between Neaira and Stephanos, and he knew that if he wanted to even remotely suggest that they had pretended to be a married couple in order to pass off their descendants as citizens, he would need to present some proof that the children of Stephanos were also Neaira's children. He does no such thing because he could not; he had no proof. His only chance of success would come from skilful manipulation of the judges, and this he could do very well. The lengthy account of the sordid details of Neaira's past as a hetaira is not meant to appeal to the judges' reason but rather to their emotions, to provoke subconscious responses, to incite condemnation and disapproval, and to pass subliminal messages about the dangers which this alien prostitute posed for the wives and daughters of Athenian citizens, and society as a whole. Later in the argumentation of the speech he verbalises these dangers, with a stark warning to the judges that unless they convict Neaira, their wives and daughters may themselves become whores.

In the sequel about Phano's failed marriages, the young woman's past, namely her first marriage and divorce, and possibly an extramarital affair after that, were the reasons why her second husband was compelled to divorce her by the Areopagos council. While Apollodoros tries to argue that Phano's divorces were the result of her alien status, he actually reveals enough details to lead the careful listener to the inevitable conclusion that her Athenian status was proven conclusively twice. First, when the arbitrator ruled in favour of the Athenian status of her son with her first huband Phrastor, he essentially accepted de facto the Athenian status and legitimate birth of his mother Phano. Then, when the Areopagos council launched an inquiry into Phano's second marriage with Theogenes, the *archon basileus*, they only found fault with the fact that she had been married before, while an ancient religious rule ordained that the wife of the *archon basileus* had to be in her first marriage, because of her religious role in the festival of the Anthesteria and probably some other Dionysiac rites. The Areopagos council would certainly have treated her with much more severity if, in addition to this violation, they believed that she was not even Athenian.

This rather substantial evidence confirming the citizen status of Phano was right before their eyes, but whether the judges could pick on it or not was not very important for Apollodoros. It did not matter so much how many of the facts and details of Phano's story the judges were prepared to believe. What mattered most was that Phano, like her alleged mother, was dragged through the mud and utterly discredited and vilified, and this perfectly suited Apollodoros' purposes. If the jury felt that such an improper woman could not possibly be the daughter of an Athenian family, then Apollodoros had effectively won the argument that she was an alien, like her mother Neaira, and that Neaira and Stephanos hard indeed broken the law and acted as a married couple, just as Apollodoros was arguing all along. Phano's past was weaponised in order to present her in an unflattering light and subconsciously suggest to the jury that this woman could not possibly be a respectable Athenian daughter, wife and mother. Of the four children whom Stephanos and Neaira allegedly presented as citizens, even though none of them were of Athenian birth, Apollodoros only focuses on Phano, leaving out the three men – Antidorides, who had the name of Stephanos' father,[54] Ariston and Proxenos – probably for this reason: it would be so much easier to drag a woman through the mud and drive home the point that such an immoral woman could not be Athenian than to stage an assault against the citizenship of three adult Athenian male citizens.

According to the slim evidence about the life of Aristagora, she must have worked as a high-end hetaira for a number of years before she was bought and set free by Hypereides. Then she must have stayed for quite some time with him as his concubine, before she decided to walk away and try to make a living seemingly using her skills with drugs and poisons. Sometime after that, litigation ensued, first the *graphe aprostasiou*, where she was acquitted. If the suggestion that Hypereides later went after her with a *graphe doroxenias* is correct, by the time of the second trial Aristagora would surely have been a middle-aged woman and her days as a high-end hetaira would be well in the past. And yet it seems that the prosecutor relied heavily upon her past as a hetaira in building the case. Aristagora's past came to haunt her probably more than a decade after she had given up prostitution.

We do not know when the trial of Timandra took place but we can easily extrapolate that she was an older woman when this happened. Timandra had already reached her floruit by 404, when she accompanied Alcibiades in his last days, so she must have been born in the 420s. Hypereides, on the other hand, did not start working as a logographer before the 370s, and so Timandra was at least in her fifties when the speech of Hypereides was composed on behalf of her opposing litigant. Without a doubt the speech brought Timandra's sordid past as a sex worker to the fore, with some shocking images of brothels and cheap sexuality that attracted the attention of later rhetoricians. We don't know what the case was about but if the Suda is transmitting the title Πρὸς Τιμάνδραν correctly, then she must have initiated this lawsuit. The opposing litigant simply took advantage of the fact that as a prominent hetaira she had a colourful past, and brought it up in court in an attempt to generate prejudice.

Women with an unconventional past were never safe from attacks on their character if they happened to be involved in litigation. Their opponent had the opportunity to weave stories about the past, sometimes wholly or partially true, and sometimes completely made up. It is most unlikely, for example, that a top-of-the-range hetaira like Neaira, who then went on to become a respectable concubine, was ever the lowly whore that Apollodoros alleges she was, offering her body to scores of men who had intercourse with her everywhere and in every sordid way possible. But he can say so without losing all credibility because, in his rich narrative, instead of focusing on the actual charges against Neaira, he went back thirty years and dredged up her past. His decision was certainly deliberate, because he was then able to weave sordid stories about the alien hetaira and the dangers she posed for the moral order of things and the rights and privileges of Athenian citizen women and men. The past was relevant because it could have a powerful emotional appeal, and in the hands of a skilled litigator a woman's past could become a weapon capable of manipulating the judges, generating prejudice and misinformation, and opening the gates for a full-scale assault on a litigant's character and reputation.

CONCLUSIONS

It should not come as a great surprise to find that gender played a crucial role in the build-up of cases for or against women, and also in those settings where female characters were presented as instrumental in a litigant's speech. The roles, expectations, lifestyles, experiences, legal standing, rights of participation in public life, and on the whole the social parameters and gender stereotypes within which Athenian women operated were very different from those of their male counterparts. What Athenian society considered to be a good woman was very different from what it considered to be a good man, and consequently litigants would emphasise different aspects of their actions and character traits. It is to be expected that positive portrayals of women would be built around their roles as indomitable guardians and defenders of the household, as caring and protective mothers, as devoted wives and dutiful daughters. Perhaps more surprisingly, positive images of Athenian women tend to favour active characters who would take matters in their own hands, when necessary and expedient, and procure solutions or at least courageously do what was right. Positive representations of Athenian women in the Attic orators do not seem to attach much value to meekness or to a passive and obedient disposition. Such stereotypes created about Athenian women in the twentieth century rather reflect the values of the times which created them.

Conversely, negative images of Athenian women in the Attic orators are built on qualities which Athenian men clearly distrusted, disapproved of and disliked in their womenfolk, like a flashy and immodest appearance, a talkative and argumentative disposition, unfaithfulness, lewd behaviour or impropriety. Often the past of women charged with such attributes would come to haunt them in court proceedings, because prosecutors would have the opportunity to weave tales of depravity, malicious conduct and activities which endangered blissfully ignorant men. Explicit images of sexuality and sensuality were intended to work at the subconscious level, appealing to the emotions rather than the reason of the jurors, and to generate prejudice and apprehension. Prosecutors often stoked up fears and insecurities in their audience about secretive powers in the hands of women, sometimes simply on account of their ability to seduce susceptible lovers and impose their will on them, and sometimes because they had skills and knowledge to which ordinary men were not privy, like love-philtres, potions, magical rites and devices, and other invisible means by which they could subdue a man's will to their own, emasculate him, and inflict upon him pain and humiliation. Understandably, such powers were seen as particularly dangerous, and it seems that Athenian juries were quite susceptible to slanderous accusations along these lines. The cases against women that we know of seem to be disproportionately built upon gender stereotypes, even in those cases where gender should have had minimal impact, as for example in alleged immigration violations. Classical Athens was a distinctly gendered society and its court documents accurately reflect this reality.

NOTES

1. See for example Lys. 16. 10–13; D. 18.267, 21. 95, 154, 36.39; Is. 2.42, al.
2. X. *Oec.* 7.2, with Pomeroy 1994: com. ad loc., compared with And. 1.124–9; see also MacKenzie 1985: 95–6; Nelsestuen 2017: 74–104; Föllinger and Stoll 2018: 143–58.
3. The much larger subject of women in vase iconography is beyond the scope of this study. Some useful insights on women's images in Greek art can be found in Eaverly 2013; Stears 2001: 107–14; 1995: 109–31; Shapiro 1995: 39–48; Marinatos 1987: 23–4; Kilmer 1993.
4. For the participation of women in ritual see Ahearne-Kroll et al. 2010; Brøns 2017: 46–64; Calame 2001; Chryssoulaki 2008: 266–285; Connelly 2007; Dillon et al. 2017; Goff 2004; 2007: 79–91; Kaltsas and Shapiro 2008; Parca and Tzanetou 2007; Rives 2013: 12946.
5. The study by Michael Gagarin (2001: 161–76) remains the most authoritative work on the subject.
6. See also the discussion in PartI, pp. 47–51.
7. Lys. 32.9: twenty minae and thirty staters, a sum total of roughly thirty minae.
8. Walters 1993: 194–214.
9. Lys. 32.18: πάντας ἡμᾶς περὶ ἐλάττονος ποιεῖ χρημάτων (you are putting all of us below money).
10. D. 27.40, 53; 29.26, 33.
11. D. 29.26: ἡ μήτηρ κατ' ἐμοῦ καὶ τῆς ἀδελφῆς, οἳ μόνοι παῖδές ἐσμεν αὐτῇ, δι' οὓς κατεχήρευσε τὸν βίον . . . (my mother, who lived her entire life in widowhood, for me and my sister who were her only children . . .).
12. D. 41. My commentary on the speech in Wolpert and Kapparis 2011, although limited in scale and scope, is the only modern commentary on the speech. Although in essence this dispute was about property inherited by the two

daughters of Polyeuktos, I have not included it in the lawsuits in Part I because by that stage the property of the two women had been fully merged with that of their husbands, probably years before this trial, and the two men were not representing their wives, but speaking for themselves.

13. While this remark demonstrates the trust of her husband in her abilities and integrity, we should not take it too literally. Free men as witnesses capable of verifying the validity of a contract, if needed, were always indispensable for legal purposes.
14. The discussion on this popular speech in the large commentary by Stephen Todd (2007) probably offers the most complete and thorough exploration of the many difficult and fascinating issues which this text raises.
15. Lys. 1.6–7: ἐπειδὴ δέ μοι παιδίον γίγνεται, ἐπίστευον ἤδη καὶ πάντα τὰ ἐμαυτοῦ ἐκείνῃ παρέδωκα, ἡγούμενος ταύτην οἰκειότητα μεγίστην εἶναι· ἐν μὲν οὖν τῷ πρώτῳ χρόνῳ, ὦ Ἀθηναῖοι, πασῶν ἦν βελτίστη· καὶ γὰρ οἰκονόμος δεινὴ καὶ φειδωλὸς καὶ ἀκριβῶς πάντα διοικοῦσα· 'But when my child was born, then I trusted her and entrusted her with all of my possessions, since I thought that this was the best marriage. At first, men of Athens, she was the best of all wives. She was a skillful and thrifty housekeeper, carefully looking after everything' (trans. Andrew Wolpert).
16. D. 59.122: τὰς μὲν γὰρ ἑταίρας ἡδονῆς ἕνεκ' ἔχομεν, τὰς δὲ παλλακὰς τῆς καθ' ἡμέραν θεραπείας τοῦ σώματος, τὰς δὲ γυναῖκας τοῦ παιδοποιεῖσθαι γνησίως καὶ τῶν ἔνδον φύλακα πιστὴν ἔχειν.
17. X. Oec. 7; see also Pomeroy's important commentary on this text (1994); Nelsestuen 2017: 74–104; Föllinger and Stoll 2018: 143–58; Larivée 2012: 276–98; Oost 1977: 225–36.
18. Ar. Ec. 213–40.
19. A. Ag. 603–10:

> ταῦτ' ἀπάγγειλον πόσει·
> ἥκειν ὅπως τάχιστ' ἐράσμιον πόλει·
> γυναῖκα πιστὴν δ' ἐν δόμοις εὕροι μολὼν
> οἵανπερ οὖν ἔλειπε, δωμάτων κύνα,
> ἐσθλὴν ἐκείνῳ, πολεμίαν τοῖς δύσφροσιν,
> καὶ τἄλλ' ὁμοίαν πάντα, σημαντήριον
> οὐδὲν διαφθείρασαν ἐν μήκει χρόνου.

'Give this message to my husband: let him come with all speed, his country's fond desire, come to find at home his wife faithful, even as he left her, a watchdog of his house, loyal to him, a foe to those who wish him ill; yes, for the rest, unchanged in every part; in all this length of time never having broken any seal' (trans. Herbert Weir Smyth).

20. It is not clear whether he conducted the *engye* with her new husband or her brothers did. It appears that in this case it did not matter to the family, because her husband and brothers were acting in unison. It could be important for us if this passage had been somewhat clearer, because it could have answered a

question which remains unanswered for us, namely whether a husband, as the woman's current *kyrios*, had the right to give her in marriage to another man, either because he wanted an amicable separation for economic or personal reasons, or because he was on his deathbed and wanted to make sure that his wife would be well looked after. The husband is not among those mentioned in the law of *engye* (D. 46.18: }ἣν ἂν ἐγγυήσῃ ἐπὶ δικαίοις δάμαρτα εἶναι ἢ πατὴρ ἢ ἀδελφὸς ὁμοπάτωρ ἢ πάππος ὁ πρὸς πατρός 'the woman given in lawful marriage by her father, brother from the same father, or paternal grandfather', and also 44.49), but perhaps we should not expect him to be mentioned explicitly in a law concerning unmarried women, and it is not beyond the realm of possibility that a man who, let's say, had to divorce his wife because he wanted to marry an *epikleros* found the wife another husband and gave her away. The few instances that we know about, like this one here, do not offer sufficient clarity on the issue.

21. D. 47.55–73.
22. The speech is wrongly attributed to Andocides. See the discussion in Edwards 1995: ad loc.
23. And. 4.13–4. The speech is probably a later antique composition and the figure of ten talents as a dowry for Hipparete is suspect, but then again, her father was the richest man in the Greek world, so it is not impossible.
24. Athen. 13.3
25. Contrast, for example, a later antique epistle falsely attributed to the Pythagorean Theano (p. 197 Thesleff), where she advises a woman whose husband has left her to stay with a hetaira that she should be patient and wait until her husband has had enough of the hetaira and is ready to return to her.
26. D. 19.196–8: ἐπειδὴ δ' ἧκον εἰς τὸ πίνειν, εἰσάγει τιν' Ὀλυνθίαν γυναῖκα, εὐπρεπῆ μέν, ἐλευθέραν δὲ καὶ σώφρονα, ὡς τὸ ἔργον ἐδήλωσεν. ταύτην τὸ μὲν πρῶτον οὑτωσὶ πίνειν ἡσυχῇ καὶ τρώγειν ἠνάγκαζον οὗτοί μοι δοκεῖ, ὡς διηγεῖτ' Ἰατροκλῆς ἐμοὶ τῇ ὑστεραίᾳ· ὡς δὲ προῄει τὸ πρᾶγμα καὶ διεθερμαίνοντο, κατακλίνεσθαι καί τι καὶ ᾄδειν ἐκέλευον. ἀδημονούσης δὲ τῆς ἀνθρώπου καὶ οὔτ' ἐθελούσης οὔτ' ἐπισταμένης, ὕβριν τὸ πρᾶγμ' ἔφασαν οὑτοσὶ καὶ ὁ Φρύνων καὶ οὐκ ἀνεκτὸν εἶναι, τῶν θεοῖς ἐχθρῶν, τῶν ἀλειτηρίων Ὀλυνθίων αἰχμάλωτον οὖσαν τρυφᾶν· καὶ 'κάλει παῖδα,' καὶ 'ἱμάντά τις φερέτω.' ἧκεν οἰκέτης ἔχων ῥυτῆρα, καὶ πεπωκότων, οἶμαι, καὶ μικρῶν ὄντων τῶν παροξυνόντων, εἰπούσης τι καὶ δακρυσάσης ἐκείνης περιρρήξας τὸν χιτωνίσκον ὁ οἰκέτης ξαίνει κατὰ τοῦ νώτου πολλάς. ἔξω δ' αὑτῆς οὖσ' ὑπὸ τοῦ κακοῦ καὶ τοῦ πράγματος ἡ γυνή, ἀναπηδήσασα προσπίπτει πρὸς τὰ γόνατα τῷ Ἰατροκλεῖ, καὶ τὴν τράπεζαν ἀνατρέπει. καὶ εἰ μὴ 'κεῖνος ἀφείλετο, ἀπώλετ' ἂν παροινουμένη· καὶ γὰρ ἡ παροινία τοῦ καθάρματος τουτουὶ δεινή. καὶ περὶ ταύτης τῆς ἀνθρώπου καὶ ἐν Ἀρκαδίᾳ λόγος ἦν ἐν τοῖς μυρίοις, καὶ Διόφαντος ἐν ὑμῖν ἀπήγγελλεν ἃ νῦν μαρτυρεῖν αὐτὸν ἀναγκάσω, καὶ κατὰ Θετταλίαν πολὺς λόγος καὶ πανταχοῦ. 'When the drinking began, Xenophron introduced an Olynthian woman – a handsome, but a freeborn and, as the event proved, a modest girl. At first, I believe, they only tried to make her drink quietly and eat dessert; so Iatrocles told me the following

day. But as the carouse went on, and they became heated, they ordered her to sit down and give them a song. The poor girl was bewildered, for she did not wish, and she did not know how, to sing. Then Aeschines and Phryno declared that it was intolerable impertinence for a captive – and one of those ungodly, pernicious Olynthians too – to give herself such airs. "Call a servant", they cried; "bring a whip, somebody." In came a flunkey with a horsewhip, and – I suppose they were tipsy, and it did not take much to irritate them, when she said something and began to cry, he tore off her dress and gave her a number of lashes on the back. Maddened by these indignities, she jumped to her feet, upset the table, and fell at the knees of Iatrocles. If he had not rescued her, she would have perished, the victim of a drunken orgy, for the drunkenness of this blackguard is something terrible. The story of this girl was told even in Arcadia, at a meeting of the Ten Thousand; it was related by Diophantus at Athens in a report which I will compel him to repeat in evidence; and it was common talk in Thessaly and everywhere.' See also D. 19.309; Aesch. 2.4.
27. Kapparis 2020: 60–80.
28. Even when she ran away from Phrynion with his household valuables, it was not her fault, according to Apollodoros. She left because she was abused and not loved as she had hoped.
29. Thus in Kapparis 1999: 46–7.
30. D. 59.54–63; see also my discussion in Kapparis 1999: ad loc.
31. D. 59.85: Λαβὲ δή μοι τὸν νόμον <τὸν> ἐπὶ τούτοις τουτονὶ καὶ ἀνάγνωθι, ἵν' εἰδῆτε ὅτι οὐ μόνον προσῆκεν αὐτὴν ἀπέχεσθαι τῶν ἱερῶν τούτων τοιαύτην οὖσαν καὶ τοιαῦτα διαπεπραγμένην, τοῦ ὁρᾶν καὶ θύειν καὶ ποιεῖν τι τῶν νομιζομένων ὑπὲρ τῆς πόλεως πατρίων, ἀλλὰ καὶ τῶν ἄλλων τῶν Ἀθήνησιν ἁπάντων. ἐφ' ᾗ γὰρ ἂν μοιχὸς ἁλῷ γυναικί, οὐκ ἔξεστιν αὐτῇ ἐλθεῖν εἰς οὐδὲν τῶν ἱερῶν τῶν δημοτελῶν. 'Now take the law on these matters and read it, so that you can see that a woman of this sort, who had committed such acts, ought to keep away not only from these rites but also from all other rites in Athens, from viewing and sacrificing and performing traditional religious duties on behalf of the city. For a woman with whom a seducer has been caught is not allowed to enter any of the public temples, into which the laws admit even the alien woman and the slave who comes as a spectator or a suppliant.'
32. D. 59.67: τόν τε νόμον ἐπὶ τούτοις παρεχόμενος, ὃς οὐκ ἐᾷ ἐπὶ ταύτῃσι μοιχὸν λαβεῖν ὁπόσαι κάθωνται ἢ πωλῶνται ἀποπεφασμένως, ἐργαστήριον φάσκων καὶ τοῦτο εἶναι, τὴν Στεφάνου οἰκίαν, καὶ τὴν ἐργασίαν ταύτην εἶναι, καὶ ἀπὸ τούτων αὐτοὺς εὐπορεῖν μάλιστα. 'He produced the law on the subject, which forbids accusations of seduction with one of those women established in brothels or visibly practising any form of prostitution, claiming that this place too, the house of Stephanos, was a brothel, and this was their trade, and they were doing very well from it.' See also Kapparis 2018: 34–46; 1999: 295–300; Hillgruber 1998: 77–8; Glazebrook 2005a: 33–52; Johnstone 2002: 229–56 (for a different interpretation of the text and the law).
33. See also the discussion in Part I, pp. 43–6.

34. Kapparis 2018: 442.
35. See the discussion and literature in Part I, pp. 29–36.
36. Apollodoros (D. 59.23) in a cryptic sentence says συνηκολούθει δὲ καὶ Νέαιρα αὑτηί, ἐργαζομένη μὲν ἤδη τῷ σώματι, νεωτέρα δὲ οὖσα διὰ τὸ μήπω τὴν ἡλικίαν αὐτῇ παρεῖναι. 'Neaira here was following along, and she was already working with her body, but she was younger because she had not yet reached the prime.' What he is trying to say in this very roundabout way, through innuendo and an unfortunate tautology, as he is trying to avoid being more explicit than necessary, is expressed in a much more straightforward manner by Procopius in his echo of this passage in the *Anecdota* (9.10), with an underage Theodora taking the place of Neaira: τέως μὲν οὖν ἄωρος οὖσα ἡ Θεοδώρα ἐς κοίτην ἀνδρὶ ξυνιέναι οὐδαμῇ εἶχεν, οὐδὲ οἷα γυνὴ μίγνυσθαι· ἡ δὲ τοῖς κακοδαιμονοῦσιν ἀνδρείαν τινὰ μισητίαν <ἂν>ἐμίσγετο. 'Before Theodora had reached her floruit she could not sleep with a man, not in the manner that women do. However, she was sleeping with some wretched men in the manner that men have intercourse.' The prospect that underage prostitutes were offering themselves to lovers only for anal (and possibly oral) sex, avoiding vaginal sex until they were ripe to take lovers, is certainly intriguing and clearly suggested by both passages. See also Kapparis 2018: 59–61.
37. See also Spatharas 2012: 846–58; 2011: 99–120.
38. The phrase ἀπὸ τριῶν τρυπημάτων τὴν ἐργασίαν πεποιῆσθαι is quoted by Hermogenes (p. 325 Rabe) with the comment that it was obelised because it was thought to be too vile and shocking (λίαν εὐτελές, καὶ εἰ σφοδρόν εἶναι δοκεῖ). See the discussion in Kapparis 1999: 402–4.
39. Tzetzes *H.* 6.35 = D.H. Fr. 23 Radermacher.
40. *AG* 6.17.
41. D.H. *Dem.* 57.
42. Eidinow 2016: 11–17.
43. Sch. Dem. 19.281, 495 A and B Dilts.
44. A thorough account of the imaginative and sometimes bold images of the body in the Attic orators and the complexity of the rhetorical strategies involving the body would be outside the purposes of this study. Our purpose here is to demonstrate through a limited number of examples how images of the female body were employed in cases involving women.
45. Aesch. 1.26, 60; Hyp. *Lyc.* Fr. 12. Jensen.
46. See the discussion and sources in Part I, pp. 76–82.
47. See the discussion in Chapter 3, pp. 174–80.
48. See Kapparis 2019a: 198–200.
49. οὐχὶ Κερκώπη μὲν ἤδη γέγον' ἔτη τρισχίλια,
    ἡ δὲ Διοπείθους ἀηδὴς Τέλεσις ἕτερα μυρία;
    Θεολύτην δ' οὐδ' οἶδεν οὐδείς, ὅτε τὸ πρῶτον ἐγένετο.
    οὐχὶ Λαῒς μὲν τελευτῶσ' ἀπέθανεν βινουμένη,
    Ἰσθμιὰς δὲ καὶ Νέαιρα κατασέσηπε καὶ Φίλα;
    Κοσσύφας δὲ καὶ Γαληνὰς καὶ Κορώνας οὐ λέγω·
    περὶ δὲ Ναΐδος σιωπῶ· γομφίους γὰρ οὐκ ἔχει.

> Is Kerkope not 3,000 years old already
> And the disgusting Telesis of Diopeithes another 10,000 years old?
> And surely no one knows when Theolyte was born.
> Did Lais not die while having sex,
> While Isthmias, Neaira and Phila have rotted away?
> I am not even going to mention women like Kossypha, Galene and Korone;
> And I'll say nothing about Nais, for she has no teeth.

50. The description of Theodote's classy establishment can be found in X. *Mem.* 3.11.
51. Demetrius, *Eloc.* 302.
52. See the discussion in Lanni 2016; Harris 2013; Adamidis 2017.
53. This is a large and highly consequential debate in our times; see for example the discussions in Jacobs 2015; Pager 2003: 937–5; Roberts 1997: 303–62; 1996: 488–99; among others.
54. As one would expect, following the Greek custom of naming the first son after the father's father. This detail, where Antidorides is the eldest son, inconveniently contradicts the earlier part of the narrative where the twin boys, Proxenos and Ariston, and the girl Phano were born in Megara before Neaira had met Stephanos (D. 59.38), but Apollodoros was not overly concerned with such minor discrepancies.

CHAPTER 4

Women's Empowerment, Social Groups and the Justice System

INTRODUCTION

The women of Athens were not a homogeneous group, as has been stated above.[1] First and foremost there were legal differences of birth and status. There were citizen women, metic women, non-resident alien women – for example transient alien workers, especially in the sex industry, or maybe even some merchants, like Lucian's rich transgender Lesbian Megilla/Megillos[2] – and certainly a very large number of slave women. Their status affected the avenues available to them for access to the legal system when necessary. While slave women had no access to the legal system or the right to a fair trial, free women, citizen or alien, had a right to a fair trial when accused of a crime, and the possibility of redress when their rights, person or property had been violated. Citizen women had different access points from aliens, with different magistrates (the polemarch for aliens, and an array of other magistrates for citizens), but the procedures and expectations during the trial were the same for both groups, at least in theory. On rare occasions, as for example in the case of homicide, ancient laws had established different penalties for the killing of citizens and non-citizens,[3] but such practices had been discontinued in laws introduced under the influence of the democracy's principle of *isonomia* (equality before the law).

But did this mean that all was equal? Perhaps not, because even if Athenian judges adhered to their oath to judge according to the laws, and to give an equal and fair hearing to both sides,[4] other factors, such as wealth, social mobility, ideology, family circumstances, looks, likeability or other personal attributes, could have an impact on the proceedings and substantially influence the verdict. These factors typically cut across lines of citizen status and complicate the picture. This is why it is necessary to take them into account as we try to reconstruct the level, avenues of access to the Athenian legal system, and actual realities and challenges which women faced when involved with Athenian justice.

Moreover, such parameters did not remain static through time. From the fall of the Peisistratids and the introduction of the moderate democracy of Kleisthenes, to the effective dissolution of the independent Athenian polis at the battlefield of Chaironeia, Athens underwent many changes. From the late archaic polis which was open to Spartan interference, to the heroic city that led the resistance to Persian autocracy at the battlefield of Marathon, the imperial metropolis and leader of the Greek world of the golden years, the defeated and humiliated superpower, and finally the affluent city which was reluctant to lead a decisive campaign against Philip before it was too late to protect the independence of the Greek city-states, Athens underwent tremendous changes and shifts of power, wealth and prestige in the course of the classical period. Such highs, lows and shifts profoundly affected the female population of Attica, their economic circumstances, their family life and their personal worldview and outlook.

A thorough exploration of the impact of these shifts on the women of Athens is a much greater topic which cannot be discussed in full here.[5] However, when considering the relationship of the women of Attica with the justice system, it is necessary to take into account these broader changes of their circumstances and outlook in life. It is therefore necessary to consider each group of the female population of Attica and the impact which such political and socioeconomic changes had on its members. Finally it is important to explore how and whether subtle changes in the way the women of Attica came to view themselves within the context of the polis may be responsible for the fact that their involvement with the justice system becomes progressively greater in the course of the fourth century. Could it be because, as circumstances and outlook changed, Athenian women felt more confident to emerge into the outside world with all its perils and dangers? This chapter will attempt to answer some of these questions, sometimes offering only tentative suggestions, because the fragmentary nature of the evidence which we have in our hands does not allow for definite conclusions. Nonetheless, this discussion needs to begin, because it is important for our understanding not only of the level and form of involvement of the women of Attica with the justice system, but of their overall standing in the institutions of the democracy.

CITIZEN WOMEN IN THE ATHENIAN POLIS

The section of the homicide law of Drakon which allows the killer of a man caught with the killer's wife, sister, mother, daughter, or concubine kept for the purpose of having free children to go unpunished does not speak about citizen or non-citizen women; it only defines women on the basis of family relations.[6] One might read the difference between the wife and the concubine in the law as one of the citizen woman versus a free alien, but such a reading could be anachronistic, applying the standards of the fourth century to the seventh.[7]

The other part of the Athenian homicide law, which has been preserved in an inscription and describes the line of the *anchisteia*, again only defines family relations with no reference to clear concepts of citizenship.[8] The only part of the Drakonian legislation which seems to be aware of a difference between citizens and non-citizens is the part where prosecutions for the killing of a citizen were tried before the Areopagos, while those for the killing of an alien were tried at the Palladion. However, there is a strong possibility that this practice came into effect at a later time when the dividing lines between citizens and aliens were more clearly drawn. This is why it is difficult to tell whether Drakon recognised Athenian citizen women as a separate entity from other free women in someone's household, as one would in the classical period.[9]

The laws of Solon certainly appear to have in mind a clearer understanding of citizenship, although caution is still necessary so as not to transport fourth-century concepts of citizenship into the archaic period. What Solon meant by terms such as δῆμος, Ἀθηναῖος or ἀνὴρ Ἀττικός was probably different from what the Athenians of the classical period understood.[10] However, his legislative work and economic rank system are built upon some concept of Athenian citizenship, which includes those who were born and lived in Athens. This concept of citizenship at the time of Solon would be unquestionably defined and safeguarded through participation in groups such as the phratry or the *genos*. Later reforms by Kleisthenes would weaken, but not eliminate, the role of the phratries and the *gene* as guardians of citizenship. To what extent women were included in this definition of citizenship is unclear. J. Gould has argued that the absence of witnesses from phratries verifying a woman's citizenship should be taken as evidence that they were not included in the structures of phratries and *gene*. Mark Golden, in response to Gould, has reinfored the traditional thesis that women were regularly presented to phratries, and there is evidence to suggest that the *phrateres* routinely offered sacrifices letting the group and the wider community know about a marriage or the birth of a son or daughter.[11] So they were somehow included in those ancient bodies, but they were not members as such in the same way as the *phrateres* (which literally expresses a male form of kinship). This might explain why *phrateres* were not called to testify on women's citizen status, but then again we only have a very small number of relevant cases, where such testimony would have made a difference (like Is. 3 or D. 57), and we cannot draw definite conclusions from these.

Athenian inheritance law, as formulated by Solon, had in mind families in their entirety, and took steps to safeguard the inheritance rights of women in their natal *oikos* (but never in their husband's *oikos*).[12] However, it still gave preference to agnatic lines, and did not expect women to be able to defend their property and inheritance rights by themselves through a direct appeal to the magistrates and the court system. The expectation was that someone would act on behalf of a woman and go to court to defend her claim and her rights. The lawgiver understood that this put women in a weak spot and tried to address this vulnerability through a series of provisions like the laws on the *epikleros*, the process of *epidikasia* for women who did not have a close male relative (father, brother, paternal grandfather) legally entitled to give them in marriage, or the *eisangelia kakoseos*, a public, risk-free prosecution through which citizens were encouraged to come forward and denounce the abuse of orphans or *epikleroi*.[13] Moreover, the lawgiver put those vulnerable groups under the charge of the archon, the most senior civil servant in the state, and gave him extensive powers to enforce these laws and protect the property and person of those who were not legally capable of protecting themselves.[14]

Were these measures enough to address some of the vulnerabilities of women and children who did not have a close male relative to speak for them? Perhaps under normal circumstances they were, and the impression we get from the orators and other texts is that, for the most part, Athenian families respected these arrangements. However, a number of instances in the corpus of the Attic orators unmistakably suggests that sometimes no law or magistrate could put a strong enough barrier against the greed or ambitions of lateral relatives who had set their eyes upon the property of an heiress or an orphan. The case of Phile is an excellent example.[15] She was indisputably and with everyone's agreement the only natural child of an affluent Athenian man named Pyrrhos and an Athenian woman whom Pyrrhos had legally married with *engye*, sealing the contract with her brother Nikodemos before no fewer than four witnesses. This contract per se ensured the legality of the marriage. Whether a dowry was given at that time or not is not legally significant, as the absence of a dowry did not affect the legality of these arrangements. At some point Pyrrhos decided that he needed a male heir and adopted his sister's son Endios. Subsequently, Pyrrhos died and it was left up to Endios to take care of the marriage of his adopted sister when she came of age. He dutifully did so, and gave her in marriage to an Athenian man named Xenokles.

Phile and Xenokles had children, but Endios died childless. In this case his substantial property should have reverted to Phile, the only remaining direct descendent of Pyrrhos. However, the brother and mother of Endios had set their eyes on the property and had their own designs for it. Their claim, although through an agnatic line, was weaker, because they were lateral relatives. The only way that they could get their hands on this property would be to remove Phile from the line of succession. But how does one remove a natural heir properly born in wedlock? The standard practice throughout history has been to present them as illegitimate. The strategy which Isaios adopted was to undermine the marriage of Phile's parents, arguing that her mother was nothing more than a hetaira, and therefore she could not have been a wife. This is a false equivalence because Athenian law did not prevent a hetaira from becoming a wife, but this is not the only such logical leap in the speech. The entire speech is built upon false equivalence, ambiguity, misinterpretation, omission and illogical conclusions presented with a very rational façade. In a truly masterful piece of oratory Isaios has left many modern scholars convinced that Phile's claim was false. One would hope that the jury which heard the case in court was more attentive, circumspect and capable of seeing through the deceptive tactics of Isaios and his ruthless clients.

We do not know whether Phile got to keep her father's property, but through a case as clear-cut as this one we get a very good idea of how vulnerable the property rights of the citizen woman could be against determined and rapacious relatives. Such vulnerabilities were not limited to female heirs; the cases of Demosthenes[16] and the sons of Diodotos[17] prove beyond reasonable doubt that when a child, regardless of gender, was the inheritor of a large property, the appetite of rapacious relatives for a slice, or sometimes the whole, of the pie would always put this child in a precarious position. The case against Diogeiton proves that the ability for self-representation in court offered no great safeguards either, as the eldest son of Diodotos, although an adult, chooses to be represented by his brother-in-law. Such trials, with so much at stake, could be daunting affairs for the ordinary citizen, especially since the orphaned heir or heiress had so much to lose while the opposing side, the lateral relatives, had everything to gain and nothing to lose, and this was often reflected in their unorthodox and ruthless tactics.

The one factor which could have made a big difference in inheritance disputes would have been a written record of births and deaths, maintained either by the city or by the demes. But even such a record could not have been entirely foolproof, as the uncertainty about the accuracy of the records meticulously kept by the demes on adult male citizens, which led to the *diapsephiseis* of Demophilos, suggests. Ultimately, where there are high profits to be made there will always be someone willing to take the risks and circumvent the rules to make these profits. Vulnerabilities in inheritance disputes were inherent in the large interests often surrounding such cases, and despite the efforts of the lawgiver to deter unjust claims, resolving these disputes before the courts was often an inevitable part of the process, and citizen as well as alien heiresses would need the support of male relatives, and perhaps the professional assistance of a seasoned litigator, if they were to prevail and keep their patrimony.

Compared to the rapid and dramatic changes in public life from the aristocratic state to the radical democracy, Athenian family law appears almost static in time.[18] At first glance it appears that Athenian families always married, had children, lived and passed on the property of the *oikos* to the next generation following a stable pattern established from time immemorial. Changes in family and inheritance law were subtle, and often dictated by broader changes in public life. The role of the archon in the affairs of the family and in family law seems to be a good example. When the *Athenaion Politeia* outlines the duties and responsibilities of the archon in family law, the citation contains a Solonean core of his responsibilities augmented by the legislation of the radical democracy.[19] However, the actual extent of his responsibilities seems to have changed substantially from the aristocratic state to the radical democracy. While the Solonean archon seems to be empowered with the authority to interfere in family affairs in defence of the interests of those who could not defend themselves, like orphans, heiresses and the elderly, when we actually watch the archon in action in the case of Demosthenes against his guardians, although he seems to agree that a serious violation has taken place, and that the orphaned Demosthenes and his sister had been deprived of their patrimony by the guardians, instead of using his legally enshrined powers to step in he actually demonstrates remarkable restraint, calls a meeting, listens, discusses, advises; but at the end of the day seeking actual redress and restoration of the property is left to the male heir of the family, Demosthenes, when he comes of age. It seems that with the passage of time the substantial powers of the archon under the aristocratic state, although not repealed, had been limited in practice by the ideology and modus operandi of the democracy, where the individual citizen was not only entitled to enforce his rights in the courts but also responsible for doing so.[20]

What such subtle changes in public life mean for the property and inheritance rights of Athenian women is a complicated question. The shift of power from the magistrate of the state to the individual citizen meant that the women themselves and those who represented their interests had more control over the proceedings, and that the women themselves became effectively more visible in the eyes of the law than they had been at the time of the aristocratic state, when women were practically invisible behind their *kyrios* and the walls of the family home. However, at the same time, by weakening the centralised powers of state officials like the archon, the democratic constitution left the citizen woman more vulnerable to the whims of family members, and sometimes those who should have been seen as the natural protectors of a lone citizen woman, her closest relatives, were actually the ones who wanted to undermine her rights and status in order to profit themselves. The inheritance cases involving women outlined in Part I of this study more often than not seem to involve rapacious relatives. In the end, the limited number of cases and the fragmentary nature of the evidence deprive us of deeper insights into such cases and into the dynamics concerning women's rights and legal protections in the wider context of the Athenian democracy. What we have to go by is a number of references by male litigants in inheritance disputes, and our imperfect knowledge of the wider legal framework and social infrastructures of the radical democracy.

In Solonean Athens the plight of the impoverished lower classes must have been severe. A series of laws intended to protect children from their own families, like laws forbidding the procuring of a free person, or allowing the father to establish a daughter in a brothel only if she had been unchaste before marriage,[21] revealed the grim realities of a society where poor people had to pawn their own freedom in order to make it through the year, and where someone's children could be viewed as a commodity in the fight for survival. Solon's legislation put a stop to such practices and offered legal protections to women and children against their own relatives. As the fortunes of Athens improved under the Peisistratids, and commerce and manufacturing made up for some of the deficiencies of the poor agricultural land of Attica and its inability to sustain a large population, it is likely that some of Solon's laws for the protection of women and children became less relevant and were eventually forgotten.

With these facts in mind we may conclude that the Solonean legislation assumed some form of citizenship for women, but it was not defined independently outside the confines of the *oikos* and Athenian property and inheritance law. This concept would evolve and increasingly the Athenian woman would come to be defined as a citizen, perhaps to some extent in contrast to the rich alien wives who entered as brides into the households of the Athenian aristocracy in the late archaic period. During the years of empire, as scores of women from other places took residence in Attica, either with their families or as unattached workers, attracted by the opportunities which the booming Athenian economy offered, the distinction between women born in Athenian families (*aste* or *politis*) and the outsiders, the others, was solidified. When Pericles introduced his consequential law in 451 limiting citizenship to persons born of two citizens (ἐξ ἀμφοῖν ἀστοῖν),[22] the law assumed a clear and self-evident definition of what a citizen man and a citizen woman were.

This simple piece of legislation effected the most substantial change in the standing of citizen women. The wider scope of this legislation is beyond our purposes to discuss here.[23] I think we can be sure that the objective of this law was not to enhance the rights and privileges of Athenian women. This may have been a side effect, but undoubtedly the main objectives had to do with important issues in public life, such as the number of citizens allowed to participate in the direct democracy of Athens and enjoy its privileges among an exploding population in the imperial capital, and the efficient administration of the polis. Nonetheless, for the brief period of twenty-two years when the law remained in effect the citizen women of Athens must have taken pride in the fact that they alone had the legal right to continue the *oikos*, and this would have raised their self-confidence and standing in the household.

The Peloponnesian war was a time of trials and suffering for the women of Attica. The bride separated from her bridegroom shortly after the wedding in Aristophanes' *Acharnians*, the woman who learned how to speak in public (Praxagora) because during the war she was one of the dispossessed who were homeless and sleeping outside near the Pnyx, or the widow who needs to rush to deliver a large order of wreaths, because she's the only earner in a household with five children after her husband was killed in the war, are not just comic figures.[24] There is nothing funny about their circumstances; surely women all around Attica, citizen and metic, were facing such challenges during the war, while its bloody battles and the major catastrophe in Sicily left thousands of households without a *kyrios*, the man expected to provide for the family and represent its interests in the world of the polis. Another critically important passage from the speech *Against Euboulides* outlines the plight of citizen women in those hard times. Euxitheos, the speaker, tells us that he came from a poor but proud citizen family, and that in the final phase of the Peloponnesian war his mother was left alone to provide for her two children while his father joined the army under Thrasyboulos, and then was captured and sold as a slave in Leukas. It would be years before Thoukritos, the speaker's father, could return to Athens, and in all that time the poor citizen woman needed to provide for her family in any way she could. We are told that she worked as a wet nurse in the affluent household of Kleinias, and during the trial of the speaker her former employers gave evidence on behalf of her son seemingly attesting that she was a citizen woman working for them out of necessity. The speaker concludes that 'poverty forces poor people to do many slavish and humble tasks'.[25]

There may have been a silver lining at the end of those difficult years. Women who, in their thousands perhaps, had learned to rely on their own skills and wits to provide for themselves and their families became less dependent on their relatives. In a scenario which seems familiar to us from the aftermath of World War II, where the fact that women had taken the place of men in the factories and the workplace while the men were at war generated changes and inspired many women with the confidence that they could make it in life without the protection of a husband or a father, we notice that more and more Athenian women seem to be entering the workforce. After all, poverty in the absence of a breadwinner husband, father or son would not go away after the end of the war, and the devastation which thirty years of bloody warfare had inflicted upon Athenian families would have consequences lasting for many years. Our evidence is limited, sketchy and sometimes anecdotal, but perhaps in the ultimate fantasy of the *Ecclesiazousai* for a society were men and women are expected to make an equal contribution to the common good and enjoy the fruits of their labours on an equal footing we may see signs of this renewed confidence in the ability of women to stand on their own two feet. As outlined in Chapter 4, in the fourth century we have evidence of citizen women working as shopkeepers, small traders, health professionals, artisans, cloth makers, nurses and caretakers, and not infrequently in the booming sex industry of the city, which was mainly populated and operated by alien workers.

The higher the percentage of women working outside the house and trying to stand on their own two feet in a competitive world, the higher was their chance of having a brush with the law. A bad customer who bought a lot of goods but did not pay in the end would need to be pursued through the courts.

In a comic but instructive scene from Aristophanes, *Frogs* two women innkeepers in the underworld recognise 'Herakles' (Dionysus dressed as Herakles) and recall that the last time he visited he left a huge bill unpaid.[26] As soon as the villainous customer is recognised one of the women goes to meet her 'protector' (προστάτης) Kleon and take the customer to court to make him pay. Such incidents would not be uncommon in businesses around town, and those run by women would need to have just as much access to the justice system as those run by men, in order to be able to pursue bad clients and debtors. A runaway slave from a business run by a woman would still need to be brought back, and it was the responsibility of the owner to make sure that this happened. In an incident described by the speaker in the speech *Against Pankleon* an unknown woman laid claim to Pankleon, amid a lot of shouting and a big argument in the marketplace, arguing that he was a runaway slave of hers. In this instance, either the unknown woman or the speaker was lying, because Pankleon was almost certainly a Plataian, and consequently an Athenian citizen. Nonetheless, the incident demonstrates that a woman business owner in a situation like this had the right and obligation to claim what was legally hers.

In the sex market perhaps the most striking case is the one that a man named Archias, who was the *kyrios* of the hetaira Nais, brought on her behalf against Philonides, one of the richest Athenian men of his time, and famous for his lavish lifestyle and heavy spending on hetairai, at a time of austerity for most Athenian families either shortly before or during the Corinthian war. In all probability the charge was rape or attempted rape, and this is the only case known to us where such a charge was brought against someone.[27] This case certainly reminds us of the fictional account of Herodas, where a procurer named Battaros takes a soldier to court for assault because the latter entered Battaros' brothel, caused a major drunken brawl and injured some of the women working there. One could continue exponentially citing incidents like these from a variety of sources. The point is that one cannot imagine a man or woman running a business without the ability to resort to the justice system when necessary in order to defend the interests of his or her business. It only makes sense that as more women ran businesses seeking financial independence, or at least trying to help out the poor finances of their household, more women would end up before a magistrate, an arbitrator or a heliastic jury, as a routine part of what was involved in running a business. As mentioned above, small claims of up to ten drachmas could be decided on the spot by the Forty, but reason suggests that business-related claims and disputes quite often exceeded this sum.[28]

While it is true that most court speeches that we have come from the fourth century, and perhaps for this reason it should not be surprising to find lawsuits involving women concentrated in fourth-century oratory, there are still some indications that women had more brushes with the law than before, for the reasons suggested above. The only fifth-century lawsuits involving a woman that we know about are the homicide prosecution brought against the stepmother (Ant. 1) and the impiety case against Aspasia. On the other hand, from the fourth century we have a rather broad array of cases, including impiety, immigration violations, inheritance disputes and sexual assault. While there is a good possibility that the nature of our evidence is distorting the picture, as undoubtedly there were at least property disputes involivng heiresses in the fifth century which we do not hear about in our sources, nonetheless, as it stands our evidence suggests that lawsuits involving women increased in number and type as the women of Attica,[29] citizen and metic, left their homes more often and made a greater contribution to the economy of the city than they did in previous times.

The horrendous losses of Athenian men during the Peloponnesian war – over a thousand at Delium, several thousand in Sicily, and many more in the long-drawn-out battles and skirmishes of the Corinthian war – forced many Athenian women to cross over traditional gender boundaries as they became the effective head of the household. Unless they were fortunate enough to have a supportive family,[30] they would need to step into roles traditionally reserved for the *kyrios*. They might need to become the main breadwinner, the indomitable defender of the interests of their children, like the daughter of Diogeiton or Kleoboule, and the person in charge of the finances and management of the household, like the prudent widow of Polyeuktos. And yet Athenian women who found themselves in this position were still bound by frustrating legal limitations, and were in need of a male relative in order to pursue someone who had harmed their interests through the courts. Although it is clear that the old Solonean law which limited the ability of women to perform financial transactions to the value of one *medimnos* of barley, roughly the amount needed for the maintenance of the household for a week,[31] had been obsolete for over a century and was never revised to reflect monetary values in coinage, there is still some uncertainty about women's ability to enter into large contracts without the presence of a male representative.[32] While wealthy hetairai like Phryne could spend large amounts of money commissioning works of art without the approval or interference of any man, ordinary Athenian women might rely on male relatives as witnesses to such transactions, like the widow of Polyeuktos who used her brothers as witnesses to all transactions in order to ensure clarity and accountability.[33] Even though it is clear that in the fourth century Athenian women were not legally barred from entering into financial contracts and transactions, still they needed male relatives to be present and act as witnesses, because if any part of a contract or financial transaction were to be disputed in future, these witnesses would be needed in the ensuing court proceedings. The very limited evidence from the Attic orators can be augmented with evidence from comedy, especially New Comedy and its Roman adaptations, like a scene from Plautus' *Asinaria* where a hilarious contract for prostitution is signed between the procuress Cleareta and the client Diabolus, an affluent merchant, for twenty minae, which he has already given to her.³⁴ This evidence suggests that there was no legal impediment to the ability of women, citizen and metic, to enter into financial agreements. However, tradition and custom certainly influenced the form of such proceedings, and it would have been prudent for a woman about to enter into a contract to have a couple of male witnesses, just in case it became necessary to follow up in the courts, where free men as witnesses would be indispensable.

METIC WOMEN IN THE ATHENIAN POLIS

The Athenian city-state operated an open immigration policy, unlike rival Sparta, which firmly discouraged outsiders from settling within the boundaries of its territory. Anyone could move to Attica, settle there and make the city their home. The numbers of alien residents in Attica probably varied depending on the economic circumstances of the city. It is reasonable to assume that in more peaceful and prosperous times there was a higher number of outsiders moving into the city, but in addition to transient workers, often employed in the sex industry, healthcare, education or retail businesses, there was always a core of alien residents who lived in Athens permanently, sometimes for generations. These families suffered the same fate as other Athenian families, and in bad times they suffered more, as they seem to have done under the Thirty, because legally they were more vulnerable.³⁵ Under the democracy, so long as the metics met the basic obligation of registering, and paying the annual fee (*metoikion*) of twelve drachmas for a man and his family, or six drachmas for an independent woman, the Athenian criminal justice system extended to them the same protections that citizens enjoyed in almost all areas. While as non-citizens they could not participate in the operations of the Athenian democracy, such as the assembly, the courts or public offices, metic men had the right to access the justice system to its highest level, the heliastic courts; to speak for themselves or through an advocate, either as prosecutors or as defendants; to appear as witnesses; and to appeal to state magistrates in defence of their interests and those of their families.³⁶ They also had to join the army and defend their host city, homes and families at the side of the citizen soldiers of Athens, and they were subject to taxation and liturgies on the same terms as citizens. In many ways the status of metic men in the Athenian democracy was similar to the status of resident aliens in modern democracies.

The Athenian state recognised and protected the marriages of metics. The fierce adultery laws which safeguarded citizen marriages applied to metics too, while the complex inheritance laws established by Solon applied to the continuation of metic *oikoi* in similar terms.³⁷ The actual terminology for marriage (συνοικεῖν) was applied equally to citizen and metic families, and the laws of the Athenian democracy protected the persons and property of metic *oikoi* just as they protected those of citizen *oikoi*.³⁸ There was only one fundamental difference between the marriages of citizens and metics for much of the classical period. Citizen families would give birth to citizens, but metic families could never give birth to citizens. However, in the years when the Periclean citizenship law was not valid, even this basic difference was blurred, and mixed families of an Athenian and a metic (typically an Athenian man and a metic woman) could give birth to citizens. Pure metic families of two non-citizens, like the Syracusan family of Lysias, could not give birth to citizens even when the Periclean citizenship law was not valid.

The rules for marriages between metics were similar to those governing the marriages of citizens. A metic woman could be given in marriage to a free non-citizen man, metic or alien, by her father, brother or paternal grandfather, during the classical period. Customs and religious practices from the place of origin of the metic family might also colour such proceedings. Since many metic women, especially freed slaves, did not have famiiles to arrange a marriage, it is quite likely that they themselves could agree to a marriage, perhaps with the assistance of a male agent, a *prostates*, who entered into a formal agreement with the future husband on their behalf.³⁹

During the years when the Periclean citizenship law was valid marriages between citizens and metics were discouraged, because the offspring of such unions would no longer be citizens. At some point in the 380s, such marriages were explicitly prohibited, with severe penalties.⁴⁰ Theoretically the legal arrangements for metic *epikleroi* were the same as those for citizen *epikleroi*, except that it was not the archon but the polemarch who would oversee the process of the *epidikasia*, and he was also in charge of accepting lawsuits for the abuse of the persons or property of metic *epikleroi* and orphans. A metic woman would become an *epikleros* at the time when the last of the male relatives who had the legal right to arrange a marriage contract on her behalf died while she was still unmarried, or married but childless.

The Athenian state, at least from the time of Solon, went to great lengths to make sure that citizen women would not be left to fend for themselves outside the protective umbrella of the *oikos*. If a citizen woman found herself without immediate male relatives to give her in marriage, the archon would oversee the process of her marriage (*epidikasia*) as an *epikleros*. And if she happened not to be sufficiently wealthy or beautiful to attract some suitor, the archon was expected to compel the nearest male relative of her father either to marry her himself, or to find her a husband and give her a dowry from his own property. The objective was that no woman should be left without a husband and the prospect of a family. Remarkably, the Athenian state was equally adamant in protecting metic women with the same set of rules. Apollodoros and the *Athenaion Politeia* citing the law agree that the rules were the same as those regulating the *epidikasia* of citizen women, with the sole difference that matters which were under the authority of the archon for citizen women would be under the authority of the polemarch for metic women (καὶ τἆλλ' ὅσα τοῖς πολίταις ὁ ἄρχων, ταῦτα τοῖς μετοίκοις ὁ πολέμαρχος).⁴¹ One more important difference between citizen and most metic women (except those whose father had been allowed to own real estate in Attica through an honorary grant of ἔγκτησις⁴²) was that the property of metic women, although sometimes very substantial, would not involve real estate. This put them in a more vulnerable position in the hands of unscrupulous relatives, because cash and valuables (ἀφανὴς οὐσία, 'invisible property') could be much more easily siphoned away, while houses or land could not be hidden or easily appropriated (φανερά οὐσία, 'visible property').

The vexed question of whether all metic women who did not have a father, paternal grandfather or brother to give them in marriage with *engye* needed to be married with *epidikasia* is not answered convincingly in our sources. We hear about marriage in metic families, and also about arrangements for metic *epikleroi* to be married with *epidikasia* under the auspices of the polemarch, but we do not know all the tantalising details. Could poor liberated slaves be given away in marriage by a *prostates*, the way a citizen woman could be given in marriage by her *kyrios*? Would the law recognise an arrangement between the woman and her future husband without the intervention and support of a *prostates*? Would marriage be an option altogether for a poor liberated slave, or would she need to be content with a more informal union as someone's concubine? We do not have easy answers to these questions. What is certain is that independent metic women with no families had the capacity to agree to live with a man as concubines of their own accord, because no legal agreement or contract was required for concubinage.⁴³ Beyond that we are in a grey area, and in all probability custom and circumstances played a major role. Greek families from other cities, like the family of Lysias,⁴⁴ would conduct marriages according to the customs of their land of origin, let's say, and from a legal perspective such marriages, with either *engye* or *epidikasia*, would be very similar to Athenian marriages, except that they would not produce future citizens. Non-Greek freeborn families from other parts of the ancient world, like Asia Minor or north Africa, might also follow their own customs. Liberated slaves were a very mixed bag, and could range from rich men like Pasion to low-end unskilled workers making three obols a day. They might follow the patterns of respectable metic families, as Pasion and his family did before his elevation to citizenship, or could live in informal unions, as the liberated slave Alke does with her partner Dion (συνῆν),⁴⁵ depending on their circumstances and aspirations. Ultimately, we need to allow for some uncertainty on this issue, partly because of limited evidence, and partly because the metic population of Attica was large and very heterogeneous, following a variety of customs and traditions from many lands and in a great variety of socioeconomic circumstances.

Rebecca Futo Kennedy in her excellent monograph on the metic women of Athens probably correctly argues against D. Whitehead that the number of single metic women in Athens was quite substantial. Kennedy emphasises 'the paradoxes and complexity of the lives of metic women or their various roles in and contributions to classical Athenian society' and states that 'metic women played a role at almost every social and economic level'.[46] The Athenian state, while willing to acknowledge and protect metic unions, might be less nervous about independent metic women floating outside the boundaries of the *oikos*. This difference from citizen women might be small and informal, since it was not the result of specific legislation but rather custom and accepted practice. And yet this was probably the single most important aspect of classical Athenian life that allowed some metic women to challenge the boundaries and limitations of their gender, seek personal development through higher education, accomplish remarkable tasks, and become writers and educators themselves; and a few of these remarkable women not only achieved recognition in their own time, but provided role models for women in the long dark centuries which were to follow. As Kennedy rightly points out, only some of these women were hetairai or other prostitutes. Some were married women, like the Epicurean Themista of Lampsakos, who incited the indignation of Cicero for having the temerity to compose an eloquent response to the great Theophrastos, and received so much attention in the works of Epicurus.[47] Some were remarkable, educated women in monogamous relations with Athenian men, like Aspasia of Miletos, the long-term partner of Perikles. An accomplished scholar, orator and intellectual, not only could she hold her own with the Athenian intellectual elite at its highest moments, but she also had students of her own, like Aeschines the Socratic, generated an entire mythology around her and remained an inspirational figure for women in later centuries.[48]

There were many other accomplished metic women of intellect. Several sources provide the names of women, mostly hetairai, who studied at the Gardens of Epicurus. These include Leontion, Mammarion, Hedeia, Erotion, Nikidion, Philainis and Boidion, some of whom were probably metics.[49] Philainis of Samos was famous for centuries after her lifetime as the author of a racy book of erotica. It was a manual which included advice on how to approach a lover in the first place and make them feel good about themselves, how to seduce someone, how to kiss and much more. This Greek Kama Sutra, which enlisted countless sexual positions, among other things, was a very popular and widely discussed piece of literature.[50] Another famous hetaira and author of the time was Gnathaina, famous for her sharp wit, who wrote a parody of the rules of conduct in philosophical schools of the time (νόμος σισσυτικός) placing those rules in the context of a rowdy symposion (νόμος συμποτικός).[51]

Around that time the mesmerising Phryne, a metic from Thespiai probably born in Athens, where her family had found refuge along with most of the population of her native city after the destruction of Thespiai by Thebes in 373,[52] was gaining notoriety and a special place in history. She never forgot her Thespian identity, and in subsequent years she made some ostentatious and pricey dedications to her native city, the most famous of which was the Thespian triad by Praxiteles, consisting of three statues, Phryne, Aphrodite and Eros. Cicero considered the statue of Eros to be the only reason why one should visit Thespiai in his time.[53] Another major art lover, whose life and activities cross the boundary from the late classical to the early Hellenistic period, was Lamia, an Athenian woman and mistress of Demetrios Poliorketes. Lamia was ostentatious in her public displays, and dedicated a painted portico to Sikyon, famous for its painters.[54]

Granted that these women were unconventional and operated outside the bounds of the *oikos*. Nonetheless, they still operated within the boundaries and limitations of their gender in a male-dominated society, and still succeeded in achieving notoriety, accomplishing remarkable feats, bettering themselves with education and culture, pushing boundaries and gaining new ground, and showing the world in their time and many centuries into the future that a woman could be more than a mother and housewife. However, as often happens with opening new frontiers, there was a reaction and a pushback, which came close to costing Aspasia and Phryne their lives. As happened with Aspasia and Socrates, when they upset many in Athens with their teachings and came to be viewed as subversive forces intent on turning the established order of things upside down by threatening time-honoured traditions, Phryne too became a symbol of new and dangerous ideas and practices, and was seen as a bad influence upon men and women in the city, especially the young. And like Aspasia and Socrates, she was prosecuted for impiety on charges which, reading between the lines, sound remarkably similar to theirs. However, unlike the great philosopher, Phryne was acquitted. Could it be because of the splendid and much-admired speech which Hypereides composed in her defence? Could it be because, sensing danger, he pulled a shocking visual stunt and laid her bare before the judges? Or could it be simply the fact that Phryne, unlike Socrates and the powerful, toxic men like Kritias and Alcibiades associated with him, was seen merely as a woman of light morals and no danger to society? We do not know the answer to this, but we do know for sure that Phryne emerged from this trial as an iconic symbol of the Golden Age of the Athenian hetaira, and would continue to inspire artists for many centuries.

In all probability, similar reasons were behind the prosecution of other metic women in the fourth century on charges of impiety. Since such charges were rarely motivated by true religious zeal, and typically came with a hidden agenda, we may assume that envy, personal animosities, fear of the impact that these unconventional women were having upon Athenian society, and probably anger at the overall state of affairs were behind these prosecutions. We are even told that Euthias had personal reasons for prosecuting Phryne, as a former jilted lover, and if we judge by the superheated reaction of Demosthenes towards

Theoris of Lemnos, we may also conclude that such emotions typically came from a place of fear and anger. Theoris, a metic like Phryne, was also pushing boundaries. She had set up a seemingly profitable business in Athens, offering healing potions, love-philtres, spells and advice, and we are told that she even offered advice to slaves on how to deceive their masters. With good reason we might think that it was that last part of her activities which raised alarms in a society where the entire economy depended on slave labour, and drew attention to her other activities. From that point forwards, presenting her as a dangerous, subversive force with dark skills and negative effects upon society would not be too difficult for the most illustrious of Greek orators.

The metic women who were prosecuted for immigration violations, with the notable exception of Neaira,[55] may have been prosecuted for similar reasons. Their conduct as free agents selling potions and drugs with arcane powers, like Aristagora, or maybe engaging in other activities which society found disquieting and dangerous, surely had something to do with their prosecutions, but again, personal motivations, as in the case of Aristagora, cannot be excluded. It seems that society in general felt some unease about free hetairai who were operating outside the bounds of the *oikos* and outside male control. This fear is expressed by Apollodoros in his argumentation in the speech *Against Neaira*. He argues that if the judges as representatives of the Athenian democracy allowed alien hetairai to do as they pleased, this would have a corrupting influence on citizen women, and it would make attractive in their eyes the option of taking up prostitution and escaping male control. So the established order would be turned upside down, with prostitutes marrying Athenian men and Athenian women taking up prostitution. The passage is typically treated as far-fetched scaremongering, and although it certainly was that, the apocalyptic vision of a future where all family and social structures have broken down might arouse some hidden fears among members of the jury, and appeal to their deepest anxieties. It is a fair bet that skilled prosecutors appealed to similar anxieties when they built other cases against those out-of-control women.

THE WORKING WOMEN OF ATHENS: LEGAL IMPLICATIONS

Richard Cudjoe opens his thorough monograph on widows in classical Athens with a list of catastrophic defeats in the history of the city and the massive toll in men's lives. He then goes on to explain that for every man killed in battle a family was left without its main breadwinner, another family was left without an heir, and countless women, many with children, were left to fend for themselves, if they did not happen to have financially able and supportive relatives. The legal position of an Athenian widow with children (or at least pregnant) was peculiar in that, unlike any other woman, she was given a choice about her fate.[56] Regardless of the wishes of the wider family, the law allowed her to choose where she would live with her children. She could remain in her husband's *oikos*, or move back with her natal family. In either case she had no inheritance rights to her husband's *oikos*, while her children remained the heirs of their father, even if she chose to go and live with her natal family. Widows in affluent households, like Kleoboule the mother of Demosthenes or the widow of Diodotos in Lysias 32, would typically not need to worry about the basic necessities of life and whether their children had been adequately provided and cared for. However, not all widows came from affluent households. Poorer women with small children and no natal family able to support them could very quickly find themselves in a terrible predicament.

Several fictional accounts, which surely reflect the struggles of real people, offer us some glimpses into the financial struggles and difficulties of widowed mothers. In a passage from the *Thesmophoriazousai* of Aristophanes a widowed mother of five is working as a wreath-seller in order to make ends meet,[57] while Lucian's dialogue between Krobyle and her daughter Korinna, whom she is planning to prostitute in order to escape poverty, outlines how hard life could have been for a working-class family after the death of the main breadwinner, in this case Korinna's blacksmith father.[58] The subject of citizen and metic women working in sectors of the economy other than the sex industry has not received adequate attention,[59] perhaps because it did not fit well into the patterns of scholarship about the women of Athens established in the 1980s. The hard-working and perfectly respectable mother who needs to go outside every day in order to provide for her family would be an anomaly in the literature on gendered spaces or the images of the queen-bee citizen woman reigning over the household, which have prevailed for decades. And yet this discussion is important and we must have it, not least because it could change forever our view of Athenian women and their place in society. This is not the place for such a major discussion; our purpose here needs to be limited to the potential interactions of working women in Attica with the law, as well as any regulatory laws which might affect them on a daily basis, and on occasion get them into trouble with the law. But before this, it is necessary to take a brief look into the shape of the female labour market, intentionally leaving out sex work, the operation of which has been discussed in considerable detail in other studies.[60]

The female labour market of Attica can be separated into two broad categories. In the one category we will find occupations which required significant training, and women would enter into these probably at a younger age and after making a conscious decision to make a lifelong commitment. Personal ambition and dedication might have something to do with it, but typically family circumstances and low economic capacity might be the most urgent motives behind a woman's decision to choose such a career path. In the other category women could come in at any age, normally motivated by dire necessity, without any particular skills except those they already possessed from regular household tasks. Women in this group and their families had not envisaged a life as working mothers, and this is why they had only received the minimal training in cooking and cloth-making which Ischomachos describes in Xenophon's *Oeconomicus*.[61] Along the way they were expected to pick up some additional skills, like good household management and basic healthcare skills for the family, which Ischomachos felt that it was his duty to teach his young wife. On the whole, women in this category were expected to be mothers and wives without the need to work outside the house. This is why when their circumstances changed, and they needed to become the breadwinners in the family, they had inadequate training for the labour market, and had to rely on their wits and whatever skills they had from the household, which typically meant that they operated at the lowest end of the job market and, to add insult to injury, they often found themselves on the receiving end of jibes and jokes by the comedians of the day.[62]

The medical professions, which included midwifery and pharmacology, would need training from a young age, and we know that women did practise these in Attica.[63] Serving as educators and instructors was also a career option for some women, even if rarely. Aspasia of Miletus is a good example of this; she certainly had students of her own.[64] Bringing up children was typically the occupation of a slave woman, but it seems that sometimes poor free women could also take on such occupations out of necessity.[65] To these professions and occupations we need to add priesthoods and other service positions in religious sites, which also required training and dedication. Other skilled occupations which required a period of learning before one could engage in them, like running a business such as an inn,[66] baking and selling bread,[67] cakes or biscuits on a professional scale, or working as a cook at inns or taverns, can perhaps be included in this group, although in this case there may be an overlap with women who did such jobs when they were forced to get out of the house and look for work using their domestic skills in cooking.

The market of entertainers and musicians was dominated by slave prostitutes to such an extent that it is difficult for us to identify free women outside the sex markets with such skills, even though they must surely have existed and would have been the preferred choice for religious festivals and other sombre occasions.[68] It is reasonable to assume that some of the women, citizen and metic, who chose some career path that would require of them to sacrifice part of family life probably wanted something more than the routine of a mother and housewife, but in most cases such aspirations were fuelled and enhanced by the desire for a more secure income. To put it bluntly, rich women did not become midwives, innkeepers or bakers in Athens, and Demosthenes classes the mother of Aeschines among the dregs of society for her activities as an instructor in some religious association.

This prejudice against working women is attested in comedy, and Aristophanes often jokes about the low-class, rough women of the marketplace.[69] Many of these women probably belonged to the other category, the ones who had not imagined their future behind a stall in the marketplace, women who were brought up to become someone's wife and mistress of his household, but by some dire necessity ended up having to provide for themselves and their families. It is fair to think that many of these women would be unprepared for the life of hardship that they experienced, and would need to toughen up and cope with the rules and demands of the outside world. Small-scale bakers and cooks, wreath-sellers, sellers of eggs, vegetables or other domestic produce, weavers and cloth-makers in a broader sense, wet-nurses, farm workers and other small earners in limited-skill jobs would need to struggle on a day-to-day basis. Their plight is eloquently described by Euxitheos in the speech *Against Euboulides*:

καὶ γὰρ εἰ ταπεινὸν ἡ τιτθή, τὴν ἀλήθειαν οὐ φεύγω· . . . πολλὰ δουλικὰ καὶ ταπεινὰ πράγματα τοὺς ἐλευθέρους ἡ πενία βιάζεται ποιεῖν, ἐφ' οἷς ἐλεοῖντ' ἄν, ὦ ἄνδρες Ἀθηναῖοι, δικαιότερον ἢ προσαπολλύοιντο. ὡς γὰρ ἐγὼ ἀκούω, πολλαὶ καὶ τιτθαὶ καὶ ἔριθοι καὶ τρυγήτριαι γεγόνασιν ὑπὸ τῶν τῆς πόλεως κατ' ἐκείνους τοὺς χρόνους συμφορῶν ἀσταὶ γυναῖκες, πολλαὶ δ' ἐκ πενήτων πλούσιαι νῦν.[70]

For even if a nurse is a lowly thing, I do not shun the truth . . . Many are the servile acts which free persons are compelled by poverty to perform, and for these they should be pitied, men of Athens, rather than be brought also to utter ruin. For, as I am informed, many women have become nurses and laborers at the loom or in the vineyards owing to the misfortunes of the city in those days, women of citizen birth, too; and many who were poor then are now rich.

The chances of a serious brush with the law were limited for women working in those lowly professions for a meagre living. Those trading in the agora could run foul of some market regulation, such as selling smuggled or contraband goods or imports from an enemy state, and be liable to a *phasis* (denunciation).[71] If convicted, their goods could be confiscated and half of the sum raised at the sale would go to the successful prosecutor. Cheating with the standard weights or selling spoiled produce which could pose a danger to public health were also offences which could result in confiscation of goods and fines. The ten *agoranomoi* and the *metronomoi* – the public magistrates overseeing the sale of goods in the agora – had the authority to fine an offender up to fifty drachmas for violations.[72] This was not a petty sum for persons selling goods in the agora. However, we are left wondering what would happen if a female offender was unable to pay such a fine. Male offenders would become debtors to the state and suffer the serious consequences of *atimia*, which included staying away from the marketplace, and thus losing their livelihood. However, none of this applied to women. If they could not or did not pay a fine, was it business as usual? We do not have any evidence to answer this question convincingly. For lack of evidence to the contrary, I would imagine that confiscation of goods would be the most serious penalty imposed upon women traders in the marketplace.

Conversely, when women were cheated of payments for goods or services, which one would imagine has always been a hazard of owning a business,[73] large or small, like their male counterparts they could launch a complaint with a magistrate, as the two innkeepers in the underworld do when they go to Aiakos, the magistrate, and demand punishment for the thief as soon as they recognise 'Herakles' (Dionysus disguised as Herakles).[74] Quite possibly the magistrate, under the threat of a fine, would have been able to push for a settlement of a minor dispute without further ado. Alternatively they could bring their case before the Forty, and if the sum was smaller than ten drachmas, the member of this body who accepted the lawsuit had the authority to decide the case there and then. One would imagine that most petty disputes in the marketplace would have been settled like this. Interestingly, the two women in Aristophanes' *Frogs* want to find their protector first, Kleon or Hyperbolos,[75] but only the magistrate appears to make the inquiries, later on. Of course, comedy is not a suitable manual for Greek law, but it still provides us with a valuable insight into the legal options of a business woman who had been cheated of due payments. She could either go direct to the magistrate and ask him to do something about it,[76] or fetch a male advocate and pursue the offender all the way to the courts if the disputed sum was larger.

The career women of Athens, if one is allowed to use this term very liberally, could get into more serious trouble with the law, and some of them were even put to death after successful prosecutions for public offences, like impiety. It appears that the higher the level and form of exposure to public life, the higher was the danger. Relatively affluent businesses, like some of the more pricey upper-end establishments in the sex industry, had the finances to support court cases with expensive advocates, as for example the case brought by Nais and her advocates against Philonides, one of the richest men in Athens, for sexual assault, or the one brought by Lais the Younger where Lysias was defending her opponent. The very public dispute for jurisdiction in the courts between the hierophant and the priestess of Demeter was probably motivated by financial interests, and resulted in more public lawsuits, which eventually led to the exile of the hierophant. The cases against Ninos and Theoris were carried out in their capacity as public servants, and at least in the case of Theoris because she clearly had a public profile and a very large presence outside the *oikos*. The same can be said about several hetairai who found themselves in trouble with the law, like Phryne, or Timandra. Their high-profile activities outside the *oikos* and the traditional bounds of female roles and expectations probably attracted unwanted attention and landed them in court. And even in those instances where it seems that it was not a high profile in public life, but rather more complex reasons, like the antagonism of men close to them, which generated the court cases against them, women like Aspasia, Neaira and Aristagora found that their past could actually be used as a weapon against them. Women in the health professions were safe from prosecution for their professional activities, because the law explicitly prohibited the prosecution of medical practitioners for any harm coming to the patient, even when it was their fault.[77]

The inevitable conclusion is that poor, low-profile women who were scraping a living through their work outside the *oikos* were typically not involved in major court cases, partly because they had no major interests to defend and partly because they were not seen as important or affluent enough to attract the unwanted attentions of a vengeful prosecutor, or a sycophant. However, when the stakes got higher and women had more substantial interests to defend, and more resources available to them to use in the pursuit of justice, they attracted more attention and found themselves the targets of prosecutions motivated by envy, anger, jealousy, hostility or simply financial interests. In such cases women became victims of their own success, or victims of the success of the men with whom they were associated, and they often faced prosecutions for offences which they had not really committed. Under the thin veneer of prosecutions for impiety or immigration violations we should always be searching for the true motives which landed these women in court. In most cases we will find that their actual level of guilt with regard to the main charge was from minimal to non-existent, and that it was simply used as an excuse to hurt them or those around them.

CONCLUSIONS

The aspirational principle of *isonomia* cultivated the illusion that the law was equal for all, but clearly differences of wealth, status and gender created substantial inequality. For the slave women of Attica the legal protections were very few, and established not to protect the slaves themselves, but to protect society and the best interests of the slave's master. When, for example, the homicide law of Drakon restricted the right to kill a slave, the law had in mind first that the slave was valuable property and should be protected on account of that, and then that society needed to be protected from the deadly miasma, the supernatural contagion which threatened anyone who came in contact with the killer or shared the same roof with them. That the law did not have in mind to protect the life of the slave as a human being becomes clearer from the fact that if the slave were to be killed by his or her master, no action against the killer was deemed necessary.[78] Likewise, when Athenian law included slaves in the law of *hybris*, the intention was not to protect the slaves from abusive behaviour, for they suffered that every day of their lives on a massive scale.[79] The intention was to protect free people from attitudes and behavioural patterns which society considered so entirely unacceptable that they could not even be directed at a slave. Slaves had no way of seeking redress for wrongs done to them, and when they did something wrong they were not put on trial, simply because they had no right to a fair trial; it was their master and not the law who meted out punishment, if the crime was reported to him and he wanted to do something about the delinquent slave. If a slave had committed a very serious crime, like murder, again he or she was not put on trial. Torture and summary execution were probably the expected course of action, as the speech of Antiphon *Against the Stepmother* makes clear.[80] The exclusion of slaves from the justice system was so complete that not even their testimony was admissible, unless it had been extracted under torture, and since torture, despite some misconceptions to the contrary, has never been a reliable tool for getting at the truth, litigants routinely blocked the testimony of slaves, even when they had reliable information.[81]

The justice system of the Athenian democracy was accessible to free persons only. Free males, citizens and non-citizens, had unfettered access on most issues, except those which had to do with immigration or the political life of the city. These matters were understandably restricted to citizens.[82] The only known restriction in private lawsuits was the limitation of laying claim to real estate to Athenian citizens, naturally, because non-citizens were not entitled to own real estate in Attica.[83] For women, initiating public lawsuits would be meaningless, perhaps with the exception of *hybris*, where conceivably a male representative could bring a prosecution on their behalf against someone who treated them with *hybris*. However, since we do not know of a single *hybris* prosecution which ever went to trial in Athens, this possibility remained theoretical.[84] On the other hand, a few women were prosecuted under public lawsuits, such as the *graphe asebeias*, or various immigration lawsuits. We can be confident that in all these cases the prosecutor would not risk a massive 1,000-drachma fine merely in order to put an unruly woman in her place. There was always more than meets the eye, personal, public and even political. Whether a metic woman and her representatives would be permitted to lay claim to the property of a close relative, who although a metic by birth might have been offered citizenship, or the right to own real estate in Attica, is not clear, since we do not know of any such case. Other than that, theoretically, metic women could defend their rights and property through private lawsuits, or respond to claims and accusations made against them, using a male representative, along similar lines to citizen women.

Although the aspiration of the Athenian legal system was to remain non-professional and easily accessible by any citizen, in practice an entire market supporting litigants in a variety of ways had evolved, and some of the prominent logographers, litigators and instructors of rhetoric had become very rich from the practice. In name they were not professional lawyers; however, in actual practice they were as professional as they come, and their superb skills came at a high cost which would be beyond the reach of poor women, citizen or metic, but available to those who could pay regardless of gender.

NOTES

1. See Chapter 1, pp. 105–24, for an outline of the level and method of access which each group had to the legal system.
2. Luc. *DMeretr.* 6.
3. For example, the homicide law of Drakon ordained that the suspected killer of a citizen was to be tried by the Areopagos, and if convicted he or she faced the death penalty. However, the suspected killer of an alien or slave was to be tried at the Palladion court, and faced exile or a fine as a penalty (probably exile for the killing of a free person and a fine for the killing of a slave). This practice had been retained in the classical period along with Drakon's homicide law.
4. The judges took the heliastic oath before their entry to office, as cited in the speech *Against Timocrates* (149–50): Ψηφιοῦμαι κατὰ τοὺς νόμους καὶ τὰ ψηφίσματα τοῦ δήμου τοῦ Ἀθηναίων καὶ τῆς βουλῆς τῶν πεντακοσίων. . . . καὶ ἀκροάσομαι τοῦ τε κατηγόρου καὶ τοῦ ἀπολογουμένου ὁμοίως ἀμφοῖν. 'I will vote according to the laws and the decrees of the Athenian people and the Council of the Five Hundred . . . and I will give both sides, the prosecutor and the defendant, a fair hearing.'
5. Some useful discussions of these shifts, especially in wartime, can be found in Fabre-Serris and Keith 2015; Humble 2004: 166–83; Loman 2004: 34–54; Sulprizio 2013: 44–63; Cudjoe 2010.
6. D. 23.53: ΝΟΜΟΣ. Ἐάν τις ἀποκτείνῃ ἐν ἄθλοις ἄκων, ἢ ἐν ὁδῷ καθελὼν ἢ ἐν πολέμῳ ἀγνοήσας, ἢ ἐπὶ δάμαρτι ἢ ἐπὶ μητρὶ ἢ ἐπ' ἀδελφῇ ἢ ἐπὶ θυγατρί, ἢ ἐπὶ παλλακῇ ἣν ἂν ἐπ' ἐλευθέροις παισὶν ἔχῃ, τούτων ἕνεκα μὴ φεύγειν κτείναντα. 'LAW. If a man kill another unintentionally in an athletic contest, or overcoming him in a fight on the highway, or unwittingly in battle, or in intercourse with his wife, or mother, or sister, or daughter, or concubine kept for procreation of legitimate children, he shall not go into exile as a manslayer on that account.' For a discussion see: Cohen 1984: 147–65; 1990: 147–65; Carey 1995: 407–17; Ogden 1997: 25–41; Kapparis 1995: 97–122.
7. For some authoritative discussions of early Greek law see Gagarin 1981; 1986.
8. *IG* i^3 104; see also Stroud 1979.
9. For a recent and thorough reappraisal of the laws of Drakon see Carey 2013: 29–51; also Gagarin 1981; Stroud 1968; Verlinsky 2017: 142–73; Mirhady 2008: 15–30; Reichardt 2003.
10. E.g. Solon Fr. 2.2–4; 5.1 West.
11. Is. 8.18: Ὅτε γὰρ ὁ πατὴρ αὐτὴν ἐλάμβανε, γάμους εἱστίασε καὶ ἐκάλεσε τρεῖς αὐτοῦ φίλους μετὰ τῶν αὐτοῦ προσηκόντων, τοῖς τε φράτερσι γαμηλίαν εἰσήνεγκε κατὰ τοὺς ἐκείνων νόμους. 'When my father married her, he held a wedding feast and invited three friends of his and his relatives, and he introduced her to his *phrateres* according to their laws.' See also Is. 3.73, 75, 76, 79; D. 57.43, 69; Sch. Ar. Ach. 146; Golden 1985: 9–13 responding to Gould 1980: 38–59.

While I do not believe that phratries routinely inscribed women in their registers, I am prepared to accept that it was customary for the *phrateres* in most Athenian phratries and *gene* to offer sacrifices and celebrate with their peers significant life events, like a marriage, the birth of a child or an adoption, thus letting the community know about this event. Is. 8.20 makes clear that, at least in the classical period, this was customary, but not required. It is certain that each phratry or *genos* had its own rules and procedures (νόμος), and therefore we must accept that there was some variation in practices with regard to such events. On phratries and *gene*, and their role in the community and Athenian public life, see Lambert 1993; Cromey 2006: 41–69; Evans 2004: 1–25; Robertson 1998: 111–20; Flower 1985: 232–5; Hedrick 1984; 1991: 241–68; 1983: 299–304; 1988: 111–17; 1989: 126–35; Bourriot 1976. On the significant Demotionid decrees see Carawan 2010: 381– 400; Thompson 1967: 51–68; Wysocki 1988: 39–46.
12. On Athenian family and inheritance laws introduced by Solon in their wider context of Solonean political and social reforms see Carey 2015: 110–28; Cudjoe and Adam-Magnissali 2010: 67–93; Flament 2007: 289–318; Frost 2002: 34–46; Gagliardi 2002: 5–59; Humphreys 2002: 340–7; L'Homme-Wéry 2005: 169–85; Lape 2002: 117–39; Leão 2005: 5–31; Leão and Rhodes 2015; Lewis 2004: 19–40; Owens 2010; Ruschenbusch 1966; Stroud 1979; Wagner-Hasel 2009: 143–81; Woodhouse 1938; Schaps 1979; 1975: 53–7; Just 1989: 53–73; Craik 1984: 6–29; Griffith-Williams 2012: 145–62; 2016: 111–16; Karnezis 1972; Katz 1992: 692–708.
13. See my previous discussion in Kapparis 2019a: 283–90.
14. It is impossible to answer the obvious question why, if Solon understood these vulnerabilities, he did not empower women to take care of their own financial and legal affairs. One might think that such an option would be unimaginable in aristocratic Athens, and that Solon legislated within the confines of acceptable social norms for each gender, families and communities as a whole. Even a visionary like Solon was restricted by prevailing social standards. For a fresh perspective on the Solonean legislation and its aims see the excellent study by Werner Riess (2018a: 61–80), with previous literature, and also Leão 2001b; 2005: 5–31; 2001a: 113–32; the new translation of the Solonean laws with notes by Leão and Rhodes (2015), and the classic work on the Solonean legislation by Ruschenbusch (1966). The larger issue is beyond our purposes to address here, but the reader could also consult Carey 2015: 110–28 (on Solon in the orators); Cudjoe and Adam-Magnissali 2010: 67–93; Humphreys 2002: 340–7; Lape 2002: 117–39; Flament 2007: 289–318; L'Homme-Wéry 2005: 169–85.
15. Is. 3; See also the discussion in Part I, pp. 73–5. For more thorough discussions of the issues involved in this case see Hatzlilambrou 2018, esp. the introduction; Griffith-Williams 2012: 145–62; 2019: 375–88.
16. D. 27–31.
17. Lys. 32.
18. Kapparis 2019a: 138–81.
19. Arist. *Ath.* 56; see also the laws quoted in D. 43.51, 54 and 75.
20. D. 30.6–7.

21. Aesch. 1.13, 14 and 184, with the discussion in Kapparis 2018: 156–8. On the law about establishing an unchaste daughter in a brothel see Glazebrook 2005a: 33–53; Frost 2002: 34–46; Rosivach 1995: 2–3.
22. Arist. *Ath*. 26.3. See also the discussion about the terms in Mossé 1985: 77–9; Patterson 1986: 49–67.
23. Arist. *Ath. Pol.* 26, 4, 1275 b 31, 1278 a 34; Plu. *Per.* 37; and also Rhodes 1981: 331–5; Patterson 1981: passim; Walters 1983: 314–36; Raaflaub 2004: 15–16, 217; Ober 1989: 81; Ogden 1996: passim; Kapparis 2005: 72–6; Blok 2017: 141–70.
24. Ar. *Ach.* 1048–68; *Ec.* 241–4; *Th.* 443–58. See also the excellent study by Richard Cudjoe (2010) on the Athenian widow, where the author assesses the demographi cost of the incessant wars in which Athens was involved, and the human cost of the losses of men in the prime of life for their families.
25. D. 57.45: πολλὰ δουλικὰ καὶ ταπεινὰ πράγματα τοὺς ἐλευθέρους ἡ πενία βιάζεται ποιεῖν. Peter Bicknell (1976: 113–15) has questioned whether this was a citizen family on the remote possibility that the grandmother of Euxitheos could have married an alien man. This is most unlikely. Athenian men sometimes took alien wives before the fourth century, but very rarely did the opposite happen. In the one instance where we know that this happened, Timokrates gave his sister in marriage to a rich man from Kerkyra (D. 24.203), and the couple went to live in the husband's city, as expected. Walter Lacey (1980: 57–61) has emphasised the high child mortality rates in poor Athenian families like Euxitheos', but also stressed that the adversities of this family offer no evidence of alien status. On the credibility of the story of Euxitheos see also Bers 2002: 232–9. I am convinced that Euxitheos was unjustly rejected by the deme on account of local politics and past resentments. The evidence he presents in favour of his citizenship is reliable and unassailable.
26. Ar. *Ra.* 549–78.
27. See also my previous discussion inKapparis 2018a: 210–13; Carey 2007: 472–3.
28. See Chapter 1, pp. 105–12.
29. This view has been broadly accepted by both Esther Eidinow (2010: 9–35) and Matthew Dillon (2002).
30. There are examples of supportive Athenian families, for example that of the widowed sister of the speaker in Lys. 3.6, who had seemingly moved into his house with her daughters after the death of her husband, or the orphaned Charmides raised by relatives (And. 1.48).
31. Is. 10.10. The very fact that this law defined the financial limitations of women not in drachmas but in pre-coinage values is a sure indication that it had lapsed into disuse centuries before the time of the orators.
32. The substantial monograph by David Schaps (1979) remains the best study on the economic rights of Athenian women. On contracts in general, see also Cohen 2006: 73–92; Lanni 2007: 225–36.
33. D. 41.9. Another good example of this can be found in the speech *Against Neaira*, where the procuress Nikarete enters into a very large financial transaction (thirty minae) with two Corinthian men according to the laws of the city (D. 59.29: κατατιθέασιν αὐτῆς τιμὴν τριάκοντα μνᾶς τοῦ σώματος τῇ Νικαρέτῃ,

καὶ ὠνοῦνται αὐτὴν παρ' αὐτῆς νόμῳ πόλεως καθάπαξ αὐτῶν δούλην εἶναι. 'They paid thirty minae, the price for her body, to Nikarete, and bought her from her according to the law of the city to be their own slave thereafter.' While, of course, Corinthian law may have been different, it would be difficult to imagine how the numerous women in the sex industry of Attica could have operated, especially in the upper end of the market, without the ability to enter into large financial transactions.

34. Plautus, *Asinaria*, scene 4.1, or lines 751–809. On prostitution contracts see Cohen 2000: 113–47 and the extensive discussion in his 2015 book.
35. The speech of Lysias *Against Eratosthenes* provides ample evidence of the vulnerability of metic families, especially wealthier ones, in the hands of a rapacious and ruthless regime which had little respect for lawful process, and saw an opportunity in these troublesome years to enrich itself from the seizure of affluent metics' properties. See also the authoritative study of Andrew Wolpert (2002) on the subject.
36. For the overall standing of metic families in Athens see the classic study by D. Whitehead (1977; 1981: 223–44), and the more recent monograph by Rebecca Futo Kennedy on metic women (2014). See also Bakewell 1999b: 43–64; 1999a: 5–22; Carey 1991: 84–9, on the legal status of metic women; Duncan-Jones 1980: 101–9; Watson 2010: 259–78. on the origins of the institution; Patterson 2000: 93–112, on the interactions of metics with the Athenian justice system. Patterson takes a more restrictive view, while in my understanding democratic Athenian courts did not disadvantage metics in their quest for justice. What was just, was just, and a judge's vote should follow it. Institutionalised inequalities in some areas, like the right to own real estate, which was restricted to citizens and privileged aliens, or the right to introduce certain lawsuits related to public life, which was explicitly limited to citizens (Ἀθηναίων ὁ βουλόμενος), were clear, and typically self-evident restrictions which metics needed to accept. However, when a metic man or woman ended up before a magistrate or arbitrator, or in court, he or she did not expect to be treated unfairly on account of his or her status. Injustice was what the Thirty did, not the magistrates and courts of the democracy.
37. However, the fact that metics could not normally own real estate in Attica would create some differences, as a metic *oikos* would be understood rather as an economic and familial unit than a physical one centred on the ancestral property.
38. For example, in D. 47.55 we read the following: τιτθή τις ἐμὴ γενομένη πρεσβυτέρα, ἄνθρωπος εὔνους καὶ πιστὴ καὶ ἀφειμένη ἐλευθέρα ὑπὸ τοῦ πατρὸς τοῦ ἐμοῦ. συνῴκησεν δὲ ἀνδρί, ἐπειδὴ ἀφείθη ἐλευθέρα. 'A nurse of mine when she got older, because she was devoted and faithful, was set free by my father. Then she married a man, when she was set free.'
39. This seems to be the case in D. 47.55; see preceding note. Whether she agreed to the marriage (συνῴκησεν ἀνδρί) or the speaker's father arranged it is hard to tell. The sequence of actions as described by Apollodoros is that first she was liberated by his father, and then she took a husband. One would imagine that the speaker's father made the formal arrangements on her behalf, now as

her *prostates*. Archippe was clearly given in marriage to Phormion, her second husband, by Pasion, her first husband, on his deathbed. No source gives a very clear description of how these metic marriages were arranged and formalised, but formal they were, and common sense suggests that independent metic women untethered to families had more of a say in these arrangements than many citizen women had in their choice of husband.

40. D. 59.16 and 52. See also Kapparis 1999: com. ad loc.
41. Arist. *Ath.* 58.3; D. 46.22; see also the full citation of the law with brief discussion in the Appendix, pp. 228–9.
42. On the honorary grant of *enktesis* see Leão 2012: 135–52; Stelzer 1971; Pečirka 1966.
43. The option of a formal contract was available, especially if a dowry (up to ten minae, by law: Harp. s.v. νοθεῖα) was involved when a non-citizen woman was given as a concubine to a citizen by her family.
44. The marriage of Kephalos to Lysias' mother was certainly a proper, lawful marriage, probably conducted in accordance with the customs of their native Syracuse, and quite possibly before Kephalos even moved to Athens, attracted by the opportunities which the markets of the city offered around the middle of the fifth century. Lysias himself married a metic woman known as the daughter of Brachyllos, his niece, and we are told by Apollodoros that he had enough respect for her and his old mother not to bring his mistress Metaneira into the family residence (D. 59.22).
45. Is. 6.19–20.
46. Kennedy 2014: 1.
47. Cic. *N.D.* 1.93 and *Fin.* 2.67–8.
48. See the discussion in Part I, pp. 39–43, and the classic monograph by Madeleine Henry (1995).
49. Poseidonios Fr. 290a.495–506; Plu. 1089c, 1097d; D.L. 10.7. Not all these women were metics. Leontion and Boidion were probably Athenian (see Kapparis 2018a: 396–7 and 421–2 for the relevant discussion), and Philainis was from Samos, and could count herself as an Athenian by the decree which offered Athenian citizenship to the Samians (*IG* ii^2 1).
50. See the discussion in Kapparis 2018a: 52–5.
51. Athen. 13.48; Kapparis 2018a: 52.
52. X. *HG* 6.3.1–5.
53. Cic. *Verr.* 2.4.4: Idem, opinor, artifex eiusdem modi Cupidinem fecit illum qui est Thespiis, propter quem Thespiae visuntur; nam alia visendi causa nulla est. 'I think the same artist (Praxiteles) made the Cupid of the same type which stands at Thespiai, and because of it one goes to see Thespiai, because there is nothing else to see at Thespiai.' See also my previous discussion of these works (2018: 321–5), and Keesling 2006: 59–76; Hoernes 2012: 55–70; Corso 1997: 123–50; 1997–8: 63–91; Cavallini 2004: 231–8.
54. Athen. 13.38 and Kapparis 2018a: 334–5.
55. As stated in Chapter 2, pp. 129–31, Neaira was caught up in the political battles of men regarding the policy of Athens towards Philip II.
56. See Cudjoe 2010: 15–169.

57. Ar. *Th.* 443–58.
58. Luc. *DMeretr.* 6.
59. A competent monograph by P. Herfst (1922) is a century old, leaving the rather brief article by Roger Brock (1994: 336–46) as the only comprehensive study on the subject in modern times. A few other studies have discussed specific aspects of women's work, like the monograph by Rebecca Futo Kennedy (2014) on metic women's labour, the very interesting book by Elizabeth Barber (1994) on cloth-making in prehistoric times, the article by Walter Scheidel (1996: 1–10) on women's agricultural labour in Greece and Rome, and two studies on images of working women (mainly woolwork) in art (Kosmopoulou 2001: 281–319; Larsson Lovén 1998: 85–95). We still need a full-scale, dedicated study on this important subject, encompassing literary sources, inscriptions and artworks.
60. E.g. Cohen 2015; Kapparis 2018a, esp. ch. 6.
61. X. *Oec.* 7.5–8: Καὶ τί ἂν, ἔφη, ὦ Σώκρατες, ἐπισταμένην αὐτὴν παρέλαβον, ἣ ἔτη μὲν οὔπω πεντεκαίδεκα γεγονυῖα ἦλθε πρὸς ἐμέ, τὸν δ' ἔμπροσθεν χρόνον ἔζη ὑπὸ πολλῆς ἐπιμελείας ὅπως ὡς ἐλάχιστα μὲν ὄψοιτο, ἐλάχιστα δ' ἀκούσοιτο, ἐλάχιστα δ' ἔροιτο; οὐ γὰρ ἀγαπητόν σοι δοκεῖ εἶναι, εἰ μόνον ἦλθεν ἐπισταμένη ἔρια παραλαβοῦσα ἱμάτιον ἀποδεῖξαι, καὶ ἑωρακυῖα ὡς ἔργα ταλάσια θεραπαίναις δίδοται; ἐπεὶ τά γε ἀμφὶ γαστέρα, ἔφη, πάνυ καλῶς, ὦ Σώκρατες, ἦλθε πεπαιδευμένη· ὅπερ μέγιστον ἔμοιγε δοκεῖ παίδευμα εἶναι καὶ ἀνδρὶ καὶ γυναικί. Τὰ δ' ἄλλα, ἔφην ἐγώ, ὦ Ἰσχόμαχε, αὐτὸς ἐπαίδευσας τὴν γυναῖκα ὥστε ἱκανὴν εἶναι ὧν προσήκει ἐπιμελεῖσθαι; Οὐ μὰ Δί', ἔφη ὁ Ἰσχόμαχος, οὐ πρίν γε καὶ ἔθυσα καὶ ηὐξάμην ἐμέ τε τυγχάνειν διδάσκοντα καὶ ἐκείνην μανθάνουσαν τὰ βέλτιστα ἀμφοτέροις ἡμῖν. "'Why, what knowledge could she have had, Socrates, when I took her for my wife? She was not yet fifteen years old when she came to me, and up to that time she had lived in leading-strings, seeing, hearing and saying as little as possible. If when she came she knew no more than how, when given wool, to turn out a cloak, and had seen only how the spinning is given out to the maids, is not that as much as could be expected? For in control of her appetite, Socrates, she had been excellently trained; and this sort of training is, in my opinion, the most important to man and woman alike." "But in other respects did you train your wife yourself, Ischomachus, so that she should be competent to perform her duties?" "Oh no, Socrates; not until I had first offered sacrifice and prayed that I might really teach, and she learn what was best for us both'" (trans. W. Heinemann). See also Pomeroy 1994: com. ad loc.; Föllinger and Stoll 2018: 143–58.
62. E.g. Ar. *V.* 35, 238, 497, 549 ff., 1388 ff., *Lys.* 456–61, *Ra.* 112–13 (where bakeries are mentioned side by side with brothels); Hermippos (an entire play entitled Ἀρτοπώλιδες, 'Bread-sellers'); Eupolis, Fr. 9; among others.
63. E. *Alc.* 393–4; Pl. *Tht.* 151 c, 161 e, *Plt.* 268 b. Aelius Dionysius (Ἀττικὰ ὀνόματα, s.v. ἰατρός) quoting Alexis, informs us that ἰάτρια was the proper Attic form for a female physician, while the commoner ἰατρίνη he considers to be non-Greek. On the qualifications and qualities of the ideal midwife the description by Soranos (*Gyn.* 1.3–4), although from centuries later, would still be broadly applicable to the realities of classical Athens. A number of medical ethics studies produced in classical Athens with male physicians in mind (e.g. Hp. *Decent.*, *Lex*, *Medic.*) would apply to female practitioners too.

64. Aesch. Socr. *Aspasia* (Fr. 15 ff. Weidmann), D. 18.259, where Demosthenes alludes to Aeschines's mother as an instructor in some rites.
65. D. 57.44–5.
66. E.g. Eup. Fr. 9; Ar. *V.* 35, *Lys.* 458, *Ra.* 549 ff.
67. Female bread-sellers appear often in classical literature, and are the butt of many jokes in comedy. As noted above, Hermippos had written a play entitled Ἀρτοπώλιδες, while jokes about female bread-sellers can be found in Anacreon (Fr. 43 Page), Aristophanes (*V.* 238, 1388, *Lys.* 458, *Ra.* 858), Lucian (*Demon.* 63, depicting a cat-fight between female bread-sellers) and elsewhere.
68. Kapparis 2018: 275–84.
69. E.g. in the famous passage of Aristophanes' *Lysistrata* (456–60) where the rough, low-class women of the marketplace are summoned to action:

> Ὦ ξύμμαχοι γυναῖκες, ἐκθεῖτ' ἔνδοθεν,
> ὦ σπερμαγοραιολεκιθολαχανοπώλιδες,
> ὦ σκοροδοπανδοκευτριαρτοπώλιδες,
> οὐχ ἕλξετ', οὐ παιήσετ', οὐκ ἀράξετε,
> οὐ λοιδορήσετ', οὐκ ἀναισχυντήσετε;
> Παύσασθ', ἐπαναχωρεῖτε, μὴ σκυλεύετε.

> On, gallant allies of our high design,
> Vendors of grain-eggs-pulse-and-vegetables,
> Ye garlic-tavern-keepers of bakeries,
> Strike, batter, knock, hit, slap, and scratch our foes,
> Be finely imprudent, say what you think of them. . . .
> Enough! retire and do not rob the dead.
> (trans. J. Lindsay)

70. D. 57.45. Trans. N. W. DeWitt.
71. For *phasis* the standard work is Douglas MacDowell 1991: 187–98. Through this procedure goods which were deemed to be illegally sold were denounced to a magistrate, and ultimately confiscated. The successful prosecutor was awarded part of the value of the confiscated goods.
72. See *Ath.* 51.1, and Rhodes 1981: 575–82; MacDowell 1978: 157–8; Fantasia 2012: 31–56; Stanley 1979: 13–19.
73. In fact, the chorus of old men in Aristophanes' *Wasps* (236–8) reminisce with pride that as young men they stole a loaf of bread from a woman bread-seller.
74. Ar. *Ra.* 549–674.
75. A standard joke about demagogues being seen as the protectors of the low classes in the agora, which Aristophanes turns into the main theme of *Knights*.
76. In a similar incident, a teenage male prostitute, Diophantos the orphan, went to the archon and demanded that he force payment from a foreigner who had not compensated him the agreed four drachmas for the encounter (Aesch. 1.158–9).
77. See Ant. *Tetralogy* 3, and the discussion in Kapparis 2019a: 218–20; Claassen 2007: 87–98; Amundsen 1973: 17–31; Amundesen and Ferngren 1977: 202–13.

78. Plato's *Euthyphro* touches upon the moral and religious dilemmas and implications in such cases. See also Rosivach 2017: 232–41; Fischer 2014: 479–94; Garver 2014: 510–27.
79. On *hybris* in Athenian law and ideology see Rowe 1993: 397–406; Fisher 1992; 1997: 44–84; 2005: 67–89; Cairns 1996: 1–32; Gagarin 1979a: 229–36; MacDowell 1976: 14–31; 1978: 129–32; Spatharas 2006: 47–67; 2009: 30–52; Todd 1993: 270–1; Harris 2004: 41–83; Lanni 2016 with the response of Alberto Maffi in his important review (2017), and also the substantial fact-checking of her views by Edward Harris in his review (2018).
80. Ant. 1.20: τῷ γὰρ δημοκοίνῳ τροχισθεῖσα παρεδόθη. 'She was tortured and handed over to the public executioner.'
81. On this contentious issue see Gagarin 1996: 1–18; Mirhady 1996: 119–31; 2000: 53–74; Thür 1996: 132–4; Kapparis 1999: 424–36.
82. The phrase Ἀθηναίων ὁ βουλόμενος 'any Athenian who wishes', as opposed to simply ὁ βουλόμενος 'anyone who wishes', indicate which types of lawsuits could only be introduced by citizens. See for example D. 21.47 (*hybris*); 24.23, 33, 63 (legislative processes); 59.16 (immigration); Is. 6.3 (laying a claim on property which included real estate); Aesch. 1.32 (denunciation of one of the orators in the assembly); Lyc. 1.121 (high treason).
83. Is. 6,3: κατὰ τὸν νόμον τοῦ κλήρου, ἐξὸν ἀμφισβητῆσαι Ἀθηναίων τῷ βουλομένῳ. 'Whoever wishes among the Athenians has the right to lay claim to the property.'
84. Edward Harris (2008: 81) understood that the *probole* was only an advisory process, and that the case *Against Meidias* (D. 21) went to court through a *graphe hybreos*. However, the critical passage from the speech itself makes unambiguously clear that the case was a *probole*, as the overwhelming majority of scholars have argued: D. 21.28: μὴ δὴ τοῦτο λέγειν αὐτὸν ἐᾶτε, ὅτι καὶ δίκας ἰδίας δίδωσ' ὁ νόμος μοι καὶ γραφὴν ὕβρεως· δίδωσι γάρ· ἀλλ' ὡς οὐ πεποίηκεν ἃ κατηγόρηκα, ἢ πεποιηκὼς οὐ περὶ τὴν ἑορτὴν ἀδικεῖ, τοῦτο δεικνύτω· τοῦτο γὰρ αὐτὸν ἐγὼ προὐβαλόμην, καὶ περὶ τούτου τὴν ψῆφον οἴσετε νῦν ὑμεῖς. 'Do not allow him to tell you that the law also permits private *dikai* and a *graphe hybreos*. Yes it does. However, he should prove that either he did not do what I am accusing him of doing, or although he did these things he has not violated the sanctity of the festival. This is what I am accusing him of through this *probole*, on which you will be casting your vote.' It could not be clearer: Demosthenes says that although the law allowed him several possibilities, such as a private lawsuit or a *graphe hybreos*, he did not choose any of these, but instead chose the *probole*, because the assault happened during the festival, and this was the most appropriate procedure. He also explicitly confirms that the case on which the jury was about to vote was the *probole*. (See also MacDowell 1990; Wolpert and Kapparis 2011: 79–83; among others.) On the issue of the viability of *hybris* prosecutions in Athens I have sided firmly with the view of Douglas MacDowell and Nick Fisher that such cases would be very difficult to prosecute, as it would be very challenging to prove attitudes, and this is why the *graphe hybreos* was a largely theoretical process (Kapparis 2019a: 223–5).

CHAPTER 5

Conclusions

Only a fraction of the legal disadvantages which restricted the lives and activities of Athenian women was actually enshrined in written law, and more often than not such provisions were not included in the statute books with the intent of legislating on the lives of Athenian women. Almost invariably they were laws reflecting 'masculine' concerns, such as the efficient administration of the *oikos*, succession and inheritance, and only incidentally affected the rights and legal standing of women. However, 'incidental' in this case does not mean 'unimportant'. For example, the basic right of an Athenian woman to marry someone of her choice, without the intervention of male relatives or the magistrates of the state, was, ironically, restricted by the same law which was intended to protect legal marriage, the traditional Athenian family, and a woman's position and property interests in it. The law explicitly defined legal rights and obligations for Athenian women primarily in relation to the concerns of their male relatives.

The laws which had established these rights were centuries old by the classical period. For the most part, they had been introduced by Solon in order to deal with family, property and succession at a very different time and under very different economic circumstances from those of classical Athens. Solon's laws were introduced at a time when the impoverished lower classes pawned their own freedom in order to survive the winter, and might even have been willing to prostitute their own children, regardless of gender. Some rigidly austere laws were necessary in order to ensure that children, male and female, were not robbed of their patrimony, regardless of their family circumstances.

The fortunes of Athens changed dramatically in the following centuries, partly because of Solon's reforms, and definitely as a result of the city's strengthened position in the Greek world in the aftermath of the Persian wars. Far from selling their freedom to survive, poor Athenians had gained significant leverage in the assembly, to the point where comedians were joking that they were actually leading the city;[1] and while this may have been a wild exaggeration, poor Athenians certainly had much improved chances of making a living in a city which offered many opportunities. Athenian families no longer prostituted their daughters in order to keep everyone alive; women and men of citizen status who were practising prostitution typically came from fatherless, broken homes, with no one to provide or care for them.

Society moved on along with the rising economic fortunes of the city in later centuries, but these statutes were barely changed. For a brief moment in 403 the Athenians considered a repeal of the laws of Solon, but this never materialised.[2] As a result, centuries-old laws, which in the fourth century might have seemed outdated, continued to regulate so many aspects of the lives of women. We may view with horror the laws on the *epikleros*, and their complete disregard for a woman's feelings or choice when it came to her own marriage and fate, but we need to bear in mind that these laws were not made with personal or emotional considerations in mind. They were practical pieces of legislation built around primarily financial concerns and intended to safeguard the *oikos* and its property, with no regard for the feelings of individuals. If anything, the law recognised that there might be no feelings or compatibility between a couple joined together through an *epidikasia*, and this is why it explicitly compelled the husband to have intercourse with his wife at least twice a month, so as to fulfil the primary purpose of the union, namely to produce an heir who would continue the *oikos*.

The laws of Solon may be praised for their caring attitude towards the well-being and fortunes of women and children in a dangerous and exploitative world, but with the passage of time, as they were not sufficiently updated, certainly not to the same extent that they were updated in public life and in political and constitutional matters, they became restrictive shackles in a rapidly changing world. Many of those laws were so incompatible with the realities of classical Athens that they were simply difficult to apply, and in time they fell into disuse. For example, the laws restricting the level of a woman's dowry, the ones on the orderly conduct of women, mentioned by Plutarch, the law severely restricting a woman's independent economic capacity, and the laws prohibiting the procuring of free persons had all been forgotten in the classical period. In the fifth and fourth centuries Athenian fathers gave as much dowry to their daughters as they saw fit, and for the rich a large dowry often functioned as a status symbol.[3] All this was a far cry from the Solonean law trying to restrict a dowry to a few household items and three garments;[4] and far from being restricted to the petty sum of one *medimnos* of barley for the amount of a transaction which a woman was entitled to complete,[5] some women in fourth-century Athens were fabulously wealthy in their own right and disposed this wealth as they pleased. Meanwhile, the laws on the orderly conduct of women were a dead letter, while the whole city was full of procurers, who were sometimes respectable and affluent citizens like the happy (εὐδαίμων) Euktemon, before he got involved with a liberated slave who was a former prostitute and procuress.[6]

Anyone who cared to read the axons of Solon in the marketplace would still find these laws inscribed in the fourth century, but none of them had been applied for a very long time. Other laws, like the ones on rape, were adapted to the realities of the classical period, and while the Solonean law itself did not even specify the monetary sum of the fine to be imposed upon a convicted defendant, obviously because drachmas were not in use in the time of Solon, anyone convicted under this law in the classical period would have been fined in drachmas. The part of Solon's laws related to women which seems to have endured is the one related to family, property and inheritance, probably because there was something reassuring in the rigid regularity of these laws, according to which Athenian *oikoi* were born, passed on and dissolved, so that the *oikos* would continue and the rights and interests of its members would be secure under the watchful eye of the quasi-mythical lawgiver.

Most of the serious restrictions which affected the lives of Athenian women, like their inability to participate in the political life of the city, to elect or be elected to office, to speak in court, appear as witnesses or sit as judges, to participate in the army in any capacity, to sit in the Council of the Five Hundred or any other board or public office, and so on, where never inscribed into law. They were mighty conventions, in place from time immemorial and woven into the fabric of the Greek city-state and the Athenian democracy, and no one could ever tell whether or when someone had instituted such rules. It seems that the concept of women participating in public life in this manner was so inconceivable that a comic poet could half-joke about it on stage[7] (and I say 'half-joke' because in the final scenes of the play the women seem to be running the city with fairness and efficiency), but no one could seriously contemplate it as a viable option in real life. It would take another two and a half millennia, and two world wars on an apocalyptic scale, where women had to get out of the house and build tanks, bombs and aeroplanes, before the notion of gender equality could gain some traction.

Within these confines at polis and *oikos* level, a free woman, citizen or metic, was expected to receive some education, typically homeschooling, which would prepare her for her role as the manager of an Athenian *oikos*. This education certainly included some reading and writing lessons, cooking instruction, the skill of making cloth out of primary materials such as wool or linen, some elementary managerial skills, and some basic healthcare information on how to look after a sick person, treat a wound and administer potions, poultices and ointments. These would allow her to fit into the roles of the wife, mother and primary caretaker of the household. Unlike educating her male siblings,[8] educating an Athenian daughter was not a legal requirement, but it was certainly a strong social convention. Likewise, securing a husband for a free woman was not a legal obligation for her *kyrios*, but it was absolutely expected of him. Once a woman in Athens, citizen or metic, reached the age of fourteen or fifteen it was part of the process of growing up for her family to start looking for a suitable husband among friends and relatives, and farther away if necessary.

A free woman was entitled to a part or the whole of her father's property, and her descendants retained these rights even after her death, but she never acquired any inheritance rights to the *oikos* of her husband. However, the extent and shape of these rights were variable and depended on the actual circumstances of the family. If the woman had male siblings, she had no automatic legal entitlement to her family's property. A father, brother or paternal grandfather was under no legal obligation to offer a dowry when arranging a woman's marriage, but again, there was an almost universal convention that a dowry, and thus a portion of the family's property, should be given to the woman. Even an illegitimate daughter would expect to receive a dowry of up to ten minae.[9] However, if the woman had no male siblings, then inheriting a part or the whole of her parental estate became a legal mandate.[10] Whether she received part or the whole of it, and whether she was viewed as a direct heiress or merely as the vessel through which the property was going to pass to the next generation, was related to the question of whether she was married with children and therefore not an *epikleros*, or childless (married or unmarried) and consequently an *epikleros*. If she was an *epikleros*, then she was the vessel through which the property of the family would be passed on to the next generation, and the real owner of her father's property would be her son when he reached his twentieth year of age and legally became the heir to his maternal grandfather.

If the woman had no natural male siblings but had been given in marriage while her father (or paternal grandfather) was alive, and she already had children when he died, then these children were viewed as heirs to their maternal grandfather, and it seems that without further ado the property of her father was merged with that of her husband to be inherited by her children one day. If she had an adopted brother, he would inherit everything, as a natural brother would. If her father died while she was still unmarried but she had an adopted brother, he could act as a natural brother and arrange a marriage for her, with one small but legally significant difference. While a natural brother was under no legal obligation to provide a dowry for his sister, an adopted brother had the legal obligation to provide a dowry. The expression of the law σὺν ταύταις made clear that in such cases the woman could not be left out of the arrangements regarding her father's property by an adopted heir.[11] However, in real life the difference was practically insignificant because both a natural and an adopted brother were urged by a strong social convention to provide a dowry when arranging the marriage of a sister, and potential husbands expected no less. If the family had more than one daughter, then all these arrangements applied equally to all of them.

The property rights and entitlements of free women, citizen or metic, as these were enshrined in the Solonean laws on inheritance and succession, could be defended before the magistrates or in the courts of the Athenian democracy by relatives and advocates representing the women, and more often than not their own interests too. When Xenokles was representing his wife Phile in the litigation with her cousin and aunt for the estate of her father, let's say, he was certainly representing his own interests too, because a win for him and his wife would guarantee that the very substantial property of his father-in-law would be merged into his existing property. Sometimes the motives of family members and advocates do not seem to be quite so mercenary. For example, it is difficult to see what the son-in-law of Diogeiton's daughter stood to gain if he won in the case which he brought against Diogeiton on behalf of his mother-in-law and her young sons. It is possible that there were some hidden motives behind such cases of which we are not informed, but then again, it is equally possible that family members sometimes acted selflessly, in order to defend the interests of a widow or an orphaned girl. In any case, the legal position of women in such situations was precarious, and this is why, in addition to the laws governing succession and inheritance, there were laws which allowed for the prosecution of people treating abusively family members who could not directly defend themselves, such as orphans and *epikleroi*.[12] These legal provisions might not be enough to safeguard the rights of women to the full extent, but the laws of the Athenian democracy, here as in many other areas of life, relied upon citizen initiatives to enforce them, and in this case undoubtedly they relied upon the selfish interests of male relatives willing to pursue anyone who tried to violate a woman's property rights, because it benefited them too.

As far as the law was concerned, the free women of Attica enjoyed the same fundamental human rights as free men with regard to their safety and protection from abusive or humiliating behaviour. They had the same right to life as men did, and killing a woman carried the same sentence as killing a man. They were also equally protected with men with regard to physical or sexual assault, verbal abuse (κακηγορία), theft, robbery or injury, and criminal law generally did not differentiate between male and female victims, or between male and female perpetrators. A crime was a crime regardless of the gender of the victim or the perpetrator, with few exceptions, like the laws of adultery, where a set of the antiquated laws of Drakon and Solon firmly placed greater responsibility, and inflicted much more severe penalties, upon the man who violated another man's *oikos*.

The immigration laws of the city, for the most part, did not differentiate on the basis of gender, but when it came to the prohibition of mixed marriages the law used different language for men and women, because their roles were by default unequal in both the enactment and the continuation of an illegal marriage. For example, since a woman could not initiate a marriage contract, the law only explored the possibility that a man could deceive a citizen and offer him an alien woman in marriage, but not the possibility that a woman could deceive a citizen and offer him an alien woman in marriage. The law on the *graphe xenias* did not differentiate along lines of gender; however, it seems that in practice only men were prosecuted because, since they could fully participate in the politics and life of the city-state by acting as citizens, the stakes were much higher in their case. With regard to religious violations the law did not differentiate between men and women. It did not matter whether a man or a woman had offended the gods; both were equally capable of doing it and invoking the wrath of the gods upon the city, and the Athenian state did not hesitate to execute both men and women after convictions in a *graphe asebeias* trial.

The difference at the level of taxation, where a metic man had to pay twice as high a *metoikion* as a woman, is somewhat deceptive because the man's payment of twelve drachmas per annum included all his family members, and the law assumed that even if he did not have a family at the time when he first registered he might acquire one in future. On the other hand, a woman's *metoikion* of six drachmas was only for herself, and the law assumed that if she got married in future she would stop paying and would be covered by her husband's payment. Again, it seems that an inequality in the law was the reflection of unequal social roles and expectations. In other areas of economic activity the overall image can be equally deceptive and murky. While the antiquated laws of Solon which limited the ability of women to conduct transactions higher than the sum needed for the weekly supply of the household (one *medimnos* of barley), and only allowed for minimal dowries, had fallen into disuse in the classical period, it is still difficult to tell how often women engaged in larger financial transactions without the presence of a male representative. Even if the law no longer required that a man would act on their behalf, one would need witnesses to verify that the transaction took place in case of a dispute, and this is why it would be prudent to have male witnesses to the transaction, especially if large sums of money were to change hands. In the markets of upper-end prostitution it was not unusual for women, procurers or hetairai, to take part in large financial transactions, and we have evidence of prostitution contracts agreed by women for large sums of money without the apparent presence of a male representative. All things considered, it appears that there was a discrepancy between legal requirements and actual practice. While the law in the classical period no longer restricted the ability of women to perform larger financial transactions, the presence of free men as witnesses would be highly recommended in case something went wrong in future and a dispute about the transaction ended up in the courts.

Women's access to public life and the institutions of the democracy seems to be just as uneven and nuanced as most of their legal rights. While they had no access to the political life of the city, they enjoyed full access to the religious life, held high priesthoods and offices, were treated as public personae in their own right in religious affairs, and were part of religious festivals and celebrations on an equal footing with their male counterparts. There were some variations, such as the five women-only festivals, or the absence of women from performances of comedy, where sometimes the lewdness of subject matter and language could be held to compromise their sense of respectability. However, women routinely had extensive access to sanctuaries, offices and festivities.

Women's direct access to the justice system is also a matter complicated by law and tradition. While the principle of *isonomia* favoured practices based on equality before the law, and we can observe a noticeable change from the time of Solon to the laws of the democracy, tradition operated as a counterforce restricting the legal dealings of women. Antiquated laws which limited women's ability to perform financial transactions and viewed them only as a part of an *oikos*, with no independent presence before the law, had either fallen into disuse or were superseded by laws of the democracy which treated women not as shadowy figures behind the man of the household, but as persons with rights and obligations of their own, personally responsible for criminal actions they perpetrated, capable of conducting financial transactions and making and spending their own money, or able to walk away from a marriage without legal barriers. On the other hand, strong traditions prevented women from appearing before a jury as witnesses or speakers for themselves or someone else.

If we understand the Athenian legal system as a three-tier structure, with the magistrates of the state at the first level, arbitrators at the second level, and trial by jury at the top and final appeal level, then women were not prevented by tradition from accessing the two lower tiers, but their presence and movements were restricted at the top tier. They could certainly appear before the magistrate and ask for his help, and they could appear as witnesses and state their case before arbitrators, even though at this level they would need to rely on male representatives to initiate the litigation, and/or to set up the public or private arbitration meeting at which a woman could appear and explain herself, her actions or her claims and demands before the arbitrator, maybe a few other witnesses and the opposing litigants. It was the small and intimate size of such meetings that made women's presence permissible by traditional standards of respectability.

Conversely, it was the large size of Athenian juries which restricted women's level of access to these bodies. They were not barred altogether from accessing the top tier of the Athenian justice system. They certainly needed to stand trial before Athenian juries as defendants if they had broken the law and were indicted. During that trial, although they could not speak in their own defence, they were certainly allocated an equal amount of time for their defence, to be used by one or more advocates representing them and speaking on their behalf. Considering that often male litigants too chose to forgo their right to speak in person and allowed a more experienced *synegoros* to do the talking on their behalf, for part or the entire time allocated to them, there was nothing unusual in the arrangement where a litigant was defended by a *synegoros* within the bounds of what was considered to be a fair trial. Women were not prevented from initiating lawsuits against men or women who had caused harm to their person or property. The only restriction was that they needed to enlist the help of a male advocate who would initiate proceedings and pursue the case all the way to the court on their behalf. These speakers could be the representative himself and possibly others too, at least theoretically speaking out of care and personal interest for the woman and her rightful claims, but not infrequently for money too, so long as the jury did not get to hear about any financial transactions between advocate and client. But to believe that Lysias took the rape case of Nais, or Hypereides spoke on behalf of Phryne, pro bono and purely out of love and affection would be naïve.

Women were also allowed and expected to lay claim to property which allegedly belonged to them. Such claims were initiated and pursued through the court system by male advocates, very often male relatives with an interest in the property. It appears that women could initiate almost any kind of private lawsuit. Things became more complicated when it came to public lawsuits. Ironically, those lawsuits which could be initiated by anyone who wished (ὁ βουλόμενος) were the ones posing most obstacles for women litigants. Women certainly did not initiate lawsuits related to the political life of the city, like a *graphe paranomon* or *eisangelia*, and we have no evidence that they even initiated other types of lawsuits in areas where they might have a greater interest, like a *graphe asebeias* or a *phasis*. There has been a persistent view ever since Edward Harris first suggested it[13] that a *graphe hybreos* could be initiated on behalf of a woman for sexual assault or rape, but there's absolutely no evidence to corroborate this possibility. In fact, the only instance we know about where a woman seems to have initiated a public lawsuit is the denunciation made by Agariste in the extraordinary events surrounding the scandal of 415. In this instance, the denunciation by Agariste was part of a larger set of denunciations and accusations, under the watchful eye of the *boule*, and without a doubt it did not carry any kind of risk for her.[14]

This is perhaps an important reason why women did not initiate public prosecutions, especially *graphai* (and *eisangelia* after 330), which carried a risk of a 1,000-drachma fine for the prosecutor who did not obtain one fifth of the votes. Any such procedure, of course, would need to be initiated by a man on behalf of a woman, and the question is who would be willing to take such a huge risk without having any personal, political or economic stake in all this. Men would not initiate such procedures on behalf of their womenfolk, because ultimately they and not the women would be responsible in the event of a bad loss. It is safe to say that public lawsuits belonged to public life and although women could find themselves prosecuted through public lawsuits, like the *graphe asebeias*, the *graphe aprostasiou* or the *graphe* for an illegal marriage, they themselves would not be able to go through male relatives and initiate such lawsuits. Even in those processes, like the *eisangelia* (before 330), or the *probole*, where the economic risk had been replaced with a two-tier process involving the initial approval of the *boule* or the assembly before the case could proceed to trial, women would be unable to bring prosecutions because they could not participate in the initial vote. I think there is little room for doubt that, even when the law did not explicitly specify this, ὁ βουλόμενος in relation to public lawsuits literally meant 'any man wishing' and that the free women of Attica could only initiate private lawsuits through a representative or advocate if their own interests or person had been violated.

The question is not whether the women of Attica understood themselves as equal with men and expected justice on equal terms, because they certainly did not. The question is whether between total exclusion and total inclusion on equal terms there were some grey shades, some areas, some avenues, some possibilities open to women, when they needed to defend fundamental rights such as their right to life, safety, sexual and personal autonomy, property and inheritance rights and the right to a happy and prosperous family life. I hope that this discussion has amply demonstrated that somewhere between total exclusion and egalitarian inclusion there were many possibilities for women to access the legal system of the Athenian democracy, enforce and protect their rights, and safeguard their persons, property and family. Representation through advocates, relatives, or professionals paid under the table was an essential part of the equation. Representation in itself does not amount and has never amounted to exclusion, as most legal systems in history have endorsed some kind of representation, whether in the form of professional legal advisors and advocates or supportive relatives and friends. In the legal system of the Athenian democracy itself the institution of advocacy (*synegoria*) was a well-established, even if somewhat disingenuous practice among male litigants, and in this respect it would surprise no one, nor would it function as any kind of inherent disadvantage, if a woman were to use a *synegoros* too. In the chequered image presented in the chapters of this volume we can see two rival forces competing with each other: on the one hand traditional perceptions of women's roles within a family, and on the other hand the individualistic concepts of equality before the law and personal responsibility for one's strengths and failings fostered by the Athenian democracy. The result was a system which allowed and welcomed women, citizen and metic, to trust the legal system of the Athenian democracy and seek to protect their person, rights and property through its mechanisms, but at the same time recognised significant restrictions in the activities of Athenian women, especially in public life. These were sometimes dictated by the laws themselves, but more often by family traditions, religion, custom and powerful social norms in operation from time immemorial.

NOTES

1. E.g. Ar. *Eq.* passim, *Ra.* 569, ff.
2. And. 1.81.
3. For example, Hipponikos gave his daughter a dowry of ten talents when she married Alcibiades (And. 4.13); the father of Demosthenes senior in his will offered his daughter a dowry of two talents, and his wife eighty minae (thirty more than she had brought with her) when she remarried (D. 27.5); Diodotos, the brother of Diogeiton, ordered in his will that if he did not return from the military campaign his wife was to get a dowry of one talent when she remarried, and his daughter another talent (Lys. 32.6).
4. Plu. *Sol.* 20–1.
5. Namely the sum required for the running of an average household for a week (Is. 10.10), as noted above.
6. Is. 6.18.
7. E.g. Ar. *Ec.* passim.
8. The law required that boys, the future citizens of the democracy, needed to be educated until the age of fourteen, and if a father failed in this duty, his son was not obligated to look after him in his old age. In the absence of a father, this duty fell upon a boy's legal guardians. See Plu. *Sol.* 22 and Vitr. 6, pr. 3 (quoting Alexis).
9. It seems that the law capped the amount of the parental estate which could go to illegitimate children at ten minae (Harp. s.v. νοθεῖα).
10. See Appendix for the relevant laws and brief commentary.
11. Is. 10.13.
12. See Appendix for a brief account of such laws.
13. Harris 1990: 370–7.
14. The denunciation of Theoris by her maid is probably different, because the maid's denunciation did not formally start the lawsuit. The maid's testimony was used by Demosthenes in building the case against Theoris, but he initiated the *graphe asebeias* which led to her conviction and death.

Appendix

THE MAIN LAWS AFFECTING THE LIVES OF ATHENIAN WOMEN

The following is a subjective selection of the main laws directly affecting the lives of Athenian women, which I hope will be useful as a reference for the discussions in other parts of this volume. The brief notes following each law are meant to provide some background and allow for a better understanding, but they are not meant to serve as a full and proper exploration of each statute. My views on these laws and their purposes are explained more extensively in my recent study on Athenian law and society (2019a), while the reader should also consult the authoritative works of MacDowell (1978), Todd (1993), Harrison (1968; 1971), Phillips (2013), Just (1989) and many more exciting works in the vast and rich bibliography on Athenian law. The comprehensive online database *NOMOI*, maintained by Mirhady and Arnaoutoglou, is an invaluable bibliographical resource, as are other online databases like *Diotima*, and the indispensable *L'Année Philologique*.

1. THE LAW ON MARRIAGE

> D. 46.18: ΝΟΜΟΣ: Ἣν ἂν ἐγγυήσῃ ἐπὶ δικαίοις δάμαρτα εἶναι ἢ πατὴρ ἢ ἀδελφὸς ὁμοπάτωρ ἢ πάππος ὁ πρὸς πατρός, ἐκ ταύτης εἶναι παῖδας γνησίους. ἐὰν δὲ μηδεὶς ᾖ τούτων, ἐὰν μὲν μὴ ἐπίκληρός τις ᾖ, τὸν κύριον ἔχειν, ἐὰν δὲ ᾖ, ὅτῳ ἂν ἐπιτρέψῃ, τοῦτον κύριον εἶναι.[1]
>
> LAW: If a woman be betrothed for lawful marriage by her father or by a brother begotten of the same father or by her grandfather on her father's

side, her children shall be legitimate. If none of them is alive, if she is not an *epikleros* (heiress), let her husband keep her, but if she is, her husband is to be the man who has been appointed.²

This was undoubtedly a Solonean law which governed Athenian marriages for centuries. It is clear that the primary concern of this law was the continuation of the *oikos* and the smooth transfer of properties from one generation to the next. Remarkably, the law, by establishing that either a close male relative (father, brother, paternal grandfather) or the archon was to arrange the marriage, removed from a free woman the option of marrying someone of her choice, and of entering into the union when and if she wished. It is almost unbelievable that an adult free woman in Athens could not actually choose a husband or get herself married, no matter how old, rich or accomplished she was.

2. THE LAW ON THE *EPIDIKASIA*

Apollodoros here first paraphrases the law, very likely word for word, and then asks the clerk of the court to read an actual extract. That his paraphrasis is very near the wording of the law is confirmed by a citation of the same law in the *Athenaion Politeia* (58.3).

> D. 46.22: Τὸν τοίνυν νόμον ἐπὶ τούτοις ἀνάγνωθι, ὃς κελεύει ἐπιδικασίαν εἶναι τῶν ἐπικλήρων ἁπασῶν, καὶ ξένων καὶ ἀστῶν, καὶ περὶ μὲν τῶν πολιτῶν τὸν ἄρχοντα εἰσάγειν καὶ ἐπιμελεῖσθαι, περὶ δὲ τῶν μετοίκων τὸν πολέμαρχον, καὶ ἀνεπίδικον μὴ ἐξεῖναι ἔχειν μήτε κλῆρον μήτε ἐπίκληρον.
>
> ΝΟΜΟΣ.
>
> Κληροῦν δὲ τὸν ἄρχοντα κλήρων καὶ ἐπικλήρων, ὅσοι εἰσὶ μῆνες, πλὴν τοῦ σκιροφοριῶνος. ἀνεπίδικον δὲ κλῆρον μὴ ἔχειν.
>
> Now in addition to this read the law which appoints that there shall be an adjudication of all heiresses, whether alien or citizen, and that in the case of those who are citizens the archon shall have jurisdiction and shall take charge of the matter, and in the case of those who are resident aliens, the polemarch; and it shall not be lawful for anyone to obtain an inheritance or an heiress without legal adjudication.
>
> 'LAW

The archon shall assign by lot days for the trial of claims to inheritances or heiresses in every month except Scirophorion; and no one shall obtain an inheritance without adjudication.'

The paraphrase of the law offers information not included in the citation but verified by the *Athenaion Politeia*, such as the fact that the same legal provisions applied to both citizen and metic women, but while everything pertinent to citizen women would be processed by the archon, matters related to metic women would be processed by the polemarch, as one would expect. The citation of the law, which is undoubtedly authentic, along with the other citations in the speech, adds the information that such cases could be introduced to the appropriate magistrate every month, except Skirophorion, the last month of the Athenian year, when magistrates were leaving office. The most consequential part of the citation is the firm statement of the law that under no circumstances could an *epikleros*, citizen or metic, and her property be secured without a formal *epidikasia*. This blanket prohibition allowing no exceptions was deemed necessary to protect vulnerable women from relatives who had their eyes on the property. By ordering a mandatory *epidikasia* the state, through the archon or the polemarch, gained control over the process, and would be in a position to reject illegal or improper claims, keep an eye on the proceedings, and make sure that the winner of the *epidikasia* would continue to follow the rules, which included mandatory intercourse with the *epikleros* twice a month for the purpose of securing an heir to her father's house, and a handover of the estate to the son of the *epikleros*, and grandson and heir of her deceased father, when he reached his twentieth year.

3. THE LAW ON THE *EPIDIKASIA* OF A POOR *EPIKLEROS*

D. 43. 54: ΝΟΜΟΣ. Τῶν ἐπικλήρων ὅσαι θητικὸν τελοῦσιν, ἐὰν μὴ βούληται ἔχειν ὁ ἐγγύτατα γένους, ἐκδιδότω ἐπιδοὺς ὁ μὲν πεντακοσιομέδιμνος πεντακοσίας δραχμάς, ὁ δ' ἱππεὺς τριακοσίας, ὁ δὲ ζευγίτης ἑκατὸν πεντήκοντα, πρὸς οἷς αὐτῆς. ἐὰν δὲ πλείους ὦσιν ἐν τῷ αὐτῷ γένει, τῇ ἐπικλήρῳ πρὸς μέρος ἐπιδιδόναι ἕκαστον. ἐὰν δ' αἱ γυναῖκες πλείους ὦσι, μὴ ἐπάναγκες εἶναι πλέον ἢ μίαν ἐκδοῦναι τῷ γ' ἑνί, ἀλλὰ τὸν ἐγγύτατα ἀεὶ ἐκδιδόναι ἢ αὐτὸν ἔχειν. ἐὰν δὲ μὴ ἔχῃ ὁ ἐγγυτάτω γένους ἢ μὴ ἐκδῷ, ὁ ἄρχων ἐπαναγκαζέτω ἢ αὐτὸν ἔχειν ἢ ἐκδοῦναι. ἐὰν δὲ μὴ ἐπαναγκάσῃ ὁ ἄρχων, ὀφειλέτω χιλίας δραχμὰς ἱερὰς τῇ Ἥρᾳ. ἀπογραφέτω δὲ τὸν μὴ ποιοῦντα ταῦτα ὁ βουλόμενος πρὸς τὸν ἄρχοντα.

LAW: In regard to all heiresses who are classified as Thetes,[3] if the nearest of kin does not wish to marry one, let him give her in marriage with a portion of five hundred drachmae, if he be of the class of Pentacosiomedimni, if of the class of Knights, with a portion of three hundred, and if of the class of Zeugitae, with one hundred and fifty, in addition to what is her own. If there are several kinsmen in the same degree of relationship, each one of them shall contribute to the portion of the heiress according to his due share. And if there be several heiresses, it shall not be necessary for a single kinsman to give in marriage more than one, but the next of kin shall in each case give her in marriage or marry her himself. And if the nearest of kin does not marry her or give her in marriage, the archon shall compel him either to marry her himself or give her in marriage. And if the archon shall not compel him, let him be fined a thousand drachmae, which are to be consecrated to Hera. And let any person who chooses denounce to the archon any person who disobeys this law.

This law concerned poorer women, who did not have a living relative legally entitled to give them in marriage, and thus they became *epikleroi*. However, since there was no property to make them an attractive marriage option for potential suitors, the law compelled the closest male relative either to marry the woman himself or to find her a husband and give her a dowry from his own property. In one such incident narrated by Andocides, the father of two young women, who died while they were still unmarried, left substantial property but also even higher debts. The orator describes how the family settled the marriage of these two women. Surprisingly, we find that their relatives were actually fighting with each other over the two women, one would imagine because they were supremely attractive.[4] The latter part of the law, which states that if the archon fails to compel the nearest relative to marry the woman, or arrange another marriage for her, he is himself liable to a very large fine of 1,000 drachmas, must be a later addition to the original Solonean law, introduced in the classical period. An archon with reduced powers in the classical period would not have the same authority to compel a citizen to do his duty, and it is reasonable to assume that he might choose to look the other way, for peace of mind, or maybe because he was corrupt. This additional clause to the Solonean law was intended to ensure that the archon would do everything within his power to compel the difficult relative to marry the poor *epikleros*, or find her another husband.

4. THE PERICLEAN CITIZENSHIP LAW

Arist. *Ath.* 26.3: ἐπὶ Ἀντιδότου (451–50 B) διὰ τὸ πλῆθος τῶν πολιτῶν Περικλέους εἰπόντος ἔγνωσαν μὴ μετέχειν τῆς πόλεως, ὃς ἂν μὴ ἐξ ἀμφοῖν ἀστοῖν ᾖ γεγονώς.

In the archonship of Antidotos after a proposal by Pericles they decided, because of the multitude of the citizens, to exclude from the city those who were not born from two citizen parents.

This was the most consequential piece of legislation introduced in the classical period for the standing of citizen women not only in the institutions of the city-state but also in family life.[5] After the introduction of this law, citizen women became the indispensable contributors of citizenship to the next generation. This law also drew a very clear line between citizen and metic women, and restricted the ability of the latter to marry Athenian men and seek full integration into Athenian society, as countless non-Athenian women had done in the past.[6] However, we should be under no illusion that the purpose of this law was to empower the citizen women of Athens. Demographic, political and, as Patterson has suggested, administrative reasons were probably behind its introduction, combined with a certain arrogance and disdain which the centre of the Athenian Empire was feeling towards outsiders flocking into the city in search of job opportunities and a better living. The Periclean citizenship law was suspended in the years of the Peloponnesian war as huge casualties left many families without legitimately born sons. Pericles himself had lost both his legitimate sons, and his only surviving son was the younger Pericles, his son by Aspasia, whom he had deprived of legitimacy with his own law in 451. The irony was not lost on ancient commentators.[7] The law was reinstated in 403, within the wider effort for a reorganisation of Athenian public life with the decree of Aristophon and Nikomenes.[8]

5. THE LAWS PROHIBITING MIXED MARRIAGES BETWEEN ATHENIANS AND NON-ATHENIANS

> D. 59.16: ΝΟΜΟΣ: Ἐὰν δὲ ξένος ἀστῇ συνοικῇ τέχνῃ ἢ μηχανῇ ἡτινιοῦν, γραφέσθω πρὸς τοὺς θεσμοθέτας Ἀθηναίων ὁ βουλόμενος οἷς ἔξεστιν. ἐὰν δὲ ἁλῷ, πεπράσθω καὶ αὐτὸς καὶ ἡ οὐσία αὐτοῦ, καὶ τὸ τρίτον μέρος ἔστω τοῦ ἑλόντος. ἔστω δὲ καὶ ἐὰν ἡ ξένη τῷ ἀστῷ συνοικῇ κατὰ ταὐτά, καὶ ὁ συνοικῶν τῇ ξένῃ τῇ ἁλούσῃ ὀφειλέτω χιλίας δραχμάς.

LAW: If an alien man lives in marriage with a citizen woman through some trickery or device, he is to be indicted to the *thesmothetai* by any Athenian who wishes and has the right to do so. If he is convicted, he is to be sold, himself and his property, and the successful prosecutor is to receive one third. Likewise, if an alien woman lives in marriage with a citizen man, the same penalties apply, and the man living in marriage with the foreign woman is to be fined one thousand drachmas.

D. 59.52: ΝΟΜΟΣ: Ἐὰν δέ τις ἐκδῷ ξένην γυναῖκα ἀνδρὶ Ἀθηναίῳ ὡς ἑαυτῷ προσήκουσαν, ἄτιμος ἔστω, καὶ ἡ οὐσία αὐτοῦ δημοσία ἔστω, καὶ τοῦ ἑλόντος τὸ τρίτον μέρος. γραφέσθων δὲ πρὸς τοὺς θεσμοθέτας οἷς ἔξεστιν, καθάπερ τῆς ξενίας.

LAW: If someone betroths an alien woman to an Athenian man under the pretense that she is his relative, he is to be disfranchised, and his property is to be confiscated, and the successful prosecutor is to receive one third. An indictment is to be brought to the *thesmothetai* by anyone who is legally entitled, as in cases of *xenia*.

These two laws, quoted by Apollodoros in different places in the speech *Against Neaira*, in all probability belonged to the same legislation, the purpose of which was to put an end to marriages between citizens and non-citizens. While in the past such marriages were discouraged, especially in the years when the Periclean citizenship law was valid, this legislation prohibits them altogether with severe penalties upon the citizen, the alien, and the man who would formally betroth an alien woman to a citizen man. The impact of this law was substantial, as can be seen from the plots of New Comedy, which are often driven by the situation where an alien woman, typically a seductive hetaira, cannot marry the Athenian youth who is in love with her and, at the very most, will need to be content if she can become his concubine.[9] On occasion a recognition plot is employed, where the woman turns out to be Athenian, and then she can marry her beloved, and the audience can have the desired happy ending.[10]

6. THE LAW ON DIVORCE

D. 59.52: κατὰ τὸν νόμον ὃς κελεύει, ἐὰν ἀποπέμπῃ τὴν γυναῖκα, ἀποδιδόναι τὴν προῖκα, ἐὰν δὲ μή, ἐπ' ἐννέ' ὀβολοῖς τοκοφορεῖν, καὶ σίτου εἰς Ὠιδεῖον εἶναι δικάσασθαι ὑπὲρ τῆς γυναικὸς τῷ κυρίῳ.

According to the law which states, if he divorces the woman, he is to return the dowry, and if he does not, he is to pay an interest of nine obols to the drachma,[11] and a *kyrios* of the woman can bring a lawsuit at the Odeon on behalf of a woman for her maintenance.

It would probably have seemed absurd in the ancient world to try and force two people to stay in an unsuitable marriage for as long as possible, as legal systems routinely do in our times, often on the basis of religious concepts of the sanctity of marriage. The Greeks understood marriage as a process with specific objectives, not as an institution or an eternal binding of souls. This is why in classical Athens the couple was divorced simply when one of the spouses said that the marriage was over, for whatever reason. There was no further ado. The only legal stipulation was that the husband needed to return the dowry in its entirety. If he failed to do so, the dowry essentially turned into a loan to the former husband, and started accumulating interest at the rate of 18 per cent from the date of the divorce. This is why, if the divorce had been initiated by the woman, she needed to appear in person before the archon and register the divorce, so that the former husband could not argue that the marriage had lasted longer than it did. From the moment the woman appeared before the archon, the husband had to start paying interest until the day that he returned the dowry. As with previous arrangements, it seems that the law was concerned only with property matters, while it was completely oblivious to other complications and considerations evolving around a divorce. The custody of the children was a father's duty, but if the family wanted to make different arrangements, the law had nothing to say on it. The legal system never interfered with guardianship or custody matters while the father of the children was alive, and assumed that it was his duty to take care of such affairs.

7. THE LAWS ON ADULTERY AFFECTING WOMEN

D. 23.53: Ἐάν τις ἀποκτείνῃ ἐν ἄθλοις ἄκων, ἢ ἐν ὁδῷ καθελὼν ἢ ἐν πολέμῳ ἀγνοήσας, ἢ ἐπὶ δάμαρτι ἢ ἐπὶ μητρὶ ἢ ἐπ' ἀδελφῇ ἢ ἐπὶ θυγατρί, ἢ ἐπὶ παλλακῇ ἣν ἂν ἐπ' ἐλευθέροις παισὶν ἔχῃ, τούτων ἕνεκα μὴ φεύγειν κτείναντα.

If someone kills in an athletic contest without intent, or by taking someone down in the street, or accidentally at war, or after catching him with his wife, mother, sister, daughter or concubine kept for the birth of free children, the killer is not to be punished under these circumstances.

D. 59.67: τόν τε νόμον ἐπὶ τούτοις παρεχόμενος, ὃς οὐκ ἐᾷ ἐπὶ ταύτῃσι μοιχὸν λαβεῖν ὁπόσαι ἂν ἐπ' ἐργαστηρίου καθῶνται ἢ πωλῶνται ἀποπεφασμένως.

He produced the law on the subject, which forbids accusations of adultery with one of those women established in brothels or visibly practicing any form of prostitution.

D. 59.87: ΝΟΜΟΣ ΜΟΙΧΕΙΑΣ. Ἐπειδὰν δὲ ἕλῃ τὸν μοιχόν, μὴ ἐξέστω τῷ ἑλόντι συνοικεῖν τῇ γυναικί· ἐὰν δὲ συνοικῇ, ἄτιμος ἔστω. μηδὲ τῇ γυναικὶ ἐξέστω εἰσιέναι εἰς τὰ ἱερὰ τὰ δημοτελῆ, ἐφ' ᾗ ἂν μοιχὸς ἁλῷ· ἐὰν δ' εἰσίῃ, νηποινεὶ πασχέτω ὅ τι ἂν πάσχῃ, πλὴν θανάτου.

After he catches the seducer, the man who caught him shall not be permitted to continue living with the woman in marriage. If he continues living with her in marriage he is to be disfranchised. And whoever is caught with a seducer shall not be permitted to enter the public temples. If she enters, she is to suffer whatever humiliation she suffers, except death, with impunity.

The first of these laws was part of Drakon's homicide law, and its purpose was not to define or penalise adultery, but only to forgive the temporary insanity of a *kyrios* who caught another man with one of the free women under his protection and in a rage killed him. There is only one such case attested in the entire classical literature, and it must be said that a closer reading of the speech of Lysias in defence of Euphiletos,[12] who claimed that he had killed his wife's lover after catching them red-handed, raises many suspicions that this was premeditated murder. Nonetheless, the impact of this piece of legislation was substantial, because it offered a broad and inclusive legal definition of the *oikos*, and instituted in law the sanctity of family life. It also defined the offence of adultery in Athenian law for centuries, but at the same time created a huge potential for abuse, because in future procurers could entrap customers with female prostitutes, and extract huge compensation from men in fear for their lives. Solon corrected this a quarter of a century later by introducing another consequential law, which excluded from the power of the adultery laws any woman who was practising any form of prostitution (D. 59.67). By doing so Solon effectively recognised the legal status of prostitution. Another Solonean law allowed a man fraudulently accused of adultery to challenge his accuser in court, and if he won, any agreement or contract made under duress was nullified (D. 59.66). At some point after the introduction of the Periclean citizenship law another piece of legislation was introduced which imposed severe penalties, such as mandatory divorce and permanent exclusion from public life and religious sites around the city, on any woman who had been caught committing adultery. While until then legal sanctions in adultery cases only affected the male party, this law also brought the citizen woman into the picture, and sanctioned an adulteress with permanent exclusion from temples and public life, a form of punishment which amounted to *atimia*.

8. THE LAWS ON SUCCESSION AND INHERITANCE DIRECTLY AFFECTING WOMEN

D. 46.14: ΝΟΜΟΣ: Ὅσοι μὴ ἐπεποίηντο, ὥστε μήτε ἀπειπεῖν μήτ' ἐπιδικάσασθαι, ὅτε Σόλων εἰσῄει τὴν ἀρχήν, τὰ ἑαυτοῦ διαθέσθαι εἶναι ὅπως ἂν ἐθέλῃ, ἂν μὴ παῖδες ὦσι γνήσιοι ἄρρενες, ἂν μὴ μανιῶν ἢ γήρως ἢ φαρμάκων ἢ νόσου ἕνεκα, ἢ γυναικὶ πειθόμενος, ὑπὸ τούτων του παρανοῶν, ἢ ὑπ' ἀνάγκης ἢ ὑπὸ δεσμοῦ καταληφθείς.[13]

LAW: Any citizen, except those who have been adopted, and have not renounced the adoption or succeeded to an estate under an epidikasia, shall have the right to dispose of his property as he wishes, if there is no legitimate male issue, unless he has been overcome by mental impairment, old age, drugs or illness, or influenced by a woman or pressured by necessity or imprisonment.

Is. 10.13: Καὶ τῷ μὲν πατρὶ αὐτῆς, εἰ παῖδες ἄρρενες μὴ ἐγένοντο, οὐκ ἂν ἐξῆν ἄνευ ταύτης διαθέσθαι· κελεύει γὰρ ὁ νόμος σὺν ταύταις κύριον εἶναι δοῦναι, ἐάν τῳ βούληται, τὰ ἑαυτοῦ·

Her father, if he had no sons, would not have been able to make a will excluding her; for the law states that he has the right to leave his property to whoever he wishes, so long as he includes her [sc. a legitimate daughter] in the arrangement.

D. 46.20: ΝΟΜΟΣ: Καὶ ἐὰν ἐξ ἐπικλήρου τις γένηται καὶ ἅμα ἡβήσῃ ἐπὶ δίετες, κρατεῖν τῶν χρημάτων, τὸν δὲ σῖτον μετρεῖν τῇ μητρί.

LAW. And if someone is the son of an epikleros, two years after he reaches manhood [i.e. 20 years old], he shall assume control of the estate and pay for his mother's living expenses.

D. 43.51 ΝΟΜΟΣ. Ὅστις ἂν μὴ διαθέμενος ἀποθάνῃ, ἐὰν μὲν παῖδας καταλίπῃ θηλείας, σὺν ταύτῃσιν, ἐὰν δὲ μή, τούσδε κυρίους εἶναι τῶν χρημάτων. ἐὰν μὲν ἀδελφοὶ ὦσιν ὁμοπάτορες· καὶ ἐὰν παῖδες ἐξ ἀδελφῶν γνήσιοι, τὴν τοῦ πατρὸς μοῖραν λαγχάνειν· ἐὰν δὲ μὴ ἀδελφοὶ ὦσιν ἢ ἀδελφῶν παῖδες, * * * ἐξ αὐτῶν κατὰ ταὐτὰ λαγχάνειν· κρατεῖν δὲ τοὺς ἄρρενας καὶ τοὺς ἐκ τῶν ἀρρένων, ἐὰν ἐκ τῶν αὐτῶν ὦσι, καὶ ἐὰν γένει ἀπωτέρω. ἐὰν δὲ μὴ ὦσι πρὸς πατρὸς μέχρι ἀνεψιῶν παίδων, τοὺς πρὸς μητρὸς τοῦ ἀνδρὸς κατὰ ταὐτὰ κυρίους εἶναι. ἐὰν δὲ μηδετέρωθεν ᾖ ἐντὸς τούτων, τὸν πρὸς πατρὸς ἐγγυτάτω κύριον εἶναι. νόθῳ δὲ μηδὲ νόθῃ μὴ εἶναι ἀγχιστείαν μήθ' ἱερῶν μήθ' ὁσίων ἀπ' Εὐκλείδου ἄρχοντος.

LAW. Whenever a man dies without making a will, if he leaves female children his estate shall go with them, but if not, the persons herein mentioned shall be entitled to his property: if there be brothers by the same father, and if there be lawfully born sons of brothers, they shall take the share of the father. But if there are no brothers or sons of brothers, their descendants shall inherit it in like manner; but males and the sons of males shall take precedence, if they are of the same ancestors, even though they be more remote of kin. If there are no relatives on the father's side within the degree of children of cousins, those on the mother's side shall inherit in like manner. But if there shall be no relatives on either side within the degree mentioned, the nearest of kin on the father's side shall inherit. But no illegitimate child of either sex shall have the right of succession either to religious rites or civic privileges, from the time of the archonship of Eucleides (403).

The law of Solon on succession prohibited a man who had legitimate sons from making a will. His property would be evenly split among his sons, and no other arrangement was permitted. However, if a man had no living son at the time of his death, he was permitted to adopt an Athenian boy or man as his heir. If he had legitimate daughters, the law stated that they could not be excluded from any property arrangements. These legal provisions in practice could result in several possible scenarios. (a) There was no adoption of a male heir and the daughter was given in marriage while her father was alive, and in time her sons were considered to be his heirs. This arrangement was eventually adopted for the two daughters of Polyeuktos, in the speech *Against Spudias* (D. 41). Each of the two daughters was given a generous dowry at the time of her marriage, and after the death of their parents they distributed the rest of the estate in equal shares. (b) A male heir was adopted and given in marriage to the daughter of the family. If this arrangement worked it was considered optimal, because the property remained in the family and the bloodline was continued. This arrangement was attempted by Polueuktos when he adopted his brother-in-law Leokrates, but it fell through after a family quarrel. Leokrates divorced his wife and walked away from the adoption, while another marriage was arranged for her to Spudias, this time without adoption. (c) A male heir was adopted into the family without marriage to the daughter. The adopted brother had the same legal right to arrange a marriage for her through *engye* as a natural brother, and was expected to offer her a dowry from her father's estate. This option was taken in the case of Phile, the daughter of Pyrrhos (Is. 3). It seems that her father died before she was of marriageable age and her adopted brother Endios gave her in marriage to an Athenian man. These arrangements went uncontested for years and only after the death of Endios, who had no children, did his brother and mother try to grab the property which rightfully belonged to his adopted sister and daughter of Pyrrhos, under the pretext that she was illegitimate. (d) If no adoption was made and the woman had no children at the time of the death of her father (and she had no living brother or paternal grandfather), whether she was married or not, she became an *epikleros*, and could be claimed in marriage by the closest male relative of her father in an order of succession which was clearly specified by the law on the *anchisteia* (D. 43.51). If she was married, she could still be removed from her husband even against her wishes or the wishes of her husband. One would imagine that this rather drastic course of action would be taken only if a large property went with a woman which a close male relative of her father wanted. If her father left no property worth the trouble, probably there would be no suitors and the woman could remain married. A law quoted by Apollodoros (D. 46.20) clarifies that eventually the legal owner of the property of the *epikleros* would be her son once he reached his twentieth year (namely when he had finished his military service and returned home). From this moment forwards he had an explicit legal obligation to provide for the maintenance of his mother. In this way the law wanted to ensure that the woman, through whom the property of her father had passed on to the next generation, would continue to be well looked after.

9. THE SOCIAL NETWORK: THE LAWS REQUIRING THE ARCHON TO PROTECT WOMEN, CHILDREN AND ORPHANS FROM ABUSE OF THEIR PERSON OR PROPERTY

D. 43.75: ΝΟΜΟΣ: Ὁ ἄρχων ἐπιμελείσθω τῶν ὀρφανῶν καὶ τῶν ἐπικλήρων καὶ τῶν οἴκων τῶν ἐξερημουμένων καὶ τῶν γυναικῶν, ὅσαι μένουσιν ἐν τοῖς οἴκοις τῶν ἀνδρῶν τῶν τεθνηκότων φάσκουσαι κυεῖν. τούτων ἐπιμελείσθω καὶ μὴ ἐάτω ὑβρίζειν μηδένα περὶ τούτους. ἐὰν δέ τις ὑβρίζῃ ἢ ποιῇ τι παράνομον, κύριος ἔστω ἐπιβάλλειν κατὰ τὸ τέλος. ἐὰν δὲ μείζονος ζημίας δοκῇ ἄξιος εἶναι, προσκαλεσάμενος πρόπεμπτα καὶ τίμημα ἐπιγραψάμενος, ὅ τι ἂν δοκῇ αὐτῷ, εἰσαγέτω εἰς τὴν ἡλιαίαν. ἐὰν δ' ἁλῷ, τιμάτω ἡ ἡλιαία περὶ τοῦ ἁλόντος, ὅ τι χρὴ αὐτὸν παθεῖν ἢ ἀποτεῖσαι.

LAW. Let the archon take charge of orphans and of heiresses and of families that are becoming extinct, and of all women who remain in the houses of their deceased husbands, declaring that they are pregnant. Let him take charge of these, and not suffer anyone to do any outrage to them. And if anyone shall commit any outrage or any lawless act against them, he shall have power to impose a fine upon such person up to the limit fixed by law. And if the offender shall seem to him to be deserving of a more severe punishment, let him summon such a person, giving him five days' notice, and bring him before the court of Heliaea, writing upon the indictment the penalty which he thinks is deserved. And if there be a conviction, let the court of Heliaea appoint for the one convicted what penalty he ought to suffer or pay.

Is. 3.46: Καὶ οὐκ [ἂν] εἰσήγγειλας πρὸς τὸν ἄρχοντα κακοῦσθαι τὴν ἐπίκληρον ὑπὸ τοῦ εἰσποιήτου οὕτως ὑβριζομένην καὶ ἄκληρον τῶν ἑαυτῆς πατρῴων καθισταμένην, ἄλλως τε καὶ μόνων τούτων τῶν δικῶν ἀκινδύνων τοῖς διώκουσιν οὐσῶν καὶ ἐξὸν τῷ βουλομένῳ βοηθεῖν ταῖς ἐπικλήροις; Οὔτε γὰρ ἐπιτίμιον ταῖς πρὸς τὸν ἄρχοντα εἰσαγγελίαις ἔπεστιν, οὐδὲ ἐὰν μηδεμίαν τῶν ψήφων οἱ εἰσαγγείλαντες μεταλάβωσιν, οὔτε πρυτανεῖα οὔτε παράστασις οὐδεμία τίθεται τῶν εἰσαγγελιῶν· ἀλλὰ τοῖς μὲν διώκουσιν ἀκινδύνως εἰσαγγέλλειν ἔξεστι, τῷ βουλομένῳ, τοῖς δ' ἁλισκομένοις <αἱ> ἔσχαται τιμωρίαι ἐπὶ ταῖς εἰσαγγελίαις ἔπεισιν.

And did you fail to bring a denunciation in the archon's court for injury to the heiress thus maltreated by the adopted son and despoiled of her paternal inheritance, especially as this is the only class of public actions which involves no risk to the party who brings it, and anyone who wishes is allowed to defend the rights of heiresses? For no fine can be inflicted for denunciations made to the archon, even if the informants fail to receive a single vote, and there are no deposits or court fees paid in any impeachments; but while the prosecutors may bring an impeachment without running any risk, extreme penalties are inflicted on those who are convicted in such impeachments.[14]

Arist. *Ath.* 56.3–7: γραφαὶ δ[ὲ καὶ δ]ίκαι λαγχάνονται πρὸς αὐτόν, ἃς ἀνακρίνας εἰς τὸ δικαστήριον εἰσάγει, [γο]νέων κακώσεως (αὗται δ' εἰσὶν ἀζήμιοι τῷ βουλομένῳ δ[ι]ώκειν), ὀρφανῶν κ[ακώ]σεως (αὗται δ' εἰσὶ κατὰ τῶν ἐπιτρόπων), ἐπικλήρου κακώσε[ως (αὗτ]αι δ' εἰσὶ κατὰ [τῶν] ἐπιτρόπων καὶ τῶν συνοικούντων), οἴκου ὀρφανικοῦ κακώσεως (εἰσὶ δὲ καὶ [αὗται κατὰ τῶν] ἐπιτρόπων), παρανοίας, ἐάν τις αἰτιᾶταί τινα παρανοοῦντα τὰ [ὑπάρχοντα ἀ]πολλύν[αι], εἰς δατητῶν αἵρεσιν, ἐάν τις μὴ θέλῃ κοινὰ [τὰ ὄντα νέμεσθ]αι, εἰς ἐπι[τρ]οπῆς κατάστασιν, εἰς ἐπιτροπῆς διαδικασίαν, εἰς [ἐμφανῶν κατάστας]ιν, ἐπίτρ[οπ]ον αὑτὸν ἐγγράψαι, κλήρων καὶ ἐπικλήρων ἐπι[δικάσαι. ἐπιμελεῖτ]αι δὲ καὶ τῶν [ὀρφ]ανῶν καὶ τῶν ἐπικλήρων, καὶ τῶν γυναικῶν ὅσαι ἂν τελευτή[σαντος τοῦ ἀνδρ]ὸς σκή[πτω]νται κύειν. καὶ κύριός ἐστι τοῖς ἀδικοῦσιν ἐπιβάλ[λειν ἢ εἰσάγειν εἰς] τὸ δικα[στή]ριον. μισθοῖ δὲ καὶ τοὺς οἴκους τῶν ὀρφανῶν καὶ τῶν ἐπικλ[ήρων, ἕως ἄν τις τετταρ]ακαιδε[κέ]τις γένηται, καὶ τὰ ἀποτιμήματα λαμβάν[ει, καὶ τοὺς ἐπιτρόπους], ἐὰν μὴ [δι]δῶσι τοῖς παισὶ τὸν σῖτον, οὗτος εἰσπράττει.

Criminal and civil law-suits are instituted before him, and after a preliminary trial he brings them in before the Jury-court: actions for ill-usage of parents (in which anybody who wishes may act as prosecutor without liability to penalty); for ill-usage of orphans (which lie against their guardians); for ill-usage of an heiress (which lie against the guardians or the relations that they live with); for injury to an orphan's estate (these also lie against the guardians); prosecutions for insanity, when one man accuses another of wasting his property when insane; actions for the appointment of liquidators, when a man is unwilling for property to be administered in partnership; actions for the institution of guardianship; actions for deciding rival claims to guardianship; actions for the production of goods or documents; actions for enrollment as trustee; claims to estates and to heiresses. He also supervises orphans and heiresses and women professing to be with child after the husband's death, and he has absolute power to fine offenders against them or to bring them before the Jury-court. He grants leases of houses belonging to orphans and heiresses until they are fourteen years of age, and receives the rents, and he exacts maintenance for children from guardians who fail to supply it.[15]

The vulnerability of women, children, orphans and *epikleroi* in the hands of ruthless relatives was not missed by Solon, and this is why he instituted a series of laws which charged the most senior civil servant of the Athenian state, the archon, with the duty of overseeing the welfare of those vulnerable members of society. The *Athenaion Politeia* suggests that the laws of Solon gave the archon a very wide range of responsibilities, which in the aristocratic state would empower him to address effectively such abuses. Under the democratic constitution the Solonean core was expanded with new provisions, while the responsibilities of the archon were to be understood within the context of his reduced authority under the democracy. While the letter of the law did not change, the way the law was understood and applied in practice had undergone significant change with the passage of time. Under the democracy the archon did not have the authority to single-handedly settle these matters. His role was to accept complains and denunciations about the ill-treatment of the person or property of women, children, orphans and *epikleroi*, and to offer practical help, such as the collection of rents and monies due to the estate of an orphan or an *epikleros*, and also legal and tactical advice on how the family could deal with this matter. In one such incident, where a complaint was launched with the archon about the abuses and improper financial practices of the guardians of Demosthenes and his sister, the archon listened, empathised and gave his tactical advice: to wait until the male heir of the household, Demosthenes, came of age and was in a position to pursue his guardians through the courts. This case illustrates how these duties of the archon were understood in actual practice. Since the initiation of lawsuits on property matters typically rested upon individual citizens, the state under the democracy expected that concerned citizens, relatives or guardians should bring such cases before the courts. In order to encourage citizens to report such abuses and pursue them through the justice system, the state had removed any element of risk for the denunciation (εἰσαγγελία) of abuse of an orphan or an *epikleros*.

10. ALL PRIESTS AND PRIESTESSES ARE EQUALLY RESPONSIBLE UNDER THE LAW

> Aesch. 3.18: Οἷον τοὺς ἱερέας καὶ τὰς ἱερείας ὑπευθύνους εἶναι κελεύει ὁ νόμος, καὶ συλλήβδην ἅπαντας καὶ χωρὶς ἑκάστους κατὰ σῶμα, τοὺς τὰ ἱερὰ μόνον λαμβάνοντας καὶ τὰς εὐχὰς ὑπὲρ ὑμῶν πρὸς τοὺς θεοὺς εὐχομένους, καὶ οὐ μόνον ἰδίᾳ, ἀλλὰ καὶ κοινῇ τὰ γένη, Εὐμολπίδας καὶ Κήρυκας καὶ τοὺς ἄλλους ἅπαντας.

> For example, the law directs that priests and priestesses be subject to audit, all collectively, and each severally and individually – persons who receive perquisites only, and whose occupation is to pray to heaven for you; and they are made accountable not only separately, but whole priestly families together, the Eumolpidae, the Ceryces, and all the rest.[16]

This law is very unusual. In fact it is perhaps the only law of the Athenian state which explicitly treats men and women equally.[17] It is an extract from the law which governed the audits (εὔθυναι) which priests and priestesses, along with all other magistrates of the Athenian state, needed to undergo at the end of their year in office. It is also the only law which makes women subject to procedures normally reserved for male citizens, such as the rigorous and unnerving audit. During this process the magistrate needed first to present all his accounts, and if they were in good standing the second phase included an overall account of one's conduct in office. This is the one area where the law had the same expectations of men and women simply because religion was the one area where women could actually cross into the public life of the city, take up public office, manage finances – sometimes quite substantial sums of money in more prosperous temples and shrines – and interact extensively with the authorities and the ordinary citizen. Understandably, they were expected to be able to provide clean accounts and defend their record and overall conduct in office like their male counterparts, and other magistrates of the Athenian state.

NOTES

1. The text as it appears here includes an emendation of the transmitted text which I proposed in my 2014 study. The reason for the transposition is that the law in

the transmitted text says the exact opposite of what it should be saying, while the transposition corrects the error, and states that a woman with children is not an *epikleros* and is to stay with her husband, while a woman without children, married or not, is an *epikleros* and is going to be given in marriage to whomever the law decides.

2. All translations of Demosthenes in the Appendix come from the Loeb translation of A. T. Murray.
3. The Thetes were the lowest of the four economic classes of Solon, the poorest Athenians.
4. And. 1.117–22.
5. See the debate in Rhodes 1981: 331–5; Patterson 1981: passim; Walters 1983: 314–36; Raaflaub 2004: 15–16, 217; Ober 1989: 81; Ogden 1996: passim; Kapparis 2005: 72–6; 2018: 141–5; Blok 2017: 141–70.
6. According to Plutarch (*Per.* 37) no less than 10 per cent of citizens in his time were born of foreign mothers (μητρόξενοι).
7. Plu. *Per.* 37.
8. D. 43.51.
9. See further my discussion in Kapparis 1999: 97–205; 2018: 145–7.
10. This is what happens, for example, in Menander's *Perikeiromene* and *Misoumenos* or Plautus' *Rudens*.
11. Namely 9 obols (= 1.5 drachmas) per 100 drachmas (= 1 mina) per month, which amounts to 18 per cent a year.
12. Lys. 1; Wolpert 2000: 415–24; Todd 2007, for a thorough study of the speech.
13. See also D. 44.68 and Is. 6.28.
14. Trans. E. S. Forster.
15. Trans. H. Rackham.
16. Trans. C. Adams.
17. Often the law implicitly treated women equally with men by not specifying gender. For example, the law did not specify gender when it came to homicide. A male and a female murderer would be held equally responsible by the courts of the Athenian democracy. This was the case with most criminal justice. A crime was a crime regardless of the gender of the perpetrator or the victim. However, where this law differs is that it explicitly includes priestesses along with priests and prescribes the same course of action for both regardless of gender.

Select Bibliography

Adamidis, Vasileios. 2017. *Character Evidence in the Courts of Classical Athens: Rhetoric, Relevance and the Rule of Law.* Abingdon: Routledge.

Adeleye, Gabriel. 1983. 'The purpose of δοκιμασία.' *Greek, Roman and Byzantine Studies* 24.

Adrados Rodriguez, Francisco, and Michail V. Sakellariou, eds. 1996. *Colloque international "Démocratie athénienne et culture" organisé par l'Académie d'Athènes en coopération avec l'UNESCO (23, 24 et 25 novembre 1992).* Athens: Akadimia Athinon.

Adshead, Katherine. 1984. 'SEG XXVII 261 and the history of the *euthyna*.' In *Studies Presented to Sterling Dow on his Eightieth Birthday*, ed. Kent J. Rigsby. Durham, NC: Duke University Press.

Ahearne-Kroll, Stephen P., Paul Andrew Holloway and James A. Kelhoffer, eds. 2010. *Women and Gender in Ancient Religions: Interdisciplinary Approaches.* Tübingen: Mohr Siebeck.

Alwine, Andrew. 2015. *Enmity and Feuding in Classical Athens.* Austin: University of Texas Press.

Amundsen, L. 1973. 'The liability of the physician in Roman law.' In *International Symposium on Society, Medicine and Law, Jerusalem, March 1972*, ed. H. Karplus. London: Brill.

Amundsen, L., and Gary B. Ferngren. 1977. 'The physician as an expert witness in Athenian law.' *Bulletin of the History of Medicine* 51.

Antonaccio, Carla M. 1999. 'Architecture and behavior: Building gender into Greek houses.' *Classical World* 93 (5).

Apostolakis, Kostas. 2007. 'Tragic patterns in forensic speeches: Antiphon 1 *Against the Stepmother*.' *Classica et Mediaevalia* 58.

Apostolakis, Kostas. 2019. *Fragmenta Comica 21: Timokles*. Göttingen: Vandenhoeck & Ruprecht.
Atack, Carol. 2017. 'The history of Athenian democracy, now: Review article.' *History of Political Thought* 38 (3).
Arthur, Marylin. 1977. 'Politics and pomegranates: An interpretation of the Homeric hymn to Demeter.' *Arethusa* 10.
Bakewell, Geoffrey. 1999a. 'Lysias 12 and Lysias 31: Metics and Athenian citizenship in the aftermath of the Thirty.' *Greek, Roman and Byzantine Studies* 40 (1).
Bakewell, Geoffrey. 1999b. 'εὔνους καὶ πόλει σωτήριος / μέτοικος: Metics, tragedy, and civic ideology.' *Syllecta Classica* 10.
Bakewell, Geoffrey. 2008. 'Forbidding marriage: *Neaira* 16 and metic spouses at Athens.' *The Classical Journal* 104 (2).
Barber, Elizabeth Wayland. 1994. *Women's Work: The First 20,000 Years: Women, Cloth and Society in Early Times*. New York: Norton.
Berent, Moshe. 2000. 'Sovereignty: Ancient and modern.' *Polis* 17 (1–2).
Bers, Victor. 2002. 'What to believe in Demosthenes 57 *Against Eubulides*.' *Hyperboreus* 8 (2).
Bevan, Elinor. 1987. 'The goddess Artemis, and the dedication of bears in sanctuaries.' *Annual of the British School at Athens* 82.
Bicknell, Peter. 1976. 'Thoukritides' mother: A note on Demosthenes 57.' *Hermes* 104.
Blass, Friedrich. 1893. *Die attische Beredsamkeit: Demosthenes*. Vol. 3, Part 1. Leipzig: Teubner.
Blok, Josine. 2001. 'Toward a choreography of women's speech in classical Athens.' In *Making Silence Speak: Women's Voices in Greek Literature and Society*, ed. André Pierre M. H. Lardinois and Laura K. McClure. Princeton: Princeton University Press.
Blok, Josine. 2002. 'Women in Herodotus' *Histories*.' In *Brill's Companion to Herodotus*, ed. Egbert J. Bakker, Irene J. F. De Jong and Hans Van Wees. Leiden: Brill.
Blok, Josine. 2017. *Citizenship in Classical Athens*. Cambridge: Cambridge University Press.
Blundell, Sue. 1995. *Women in Ancient Greece*. Cambridge, MA: Harvard University Press.
Blundell, Sue. 1998. *Women in Classical Athens*. London: Bristol Classical Press.
Blundell, Sue, and Lloyd Llewellyn-Jones, eds. 2002. *Women's Dress in the Ancient Greek World*. Swansea: Classical Press of Wales.
Bourriot, Félix. 1976. *Recherches sur la nature du genos: Étude d'histoire sociale athénienne, périodes archaïque et classique*. Paris: Champion.

Brickhouse, Thomas C., and Nicholas D. Smith. 1988. *Socrates on Trial.* Oxford: Clarendon Press.

Brickhouse, Thomas C., and Nicholas D. Smith. 2002. *The Trial and Execution of Socrates: Sources and Controversies.* Oxford: Oxford University Press.

Brisson, Luc, Marie-Hélène Congourdeau and Jean-Luc Solère, eds. 2008. *L'embryon: Formation et animation: Antiquité grecque et latine, tradition hébraïque, chrétienne, et islamique.* Paris: Vrin.

Brock, Roger. 1994. 'The labour of women in Classical Athens.' *Classical Quarterly* 44.

Brøns, Cecilie. 2017. 'Power through textiles: Women as ritual performers in ancient Greece.' In *Women's Ritual Competence in the Greco-Roman Mediterranean*, ed. Matthew Dillon, Esther Eidinow and Lisa Maurizio. Abingdon: Routledge.

Brulé, Pierre. 2001. *Les femmes grecques à l'époque classique,.* Paris: Hachette. (Trans. 2003. *Women of Ancient Greece*, trans. Antonia Nevill. Edinburgh: Edinburgh University Press.)

Burnyeat, Myles F. 1994. 'Did the ancient Greeks have the concept of human rights?' *Hyperboreus* 1 (1).

Burnyeat, Myles F. 1997. 'The impiety of Socrates.' *Ancient Philosophy* 17 (1).

Cairns, Douglas L. 1996. '*Hybris*, dishonour, and thinking big.' *The Journal of Hellenic Studies* 116.

Calame, Claude. 2001. *Choruses of Young Women in Ancient Greece: Their Morphology, Religious Role, and Social Functions*, trans. Derek Burton Collins and Janice Orion, rev. edn. Lanham, MD: Rowman and Littlefield.

Calderini, Aristide. 1908. *La manomissione e la condizione dei liberti in Grecia.* Milan: Umberto Allegretti.

Campa, Naomi T. 2018. 'Positive freedom and the citizen in Athens.' *Polis* 35 (1).

Campa, Naomi T. 2019. '*Kurios, kuria* and the status of Athenian women.' *The Classical Journal* 114 (3).

Canevaro, Mirko. 2013. *The Documents in the Attic Orators: Laws and Decrees in the Public Speeches of the Demosthenic Corpus.* Oxford: Oxford University Press.

Cantarella, Eva. 1986. 'Women's position in classical Athens.' *Archaiologia* 21.

Cantarella, Eva. 1987. *Pandora's Daughters: The Role and Status of Women in Greek and Roman Antiquity*, trans. Maureen B. Fant with a foreword by Mary R. Lefkowitz. Baltimore: Johns Hopkins University Press.

Canto, Monique. 1994. 'The politics of women's bodies: Reflections on Plato.' In *Feminist Interpretations of Plato*, ed. Nancy Tuana. University Park: Pennsylvania State University Press.

Carawan, Edwin. 1985. Ἀπόφασις and εἰσαγγελία: The role of the Areopagus in Athenian political trials.' *Greek, Roman and Byzantine Studies* 26: 114–40.

Carawan, Edwin. 1987. '*Eisangelia* and *euthyna*: The trials of Miltiades, Themistocles, and Cimon.' *Greek, Roman and Byzantine Studies* 28.
Carawan, Edwin. 1991. 'ΕΦΕΤΑΙ and Athenian courts for homicide in the age of orators.' *Classical Philology* 86: 1–16.
Carawan, Edwin. 1998. *Rhetoric and the Law of Draco*. New York: Oxford University Press.
Carawan, Edwin. 2010. 'διαδικασίαι and the Demotionid problem.' *Classical Quarterly* n.s. 60 (2).
Carey, Christopher. 1991. 'Apollodorus' mother: The wives of enfranchised aliens in Athens.' *Classical Quarterly* 41.
Carey, Christopher. 1995. 'The witness's *exomosia* in the Athenian courts.' *Classical Quarterly* 45 (1).
Carey, Christopher. 2004. 'Antiphon's daughter.' In *Law, Rhetoric, and Comedy in Classical Athens: Essays in Honour of Douglas M. MacDowell*, ed. Douglas L. Cairns and Ronald A. Knox. Swansea: Classical Press of Wales.
Carey, Christopher, ed. 2007. *Lysiae Orationes cum fragmentis*. Oxford: Clarendon Press.
Carey, Christopher. 2013. 'In search of Drakon.' *Cambridge Classical Journal* 59.
Carey, Christopher. 2015. 'Solon in the orators.' *Trends in Classics* 7 (1).
Cavallini, Eleonora. 2004. 'Il processo contro Frine: L'accusa e la difesa.' *Labeo* 50.
Cavallini, Eleonora. n.d. 'Phryne in modern art, cinema and cartoon.' http://www.24grammata.com/wp-content/uploads/2011/12/Cavallini-Phryne-24grammata.com_.pdf.
Chambet, Daniel. 2007. 'Les fantômes de Praxitèle.' *Esprit* 8.
Che, Jayoung. 2017. 'Citizenship and the social position of Athenian women in the classical age: A prospect for overcoming the antithesis of male and female.' *Athens Journal of History* 3 (2).
Christ, Matthew R. 1998. *The Litigious Athenian*. Baltimore: Johns Hopkins University Press.
Chryssoulaki, Stella. 2008. 'The participation of women in the worship and festivals of Dionysos.' In *Worshiping Women: Ritual and Reality in Classical Athens*, ed. Nikolaos Kaltsas and Harvey Alan Shapiro. Athens: Ethniko Archaiologiko Mouseio.
Claassen, Jo-Marie. 2007. 'Medical negligence in ancient legal codes.' *Akroterion* 52.
Cleland, Liza, Mary Harlow and Lloyd Llewellyn-Jones, eds. 2005. *The Clothed Body in the Ancient World*. Oxford: Oxbow Books.
Cohen, David J. 1984. The Athenian law of adultery. *Revue Internationale des Droits de l'Antiquité* 31.
Cohen, David J. 1989a. 'Seclusion, separation, and the status of women in classical Athens.' *Greece and Rome*.

Cohen, David J. 1989b. 'The prosecution of impiety in Athenian law.' In *Symposion 1985: Vorträge zur griechischen und hellenistischen Rechtsgeschichte (Ringberg, 24.–26. Juli 1985)*, ed. Gerhard Thuer. Cologne: Böhlau.

Cohen, David J. 1990. 'The social context of adultery at Athens.' In *Nomos: Essays in Athenian Law, Politics and Society*, ed. Paul Cartledge, Paul Millett and Stephen Randolph Todd. Cambridge: Cambridge University Press.

Cohen, David J. 1995. *Law, Violence, and Community in Classical Athens*. Cambridge: Cambridge University Press.

Cohen, Edward E. 2000. '"Whoring under contract": The legal context of prostitution in fourth-century Athens.' In *Law and Social Status in Classical Athens*, ed. Virginia J. Hunter and Jonathan C. Edmondson. Oxford: Oxford University Press.

Cohen, Edward E. 2006. 'Consensual contracts at Athens.' In *Symposion 2003*, ed. Hans Rupprecht. Vienna: Verlag der Österreichischen Akademie der Wissenschaften.

Cohen, Edward E. 2015. *Athenian Prostitution: The Business of Sex*. New York: Oxford University Press.

Cohen, Edward E. 2016. 'The Athenian businesswoman.' In *Women in Antiquity: Real Women Across the Ancient World*, ed. St. L. Budin and J. MacIntosh Turfa. Abingdon: Routledge.

Cohn-Haft, Louis. 1995. 'Divorce in classical Athens.' *The Journal of Hellenic Studies* 115.

Cole, Susan Guettel. 2004. *Landscapes, Gender, and Ritual Space: The Ancient Greek Experience*. Berkeley: University of California Press.

Collins, Derek Burton. 2001. 'Theoris of Lemnos and the criminalization of magic in fourth-century Athens.' *Classical Quarterly* n.s. 51 (2).

Compton-Engle, Gwendolyn Leigh. 2005. Stolen cloaks in Aristophanes' Ecclesiazusae.' *Transactions of the American Philological Association* 135.

Connelly, Joan Breton. 2007. *Portrait of a Priestess: Women and Ritual in Ancient Greece*. Princeton: Princeton University Press.

Connelly, Joan Breton. 2008. 'Priestesses – women in cult: In divine affairs – the greatest part: Women and priesthoods in classical Athens.' In *Worshiping Women: Ritual and Reality in Classical Athens*, ed. Nikolaos Kaltsas and Harvey Alan Shapiro. Athens: Ethniko Archaiologiko Mouseio.

Connor, W. Robert. 1991. 'The other 399: Religion and the trial of Socrates.' In *Georgica: Greek Studies in Honour of George Cawkwell*, ed. Michael Attyah Flower and Mark Toher. London: Institute of Classical Studies.

Cooper, Craig. 1995. 'Hyperides and the trial of Phryne.' *Phoenix* 49 (4).

Corner, Sean. 2011. 'Bringing the outside in: The ἀνδρών as brothel and the symposium's civic sexuality.' In *Greek Prostitutes in the Ancient Mediterranean, 800 BCE–200 CE*, ed. Allison Mary Jane Glazebrook and Madeleine Mary Henry. Madison: University of Wisconsin Press.

Corpataux, Jean-François. 2009. 'Phryné, Vénus et Galatée dans l'atelier de Jean-Léon Gérôme.' *Artibus et Historiae* 30 (59).
Corso, Antonio. 1997. 'The monument of Phryne at Delphi.' *Numismatica e Antichità Classiche* 26.
Corso, Antonio. 1997–8. 'Love as suffering: The Eros of Thespiae of Praxiteles.' *Bulletin of the Institute of Classical Studies of the University of London* 42.
Cox, Cheryl Anne. 1992. 'On Roger Just's *Women in Athenian Law and Life.*' *The Ancient History Bulletin* VI.
Cox, Cheryl Anne. 1998. *Household Interests: Property, Marriage Strategies, and Family Dynamics in Ancient Athens.* Princeton: Princeton University Press.
Craik, Elizabeth M. 1984. 'Marriage in ancient Greece.' In *Marriage and Property,* ed. Elizabeth M. Craik and John Selby Watson. Aberdeen: Aberdeen University Press.
Cromey, Robert. 2006. 'Apollo Patroos and the phratries.' *L'Antiquité Classique* 75.
Crummy, Nina. 2010. 'Bears and coins: The iconography of protection in Late Roman infant burials.' *Britannia* 41.
Cudjoe, Richard V. 2005. 'The purpose of the *epidikasia* for an *epikleros* in classical Athens.' *Dike* 8.
Cudjoe, Richard V. 2010. *The Social and Legal Position of Widows and Orphans in Classical Athens.* Athens: Centre for Ancient Greek and Hellenistic Law; Panteion University of Social and Political Sciences.
Cudjoe, Richard V., and Sophia Adam-Magnissali. 2010. 'Family law in [Demosthenes] 43: *Against Makartatos,* 75.' Ἐπετηρὶς τοῦ Κέντρου Ἐρεύνης τῆς Ἱστορίας τοῦ Ἑλληνικοῦ Δικαίου 42.
Dasen, Véronique, ed. 2007. *L'embryon humain à travers l'histoire: Images, savoirs et rites: Actes du colloque international de Fribourg, 27–29 octobre 2004.* Gollion: Infolio.
Davidson, James. 2006. 'Making a spectacle of her(self): The Greek courtesan and the art of the present.' In *The Courtesan's Arts: Cross-Cultural Perspectives,* ed. M. Feldman and B. Gordon. Oxford: Oxford University Press.
Davidson, James. 2013. 'Bodymaps: Sexing space and zoning gender in ancient Athens.' In *Gender and the City Before Modernity,* ed. Lin Foxhall and Gabriele Neher. Malden, MA: Wiley-Blackwell.
Delli Pizzi, Aurian. 2011. 'Impiety in epigraphic evidence.' *Kernos* 24.
Des Bouvrie, Synnøve. 1990. *Women in Greek Tragedy: An Anthropological Approach.* Oxford: Oxford University Press.
Deslauriers, Marguerite. 2003. 'Aristotle on the virtues of slaves and women.' *Oxford Studies in Ancient Philosophy* 25.
Develin, Robert. 1991. 'Euboulides' office and the *diapsephisis* of 346/5 B.C.' *Classica et Mediaevalia* 42.
Dillon, Matthew. 2002. *Girls and Women in Classical Greek Religion.* Abingdon: Routledge.

Dillon, Matthew, Esther Eidinow and Lisa Maurizio, eds. 2017. *Women's Ritual Competence in the Greco-Roman Mediterranean.* Abingdon: Routledge.

Dixon, Suzanne. 1983. 'A family business: Women's role in patronage and politics at Rome 80–44 B.C.' *Classica et Mediaevalia* 34.

DuBois, Page. 1992. 'Eros and the woman.' *Ramus* 21.

Duncan-Jones, Richard P. 1980. 'Metic numbers in Periclean Athens.' *Chiron* X.

Durand, Bernard, and Leah Otis-Cour, eds. 2002. *La torture judiciaire: Approches historiques et juridique.* Lille: Centre d'Histoire Judiciaire.

Easterling, Patricia E. 1987. 'Women in tragic space.' *Bulletin of the Institute of Classical Studies of the University of London* 34.

Eaverly, Mary Ann. 2013. *Tan Men/Pale Women: Color and Gender in Archaic Greece and Egypt: A Comparative Approach.* Ann Arbor, MI: University of Michigan Press.

Edwards, Michael J., ed. and trans. 1995. *Greek Orators. 4: Andocides.* Warminster: Aris & Phillips.

Edwards, Michael J. 2004. 'Narrative levels in Antiphon 1, *Against the Stepmother.*' In *Registros lingüísticos en las lenguas clásicas,* ed. Antonio López Eire and Agustín Ramos Guerreira. Salamanca: Ediciones Universidad de Salamanca.

Edwards, Michael J., ed. 2007. *Isaeus.* Austin: University of Texas Press.

Edwards, Michael J. 2017. 'Tragedy in Antiphon 1, *Against the Stepmother.*' In *Theatre World: Critical Perspectives on Greek Tragedy and Comedy: Studies in Honour of Georgia Xanthakis-Karamanos,* ed. A. Fountoulakis, Markantonatos and G. Vasilaros. Berlin: De Gruyter.

Efstathiou, Athanasios. 2007. '*Euthyna* procedure in 4th c. Athens and the case on the false embassy.' *Dike* 10.

Eidinow, Esther. 2010. 'Patterns of persecution: "Witchcraft" Trials in Classical Athens.' *Past and Present* 208 (1).

Eidinow, Esther. 2016. *Envy, Poison, and Death: Women on Trial in Classical Athens.* Oxford: Oxford University Press.

Evans, Nancy A. 2004. 'Feasts, citizens, and cultic democracy in Classical Athens.' *Ancient Society* 34.

Fabre-Serris, Jacqueline, and Alison M. Keith, eds. 2015. *Women and War in Antiquity.* Baltimore: Johns Hopkins University Press.

Fantasia, Ugo. 2012. 'I magistrati dell'*agora* nelle città greche di età classica ed ellenistica.' In *"Agora" greca e "agorai" di Sicilia,* ed. Carmine Ampolo. Pisa: Ediciones della Normale.

Fantham, Elaine, Helene Peet Foley, Natalie Boymel Kampen, Sarah B. Pomeroy and H. Alan Shapiro. 1994. *Women in the Classical World: Image and Text.* New York: Oxford University Press.

Faulkner, Andrew. 2011. *The Homeric Hymns: Interpretative Essays.* Oxford: Oxford University Press.

Faulkner, Robert. 2007. *The Case for Greatness: Honorable Ambition and Its Critics.* New Haven: Yale University Press.
Fauth, Wolfgang. 1984. 'Arktos in den griechischen Zauberpapyri.' *Zeitschrift für Papyrologie und Epigraphik* 57.
Fehr, Burkhard. 2009. '*Pornos* and the pleasure of rest: Some thoughts on body language in ancient Greek art and life.' In *An Archaeology of Representations: Ancient Greek Vase-Painting and Contemporary Methodologies*, ed. Dimitiros Yatromanolakis. Athens: Ekdoseis Kardamitsa.
Feldman, Martha, and Bonnie Gordon. 2006. *The Courtesan's Arts: Cross-Cultural Perspectives.* Oxford: Oxford University Press .
Feyel, Christophe. 2009. *Dokimasía: La place et le rôle de l'examen préliminaire dans les institutions des cités grecques.* Paris: De Boccard.
Filonik, Jakub. 2013. 'Athenian impiety trials: A reappraisal.' *Dike* 16.
Filonik, Jakub. 2016. 'Impiety avenged: Rewriting Athenian history.' In *"Splendide Mendax": Rethinking Fakes and Forgeries in Classical, Late Antique, and Early Christian Literature*, ed. Edmund P. Cueva and Javier Martínez. Groningen: Barkhuis.
Finnegan Rachel. 1990. 'Women in Aristophanic comedy.' *Platon* 42.
Finnegan, Rachel. 1995. *Women in Aristophanes.* Amsterdam: Adolf M. Hakkert.
Fischer, Norman J. 2014. 'Euthyphro's choice.' *Philosophy and Literature* 38 (2).
Fisher, Nick. 1992. *Hybris: A Study in the Values of Honour and Shame In Ancient Greece.* Warminster: Aris & Phillips.
Fisher, Nick. 1997. '*Hybris*, status and slavery.' In *The Greek World*, ed. Anton Powell. London: Routledge.
Fisher, Nick, ed. 2001. *Against Timarchos/Aeschines.* New York: Oxford University Press.
Fisher, Nick. 2005. 'Body-abuse: The rhetoric of *hybris* in Aechines' *Against Timarchos.*' In *La violence dans les mondes grec et romain: Actes du colloque international Paris, 2–4 mai 2002*, ed. Jean-Marie Bertrand. Paris: Éditions de la Sorbonne
Flacelière, R. 1965. *Daily Life in Ancient Greece at the Time of Pericles*, trans Peter Green. New York: Macmillan.
Flament, Christophe. 2007. 'Que nous reste-t-il de Solon? Essai de déconstruction du père de la πάτριος πολιτεία.' *Les Études Classiques* 75 (4).
Fletcher, Judith. 1999. 'Sacrificial bodies and the bodies of the text in Aristophanes' *Lysistrata.*' *Ramus* 28 (2).
Fletcher, Judith. 2012. 'The women's decree: Law and its other in *Ecclesiazusae.*' In *No Laughing Matter: Studies in Athenian Comedy*, ed. Christopher W. Marshall and George Adam Kovacs. London: Bristol Classical Press.

Florence, Monica. 2014. 'The body politic: Sexuality in Greek and Roman comedy and mime.' In *A Companion to Greek and Roman Sexualities*, ed. Thomas K. Hubbard. Oxford: Blackwell.

Flower, Michael Attyah. 1985. 'IG II FD.2344 and the size of phratries in classical Athens.' *Classical Quarterly* 35.

Foley, Helene Peet, ed. 1981. *Reflections of Women in Antiquity*. New York: Gordon & Breach.

Foley, Helene Peet. 1994. *The Homeric Hymn to Demeter: Translation, Commentary, and Interpretive Essays*. Princeton: Princeton University Press.

Foley, Helene Peet. 2014. Performing gender in Greek Old and New Comedy.' In *The Cambridge Companion to Greek Comedy*, ed. Martin Revermann. Cambridge: Cambridge University Press.

Föllinger, Sabine, and Oliver Stoll. 2018. 'Die wirtschaftliche Effizienz von Ordnung und personalen Beziehungen: Ein neuer Blick auf Xenophons *Oikonomikos*.' In *"Emas Non Quod Opus Est, Sed Quod Necesse Est": Beiträge zur Wirtschafts-, Sozial-, Rezeptions- und Wissenschaftsgeschichte der Antike: Festschrift für Hans-Joachim Drexhage zum 70. Geburtstag*, ed. Kai Ruffing and Kerstin Dross-Krüpe. Wiesbaden: Harrassowitz.

Foxhall, Lin. 1989. 'Household, gender and property in classical Athens.' *Classical Quarterly* 39.

Foxhall, Lin. 1996. 'The law and the lady: Women and legal proceedings in classical Athens.' In *Greek Law in Its Political Setting: Justifications Not Justice*, ed. Lin Foxhall and Andrew D. E. Lewis. Oxford: Oxford University Press.

Foxhall, Lin, and Andrew D. E. Lewis, eds. 1996. *Greek Law in Its Political Setting: Justifications Not Justice*. Oxford: Oxford University Press.

Frankfurter, David. 2014. 'The social context of women's erotic magic in antiquity.' In *Daughters of Hecate: Women and Magic in the Ancient World*, ed. Kimberly B. Stratton and Dayna S. Kalleres. Oxford: Oxford University Press.

Frost, Frank. 2002. 'Solon Pornoboskos and Aphrodite Pandemos.' *Syllecta Classica* 13 (1).

Fulkerson, Laurel. 2013. 'Alcibiades πολύτροπος: Socratic philosopher and tragic hero?' *Histos* 7.

Gagarin, Michael. 1979a. 'The Athenian law against *hybris*.' In *Arktouros: Hellenic Studies Presented to Bernard M. W. Knox on the Occasion of His 65th Birthday*, ed. Glen Warren Bowersock, Walter Burkert and Michael C. J. Putnam. Berlin: De Gruyter.

Gagarin, Michael. 1979b. 'The prosecution of homicide in Athens.' *Greek, Roman and Byzantine Studies* 20.

Gagarin, Michael. 1981. *Drakon and Early Athenian Homicide Law*. New Haven: Yale University Press.

Gagarin, Michael. 1990. '*Bouleusis* in Athenian homicide law.' In *Symposion 1988: Vorträge zur griechischen und hellenistischen Rechtsgeschichte*, ed. Giuseppe Nenci and Gerhard Thür. Cologne: Böhlau.
Gagarin, Michael. 1986. *Early Greek Law*. Berkeley: University of California Press.
Gagarin, Michael. 1996. 'The torture of slaves in Athenian law.' *Classical Philology* 91 (1).
Gagarin, Michael. 1998. 'Women in Athenian courts.' *Dik* 1.
Gagarin, Michael. 2000. 'The *basileus* in Athenian homicide law.' In *Polis and Politics: Studies in Ancient Greek History Presented to Mogens Herman Hansen on his Sixtieth Birthday, August 20, 2000*, ed, Pernille Flensted-Jensen, Thomas Heine Nielsen and Lene Rubinstein. Copenhagen: Museum Tusculanum Press.
Gagarin, Michael. 2001. 'Women's voices in Attic oratory.' In *Making Silence Speak: Women's Voices in Greek Literature and Society*, ed. André Pierre M. H. Lardinois and Laura K. McClure. Princeton: Princeton University Press.
Gagarin, Michael. 2008. 'Women and property at Gortyn.' *Dike* 11.
Gagarin, Michael. 2010. *Antiphon the Athenian: Oratory, Law, and Justice in the Age of the Sophists*. Austin: University of Texas Press.
Gagarin, Michael. 2012. 'Women and the law in Gortyn.' *Index* 40.
Gagliardi, Lorenzo. 2002. 'Per un'interpretazione della legge di Solone in materia successoria.' *Dike* 5.
Garver, Eugene. 2014. 'Euthyphro prosecutes a human rights violation.' *Philosophy and Literature* 38 (2).
Gasparo, Giulia Sfameni. 1986. *Misteri e culti mistici di Demetra*. Rome: L'Erma di Bretschneider.
Gernet, Louis. 1955. *Droit et société dans la Grèce ancienne*. Paris: Recueil Sirey.
Gerolemou, Maria. 2011. *Bad Women, Mad Women: Gender und Wahnsinn in der griechischen Tragödie*. Tübingen: Narr.
Geschiere, Peter. 2009. *The Perils of Belonging: Autochthony, Citizenship, and Exclusion in Africa and Europe*. Chicago: University of Chicago Press.
Gilhuly, Kate, and Nancy Worman, eds. 2014. *Space, Place, and Landscape in Ancient Greek Literature and Culture*. Cambridge: Cambridge University Press.
Gilmore, David D. 1987. *Honor and Shame and the Unity of the Mediterranean*. Washington, DC: American Anthropological Association.
Glazebrook, Allison. 2005a. 'Prostituting female kin (Plut. *Sol.* 23.1–2).' *Dike* 8.
Glazebrook, Allison. 2005b. 'The making of a prostitute: Apollodoros's portrait of Neaira.' *Arethusa* 38 (2).
Glazebrook, Allison. 2011. 'Πορνεῖον: prostitution in Athenian civic space.' In *Greek Prostitutes in the Ancient Mediterranean, 800 BCE–200 CE*, ed. Allison Glazebrook and Madeleine Mary Henry. Madison: University of Wisconsin Press.

Goff, Barbara. 2004. *Citizen Bacchae: Women's Ritual Practice in Ancient Greece.* Berkeley: University of California Press.

Goff, Barbara. 2007. 'Improvising on the Athenian stage: Women's ritual practice in drama.' In *Finding Persephone: Women's Rituals in the Ancient Mediterranean,* ed. Maryline G. Parca and Angeliki Tzanetou. Bloomington: Indiana University Press.

Golden, Mark. 1985. 'Donatus and Athenian phratries.' *Classical Quarterly* 35.

Goldhill, Simon. 1994. 'Representing democracy: Women at the Great Dionysia.' In *Ritual, finance, politics: Athenian democratic accounts presented to David Lewis,* ed. Robin Osborne and Simon Hornblower. Oxford: Clarendon Press.

Gomme, A. W. 1925. 'The position of women in Athens in the 5th and 4th century.' *Classical Philology* XX.

Gould, J. 1980. 'Law, custom, and myth: Aspects of the social position of women in classical Athens.' *The Journal of Hellenic Studies* 100.

Griffith-Williams, Brenda. 2012. '*Oikos,* family feuds and funerals: Argumentation and evidence in Athenian inheritance disputes.' *The Classical Quarterly* 62 (1).

Griffith-Williams, Brenda. 2013. *A Commentary on Selected Speeches of Isaios.* Leiden: Brill.

Griffith-Williams, Brenda. 2016. '"She was treated abominably, gentlemen": Women in the Athenian inheritance law.' In *The Material Side of Marriage: Women and Domestic Economies in Antiquity,* ed. R. Berg. Rome: Institutum Romanum Finlandiae.

Griffith-Williams, Brenda. 2019. 'Families and family relationships in the speeches of Isaios and in Middle and New Comedy.' In *Poet and Orator: A Symbiotic Relationship in Democratic Athens,* ed. A. Volonaki and E. Markantonatos. Berlin: De Gruyter.

Griffith-Williams, Brenda. 20120. 'The two Mantitheuses in Demosthenes 39 and [Demosthenes] 40: A case of Athenian identity theft?' In *The Making of Identities in Athenian Oratory,* ed. Jakub Filonik, Brenda Griffith-Williams and Janek Kucharski. Abingdon: Routledge.

Günther, Linda-Marie. 1994. 'Aspasia und Perikles: Rufmord im klassischen Athen.' In *Reine Männersache? Frauen in Männerdomänen der antiken Welt,* ed. Maria H. Dettenhofer. Cologne: Böhlau.

Haley, Shelley P. 1985. 'The five wives of Pompey the Great.' *Greece and Rome* 32.

Hall, Edith. 2016. 'Citizens but second class: Women in Aristotle's *Politics* (384–322 B.C.E.).' In *Patriarchal Moments: Reading Patriarchal Texts,* ed. Cesare Cuttica and Gaby Mahlberg. London: Bloomsbury Academic.

Hamel, Debra Louise. 2003. *Trying Neaira: The True Story of a Courtesan's Scandalous Life in Ancient Greece.* New Haven: Yale University Press.

Hammond, N. G. L. 1985. 'Arbitration in ancient Greece.' *Arbitration International* 1 (2).
Hansen, Mogens Herman. 1975. *Eisangelia: The sovereignty of the People's Court in Athens in the Fourth Century B.C. and the Impeachment of Generals and Politicians.* Odense: Odense University Press.
Hansen, Mogens Herman. 1976. Ἀπαγωγή, ἔνδειξις, *and* ἐφήγησις *against* κακοῦργοι, ἄτιμοι *and* φευγόντες*: A Study in the Athenian Administration of Justice in the Fourth Century B.C.* Odense: Odense University Press.
Hansen, Mogens Herman. 1980. 'Eisangelia in Athens: A reply.' *The Journal of Hellenic Studies* 100.
Hansen, Mogens Herman. 1996. 'The trial of Sokrates from the Athenian point of view.' In *Colloque international "Démocratie athénienne et culture" organisé par l'Académie d'Athènes en coopération avec l'UNESCO (23, 24 et 25 novembre 1992)*, ed. Francisco R. Adrados and Michel B. Sakellariou. Athens: Akadimia Athinon.
Hansen, Mogens Herman. 2002. 'The trial of Sokrates: From my point of view.' In *"Noctes Atticae": 34 Articles on Graeco-Roman Antiquity and Its Nachleben: Studies Presented to Jørgen Mejer on his Sixtieth Birthday, March 18, 2002*, ed. Bettina Amden. Copenhagen: Museum Tusculanum Press.
Hanson, Ann Ellis. 2008. 'The gradualist view of fetal development.' In *L'embryon: Formation et animation: Antiquité grecque et latine, tradition hébraïque, chrétienne et islamique*, ed. Luc Brisson, Marie-Hélène Congourdeau and Jean-Luc Solère. Paris: Vrin.
Harris, Edward M. 1990. 'Did the Athenians regard seduction as a worse crime than rape?' *Classical Quarterly* 40.
Harris, Edward M. 1992. 'Women and lending in Athenian society: A *horos* re-examined.' *Phoenix* XLVI.
Harris, Edward M. 2004. 'Did rape exist in classical Athens? Further reflections on the laws about sexual violence.' *Dike* 7.
Harris, Edward M., trans. 2008. *Demosthenes, Speeches 20–22*, ed. M Gagarin. Austin: University of Texas Press.
Harris, Edward M. 2013. *The Rule of Law in Action in Democratic Athens.* Oxford: Oxford University Press.
Harris, Edward M. 2014. 'Wife, household, and marketplace: The role of women in the economy of classical Athens.' In *Donne che contano nella storia greca*, ed. Umberto Bultrighini and Elisabetta Dimauro. Lanciano: Carabba.
Harris, Edward M. 2018. Review of Lanni, *Law and Order in Ancient Athens. Journal of Hellenic Studies* 138.
Harrison, A. R. W. 1968. *The Law of Athens, I: The Family and Property.* Oxford: Clarendon Press.
Harrison, A. R. W. 1971. *The Law of Athens, II: Procedure.* Oxford: Clarendon Press.

Hartmann, Elke. 2002. *Heirat, Hetärentum und Konkubinat im klassischen Athen.* Frankfurt am Main: Campus.

Hatzilambrou, Rosalia. 2018. *Isaeus' On the Estate of Pyrrhus (Oration 3).* Newcastle upon Tyne: Cambridge Scholars.

Havelock, Christine Mitchell. 1995. *The Aphrodite of Knidos and Her Successors: A Historical Review of the Female Nude in Greek Art.* Ann Arbor, MI: University of Michigan Press.

Hedrick, Charles W. 1983. 'Old and new on the Attic phratry of the Therrikleidai.' *Hesperia* 52.

Hedrick, Charles W. 1984. *The Attic Phratry.* Philadelphia, PA: University of Pennsylvania Press.

Hedrick, Charles W. 1988. 'An honorific phratry inscription.' *American Journal of Philology* 109.

Hedrick, Charles W. 1989. 'The phratry from Paiania.' *Classical Quarterly* 39.

Hedrick, Charles W. 1991. 'Phratry shrines of Attica and Athens.' *Hesperia* 60.

Helfer, Ariel. 2017. *Socrates and Alcibiades: Plato's Drama of Political Ambition and Philosophy.* Philadelphia, PA: University of Pennsylvania Press.

Henderson, Jeffrey. 1991. 'Women and the Athenian dramatic festivals.' *Transactions of the American Philological Association* 121.

Henry, Madeleine Mary. 1984. *Menander's Courtesans and the Greek Comic Tradition.* Frankfurt am Main: Peter Lang.

Henry, Madeleine Mary. 1995. *Prisoner of History: Aspasia of Miletus and Her Biographical Tradition.* Oxford: Oxford University Press.

Herfst, P. 1922. *Le travail de la femme dans la Grèce ancienne.* Utrecht: Oostnoek.

Herman, G. 2006. *Morality and Behaviour in Democratic Athens: A Social History.* Cambridge: Cambridge University Press.

Hillgruber, Michael. 1998. *Die zehnte Rede des Lysias: Einleitung, Text und Kommentar mit einem Anhang über die Gesetzesinterpretationen bei den attischen Rednern.* Berlin: De Gruyter.

Hoernes, Matthias. 2012. 'Bilder und Konstruktionen einer Hetäre: "Und Phryne soll nicht durch die Gerichtsrede des Hypereides, sondern durch den Anblick ihres Körpers gerettet worden sein".' In *Gefährtinnen: Vom Umgang mit Prostitution in der griechischen Antike und heute*, ed. Florian Martin Müller, Veronika Sossau and Faika A. El-Nagashi. Innsbruck: Innsbruck University Press.

Humble, Noreen M. 2004. 'Reality and ideology in the representation of women and war in Xenophon.' *The Ancient World* 35 (2).

Humphreys, Sally C. 1983. 'The date of Hagnias' death.' *Classical Philology* 78.

Humphreys, Sally C. 2002. 'Solon on adoption and wills.' *Zeitschrift der Savigny-Stiftung für Rechtsgeschichte: Romanistische Abteilung* 119.

Hunter, Virginia J. 1989. 'Women's authority in classical Athens.' *Échos du Monde Classique = Classical Views* 33.

Hunter, Virginia J. 1993. 'Agnatic kinship in Athenian law and Athenian family practice: Its implications for women.' In *Law, Politics and Society in the Ancient Mediterranean World*, ed. Baruch Halpern and Deborah W. Hobson. Sheffield: Sheffield Academic Press.

Hunter, Virginia J. 1994. *Policing Athens: Social Control in the Attic Lawsuits, 420–320 BC.* Princeton: Princeton University Press.

Inglis, Kristen Anne. 2011. 'Aristotle on the virtues of slaves, women, and children.' Cornell University, PhD diss.

Isaacs, Sonia E. 2010. 'Homeward bound: Gendered spatial arrangements in classical Athenian houses.' University of Washington, PhD diss.

Isager, Signe. 1981. 'The marriage pattern in classical Athens: Men and women in Isaios.' *Classica et Mediaevalia* 33.

Isager, Signe, and Mogens Herman Hansen. 1975. *Aspects of Athenian Society in the Fourth Century BC: A Historical Introduction to and Commentary on the Paragraphe Speeches and the Speech Against Dionysodorus in the Corpus Demosthenicum (XXXII–XXXVIII and LVI).* Odense: Odense University Press.

Jacobs, James B. 2015. *The Eternal Criminal Record.* Cambridge, MA: Harvard University Press.

Jameson, Michael Hamilton. 1997. 'Women and democracy in fourth-century Athens.' In *Esclavage, guerre, économie en Grèce ancienne: Hommages à Yvon Garlan*, ed. Pierre Brulé and Jacques Oulhen. Rennes: Presses Universitaires de Rennes.

Jenks, Rod. 2004. 'Socratic piety and Socrates' defense.' *The Modern Schoolman* 82 (4).

Johnstone, Steven. 1998. 'Cracking the code of silence: Athenian legal oratory and the histories of slaves and women.' In *Women and Slaves in Greco-Roman Culture: Differential Equations*, ed. Sandra R. Joshel and Sheila Murnaghan. London: Routledge.

Johnstone, Steven. 2002. 'Apology for the manuscript of Demosthenes 59.67.' *American Journal of Philology* 123 (2).

Johnstone, Steven. 2003. 'Women, property, and surveillance in classical Athens.' *Classical Antiquity* 22 (2).

Just, Roger. 1989. *Women in Athenian Law and Life.* London: Routledge.

Kaltsas, Nikolaos, and Harvey Alan Shapiro, eds. 2008. *Worshiping Women: Ritual and Reality in Classical Athens.* Athens: Ethniko Archaiologiko Mouseio.

Kapparis, Konstantinos. 1994. 'Was *atimia* for debts to the state inherited through women?' *Revue Internationale des Droits de l'Antiquité*, 3rd series, 41.

Kapparis, Konstantinos. 1995. 'When were the Athenian adultery laws introduced?' *Revue Internationale des Droits de l'Antiquité*, series 3, 42.

Kapparis, Konstantinos. 1998. 'Assessors of magistrates (*paredroi*) in classical Athens.' *Historia* 47.

Kapparis, Konstantinos. 1999. *Apollodoros: Against Neaira*. Berlin: De Gruyter.
Kapparis, Konstantinos. 2002. *Abortion in the Ancient World*. London: Duckworth.
Kapparis, Konstantinos. 2005. 'Immigration and citizenship procedures in Athenian law.' *Revue Internationale des Droits de l'Antiquité*, 3rd series, 52.
Kapparis, Konstantinos. 2014 'The Demosthenic edition of Mervin Dilts, and the textual transmission of Apollodoros.' In *Demosthenica libris manu scriptis tradita*, ed. Jana Grusková and Herbert Bannert. Vienna: Austrian Academy of Sciences Press.
Kapparis, Konstantinos. 2015. Review of Canevaro, *The Documents in the Attic Orators*. *Gnomon* 87: 40–3.
Kapparis, Konstantinos. 2018a. *Prostitution in the Ancient Greek World*. Berlin: De Gruyter.
Kapparis, Konstantinos. 2018b. 'The social and legal position of metics, foreigners, and slaves.' In *The Oxford Handbook of Demosthenes*, ed. Gunther Martin. Oxford: Oxford University Press.
Kapparis, Konstantinos. 2019a. *Athenian Law and Society*. London: Routledge.
Kapparis, Konstantinos. 2019b. 'Women in the dock: Body and feminine attire in women's trials.' In *The Ancient Art of Persuasion Across Genres and Topics*, ed. S. Papaioannou, A. Serafim and K. N. Demetriou. Leiden: Brill.
Kapparis, Konstantinos. 2020. 'Constructing gender identity: Women in Athenian trials.' In *The Making of Identities in Athenian Oratory*, ed. Brenda Griffith-Williams, Jakub Filonik, and Janek Kucharski. Abingdon: Routledge.
Karbowski, Joseph Anthony. 2012. 'Slaves, women, and Aristotle's natural teleology.' *Ancient Philosophy* 32 (2).
Karnezis, I. E. 1972. *The ἐπίκληρος (Heiress): A Contribution to the Interpretation of the Attic Orators and to the Study of the Private Life of Classical Athens*. Athens: privately printed.
Karnezis, I. E. 1979. 'The non-*aphairesis* of the *epikleros* and the testamentary *engyetè* woman in classical Athens.' *Athina* 77.
Katz, Marylin A. 1992. 'Patriarchy, ideology and the *epikleros*.' *Studi Italiani di Filologia Classica* 10.
Katz, Marylin A. 1995. 'Ideology and "the status of women" in ancient Greece.' In *Women in Antiquity: New Assessments*, ed. Richard Hawley and Barbara Mary Levick. London: Routledge.
Keesling, Catherine Marie. 2006. 'Heavenly bodies: Monuments to prostitutes in Greek sanctuaries.' In *Prostitutes and Courtesans in the Ancient World*, ed. Christopher A. Faraone and Laura K. McClure. Madison: University of Wisconsin Press.
Kennedy, Rebecca Futo. 2014. *Immigrant Women in Athens: Gender, Ethnicity, and Citizenship in the Classical City*. Abingdon: Routledge.
Keuls, Eva C. 1985. *The Reign of the Phallus: Sexual Politics in Ancient Athens*. New York: Harper & Row.

Kilmer, Martin F. 1993. *Greek Erotica on Attic Red-Figure Vases*. London: Duckworth.
King, H. T., and Marc A. LeForestier. 1994. 'Arbitration in ancient Greece.' *Dispute Resolution Journal* 49 (3).
Kondo, Kazutaka. 2015. 'Reputation and virtue: The rhetorical achievement of Socrates in Xenophon's *Apology*.' *Interpretation* 42 (1).
Konstantinou, Ariadne. 2018. *Female Mobility and Gendered Space in Ancient Greek Myth*. London: Bloomsbury Academic.
Kosmopoulou, Angeliki. 2001. '"Working women": Female professionals on classical Attic gravestones.' *Annual of the British School at Athens* 96.
Kuenen-Janssens, L. J. T. 1941. 'Some notes upon the competence of the Athenian woman to conduct a transaction.' *Mnemosyne* 9.
L'Homme-Wéry, Louise-Marie. 2005. 'Le rôle de la loi dans la pensée politique de Solon.' In *Le législateur et la loi dans l'Antiquité: Hommage à Françoise Ruzé: Actes du colloque de Caen, 15–17 mai 2003*, ed. Pierre Sineux. Caen: Presses Universitaires de Caen.
Lacey, Walter Kirkpatrick. 1980. 'The family of Euxitheus (Demosthenes LVII).' *Classical Quarterly* 30.
Lambert, S. D. 1993. *The Phratries of Attica*. Ann Arbor, MI: University of Michigan Press.
Lanni, Adriaan. 2007. 'Athenian approaches to legal predictability in contract cases.' In *Symposion 2005*, ed. E. Cantarella. Vienna: Verlag der Österreichischen Akademie der Wissenschaften.
Lanni, Adriaan. 2016. *Law and Order in Ancient Athens*. Cambridge: Cambridge University Press.
Lanni, Adriaan. 2017. 'Collective sanctions in classical Athens.' In *Ancient Law, Ancient Society*, ed. Dennis P. Kehoe and Thomas A. J. McGinn. Ann Arbor, MI: University of Michigan Press.
Lännström, Anna C. 2013. 'Socrates' moral impiety and its role at the trial: A reading of Euthyphro 6A.' *Polis* 30 (1).
Lape, Susan. 2002. 'Solon and the institution of the "democratic" family form.' *The Classical Journal* 98 (2).
Lape, Susan. 2010. *Race and Citizen Identity in the Classical Athenian Democracy*. Cambridge: Cambridge University Press.
Larivée, Annie. 2012. '"Gender trouble" in Xenophon and Plato.' *New England Classical Journal* 39 (4).
Larson, Stephanie. 2005. 'Kandaules' wife, Masistes' wife: Herodotus' narrative strategy in suppressing names of women (Hdt. 1.8–12 and 9.108–13).' *The Classical Journal* 101 (3).
Larsson Lovén, Lena. 1998. '"Lanam fecit": Woolworking and female virtue.' In *Aspects of Women in Antiquity: Proceedings of the First Nordic Symposium on Women's Lives in Antiquity, Göteborg, 12–15 June 1997*, ed. Lena Larsson Lovén and Agneta Strömberg. Jonsered: Åströms Förl.

Leão, Delfim Ferreira. 2001a. 'Matrimónio, amor e sexo na legislação de Sólon.' *Humanitas* 53.

Leão, Delfim Ferreira. 2001b. *Sólon: Ética e política.* Lisbon: Fundação Calouste Gulbenkian.

Leão, Delfim Ferreira. 2005. 'Sólon e a legislação em matéria de direito familiar.' *Dike* 8.

Leão, Delfim Ferreira. 2012. 'The myth of autochthony, Athenian citizenship and the right of *enktesis*.' In *Symposion 2011*, ed. B. Legras and G. Thür. Vienna: Verlag der Österreichischen Akademie der Wissenschaften.

Leão, Delfim Ferreira, and Peter Rhodes. 2015. *The Laws of Solon: A New Edition with Introduction, Translation and Commentary.* London: I. B. Tauris.

Lee, Mireille Michelle. 2005. 'Constru(ct)ing gender in the feminine Greek *peplos*.' In *The Clothed Body in the Ancient World*, ed. Liza Cleland, Mary Harlow and Lloyd Llewellyn-Jones. Oxford: Oxbow Books.

Lee, Mireille Michelle. 2015. *Body, Dress, and Identity in Ancient Greece.* Cambridge: Cambridge University Press.

Lefkowitz, Mary R. 1981. *Heroines and Hysterics.* New York: St. Martin's Press.

Lefkowitz, Mary R. 2008. 'Ancient Greek women and the gods.' In *Worshiping Women: Ritual and Reality in Classical Athens*, ed. Nikolaos Kaltsas and Harvey Alan Shapiro. Athens: Ethniko Archaiologiko Mouseio.

Lehoux, Élise, and Nicolas Siron. 2016. 'Montrer, démontrer: Phryné et le dévoilement de la vérité.' *Cahiers Mondes anciens* 8.

Lepri Sorge, Luisa. 1987. 'Ancora in terma di *ephesis*: La *dokimasia* degli arconti, VI.' In *Studi in onore di Arnaldo Biscardi, V.* Milan: Istituto Editoriale Cisalpino, La Goliardica.

Levin, Susan B. 2000. 'Plato on women's nature: Reflections on the *Laws*.' *Ancient Philosophy* 20 (1).

Lewis, John. 2004. 'Slavery and lawlessness in Solonian Athens.' *Dike* 7.

Lipsius, Justus H. 1905. *Das attische Recht und Rechtsverfahren.* 3 vols. Leipzig: Reisland.

Llewellyn-Jones, Lloyd. 2003. *Aphrodite's Tortoise: The Veiled Woman of Ancient Greece.* Swansea: Classical Press of Wales.

Llewellyn-Jones, Lloyd. 2011. 'Domestic abuse and violence against women in ancient Greece.' In *Sociable Man: Essays on Ancient Greek Social Behaviour in Honour of Nick Fisher*, ed. Stephen D. Lambert and Douglas L. Cairns. Swansea: Classical Press of Wales.

Loman, Pasi. 2004. 'No woman no war: Women's participation in ancient Greek warfare.' *Greece and Rome*, 2nd series, 51 (1).

McBrayer, Gregory A. 2017. 'Corrupting the youth: Xenophon and Plato on Socrates and Alcibiades.' *Kentron* 33.

McCannon, Bryan C. 2011. 'Jury size in classical Athens: An application of the Condorcet jury theorem.' *Kyklos* 64 (1).

MacDowell, Douglas M., ed. 1962. *On the Mysteries*. Oxford: Oxford University Press.
MacDowell, Douglas M. 1963. *Athenian Homicide Law in the Age of the Orators*. Manchester: Manchester University Press.
MacDowell, Douglas M. 1976. '*Hybris* in Athens.' *Greece and Rome* 32.
MacDowell, Douglas M. 1978. *The Law in Classical Athens*. Ithaca, NY: Cornell University Press.
MacDowell, Douglas M. 1990. *Demosthenes, Against Meidias (Oration 21)*. Oxford: Oxford University Press.
MacDowell, Douglas M. 1991. 'The Athenian procedure of *phasis*.' In *Symposion 1990: Vorträge zur griechischen und hellenistischen Rechtsgeschichte*. Cologne: Böhlau (= Douglas M. MacDowell. 2018. *Studies on Greek Law, Oratory and Comedy*, ed. Ilias Arnaoutoglou, Dimos Spatharas and Konstantinos Kapparis. Abingdon: Routledge).
MacDowell, Douglas M. 2000. 'The length of trials for public offenses in Athens.' In *Polis and Politics: Studies in Ancient Greek History*, ed. John. M. Camp. Copenhagen: Museum Tusculanum Press (= Douglas M. MacDowell. 2018. *Studies on Greek Law, Oratory and Comedy*, ed. Ilias Arnaoutoglou, Dimos Spatharas and Konstantinos Kapparis. Abingdon: Routledge).
MacDowell, Douglas M. 2018. *Studies on Greek Law, Oratory and Comedy*, ed. Ilias Arnaoutoglou, Dimos Spatharas and Konstantinos Kapparis. Abingdon: Routledge.
McHardy, Fiona. 2004. 'Women's influence on revenge in ancient Greece.' In *Women's Influence on Classical Civilization*, ed. F. McHardy and E. Marshall. Abingdon: Routledge.
McHardy, Fiona. 2005. 'From treacherous wives to murderous mothers: Filicide in tragic fragments.' In *Lost Dramas of Classical Athens: Greek Tragic Fragments*, ed. Fiona McHardy, James Robson and David Harvey. Exeter: University of Exeter Press,.
MacKenzie, D. C. 1985. 'The wicked wife of Ischomachus . . . again.' *Échos du Monde Classique = Classical Views* 29.
McLaren, Angus. 1990. *A History of Contraception: From Antiquity to the Present Day*. Oxford: Blackwell.
Maffi, Alberto. 1985. 'Contributo all'esegesi delle orazioni demosteniche Contro Beoto (39 e 40).' *Bullettino dell'Istituto di Diritto Romano* 88.
Maffi, Alberto. 1990. 'E' esistita l'aferesi dell' *epikleros*?' In *Symposion 1988: Vorträge zur griechischen und hellenistischen Rechtsgeschichte: Siena – Pisa, 6.-8. Juni 1988)*, ed. Giuseppe Nenci and Gerhard Thür. Cologne: Böhlau.
Maffi, Alberto. 2017. Review of Lanni, *Law and Order in Ancient Athens. Bryn Mawr Classical Review* 22 (10).
Marinatos, Nannó. 1987. 'Role and sex division in ritual scenes of Aegean art.' *Journal of Prehistoric Religion* 1.

Mélèze-Modrzejewski, Joseph. 1981. 'La structure juridique du mariage grec.' In *Scritti in onore di Orsolina Montevecchi*, ed. Edda Bresciani. Bologna: Clueb.

Miles, J. 1951. 'The marriage of Plangon (Dolly).' *Hermathena* 77.

Millis, Benjamin Willard. 2015. *Anaxandrides: Introduction, Translation, Commentary*. Heidelberg: Verlag Antike.

Mirhady, David Cyrus. 1996. 'Torture and rhetoric in Athens.' *The Journal of Hellenic Studies* 116.

Mirhady, David Cyrus. 2000. 'The Athenian rationale for torture.' In *Law and Social Status in Classical Athens*, ed. Virginia J. Hunter and Jonathan C. Edmondson. Oxford: Oxford University Press.

Mirhady, David Cyrus. 2002. 'Athens' democratic witnesses.' *Phoenix* 56 (3–4).

Mirhady, David Cyrus. 2008. 'Drakonian procedure.' In *Epigraphy and the Greek Historian*, ed. Craig Richard Cooper. Toronto: University of Toronto Press.

Miyazaki, Makoto. 1996. 'On public arbitration in Athens.' *Journal of Classical Studies* 44.

Morales, Helen L. 2011. 'Fantasising Phryne: The psychology and ethics of ekphrasis.' *Cambridge Classical Journal* 57.

Morris, Ian. 1998. 'Remaining invisible: The archaeology of the excluded in classical Athens.' In *Women and Slaves in Greco-Roman Culture: Differential Equations*, ed. Sandra R. Joshel and Sheila Murnaghan. London: Routledge.

Mossé, Claude. 1985. 'ΑΣΤΗ ΚΑΙ ΠΟΛΙΤΙΣ.' *Ktèma* 10.

Mossé, Claude. 1993. *Le citoyen dans la Grèce antique*. Paris: Nathan.

Muir, Steven. 2018. 'Greek piety and the charge against Socrates.' *Mouseion* 15 (3).

Mulhern, E. V. 2016. 'Roma(na) matrona.' *The Classical Journal* 112 (4).

Mustakallio, Katariina. 2012. 'Women outside their homes: The female voice in early Republican memory: Reconsidering Cloelia et Veturia.' *Index* 40.

Nadareishvili, Ketevan. 2003. 'Women in the law of democratic Athens.' *Phasis* 5–6.

Nehamas, Alexander. 2007. 'Beauty of body, nobility of soul: The pursuit of love in Plato's *Symposium*.' In *Maieusis: Essays on Ancient Philosophy in Honour of Myles Burnyeat*, ed. Dominic Scott. Oxford: Oxford University Press.

Neils, Jenifer. 2008. 'Festivals: Adonia to Thesmophoria: Women and Athenian festivals.' In *Worshiping Women: Ritual and Reality in Classical Athens*, ed. Nikolaos Kaltsas and Harvey Alan Shapiro. Athens: Ethniko Archaiologiko Mouseio.

Nelsestuen, Grant A. 2017. '*Oikonomia* as a theory of empire in the political thought of Xenophon and Aristotle.' *Greek, Roman and Byzantine Studies* 57 (1).

O'Connell, Peter A. 2017. *The Rhetoric of Seeing in Attic Forensic Oratory*. Austin: University of Texas Press.

O'Sullivan, L. L. 1997. 'Athenian impiety trials in the late fourth century B.C.' *Classical Quarterly* n.s. 47 (1).
O'Sullivan, Patrick. 2011. 'Sophistic ethics, old atheism, and *Critias* on religion.' *Classical World* 105 (2).
Oakley, John H. 2008. 'Death: Women in Athenian ritual and funerary art.' In *Worshiping Women: Ritual and Reality in Classical Athens*, ed. Nikolaos Kaltsas and Harvey Alan Shapiro. Athens: Ethniko Archaiologiko Mouseio.
Ober, Josiah. 1989. *Mass and Elite in Democratic Athens: Rhetoric, Ideology and the Power of the People*. Princeton: Princeton University Press.
Ogden, Daniel. 1996. *Greek Bastardy in the Classical and Hellenistic Periods*. Oxford: Oxford University Press.
Ogden, Daniel. 1997. 'Rape, adultery and the protection of bloodlines in classical Athens.' In *Rape in Antiquity: Sexual Violence in the Greek and Roman Worlds*, ed. Susan Deacy and Karen F. Peirce. Swansea: Classical Press. of Wales.
Omitowoju, Rosanna. 2016. 'The crime that dare not speak its name: Violence against women in the Athenian courts.' In *The Topography of Violence in the Greco-Roman World*, ed. Werner Riess and Garrett G. Fagan. Ann Arbor, MI: University of Michigan Press.
Oost, S. I. 1977. 'Xenophon's attitude toward women.' *Classical World* 71.
Oranges, A. 2016. 'L'accusa di corruzione nel contesto di euthyna: Verifica delle finanze e della fedeltà democratica dei magistrati.' *Anthesteria* 5.
Osborne, Robin. 1997. 'Law, the democratic citizen and the representation of women in classical Athens.' *Past and Present* 155.
Osborne, Robin. 2011. *The History Written on the Classical Greek Body*. Cambridge: Cambridge University Press .
Owens, Ron. 2010. *Solon of Athens: Poet, Philosopher, Soldier, Statesman*. Eastbourne: Sussex Academic Press.
Pager, Devah. 2003. 'The mark of a criminal record.' *American Journal of Sociology* 108 (5).
Palagia, Olga. 2008. 'Athena: Women in the cult of Athena.' In *Worshiping Women: Ritual and reality in Classical Athens*, ed. Nikolaos Kaltsas and Harvey Alan Shapiro. Athens: Ethniko Archaiologiko Mouseio.
Paoli, Ugo Enrico. 1943. 'L'ἐπίκληρος attica nella palliata romana.' *Atene e Roma* 11.
Papadimitriou, I. 1959. 'Ἀνασκαφαι Βραυρῶνος.' *Πρακτικὰ τῆς ἐν Ἀθήναις Ἀρχαιολογικῆς ἑταιρείας*.
Papadopoulou, Thaleia. 2008. 'Ἀνθρωπολογία, κοινωνιολογία και λογοτεχνική παράδοση: το γυναικείο στοιχείο στην αρχαία ελληνική τραγωδία.' In *Ἀρχαία ελληνική τραγωδία: θεωρία και πράξη*, ed. Andreas Markantonatos and Christos Tsangalis. Athens: Gutenberg.

Papaioannou, Sophia, Andreas Serafim and Beatrice da Vela, eds. 2017. *The Theatre of Justice: Aspects of Performance in Greco-Roman Oratory and Rhetoric.* Leiden: Brill.

Papaioannou, Sophia, Andreas Serafim, and Kyriakos Demetriou. 2019. *The Ancient Art of Persuasion Across Genres and Topics.* Leiden: Brill.

Papet, E. 2007. 'Phryné au XIXe siècle: La plus jolie femme de Paris?' In *Praxitele*, ed. A. Pasquier and J.-L. Martinez. Paris: Musée du Louvre.

Parca, Maryline G., and Angeliki Tzanetou, eds. 2007. *Finding Persephone: Women's Rituals in the Ancient Mediterranean.* Bloomington: Indiana University Press.

Parker, Robert. 1991. 'The Hymn to Demeter and the Homeric Hymns 1.' *Greece and Rome* 38 (1).

Patterson, Cynthia. 1976. 'Pericles' citizenship law of 451/0 B.C.' University of Pennsylvania, PhD diss.

Patterson, Cynthia. 1981. *Pericles' Citizenship Law of 451–50 B.C.* New York: Arno Press.

Patterson, Cynthia. 1986. '*Hai Attikai*: The other Athenians.' *Helios* 13 (2).

Patterson, Cynthia. 1990. 'Those Athenian bastards.' *Classical Antiquity* 9 (1).

Patterson, Cynthia. 1991. 'Marriage and the married woman in Athenian law.' In *Women's History and Ancient History*, ed. Sarah B. Pomeroy. Chapel Hill: University of North Carolina Press.

Patterson, Cynthia. 1993. 'The case against Neaira and the public ideology of the Athenian family.' In *Athenian Identity and Civic Ideology*, ed. Alan L. Boegehold and Adele C. Scafuro. Baltimore: Johns Hopkins University Press.

Patterson, Cynthia. 1998. *The Family in Greek History.* Cambridge, MA: Harvard University Press.

Patterson, Cynthia. 2000. 'The hospitality of Athenian justice: The metic in court.' In *Law and Social Status in Classical Athens*, ed. Virginia J. Hunter and Jonathan C. Edmondson. Oxford: Oxford University Press.

Patterson, Cynthia. 2006. '"Citizen cemeteries" in classical Athens?' *Classical Quarterly* n.s. 56 (1).

Patterson, Cynthia. 2007. 'Other sorts: Slaves, foreigners, and women in Periclean Athens.' In *The Cambridge Companion to the Age of Pericles*, ed. Loren J. Samons II. Cambridge: Cambridge University Press.

Pečirka, J. 1966. *The Formula for the Grant of Enktesis in Attic Inscriptions.* Prague: Universita Karlova.

Pecorella Longo, Chiara. 2002. 'Aristofane e la legge sull'*eisangelia*.' *Prometheus* 28 (3).

Perlman, Paula J. 1989. 'Acting the she-bear for Artemis.' *Arethusa* 22.

Phillips, David. 2008. *Avengers of Blood: Homicide in Athenian Law and Custom from Draco to Demosthenes.* Stuttgart: Steiner.

Phillips, David. 2013. *The Law of Ancient Athens*. Ann Arbor, MI: University of Michigan Press.
Piccirilli, Luigi. 1983. '*Eisangelia* e condanna di Temistocle.' *Civiltà Classica e Cristiana* 6.
Pomeroy, Sarah B. 1975. *Goddesses, Whores, Wives, and Slaves: Women in Classical Antiquity.* New York: Schocken.
Pomeroy, Sarah B., ed. 1991. *Women's History and Ancient History.* Chapel Hill: University of North Carolina Press.
Pomeroy, Sarah B., trans. 1994. *Xenophon, Oeconomicus: A Social and Historical Commentary.* New York: Oxford University Press.
Pomeroy, Sarah B. 1997. *Families in Classical and Hellenistic Greece: Representations and Realities.* Oxford: Oxford University Press.
Pritchard, David M. 2004. 'A woman's place in classical Athens: An overview.' *Ancient History: Resources for Teachers* 34 (2).
Pritchard, David M. 2014. 'The position of Attic women in democratic Athens.' *Greece and Rome,* 2nd series, 61 (2).
Raaflaub, Kurt A. 2004. *The Discovery of Freedom in Ancient Greece,* trans. Renate Franciscono; rev. by the author. Chicago: University of Chicago Press.
Rahe, Paul A. 1984. 'The primacy of politics in classical Greece.' *American Historical Review* 89.
Rehm, Rush. 1999. 'The play of space: Before, behind, and beyond in Euripides' *Heracles.*' *Illinois Classical Studies* 24–5.
Reichardt, Tobias. 2003. *Recht und Rationalität im frühen Griechenland.* Würzburg: Königshausen und Neumann.
Reinsberg, Carola. 1989. *Ehe, Hetärentum und Knabenliebe im antiken Griechenland.* Munich: Beck.
Rhodes, P. J. 1979. '*Eisangelia* in Athens.' *The Journal of Hellenic Studies* 99.
Rhodes, P. J. 1981. *A Commentary on the Aristotelian Athenaion Politeia.* Oxford: Oxford University Press.
Rhodes, P. J. 2011. *Alcibiades: Athenian Playboy, General and Traitor.* Barnsley: Pen & Sword.
Richter, D. C. 1971. 'The position of women in classical Athens.' *The Classical Journal* 67.
Riess, Werner. 2008. 'Private violence and state control: The prosecution of homicide and its symbolic meanings in fourth-century BC Athens.' In *Sécurité collective et ordre public dans les sociétés anciennes,* ed. Hans Van Wees, Pierre Ducrey and Cédric Brélaz. Geneva: Fondation Hardt.
Riess, Werner. 2012. *Performing Interpersonal Violence: Court, Curse, and Comedy in Fourth-Century BCE Athens.* Berlin: De Gruyter.
Riess, Werner. 2018a. 'Solon: Der erste europäische Krisenmanager und Reformer?' In *Colloquia Attica: Neuere Forschungen zur Archaik, zvum athenischen Recht und zur Magie,* ed. Werner Riess. Stuttgart: Steiner.

Riess, Werner, ed. 2018b. *Colloquia Attica: Neuere Forschungen zur Archaik, zvum athenischen Recht und zur Magie.* Stuttgart: Steiner.

Rives, James. 2013. 'Women and animal sacrifice in public life.' In *Women and the Roman City in the Latin West*, ed. Emily A. Hemelrijk and Greg Woolf. Leiden: Brill.

Roberts, Julian V. 1996. 'Public opinion, criminal record, and the sentencing process.' *American Behavioral Scientist* 39 (4).

Roberts, Julian V. 1997. 'The role of criminal record in the sentencing process.' *Crime and Justice* 22.

Robertson, Noel. 1998. 'Phratries and τρίττυες: The early organization of Attica.' In *Ancient History in a Modern University: Proceedings of a Conference Held at Macquarie University, 8–13 July 1993 to Mark Twenty-Five Years of the Teaching of Ancient History at Macquarie University and the Retirement from the Chair of Professor Edwin Judge*, ed. Tom W. Hillard. North Ryde: Ancient History Documentary Research Centre, Macquarie University.

Roebuck, Derek. 2001. *Ancient Greek Arbitration.* Oxford: Holo Books.

Rosen, Ralph M. 1997. 'The gendered polis in Eupolis' *Cities.*' In *The City as Comedy: Society and Representation in Athenian Drama*, ed. Gregory W. Dobrov. Chapel Hill: University of North Carolina Press.

Rosivach, Vincent J. 1995. 'Solon's brothels.' *Liverpool Classical Monthly* 20.

Rosivach, Vincent J. 2017. 'Euthyphron's prosecution of his father in the *Euthyphron.*' *Classical Philology* 112 (2).

Rowe, Galen O. 1993. 'The many facets of *hybris* in Demosthenes' *Against Meidias.*' *American Journal of Philology* 114.

Roy, James. 1997. 'An alternative sexual morality for classical Athens.' *Greece and Rome*, 2nd series, 44 (1).

Rubinstein, Lene. 1993. *Adoption in IV. Century Athens.* Copenhagen: Museum Tusculanum Press.

Rubinstein, Lene. 2000. *Litigation and Cooperation: Supporting Speakers in the Courts of Classical Athens*.: Wiesbaden: Steiner.

Rubinstein, Lene. 2003. 'Volunteer prosecutors in the Greek world.' *Dike* 6.

Rubinstein, Lene (with response by J. Fournier). 2012. 'Individual and collective liabilities of boards of officials in the late classical and early Hellenistic period.' In *Symposion 2011*, ed. B. Legras and G. Thür. Vienna: Verlag der Österreichischen Akademie der Wissenschaften.

Rubinstein, Lene. 2018a. 'The Athenian amnesty of 403/2 and the "forgotten" amnesty of 405/4.' In *Colloquia Attica: Neuere Forschungen zur Archaik, zum athenischen Recht und zur Magie*, ed. Werner Riess. Stuttgart: Steiner.

Rubinstein, Lene. 2018b. 'Summary fines in Greek inscriptions and the question of "Greek law".' In *Ancient Greek Law in the 21st Century*, ed. Paula Perlman. Austin: University of Texas Press.

Rudhardt, Jean. 1962. 'La reconnaissance de la paternité, sa nature et sa portée dans la société athénienne.' *Museum Helveticum* XIX.
Ruschenbusch, Eberhard. 1966. Σόλωνος νόμοι: *Die Fragmente des solonischen Gesetzeswerkes mit einer Text-und Überlieferungsgeschichte*. Wiesbaden: Steiner.
Sabetai, Victoria. 2008. 'Birth, childhood, and marriage: Women's ritual roles in the cycle of life.' In *Worshiping Women: Ritual and Reality in Classical Athens*, ed. Nikolaos Kaltsas and Harvey Alan Shapiro. Athens: Ethniko Archaiologiko Mouseio.
Sainte Croix, G. E. M. de. 1970. 'Some observations on the property rights of Athenian women.' *Classical Review* 20.
Samuel, Alan Edouard. 1965. 'The role of *paramone* clauses in ancient documents.' *The Journal of Juristic Papyrology* 15.
Sanders, Ed. 2014. *Envy and Jealousy in Classical Athens: A Socio-Psychological Approach*. Oxford: Oxford University Press.
Saunders, Trevor J. 1997. 'Plato on women in the *Laws*.' In *The Greek World*, ed. Anton Powell. London: Routledge.
Scafuro, Adele C. 1997. *The Forensic Stage: Settling Disputes in Graeco-Roman New Comedy*. Cambridge: Cambridge University Press.
Scafuro, Adele C. 2003. 'The rigmarole of the parasite's contract for a prostitute in *Asinaria*: Legal documents in Plautus and his predecessors.' *Leeds International Classical Studies* 3 (4).
Schaps, David M. 1975. 'Women in Greek inheritance law.' *Classical Quarterly* 25.
Schaps, David M. 1977. 'The woman least mentioned: Etiquette and women's names.' *Classical Quarterly* 27.
Schaps, David M. 1979. *Economic Rights of Women in Ancient Greece*. Edinburgh: Edinburgh University Press.
Schaps, David M. 1998. 'What was free about a free Athenian woman?' *Transactions of the American Philological Association* 128.
Scheidel, Walter. 1996. 'The most silent women of Greece and Rome: Rural labour and women's life in the ancient world (II).' *Greece and Rome* 43 (1).
Schnurr-Redford, Christine. 1996. *Frauen im klassischen Athen: Sozialer Raum und reale Bewegungsfreiheit*. Berlin: Akademie.
Schönbauer, Ernst. 1964. '*Paragraphe, diamartyria, exceptio, praescriptio*: Zur antiken Einrede der Unzulässigkeit des Streitverfahrens.' *Anzeiger der osterreichischen Akademie der Wissenschaften in Wien, Phil.-hist. Klasse* 101.
Sealey, Raphael. 1981. 'Ephialtes, eisangelia and the council.' In *Classical Contributions: Studies in Honour of Malcolm Francis McGregor*, ed. Gordon S. Shrimpton and D. J. McCargar. Locust Valley, NY: Augustin.
Sealey, Raphael. 1990. *Women and Law in Classical Greece*. Chapel Hill: University of North Carolina Press.
Seltman, C. 1955. 'The status of women in Athens.' *Greece and Rome* 2.
Serafim, Andreas. 2017. *Attic Oratory and Performance*. Abingdon: Routledge.

Sezer, Devrim. 2015. 'Medea's wounds: Euripides on justice and compassion.' *History of Political Thought* 36 (2).

Shapiro, Harvey Alan. 1995. 'The cult of heroines: Kekrops' daughters.' In *Pandora: Women in Classical Greece*, ed. Ellen D. Reeder. Princeton: Princeton University Press.

Shaw, M. 1975. 'The female intruder: women in fifth-century drama.' *Classical Philology* 70 (4).

Shaw King, Lida, 1903. 'The cave at Vari: IV.' *American Journal of Archaeology* 7.

Shear, T. Leslie. 1995. 'Bouleuterion, Metroon, and the archives at Athens.' In *Studies in the Ancient Greek Polis*, ed. Mogens Herman Hansen and Kurt A. Raaflaub. Stuttgart: Steiner.

Shero, L. R. 1932. 'Xenophon's portrait of a young wife.' *Classical World* 26.

Sickinger, James P. 1994. 'Inscriptions and archives in classical Athens.' *Historia* 43 (3).

Sickinger, James P. 1999. *Public Records and Archives in Classical Athens*. Chapel Hill: University of North Carolina Press.

Sickinger, James P. 2002. 'Literacy, orality, and legislative procedure in classical Athens.' In *Epea and Grammata: Oral and Written Communication in Ancient Greece*, ed. Ian Worthington and John Miles Foley. Leiden: Brill.

Sickinger, James P. 2004. 'The laws of Athens: Publication, preservation, consultation.' In *The Law and the Courts in Ancient Greece*, ed. Edward Monroe Harris and Lene Rubinstein. London: Duckworth.

Silver, Morris. 2015. '"Living apart", *apeleutheroi* and *paramone*-clause: A response to Canevaro and Lewis.' *Incidenza dell'Antico* 13.

Silver, Morris. 2018. *Slave-Wives, Single Women and 'Bastards' in the Ancient Greek World: Law and Economics Perspectives*. Oxford: Oxbow Books.

Siropoulos, Spiridon D. 2000. 'The prominence of women in tragedy: *Alcestis* and the *oikos*.' Ἑλληνικά 50 (2).

Skov, G. E. 1975. 'The priestess of Demeter and Kore and her role in the initiation of women at the festival of the Haloa at Eleusis.' *Temenos* 11.

Sosin, Joshua D. 2015. 'Manumission with *paramone*: Conditional freedom?' *Transactions of the American Philological Association* 145 (2).

Sosin, Joshua D. 2016. 'A metic was a metic.' *Historia* 65 (1).

Sourvinou-Inwood, Christiane. 1995. 'Male and female, public and private, ancient and modern.' In *Pandora: Women in Classical Greece*, ed. Ellen D. Reeder. Princeton: Princeton University Press.

Spaeth, Barbette Stanley. 2014. 'From goddess to hag: The Greek and Roman witch in classical literature.' In *Daughters of Hecate: Women and Magic in the Ancient World*, ed. Kimberly B. Stratton and Dayna S. Kalleres. Oxford: Oxford University Press.

Spatharas, Dimos. 2006. 'Λυσίας, Κατα Τείσιδος (απ. 17 Gernet-Bizos): μια ερμηνευτική προσέγγιση.' *Αριάδνη* = *Ariadne* 12.

Spatharas, Dimos. 2008. 'ταῦτ' ἐγω μαρτύρομαι: Bystanders as witnesses in Aristophanes.' *Mnemosyne*, 4th series, 61 (2).
Spatharas, Dimos., ed. 2009. *Κατα Λοχίτου / Ισοκράτης: εισαγωγή, κείμενο, μετάφραση, ερμηνευτικό υπόμνημα Δήμος Γ. Σπαθάρας*. Athens: Smili.
Spatharas, Dimos. 2011. 'Kinky stories from the rostrum: Storytelling in Apollodorus' *Against Neaira*.' *Ancient Narrative* 9.
Spatharas, Dimos. 2012. '"Liaisons dangereuses": Procopius, Lysias and Apollodorus.' *Classical Quarterly* n.s. 62 (2).
Spatharas, Dimos. 2017. 'The mind's theatre: Envy, *hybris* and *enargeia* in Demosthenes' *Against Meidias*.' In *The Theatre of Justice: Aspects of Performance in Greco-Roman Oratory and Rhetoric*, ed. Sophia Papaioannou, Andreas Serafim and Beatrice da Vela. Leiden: Brill.
Stanley, Phillip V. 1979. '*Agoranomoi* and *metronomoi*: Athenian market officials and regulations.' *The Ancient World* 2.
Stears, Karen. 1995. 'Dead woman's society: Constructing female gender in classical Athenian funerary sculpture.' In *Time, Tradition, and Society in Greek Archaeology: Bridging the "Great Divide*. London: Routledge.
Stears, Karen. 2001. 'Spinning women: Iconography and status in Athenian funerary sculpture.' In *Les pierres de l'offrande: Autour de l'œuvre de Christoph W. Clairmont: Actes*, ed. Geneviève Hoffmann and Adrienne Lezzi-Hafter. Zurich: Akanthus.
Stehle, Eva M. 2002. 'The body and its representations in Aristophanes' *Thesmophoriazousai*: where does the costume end?' *American Journal of Philology* 123 (3).
Stelzer, E. 1971. 'Untersuchungen zur Enktesis im attischen Recht.' Munich, diss.
Stone, Isidor F. 1988. *The Trial of Socrates*. Boston, MA: Little, Brown.
Stratton, Kimberly B. 2014. 'Interrogating the magic–gender connection.' In *Daughters of Hecate: Women and Magic in the Ancient World*, ed. Kimberly B. Stratton and Dayna S. Kalleres. Oxford: Oxford University Press.
Stratton, Kimberly B., and Dayna S. Kalleres, eds. 2014. *Daughters of Hecate: Women and Magic in the Ancient World*. Oxford: Oxford University Press.
Stroud, Ronald S. 1968. *Drakon's Law on Homicide*. Berkeley: University of California Press.
Stroud, Ronald S. 1979. *The Axones and Kyrbeis of Drakon and Solon*. Berkeley: University of California Press.
Stuttard, David. 2018. *Nemesis: Alcibiades and the Fall of Athens*. Cambridge, MA: Harvard University Press.
Sulprizio, Chiara. 2013. 'You can't go home again: War, women, and domesticity in Aristophanes' *Peace*.' *Ramus* 42 (1–2).
Summons, Bianca. 2005. 'Gender reversal in Greek tragedy.' *Pegasus* 48.
Taaffe, Lauren Kathleen. 1993. *Aristophanes and Women*. London: Routledge.

Ténékidès, G. 1988. 'La cité d'Athènes et les droits de l'homme: Protecting human rights.' In *Protecting Human Rights: The European Dimension: Studies in Honour of G. J. Wiarda*, ed. Franz Matscher and Herbert Petzold. Cologne: Heymanns.

Tetlow, Elisabeth Meier. 2004. *Women, Crime, and Punishment in Ancient Law and Society. Vol. 2: Ancient Greece.* London: Continuum.

Thompson, Wesley E. 1967. 'An interpretation of the Demotionid decrees.' *Symbolae Osloenses* 42.

Thür, Gerhard. 1996. 'Reply to D. C. Mirhady: Torture and rhetoric in Athens.' *The Journal of Hellenic Studies* 116.

Thür, Gerhard. 2005. 'The role of the witness in Athenian law.' In *The Cambridge Companion to Ancient Greek Law*, ed. Michael Gagarin and David J. Cohen. Cambridge: Cambridge University Press.

Tiverios, Michalis. 2008. 'Demeter: Women of Athens in the worship of Demeter: Iconographic evidence from archaic and classical times.' In *Worshiping Women: Ritual and Reality in Classical Athens*, ed. Nikolaos Kaltsas and Harvey Alan Shapiro. Athens: Ethniko Archaiologiko Mouseio.

Todd, Stephen C. 1993. *The Shape of Athenian Law.* Oxford: Oxford University Press.

Todd, Stephen C. 2007. *A Commentary on Lysias, Speeches 1–11.* Oxford: Oxford University Press.

Todd, Stephen C. 2010. 'The Athenian procedure(s) of *dokimasia*.' In *Symposion 2009*, ed. Gerhard Thür. Vienna: Verlag der Österreichischen Akademie der Wissenschaften.

Totaro, Piero. 2015. '*Onomastì komodeîn* nella parodo lirica del *Pluto* di Aristofane.' In *Studi sulla commedia attica*, ed. Matteo Taufer. Freiburg: Rombach.

Tulin, Alexander. 1996. *Dike phonou: The Right of Prosecution and Attic Homicide Procedure.* Stuttgart: Teubner.

Tulin, Alexander. 1999. 'Slave witnesses in Antiphon 5.48.' *Scripta Classica Israelica* 18.

Turner, Victoria, and Ian Jenkins. 2009. *The Greek Body.* Malibu, CA: J. Paul Getty Museum.

Verlinsky, Alexander. 2017. 'Draco's constitution in the Athenaion Politeia 4: Is it an interpolation or an author's later addition?' *Hyperboreus* 23 (1).

Vester, Christina. 2009. 'Bigamy and bastardy, wives and concubines: Civic identity in *Andromache*.' In *The Play of Texts and Fragments: Essays in Honour of Martin Cropp*, ed. J. Robert C. Cousland and James R. Hume. Leiden: Brill.

Vickers, Michael J. 2008. *Sophocles and Alcibiades: Athenian Politics in Ancient Greek Literature.* Stocksfield: Acumen.

Vikela, Evgenia. 2008. 'Artemis: The worship of Artemis in Attica: Cult places, rites, iconography.' In *Worshiping Women: Ritual and Reality in Classical*

Athens, ed. Nikolaos Kaltsas and Harvey Alan Shapiro. Athens: Ethniko Archaiologiko Mouseio.
Wagner-Hasel, Beate. 2009. 'Brautgut oder Mitgift? Das textile Heiratsgut in den Solonischen Aufwandbestimmungen.' In *Der Wert der Dinge: Güter im Prestigediskurs*, ed. Berit Hildebrandt and Caroline Veit. Munich: Utz.
Walbank, Michael B. 1981. 'Artemis, bear-leader.' *Classical Quarterly* 31.
Walcot, Peter. 1978. *Envy and the Greeks: A Study of Human Behavior*. Warminster: Aris & Phillips.
Walcot, Peter. 1994. 'Separatism and the alleged conversation of women.' *Classica et Mediaevalia* 45.
Wallace, Robert W. 1989. *The Areopagus Council, to 307 B.C.* Baltimore: Johns Hopkins University Press.
Wallace, Robert W. 1994. 'Private lives and public enemies: Freedom of thought in classical Athens.' In *Athenian Identity and Civic Ideology*, ed. Alan L. Boegehold and Adele C. Scafuro. Baltimore: Johns Hopkins University Press.
Wallace, Robert W. 1996. 'Book burning in ancient Athens.' In *Transitions to Empire: Essays in Greco-Roman History*, ed. Robert W. Wallace and Edward M. Harris. Norman, OK: University of Oklahoma Press.
Walters, Kenneth R. 1983. 'Perikles' citizenship law.' *Classical Antiquity* 2.
Walters, Kenneth R. 1993. 'Women and power in classical Athens.' In *Woman's Power, Man's Game: Essays on Classical Antiquity in Honor of Joy K. King*, ed. Mary DeForest. Wauconda, IL: Bolchazy-Carducci.
Waterfield, Robin. 2012. 'Xenophon on Socrates' trial and death.' In *Xenophon: Ethical Principles and Historical Enquiry*, ed. Fiona Hobden and Christopher J. Tuplin. Leiden: Brill.
Watson, James. 2010. 'The origin of metic status at Athens.' *Cambridge Classical Journal* 56.
Weißenberger, Michael. 1987. *Die Dokimasiereden des Lysias (orr. 16, 25, 26, 31)*. Frankfurt: Athenäum.
Westermann, W. L. 1948. 'The *paramone* as general service contract.' *The Journal of Juristic Papyrology* 2.
Westgate, Ruth. 2015. 'Space and social complexity in Greece from the early Iron Age to the classical period.' *Hesperia* 84 (1).
White, James Boyd. 1985. *Heracles' Bow: Essays on the Rhetoric and Poetics of Law*. Madison: University of Wisconsin Press.
Whitehead, D. 1977. *The Ideology of the Athenian Metic*. Cambridge: Cambridge Philological Society.
Whitehead, D. 1981. 'Xenocrates the metic.' *Rheinisches Museum für Philologie* 124.
Whitehead, D. 1986a. 'Women and naturalisation in fourth-century Athens: The case of Archippe.' *Classical Quarterly* 36.
Whitehead, D. 1986b. 'The ideology of the Athenian metic: Some pendants and a reappraisal.' *Proceedings of the Cambridge Philological Society* 32.

Whitmarsh, Tim. 2015. *Battling the Gods: Atheism in the Ancient World.* New York: Knopf.

Wickkiser, Bronwen L. 2008. *Asklepios, Medicine, and the Politics of Healing in Fifth-Century Greece: Between Craft and Cult.* Baltimore: Johns Hopkins University Press.

Wohl, Victoria Josselyn. 2010. 'A tragic case of poisoning: Intention between tragedy and the law.' *Transactions of the American Philological Association* 140 (1).

Wolff, Hans Julius. 1966. *Die attische Paragraphe.* Weimar: Böhlau.

Wolpert, Andrew. 2000. 'Lysias 1 and the politics of the οἶκος.' *The Classical Journal* 96 (4).

Wolpert, Andrew. 2002. *Remembering Defeat: Civil War and Civic Memory in Ancient Athens.* Baltimore: Johns Hopkins University Press.

Wolpert, Andrew, and Konstantinos Kapparis, eds. and trans. 2011. *Legal Speeches of Democratic Athens: Sources for Athenian History.* Indianapolis, IN: Hackett.

Woodhouse, William John. 1938. *Solon the Liberator: A Study of the Agrarian Problem in Attica in the Seventh Century.* Oxford: Oxford University Press.

Worthington, Ian. 2003. 'The length of an Athenian public trial: A reply to Professor MacDowell.' *Hermes* 131 (3).

Wright, F. A. 1923. *Feminism in Greek Literature from Homer to Aristotle.* London: Routledge.

Wysocki, Leszek. 1988. 'The so-called Demotionid decrees.' *Eos* 76.

Yamauchi, Akiko. 2005. 'Oaths and disputes in fourth-century Athenian society.' *Journal of Classical Studies* 53.

Yates, Velvet. 2015. 'Biology is destiny: The deficiencies of women in Aristotle's biology and *Politics*.' *Arethusa* 48 (1).

Zeitlin, Froma I. 1981. 'Travesties of gender and genre in Aristophanes' *Thesmophoriazousae*.' In *Reflections of Women in Antiquity*, ed. Helene Peet Foley. New York: Gordon & Breach.

Zoumpoulakis, Stavros, ed. 2015. *Δικαιοσύνη καὶ δίκαιο.* Athens: Artos Zois.

Index of Ancient Authors

Achilles Tatius 2.38.5: 101
Aeschines 1.2: 97, 210; 14: 210; 18: 51; 26: 172, 185; 45–50: 152; 60: 172, 185; 62: 92; 112: 154; 119: 152; 132 ff.: 152; 158–9: 215; 184: 211; 2.4: 184; 3.18: 240–1; 197: 151
Aeschines Socraticus Fr. 15 Weidmann: 215; Fr. 25 Dittmar: Fr. 25: 39–43
Aeschylus *Ag.* 603–10: 182
Alciphron 1.32: 76–82; 4.3–5: 100
Ammonius 60 Nickau: 94
Amphis Fr. 23: 123
Anaxandrides, *Gerontomania*, Fr. 9: 53–6
Anaximenes *FGrH* 72 T 17a: 100
Andocides 1.16: 94; 43: 123; 81: 226; 110: 153; 117–22: 98, 241; 124–9: 19, 181; 4.13–14: 121, 183, 226
Anon. Seguerianus *Ars Rhet.* 215 Hammer: 76–82, 100
Antiphon 1. *passim*: 12, 84–5, 118, 123, 148–9, 156, 162, 170, 173, 176, 177, 208; 1.20: 216; 4 passim: 215; 5.29–55: 152; 5.82–5: 151; Fr. 25a: 26

Apollodoros *FGrH* 244 F 210: 97
Aristophanes *Ach.* 526–37: 92; 1048–68: 211; *Ec.* 213–40: 182, 211; 241–5: 95; *Eq.* passim: 226; *Lys.* 1–253: 19; 456–61: 214, 215; *Ra.* 112–13: 214; 549–78: 19, 121, 195–6, 211, 215; 549–674: 215; 569–70: 91, 226; *Th.* 443–58: 211, 214; *Plu.* 102–15: 98; 179: 75–6; *V.* 35, 236–8: 214–15; 418: 92; 497, 549 ff.: 214; Fr. 317–44: 19
Aristotle *Athenaion Politeia* 26.3–4: 211, 230–1; 43.5: 151; 47.2: 91; 53.1–4: 121, 152; 53.4–7: 121; 56: 210; 58.3: 94, 213, 228–9; *Pol.* 1275 b 31: 211; 1278 a 34: 211
Athenaios 5.53: 122; 13.3: 183; 13.22: 153; 13.38: 213; 13.46: 96; 13.48: 213; 13.50: 29–36, 55, 97, 174; 13.51: 95, 215; 13.52: 29, 30, 35, 53, 54, 55, 92, 96, 97, 174, 186, 206, 213; 13.59: 76–82, 100; 13.60: 100, 153; 13.62: 75–6, 95, 99; 13.171: 76–82; 15.32: 29–36; 15.58: 91; *Epit.* 2.2 117: 39–43

Chorikios 29.2.45, 76: 100
Cicero *N.D.* 1.93.3: 95; *Ver.* 2.4.4: 213
Cratinus Fr. 241: 93

Deinarchos; Fr. 33 Conomis: 69–72,
    142; 35: 56–60; 55: 52; 57: 51–2;
    58–9: 56; 60: 36–8; 65–6: 152
Demetrius, *Eloq.* 302: 88–90, 186
Demosthenes 15.29:123;18.46:
    92; 61: 92; 199: 92; 245: 92;
    259: 215; 267: 181; 19.61, 95,
    197, 223, 250, 268, 315: 92;
    196–8: 183; 245 ff.: 152; 309:
    184; 21. 8–9: 151; 28: 216;
    47: 216; 84–95: 122, 181; 94:
    122; 154: 181; 197: 92; 22.37:
    154; 59: 92; 23.53: 188–9, 209,
    233–4; 119: 92; 24.6, 195: 92;
    24, 33, 63: 216; 149–50: 209;
    25. 56–8: 91, 123, 152; 66: 92;
    79–80: 85–8; 27–33 passim: 50;
    27.5: 226; 40, 53: 181; 56: 123;
    29.26–33:19, 181; 30.6–7: 95;
    30.6–7: 210; 26: 121; 36.49:
    181; 39.2: 69–72; 39.13: 69–72;
    40 passim: 43–6; 40.9: 69–72;
    10–11: 17, 69–72; 41 passim:
    181; 9: 211; 43.7: 123; 51: 210,
    234–7, 241; 54: 210, 229–31;
    75: 210, 234–7; 44.68: 241;
    45.8: 152; 55: 152; 79: 92;
    46.14: 101, 234–7; 18: 183,
    227–8, 240–1; 20: 234–7; 22:
    213, 228–9; 26: 122; 47. 55–73:
    183; 55: 212; 57: 123; 48.16:
    101; 53.18:152; 55.36:17; 48:
    94; 57.8: 67; 43: 209; 44–5:
    215; 68: 94; 69:209; 59. 14–15:
    17, 16: 152, 213, 216, 231–2;
    18–22: 89; 19: 92; 22: 213; 23:
    184; 27–48: 152; 28: 152; 29:
    211; 32: 122; 40: 92; 45–8: 17,
    151; 50: 164; 52: 213, 231–3;
    54–63: 184; 67–71: 51, 184,
    233–4; 85: 184; 87: 233–4;
    107–26: 97, 152; 113: 136;
    116–17: 56–60; 122: 160, 182
Diogenes Laertius 10.7: 213
Dionysios Halicarnasseus *de Din*
    11:56–60; 12: 36, 51, 52–3,
    56; Dem. 57: 185; Fr. 23
    Radermacher: 185

Euboulos Fr. 97 (98 Hunter): 19
Eupolis Fr. 9: 215
Euripides *Alc.* 393–4: 214
Eustathios *Com. Il.* 4.579: 100

Galen *Comm. Hip. Epid.* 2, 17a 371
    Kühn: 25

Hermippus Fr. 68a1 Wehrli: 100
Herodas 2: 76, 119; 6: 101
Hippocrates: *Epid.* 2.2.19: 23–6
Hypereides Fr. 13–26: 29–36; 24:
    97; 125: 67–8; 164–165: 88–90;
    171–8: 76–82, 100

Idomeneus *FGrH* 338 F 4 : 32, 91
IG I³ 104: 189, 209
IG ii² 1: 213; 1514 col. II. 58: 95;
    1516, col. II, 34: 95; 1523, col. II,
    20: 95; 1524, face B, col. II, 194:
    95; 1527, face B, 25: 95; 1622:
    93; 4358: 95; 5492: 95; 6218: 95
Isaios 2. 6–10: 161; 42: 181; 3 passim:
    73–5, 14–7, 154; 3.3: 93; 26:
    123; 30: 94; 46: 234–7; 73–5,
    143–7; 73: 209; 75: 209; 76:
    209; 78: 121; 79: 209; 5.16: 93;
    6.3: 216; 4: 93; 18: 226; 19–20:
    213; 28: 243; 7.3: 93; 8.18: 209;
    10.10: 143, 153, 196, 218, 211,
    222, 226; 13: 226, 234–7

Isocrates 5.14: 92; 6.32: 123; 11.168: 152; 17.125: 91; 18.2–3: 92;

Juvenal *Sat.* 6.117: 101

Lucian *DMeretr. 2*: 152, 209, 214
Lycurgus 1. 2: 152; 66: 122
Lysias 1. 6–7: 182; 9: 18; 12.5 ff.: 91; 12.66: 91; 67: 91; 13.47: 91; 16.10–13: 181; 23.10–11: 92, 121; 23.13–14: 92; 32 passim: 47–51, 210; 32.6: 226; 7: 95; 9: 181; 18: 181; Fr. 20–3 Carey: 23–6; Fr. 25–9: 26–9; Fr. 208: 92, 95; Fr. 257: 69; Fr. 299: 75–6; Fr. 309: 82–3; Fr. 708: 53–6

Marcellinus, *Scholia in Hermog.* 4.324 Walz: 68–9
Messala Fr. 22:100

Nicochares, Fr. 4: 99

P. Vindob. Gr. 29816, F. 1, col. 1, 1–14: 26–9
P. Vindob. Gr. 29816, Fr. 2, col. 2, 2–8: 26–9
P. Vindob. Gr. 29816, F. 4, 1–8: 26–9
Prolegomena on the Staseis, 7,15 Walz: 23–6
Plato *Ap.* 19 b 4–c 7: 93; *Euthphr.* Passim: 216; *Grg.* 483 b : 123; *Mx.* 835 e ff.: 93; *Tht.* 151 c: 214; 268 b: 214
Plato Comicus, Fr. 65: 99
Plautus *Asinaria* 751–809: 212
Plutarch: 833 A: 26–9; 833 E–F: 91, 98; 834 A: 91; 849 D : 91; 1097 D: 213; *Dem.* 14.6.2: 85–8; *Pel.* 10.6: 56–60; *Per.* 24: 95; 32: 39–43; 37: 211, 241; *Sol.* 20–1: 226; 22: 226
Poseidonios Fr. 290a.495–506: 213
Ptolemy Gramm. *De Differentia Vocabulorum* 397.26: 94

Quintilian *Inst.* 1.5.61: 100; 2.15.9: 100

Scholia in Ar. Ach. 146: 209
Scholia Demosthenica 19.281, 495 A and B Dilts: 69–72, 185
SEG 16.39: 98
Sopater ed. H. Rabe *RHM* 64 [1909] 576: 23–6
Sopater *Commentary on Hermogenes*, 5,3 Walz: 23–6
Sophocles *OT* 14–77: 151
Soranos *Gyn.* 1.3–4: 214
Syrian. *ad Herm.* 4 p. 120 Walz: 76–82

Terence *Heautontimorumenos* 389–95: 152
Timokles, Fr. 23: 153
Theon *Progymnasmata* 2,69, Spengel: 23–6
Theon. *Progymnasmata* 1,162 Walz: 29–36
Theon *Prolegomena* 68 Spengel: 91
Theopompos *FGrH* 115 F 120: 26–9
Thucydides 8. 25–30: 98; 68: 91

Vat. Gr. 7, Fr. 88 Ucciardello: 26–9

Xenophon *H.G.* 2.3.2: 98; 2.4.1–18: 97; 6.4.19–20: 97; 6.3. 1–5: 213; *Mem.* 3.11: 101, 186; *Oec.* 7.2: 5–8, 19, 160, 181, 214; 9.5.3: 18; 9.6.6: 18

General Index

abortion, 23–6
advocate, 2–4, 8, 15–17, 29, 41–3, 51–2, 54, 69, 73, 76, 78, 80, 82, 91, 99, 105–9, 111–12, 114–19, 122–3, 126, 128, 130, 133, 145, 147, 150–3, 156–7, 161, 172, 180, 182, 191–4, 196, 197, 206, 208, 221, 223–5
Alcibiades, 43, 86, 88, 95, 96, 108, 121, 124, 138, 140, 141, 153, 156, 162, 179, 201, 226
alien, 14, 29, 33, 36, 68, 76, 81, 87, 91, 92, 106, 117, 121, 127, 129, 130, 131–6, 142, 146, 165, 168, 177, 178, 179, 180, 184, 187, 188, 189, 191, 193, 194, 197, 198, 202, 209, 211, 212, 221, 222, 228, 231, 232
amplifiatio, 97
andronitis, 18
Anteia, 53, 54, 55, 96, 97
Antigenes, 23–6
Antiphon, 26–8
Antiphon's daughter, 26–9
aphairesis eis eleutherian, 92, 134
Aphyai, 29–36, 55, 174
Apollodoros, 3, 4, 12, 17, 35, 41, 54, 55, 56, 58, 59, 63, 68, 75, 89, 97, 114, 119, 122, 130, 131, 133, 135, 152, 160, 163, 164, 165, 168, 169, 171, 173, 174, 175, 177, 178, 179, 180, 184, 185, 186, 198, 202, 212, 213, 228, 232, 237
apostasiou, 46, 47, 52, 92, 125, 132, 133
aprostasiou graphe, 30, 34, 91, 92, 132, 179, 225
arbitration/arbitrator, 2, 10, 17, 44, 92, 107, 109–12, 117–18, 121, 122, 127–8, 134, 145, 178, 195, 212, 223
archon, 38, 106, 108, 112, 114, 118, 121, 144, 162, 178, 190, 191, 192, 198, 215, 228–31, 236, 237–40, 253
Aristagora, 29–36, 47, 55, 90, 133, 167, 169, 170, 174, 179, 202, 207
Artemis at Brauron, 82–3
Aspasia, 11, 39–43, 79, 80, 93, 95, 129, 137, 138, 196, 200, 201, 204, 207, 215, 231
Athena's priestess, 60–6

bebaioseos dike, 90
biaion dike, 75–6, 127

Boiotos, 12, 43–6, 69, 71, 92, 98, 110, 128, 142, 165, 174

citizen/citizenship, 1, 4, 8, 9, 10, 11, 14, 16, 17, 33, 34, 57, 64, 65, 68, 72, 75, 91, 92, 94, 98, 105, 106, 108, 113, 114, 115, 117, 118, 120, 121, 125, 127, 128, 129, 130, 131, 132, 133, 135, 136, 140, 142, 146, 150, 153, 154, 155, 157, 160, 161, 165, 166, 168, 171, 178, 179, 183, 187–99, 209, 211, 212, 213, 216, 218, 219–22, 225, 226, 228, 229, 230, 231, 240, 241, 254, 255, 259, 272
collective responsibility, 9–10, 115, 127, 148–51, 222, 240

Damasandra, 95
Demeter's priestess at Eleusis, 56–60
Demetria, 46–7, 133
democracy/democratic, 1–2, 4, 7, 8–12, 14, 16, 19, 28, 73, 106, 112–17, 120, 125, 129, 137, 149–50, 153, 155, 187–8, 191–3, 197, 202, 208, 212, 219, 221–3, 225, 226, 241, 259
diadikasia, 56, 58, 59, 60, 108, 144, 145
diamartyria, 30, 34, 36, 38, 53, 74, 92, 95, 146, 154
dikasterion/dikastes, 1, 2, 10, 105, 109, 111, 112, 114, 115–18, 126, 128
Diodotos, 47–51, 158, 159, 191, 228
Diodotos' wife, 12, 47–51, 145, 156, 203
Diogeiton, 47–51, 159, 221, 226

Diogeiton's daughter (wife of Diodotos), 12, 47–51, 123, 145, 158, 159, 196, 221
divorce, 6, 25, 107, 108, 112, 121, 129, 145, 161, 162, 164, 165, 166, 178, 183, 232–6
dokimasia, 19, 57, 72, 137, 152–3, 242
doroxenias graphe, 31, 33, 34, 167, 179
drama, 1, 5, 13, 16, 84, 93, 111, 126, 134, 156, 160, 170

Endios, 45, 73–5, 99, 118, 145, 146, 154, 190, 236
engye, 74, 75, 99, 146, 159, 166, 182, 183, 190, 199
epidikasia, 26, 29, 52, 58, 90, 145, 147, 190, 196, 199, 218, 228–30, 235
epikleros/heiress, 10, 26, 28, 29, 36–8, 51–3, 66, 73–4, 83–4, 90, 92, 98, 110, 116, 123, 144–6, 147, 154, 183, 190–2, 196, 198, 218, 220, 228–30, 235–7, 239–41
Eratosthenes, 28
ethopoeia, 10, 148
Euboulides, 67, 142, 194, 205
Euthias, 43, 76–82, 100, 158, 174, 201
euthyna, 19, 72, 125, 151, 153, 157, 240
Euxitheos, 67, 142, 194, 205, 211

foreign/foreigner, 30, 59, 60, 75, 78, 98, 119, 130, 132, 133, 139, 215, 231, 241

gynaeconitis, 4, 12, 18–19

Haloa, 56–60
health professionals, 202–7
Hedyle, 52–3, 133
Hegelochos, 51–2
hetaira, 31, 32, 33, 35, 36, 45, 46,
    47, 52, 53, 54, 55, 56, 67, 68,
    69, 73, 74, 75, 76, 77, 78, 80,
    81, 88, 89, 90, 95, 96, 99, 106,
    111, 117, 119, 130, 131, 133,
    134, 135, 136, 139, 140, 141,
    146, 163, 165, 166, 167, 168,
    169, 173, 174, 175, 177, 178,
    179, 183, 190, 195, 196, 200,
    201, 202, 206, 222, 232
hierophant, 56–60, 206
Hipparete, 143, 162, 183
household, 5, 6, 7, 11, 18, 19, 33,
    49, 50, 74, 75, 89, 132, 133,
    134, 140, 145, 153, 158, 159,
    160, 161, 164, 166, 176, 180,
    184, 189, 193, 194, 196, 203,
    204, 205, 218, 219, 222, 223,
    226, 239
Hyperbolos, 8, 206
Hypereides, 4, 11, 34, 43, 76–82,
    111, 114, 115, 117, 153,
    167, 168, 170, 173, 174, 179,
    201, 224

immigrant/immigration, 29, 30, 33,
    34, 36, 47, 53, 92, 105, 125,
    131–6, 150, 151, 167, 181, 196,
    197, 202, 207, 208, 216, 221
isonomia, 8, 113, 114, 120, 187,
    207, 223
isopoliteia, 8, 114, 120

Kallaischros, 29
Kleon, 8, 108, 118, 206
Klytemestra, 1, 84, 147–9, 160,
    170

Lais, 29, 30, 35, 53–6, 92, 96, 97,
    174, 186, 206
Lakedaimonios' sister, 67, 72, 98,
    118, 121, 142, 151
legal system (Athens), 1–2, 4, 7–9,
    11–16, 33, 99, 105, 106, 109,
    113–15, 117, 119–22, 150, 187,
    193, 195, 197, 199, 207–9, 212,
    215, 223, 225, 272, 273
logographer (*logographos*), 2–4, 8,
    45, 48, 60, 105, 115, 117, 120,
    165, 179, 208

magic, 85–8, 170, 171, 181
magistrate, 2, 9–10, 72, 106–9, 112,
    114, 117–18, 120–1, 125–8, 144,
    149, 153, 157, 187, 189–90, 192,
    195, 197, 205, 206, 212, 215,
    217, 221, 229, 240
Mantias, 12, 17, 44, 45, 69, 72, 93,
    94, 110, 128, 142, 165, 166,
    167
Mantitheos, 43–6, 69, 72, 81, 82,
    92, 110, 128, 142, 165, 166,
    167, 172, 174
manumission, 47, 95, 110, 133,
    134, 151
market, 6, 7, 11, 109, 117, 140,
    166, 167, 171, 173, 195, 202–7,
    208, 212–15, 219, 222
marriage, 18, 37, 38, 44, 47, 68, 73,
    74, 75, 83, 84, 90, 92, 98, 108,
    121, 129, 130, 132, 134, 135,
    136, 146, 154, 159, 161, 162,
    167, 178, 182, 183, 190, 192,
    197, 198, 199, 211, 212, 215,
    217, 218, 220, 221–2, 223, 225,
    227–34, 236, 237, 241
Menekles, 69–72, 98, 118, 142, 156,
    161, 171
Metaneira, therapy, 96, 97, 174, 213

metic, 8, 11, 15, 20, 33–4, 91, 106, 108, 117–19, 123, 129, 132–4, 152, 160, 187, 191, 194, 196–209, 212–14, 219–20, 222, 235, 229, 231
metoikion, 32, 33, 34, 91, 119, 132, 133, 197, 199, 222, 228
miasma, 124, 151, 207
Mika, 67–8

Nais, 4, 75–6, 79, 119, 120, 186, 195, 206, 224
Neaira, 12, 17, 41, 43, 46–7, 55–6, 58, 60, 67, 68, 75, 89, 90, 94, 96, 97, 110, 114, 119, 129, 130, 131, 133, 134, 135, 142, 152, 153, 156, 163, 164, 168, 169, 171, 173, 174, 175, 177, 178, 179, 180, 185, 186, 202, 207, 211, 213, 232
Nikomache, 68–9
Ninos, 69–72, 82, 98, 118, 131, 142, 171, 206
notheia, 34, 91, 99

oikos, 5, 7, 9–10, 15, 16, 17, 33, 45, 49, 87, 113, 116, 132–4, 141–4, 150–1, 161, 189, 191, 193, 198, 200–3, 206–7, 212, 217–21, 223, 228, 234
Okimon, 30, 55, 174
Onomakles, 73
ostracism, 153

paragraphe, 38, 92, 127
paramone, 47, 95, 122, 151
paredros/assessor, 63, 97
performance (in court), 4, 18, 149, 158, 223
Periclean citizenship law, 132, 135, 150, 198, 230–4

Pericles, 39–43, 93, 129, 132, 135, 138, 150, 193, 198, 230–2, 234
personal responsibility (law), 9–10, 115, 127, 148–51, 222, 240
Phano, 156, 164–5, 177, 186
Phile, 3, 12, 45, 73, 74, 75, 97, 98, 99, 118, 145, 146, 147, 154, 156, 160, 174, 176, 190, 191, 221, 234, 236
Philonides, 4, 75–6, 196, 206
philtre, 35, 71, 87, 141, 162, 170, 173, 181, 202
Phryne, 4, 11, 41, 42, 43, 71, 76–82, 90, 99, 100, 111, 114, 117, 131, 138, 139, 140, 141, 173, 174, 196, 200, 201, 202, 206, 224
Phrynichos' daughter, 82–3
Plangon, 12, 17, 43–6, 69, 70, 72, 94, 99, 110, 128, 156, 165–7, 174, 175
poison, 35, 36, 71, 84, 85, 86, 169–72, 179
polemarch, 107, 152, 187, 198, 199, 228, 229
poletai, 34
polis, 5, 7–8, 15, 16, 17, 18, 33, 39, 63, 68, 89, 125, 132, 139, 141, 153, 188, 193–4
politics, 6, 8, 9, 10, 14, 16, 19, 26, 41, 43, 58, 68, 72, 76, 86, 98, 114, 115, 118, 119, 120, 121, 126, 129, 130, 131, 132, 143, 147, 162, 163, 188, 208, 210, 211, 213, 224, 231
Polyeuktos' daughters, 182, 236
Polyeuktos' wife, 50, 159, 160, 176, 196
pornikon telos, 133

priestess, 56–66, 69–72, 85–8, 97, 98, 118, 137, 142, 152, 171, 206, 240–1
property, 5–6
prostates, 73, 91, 108, 198, 199, 213
prostitution, 11, 35, 36, 45, 46, 47, 53, 75, 76, 79, 88, 89, 90, 96, 119, 122, 123, 130, 133, 136, 139, 156, 165, 167–9, 174, 175, 177, 178, 179, 184, 185, 196, 200, 202, 203, 212, 215, 217, 218, 222, 233, 234
Pyrrhos' daughter/Phile, 12, 45, 73–5, 98–9, 118, 145, 146, 147, 154, 190, 191, 221, 236
Pyronides, 29

race, 11, 19, 20, 105, 150, 151, 156, 169, 174, 177
rape, 75–6, 162, 195, 219, 224
religion, 6, 40, 43, 58, 59, 60, 64, 65, 66, 72, 79, 82, 86, 87, 88, 97, 124, 125, 131, 136–43, 151, 157, 169, 171, 172, 178, 194, 196, 201, 204, 216, 222, 225, 240, 242, 252, 254, 256
representative/representation (legal), 2–4, 8, 15–17, 29, 41–3, 51–2, 54, 69, 73, 76, 78, 80, 82, 91, 99, 105–9, 111–12, 114–19, 122–3, 126, 128, 130, 133, 145, 147, 150–3, 156–7, 161, 172, 180, 182, 191–4, 196, 197, 206, 208, 221, 223–5

Satyros, 83–4
scrutiny, 9, 19, 51, 57, 72, 125, 151, 152–3, 157, 240, 242
sexual assault, 4, 75–6, 127, 196, 206, 221, 224 him

Sinope, 56–60
slave/slavery, 8, 11, 14, 17, 18, 20, 47, 54, 84, 85, 87, 91, 92, 94, 95, 96, 106, 107, 110, 117, 118, 119, 123, 125, 127, 128, 133, 134, 135, 138, 141, 151, 162, 168, 170, 173, 177, 184, 187, 194, 195, 198, 199, 202, 204, 208, 209, 212, 218
space studies, 5, 214, 219
speechwriter, 2–4, 8, 45, 48, 60, 105, 115, 117, 120, 165, 179, 208
spider, 31, 35–6, 170
Stephanos, 41, 68, 110, 119, 130, 131, 133, 134, 171, 173, 177, 178, 179, 184, 186
stepmother, 12, 84, 118, 123, 148, 149, 156, 162, 170, 173, 176, 177, 208
synegoria/synegoros, 2–4, 8, 15–17, 29, 41–3, 51–2, 54, 69, 73, 76, 78, 80, 82, 91, 99, 105–9, 111–12, 114–19, 122–3, 126, 128, 130, 133, 145, 147, 150–3, 156–7, 161, 172, 180, 182, 191–4, 196, 197, 206, 208, 221, 223–5

theoisechthria (enemy of the gods), 35
Theokleia, 53, 54
Theomnestos, 3, 17, 113, 114, 152
Theoris of Lemnos, 35, 36, 71, 82, 85–8, 92, 100, 121, 131, 141, 156, 158, 169, 170, 171, 202, 206, 226
Thesmothetai, 120, 231, 232
Timandra, 88–90
Timarchos, 3, 51, 66, 114, 152, 172

transgression, 1, 16, 17, 57, 59, 60, 115

violence, 1, 76, 147–9, 150

working women, 6–7, 202–2

xenias graphe, 33, 34, 92, 151, 167, 179, 222

Xenokles, 3, 12, 73–5, 99, 118, 146, 154, 193, 221

Zobia, 91–2

EU representative:
Easy Access System Europe
Mustamäe tee 50, 10621 Tallinn, Estonia
Gpsr.requests@easproject.com

www.ingramcontent.com/pod-product-compliance
Lightning Source LLC
Chambersburg PA
CBHW051605230426
43668CB00013B/1989